THE MOST TRUSTED NAME IN TRAVEL: **FROMMER'S**

FROMMER'S EasyGuide to
ROME, FLORENCE & VENICE 2019

By Donald Strachan, Stephen Keeling,
and Elizabeth Heath

FROMMER'S STAR RATINGS SYSTEM

Every hotel, restaurant, and attraction listed in this guide has been ranked for quality and value. Here's what the stars mean:

★ Recommended
★★ Highly Recommended
★★★ A must! Don't miss!

AN IMPORTANT NOTE

The world is a dynamic place. Hotels change ownership, restaurants hike their prices, museums alter their opening hours, and busses and trains change their routings. And all of this can occur in the several months after our authors have visited, inspected, and written about, these hotels, restaurants, museums and transportation services. Though we have made valiant efforts to keep all our information fresh and up-to-date, some few changes can inevitably occur in the periods before a revised edition of this guidebook is published. So please bear with us if a tiny number of the details in this book have changed. Please also note that we have no responsibility or liability for any inaccuracy or errors or omissions, or for inconvenience, loss, damage, or expenses suffered by anyone as a result of assertions in this guide.

Previous Page: Gondolas await the dawning day on Venice's Grand Canal.

Current Page: Art lovers stroll through the vast Vatican Museums in Rome.

CONTENTS

The gleaming baroque dome of Santa Maria della Salute (p. 274), an iconic presence in Venice's skyline.

A LOOK AT ROME, FLORENCE & VENICE

The classic itinerary that forms the heart of this guidebook—Rome, Florence, and Venice—showcases three of the world's most magical destinations. The highlights are legendary: In Rome, thrill to the ruins of the Roman Forum, best reached by first ascending the Capitoline steps designed by Michelangelo; the treasures of the Vatican; the elegant bones of the once-mighty Colosseum; and the Pantheon, designed by Hadrian in the 2nd century. In Florence, Michelangelo's "David" stands tall in the Accademia Museum, and the Ufizzi and the Pitti Palace are packed with priceless art. In Venice, float on the canal on a gondola or watch the world go by from a cafe seat on the Piazza San Marco. Italy can support a lifetime of travel, but our EasyGuide approach gives you all the tools you need to make your trip as pleasurable and uncomplicated as possible. *Buon viaggio!*

Ringed with statues, Piazza della Signorina is the medieval heart of Florence, with several world-class art museums only steps away.

The interior of Saint Peter's Basilica (p. 88) in Vatican City; one of the holiest sites in all Christendom, the church was built on the tomb of St. Peter.

The Roman Colosseum (p. 102), inaugurated in A.D. 80, was once the site of bloody gladiator contests and wild animal fights. It could also be flooded for mock naval battles.

The double spiral staircase at the Vatican Museums (p. 90), inspired by a 1505 design by Bramante, allows visitors to pass in both directions without encountering one another.

Now a jumble of ruins and fragments, the Roman Forum (p. 100) was once the center of commercial, political, and religious life in the ancient Empire.

Neptune presides over the baroque Trevi Fountain (p. 116), where tossing in a coin is supposed to guarantee a return trip to Rome.

Artisanal gelato (p. 83) in a range of flavors. At least one cone (cono) or small cup (coppetta) per day is practically a requirement when visiting Rome, especially in the summer!

The "School of Athens" by Raphael Sanzio adorns the Stanze di Raffaello (Raphael Rooms) of the Vatican Museums (p. 90), in what was once the library and office of Pope Julius II.

Sunny Santa Maria Square lies at the heart of Trastevere (p. 47), one of Rome's most youthful, Bohemian neighborhoods, full of offbeat shops, little trattorias, and wine bars.

Al Ceppo (p. 75) restaurant is renowned for its grilled and roasted meats, but be sure to save room for dessert!

The ancient ruins of Pompeii, reachable via a day trip from Rome, reveal the preserved Roman city, including plaster casts of Vesuvius's victims in their moments of death in August, A.D. 79. See p. 141.

St. Peter's Basilica (p. 88) and the Vatican, viewed from the Tiber River; a climb to the top of the dome offers breathtaking views of Rome.

FLORENCE

A local vibe pervades in the neighborhoods of Oltrarno, San Niccolò, and San Frediano, collectively known as Florence's lively "Left Bank." See p. 151.

Fresh produce, exotic spices, pizza vendors, and gourmet food stalls are all on hand at Florence's Mercato Centrale (p. 204).

Florence's Duomo (p. 178), with its elaborate 19th-century facade, is topped by Brunelleschi's marvelous 15th-century dome and overlooks Piazza del Duomo.

Rustic Tuscan fare and ambience, plus an extensive wine list, are the hallmarks of Coquinarius Enoteca, located 2 blocks from Piazza del Duomo (p. 175).

The art collection of the Vasari Corridor (p. 188), an elevated walkway built for Duke Cosimo Medici I.

"Primevera" painting in the Botticelli room in the Uffizi Gallery (p. 181).

The walk, cab, or bus ride up to Piazzale Michelangelo (p. 199) affords splendid views of the Duomo and the rest of Florence.

Siena's Palazzo Publica and scallop-shell-shaped Piazza del Campo in Siena have changed little since the mid-1300s, when the Black Death decimated the city, located just over an hour from Florence. See p. 212.

Piazza della Cisterna (p. 218), built around a well dating to 1237, is a focal point of San Gimignano, a picturesque town near Siena known for its medieval defensive towers.

VENICE

A fixture on the Venice skyline, Santa Maria della Salute (p. 274) was built in the 1630s to offer thanks for the city's deliverance from the Black Death.

Venice's Castello neighborhood (p. 269) is one of the city's six water-bound sestiere, or districts.

Colorful houses line Burano (p. 281), an island in the Venetian Lagoon known for its lacemaking tradition.

A reveler in an elaborate Carnevale (p. 284) costume at the Piazza San Marco; the pre-Lenten festival takes place over 10 days leading up to Fat Tuesday.

Handcrafted, hand-painted papier-maché Carnevale masks are created in several traditional botteghe shops in Venice.

In business since 1871, Trattoria Da Fiori offers up-to-date renditions of classic Venetian dishes.

Overpriced, but not overrated, a gondola ride (p. 230) through the canals of Venice is every bit as romantic as it looks.

The Mercato Rialto (p. 259) is Venice's biggest open-air market, and its vast array of fish and seafood stalls harkens to the days when it was one of the Mediterranean's great fish bazaars.

Reopened in 2003 after a devastating fire, Venice's Teatro La Fenice (p. 268) is one of Europe's great opera houses.

A ringside seat at a cafe on Piazza San Marco (p. 267) makes for memorable people-watching on Venice's busiest square.

Eastern influence on Venetian history is in evidence in these Byzantine mosaics on the facade of Basilica di San Marco (p. 261).

There's no proof that any family named Capulet ever lived here, but *Romeo and Juliet* fans still come to Verona to visit Casa di Giulietta (p. 293), a 14th-century house with a picture-perfect balcony.

THE BEST OF ROME, FLORENCE & VENICE

By Donald Strachan

I taly is a country that needs no fanfare to introduce it. The mere name conjures up vivid images: the grand ruins of Ancient Rome, the paintings and panoramas of Florence, the secret canals and noble palaces of Venice. For centuries, visitors have headed to Italy looking for their own slice of the good life, and these three cities supply the highpoint of any trip around the country.

Nowhere in the world is the impact of the Renaissance felt more than in its birthplace, **Florence,** a repository of art icons left by Masaccio, Botticelli, Leonardo da Vinci, Michelangelo, and many others. Much of the "known world" was once ruled from **Rome,** a city mythically founded by twins Romulus and Remus in 753 B.C. There's no place with more artistic monuments—not even **Venice,** a seemingly impossible floating city whose beauty and history was shaped by centuries of trade with the Byzantine world to the east.

And there's more. Long before Italy was a country, it was a loose collection of city-states. Centuries of alliance and rivalry left a legacy dotted across the hinterlands of these three great cities, and much of it lies within easy day-trip distance. It is a short hop from Venice to the "Venetian Arc": **Verona,** with its Shakespearean romance and an intact Roman Arena; or **Padua** and its sublime Giotto frescoes. In **Siena,** an hour from Florence, ethereal art and Gothic palaces seem barely altered since the city's heyday in the 1300s. South of Rome, **Pompeii**—preserved under volcanic ash for 2 millennia after Vesuvius' eruption in A.D. 79—remains the best place to get up close with the world of the ancients.

St. Mark's Square in Venice.

ITALY'S best AUTHENTIC EXPERIENCES

o **Dining Italian Style:** There is no pastime here more cherished than eating—even better, eating outdoors, preferably with a view of a medieval church or Renaissance piazza. There's no such thing as a single "Italian" cuisine: You'll discover that each region and city has its own beloved recipes, handed down over generations. *Buon appetito!*

o **Catching an Opera at Verona's Arena:** In summer, Italians enjoy their opera under the stars. The setting for Italy's largest and most famous outdoor festival is the ancient **Arena di Verona,** a Roman amphitheater grand enough to accommodate as many elephants as required for a performance of *Aïda.* See p. 293.

o **Shopping at Rome's Mercato di Testaccio:** The 2012 opening of a new, modern version of Testaccio's historic market signaled a rebirth of this gritty, authentic neighborhood. The bustling market is a culinary and cultural treat, where local chefs jostle elbow-to-elbow with feisty *signore,* clamoring for the best *pomodori, mozzarella di bufala,* and *trippa* (tripe). Sustain yourself with delectable street food as you soak up this slice of real Rome. See p. 132.

- **Exploring Florence's Diverse Cocktail Scene:** You can tailor your sipping the way you like it: straight up with one of the world's great views at **La Terrazza;** casual and creative at **Lo Sverso;** vintage and quirky at **Mayday;** or crafted by one of Italy's most inventive mixologists at **Bitter Bar.** See p. 208.

THE best TASTES OF ITALY

- **Bonci Pizzarium, Rome:** Chef-entrepreneur Gabriele Bonci elevates the simple slice of pizza to extraordinary levels. There's nothing fussy about the place, or the prices, but every single ingredient is carefully sourced and expertly prepared—as you can tell from the first bite. See p. 70.
- **Mercato Centrale, Florence:** Not really a restaurant . . . more the food hall of your dreams, with a constant buzz from noon until nighttime. Pick and choose from multiple kiosks preparing the best Tuscan and modern Italian food and wash it all down with a fine wine from the well-stocked enoteca. See p. 170.
- **Ai Artisti, Venice:** Venice's culinary rep is founded on the quality of fish sold at its famous market. Both *primi* and *secondi* at Ai Artisti feature the freshest catch from the lagoon and farther afield. See p. 253.
- **Florence's Vegetarian Dining Scene:** The days when you had to be a carnivore to fully enjoy a meal in the Renaissance city are long gone. The

Food shopping at Florence's Mercato Centrale.

modern menu at **Vagalume** (p. 171) is populated with veggie dishes to fit any appetite, and **A Crudo** (p. 172) serves vegetarian tartare alongside classic and reinvented meat versions. Vegans, as well as celiacs, are looked after by the inventive menu at **Brac** (p. 171).

o **Cicchetti & a Spritz in Venice:** *Cicchetti*—tapaslike small servings, usually eaten while standing at a bar—are a Venetian tradition. To make the experience complete, accompany them with a spritz made with Aperol and sparkling prosecco wine from the Veneto hills. To find some of the best spots, head for the San Polo side of the Rialto Bridge. See p. 246.

ITALY'S best HOTELS

o **Villa Spalletti Trivelli, Rome:** Recent upgrades have only enhanced the unique experience of staying in an Italian noble mansion in the middle of the capital. Opulence and impeccable service comes at a price, of course. When our lottery numbers come up, we will be booking a stay here. See p. 63.

o **Mediterraneo, Rome:** Upscale Art Deco Hotel Mediterraneo is the flagship of a trio of hotels near Termini Station run by the Bettoja

A suite at Villa Spalletti Trivelli, Rome.

family. Others are even more budget-friendly, but all offer vintage charm, old-school comforts, and warm service from a loyal longtime staff. They don't make 'em like this anymore. See p. 65.

o **Metropole, Venice:** The Grand Old Lady of Venetian hospitality, transformed from a medieval building into a luxury hotel in the 19th century, remains a chic choice, filled with antiques and Asian art. See p. 238.

o **Palazzo Tolomei, Florence:** A palace where Raphael once stayed—perhaps even giving its owners a painting to pay his rent—sounds grand indeed, and you won't be disappointed. The Renaissance layout and a baroque redecoration from the 1600s are gloriously intact. See p. 157.

On top of Pisa's Leaning Tower.

ITALY'S best FOR FAMILIES

o **Climbing Pisa's Wonky Tower:** Are we walking up or down? Pleasantly disoriented kids are bound to ask, as you spiral your way to the rooftop viewing balcony atop the world's most famous pieces of botched engineering. Pisa is an easy day trip from Florence; eight is the minimum age for heading up its *Torre Pendente*, or Leaning Tower. See p. 216.

o **Boat Tripping on the Venice Lagoon:** Who doesn't like a day boating on a lake, any lake? Throw in the floating city and its bell tower of San Marco as fixtures on the horizon, and you have one unforgettable family moment. See p. 280.

o **Rooting for Fiorentina Soccer:** Forget lions battling gladiators in Rome's Colosseum, or Guelphs fighting Ghibellines in medieval lanes. For a modern showdown, hit a Florence soccer game. Home side Fiorentina plays Serie A matches at the city's Stadio Comunale alternate weekends from September to June. Wear something lilac—the team's nickname is *i viola* ("the purples"). See p. 202.

o **Visiting Rome's Centrale Montemartini:** Industrial chic meets ancient marble in this unique museum, where Greek and Roman statues are displayed in the restored rooms of Rome's first public electricity plant. The museum always has drawing and painting materials onsite, and guided tours for children are available on request. On Sundays, admission is free for kids 11 and under. See p. 125.

o **Taste-Testing at an Artisan Gelateria:** When it comes to Italian ice cream, choose carefully—Smurf-blue or bubble-gum-pink flavors are a sure sign of color enhancers, and beware of ice crystals and fluffy heaps that betray additives and pumped-in air. Authentic artisan *gelaterie* make good stuff from scratch daily, with fresh seasonal produce: Look for a short, all-natural ingredient list posted proudly for all to see. Believe us, you'll taste the difference. See "Gelato," p. 83, 173, and 258.

The Venice lagoon, with the domes of St. Mark's in the background.

ITALY'S best MUSEUMS

o **Vatican Museums, Rome:** The 100 galleries of the Musei Vaticani are loaded with papal treasures accumulated over the centuries. Musts include the Sistine Chapel, such ancient Greek and Roman sculptures as "Laocoön"

Florence's Galleria degli Uffizi.

and "Belvedere Apollo," and room after room of Raphael's frescoes, including his masterful "School of Athens." See p. 90.

o **Galleria degli Uffizi, Florence:** This U-shaped High Renaissance building designed by Giorgio Vasari was the administrative headquarters, or *uffizi* (offices), for the Medici dukes of Tuscany. It's now the crown jewel of Europe's art museums, housing the world's greatest collection of Renaissance paintings, including icons by Botticelli, Leonardo da Vinci, and Michelangelo. See p. 181.

o **Accademia, Venice:** The "Academy" houses an unequalled array of Venetian paintings, exhibited chronologically from the 13th to the 18th century. Walls are hung with works by Bellini, Carpaccio, Giorgione, Titian, and Tintoretto. See p. 270.

o **Galleria Borghese, Rome:** Housed amid the frescoes and decor of a 1613 palace in the heart of the Villa Borghese, this gem of a building is merely the backdrop for its collections, which include masterpieces of baroque sculpture by a young Bernini and Canova, and paintings by Caravaggio and Raphael. See p. 118.

o **Santa Maria della Scala, Siena:** The building is as much the star as the artworks—the frescoed wards, ancient chapels, sacristy, and labyrinthine basement of a medieval hospital that was still healing patients until the 1990s. See p. 214.

ITALY'S best FREE THINGS TO DO

o **Watching the Sun Rise over the Roman Forum:** A short stroll from the Capitoline Hill down Via del Campidoglio to Via di Monte Tarpeo brings you to a perfect outlook: The terrace behind the Michelangelo-designed square, an ideal photo op when the sun rises behind the Temple of Saturn, illuminating the archaeological complex below in pink-orange light. Early risers can reward themselves with breakfast from the bakeries of the nearby Jewish Ghetto. See p. 100.

o **Basking in the Lights of the Renaissance:** At dusk, make the steep climb up to the ancient church of San Miniato al Monte, Florence. Sit down on the steps and watch the city begin its evening twinkle. See p. 200.

o **Treading the Gothic Streets of Siena:** The shell-shaped Piazza del Campo stands at the heart of one of Europe's best-preserved medieval cities. Steep canyonlike streets, icons of Gothic architecture like the Palazzo Pubblico, and ethereal Madonnas painted on shimmering gold altarpieces transport you back to a time before the Renaissance. See p. 212.

o **Gazing in Wonder at Caravaggio's Greatest Paintings:** Rome's French church, San Luigi dei Francesi, is home to three panels by bad-boy of the baroque, Michelangelo Merisi da Caravaggio. His "Calling of St. Matthew," painted at the height of his fame (and powers), incorporates uncompromising realism and his trademark *chiaroscuro* (extremes of light and dark) style. See p. 109.

o **Discovering You're Hopelessly Lost in Venice:** You haven't experienced Venice until you have turned a corner convinced you're on the way to somewhere, only to find yourself smack against a canal with no bridge, or in a little courtyard with no way out. All you can do is shrug, smile, and give the city's maze of narrow streets another try. Because getting lost in Venice is a pleasure. See p. 260.

Inside the Pantheon, Rome.

undiscovered ITALY

o **San Frediano, Florence:** Most Florentines have abandoned their *centro storico* to the visitors, but the Arno's Left Bank in San Frediano has plenty of local action after dark. Dine at **iO** (p. 172), slurp a gelato by the river at **La Carraia** (p. 174), then sip fine wines until late at **Il Santino** (p. 209) or catch an offbeat gig at **Libreria–Café La Cité** (p. 206).

o **Cannaregio, Venice:** This residential neighborhood has silent canals, elegantly faded mansions, hidden churches graced by Tiepolo paintings, and the old Ghetto Nuovo, a historic area of Jewish bakeries, restaurants, and synagogues. It's all a great escape from the chaos around San Marco. See chapter 9.

o **The *Aperitivo* Spots & Craft Beer Bars of Rome:** Don't confuse *aperitivo* with happy hour: Predinner cocktails tickle appetites, induce conversation and flirting, and allow free access to all-you-can-eat buffets if you buy one drink. And Romans are increasingly turning to artisan-brewed beers for their one drink. See p. 134.

o **The View from T Fondaco dei Tedeschi:** This Venice department store—renovated in 2016 by stellar architect Rem Koolhas, no less—was once an elegant *palazzo* beside the Grand Canal. The views from its free rooftop deck are even more spectacular than the opulent goods inside. See p. 268.

Aperitivo time in Rome.

o **An Unexpected Insight into Brunelleschi's Genius:** Tucked away on the top floor of Florence's Spedale degli Innocenti is a window with a cutaway view into the ceiling of a Brunelleschi-designed chapel below. From this angle, you can see every strut, joint, and Renaissance nail holding it up. Fascinating. See p. 196.

SUGGESTED ITINERARIES

By Donald Strachan

taly is so vast and treasure-filled, it's hard to resist the temptation to pack too much into too short a time. This is a dauntingly diverse destination, and you can't even skim the surface in one or two weeks—so relax, don't try. If you're a first-time visitor with limited time, we suggest you max out on the classic trio: Rome, Florence, and Venice can be packed into one very busy week, better yet in two.

How can you accomplish that? Well, in addition to having one of Europe's better highway networks (called *autostrade*), Italy has one of the continent's most efficient high-speed rail networks. Rome is a key hub of this 21st-century transportation empire; from Rome's Termini station, Florence can be reached in only 91 minutes. If you're city-hopping, you need never rent a car. Key routes (which include the Venice–Florence–Rome line) are served by comfortable, fast trains. You'll only require a rental car for rural detours.

The following itineraries take you to some of our favorite places. The pace may be a bit breathless for some visitors, so skip a stop occasionally to enjoy some chill-out time—after all, you're on vacation. Of course, you can also use any of our itineraries as a jumping-off point to develop your own adventure.

ROME, FLORENCE & VENICE IN 1 WEEK

Let's be realistic: It's impossible to see Italy's three iconic cities fully in a week. However, a fast, efficient rail network along the Rome–Florence–Venice line means it's surprisingly easy to see some of the best they offer. This weeklong itinerary treads the familiar highlights, but there's a reason why they're Italy's most-visited sights—they're sure to provide memories that will last a lifetime.

Days 1, 2 & 3: Rome: The Eternal City ★★★

You could spend a month touring Italy's capital, but 3 days is enough to get the flavor of it. There are two essential areas to focus on. The first is the legacy of Imperial Rome, including

Italy in 1 Week

Days 1–3 Rome
Days 4–5 Florence
Days 6–7 Venice

2

SUGGESTED ITINERARIES | Rome, Florence & Venice in 1 Week

the **Forum, Campidoglio,** and **Colosseum** (p. 95). Bookend your day with the Forum and Colosseum (one first, the other last) to avoid the busiest crowds; the same ticket is good for both. On **Day 2,** tackle **St. Peter's Basilica** and the **Vatican Museums** (p. 90), with a collection unlike any other in the world (including Michelangelo's **Sistine Chapel**). On **Day 3,** it's a toss-up: Choose between the underground catacombs of the **Via Appia Antica** (p. 126); or the well-trod streets of the **Centro Storico** (p. 107) and the **Tridente** (p. 112), where you can wander from Piazza Navona to the Pantheon, the Spanish Steps, and the Trevi Fountain. Spend your evenings in the bars of **Campo de' Fiori** or **Monti**

(p. 111) and the restaurants of **Trastevere** (p. 79) or **Testaccio** (p. 81). At the end of Day 3, catch the late train to Florence. Be sure to buy tickets in advance—on the high-speed network, walk-up fares are much more expensive than prebooked tickets.

Days 4 & 5: Florence: Cradle of the Renaissance ★★★

You have 2 whole days to explore the city of Giotto, Leonardo, Botticelli, and Michelangelo. Start with their masterpieces at the **Uffizi** (p. 181; definitely prebook tickets, months ahead if possible), then explore the **Duomo** complex (p. 175): Scale Brunelleschi's ochre dome and follow up with a visit to the adjoining **Battistero di San Giovanni,** the **Museo dell'Opera del Duomo,** and the **Campanile di Giotto** (p. 178). Start the next day with "David" at the **Accademia** (p. 193). Spend the rest of your day getting to know the intimate wall paintings of **San Marco** (p. 194), paintings hanging at the **Palazzo Pitti** (p. 198), and Masaccio's revolutionary frescoes in the **Cappella Brancacci** (p. 200). In the evenings, stay south of the Arno, in **San Frediano** or **San Niccolò,** for lively wine bars and better restaurants than you generally find in the historic center (p. 150).

Days 6 & 7: Venice: The City That Defies the Sea ★★★

Head to Venice via early train in the morning. You'll ride into the heart of Venice on a *vaporetto* (water bus), taking in the **Grand Canal,** the world's greatest main street. Begin your sightseeing at **Piazza San Marco** (p. 267): The **Basilica di San Marco** is right there, and after

Rome's Flavian Amphitheater, better known as the Colosseum.

exploring it, visit the nearby **Palazzo Ducale** (**Doge's Palace;** p. 265) before walking over the **Bridge of Sighs.** Begin your evening with the classic Venetian *aperitivo,* an Aperol spritz (Aperol with sparkling prosecco wine and soda) followed by *cicchetti* (Venetian tapas) before a late dinner. Make your second day all about the city's art: the **Gallerie dell'Accademia** (p. 270), the modern **Peggy Guggenheim Collection** (p. 272), and **San Rocco** (p. 276). Catch the latest train you can back to Rome. Or add another night; you can never stay too long in Venice.

The Bridge of Sighs, the Doge's Palace, Venice.

A 2-WEEK ITINERARY

It's obviously difficult to see the top sights of Italy—and to see them properly—in just 2 weeks. But in this itinerary, we show you some of the best of them. We'll add some significant detours from the Rome–Florence–Venice trail, heading south to Pompeii, Europe's most complete Roman ruins; north to Pisa (for the Leaning Tower and more); and making day trips to Padua (with its Giotto frescoes), and Verona (city of lovers since *Romeo and Juliet*).

Days 1, 2 & 3: Rome ★★★

Follow the Rome itinerary suggested in "Italy in 1 Week," above. Rome will actually be your base for 5 days (days 4 and 5 will be day trips from Rome); for this longer stay, you should consider apartment rental rather than a hotel room in the capital; see "Self-Catering Apartments," p. 54.

Day 4: Pompeii: A Day Trip to Europe's Best-Preserved Roman Ruins ★★

Early on **Day 4,** take the high-speed Frecciarossa or Italo train from Rome to Naples (1½ hr.), then a Circumvesuviana train 24km (15 miles) southeast of Naples to wander the archaeological remains at **Pompeii** (p. 143). If you can, pack water and a lunch—onsite services aren't great.

Italy in 2 Weeks

Days 1–3 Rome
Day 4 Pompeii
Day 5 Tivoli
Days 6–7 Florence
Day 8 Siena
Day 9 San Gimignano
Day 10 Pisa
Days 11–12 Venice
Day 13 Padua
Day 14 Verona

Buried for almost 2,000 years, after nearby Vesuvius erupted in A.D. 79, Pompeii exhibits some of the great archaeological treasures of Italy, including the patrician **Casa dei Vettii** and the frescoed **Villa dei Misteri.** You'll return to Rome for overnight. *Tip:* This is a very long day; it may be easier to do as an escorted visit by bus from Rome. Several operators offer it; ask at your hotel or at one of Rome's tourist information points (see "Visitor Information," p. 45).

Day 5: Tivoli: A Day Trip to Rome's Imperial Villa ★★

Take your foot off the gas with a more relaxed day trip, 32km (20 miles) northeast of Rome to **Tivoli** (p. 139). Emperor Hadrian's serene rural retreat here, the **Villa Adriana** (p. 139), is the grandest retirement residence you'll ever see, complete with theaters, baths, fountains, and gardens. This emperor had a good eye for design.

Days 6 & 7: Florence ★★★

Take an early train to Florence (or depart the evening before). Follow the itinerary in "Rome, Florence & Venice in 1 Week," p. 10, then use Florence as your base for 3 more days, as you explore Siena, San Gimignano, and Pisa.

Day 8: A Day Trip to Gothic Siena ★★★

It's just over an hour to **Siena** (p. 211) on the *rapida* bus from Florence. On arrival, set out immediately for **Piazza del Campo,** the shell-shaped main square, including its art-filled **Museo Civico** (inside the **Palazzo Pubblico**). You still have time to squeeze in a fast look at the **Duomo** and **Museo dell'Opera Metropolitana,** where you'll find Sienese master Duccio's giant "Maestà" painting. Stop on the Campo for a late afternoon drink, then grab an early dinner at a restaurant in Siena's atmospheric back streets. The last bus back to Florence departs at 8:45pm, arriving back in Florence at 10pm (the last bus on weekends is usually 7:10pm).

Day 9: San Gimignano: A Town Stuck in the 1300s ★★

It's another long day on buses, but well worth it to see one of the most perfectly preserved Gothic towns in Europe. You change buses in Poggibonsi for the last, outrageously pretty leg through vine-clad hills to **San Gimignano** (p. 217). In its medieval heyday, the "city of beautiful towers" had over 70 turrets spiking the sky above its tiny, crowded plot. Now just a handful remain, including the **Torre Grossa** (which you can climb). The frescoed **Collegiata** is the essential art stop. You can dine early at **Chiribiri** (it's open all day), then leave on the late bus. Or consider renting a car: The roads of central Tuscany are pretty any time of year, and there's good signposted parking on San Gimignano's outskirts.

Michelangelo's "David" in the Accademia, Florence.

Day 10: Pisa & Its Leaning Tower ★★

A fast train from Florence takes only 45 minutes to Pisa, with its set-piece piazza, one of the most photographed slices of real estate on the planet. Pisa's **Campo dei Miracoli** ("Field of Miracles") is home to the **Leaning Tower** (p. 216), of course; book a slot ahead of time if you want to climb it. A combination ticket admits you to the rest of the piazza's sights, including the **Duomo,** with its Arab-influenced Pisan-Roman-esque façade, and the **Battistero,** with its carved pulpit and crazy acoustics. Head away from the piazza for dining *alla pisana*—the "real Pisa" lies in the warren of streets around the market square, **Piazza delle Vettovaglie.** Finish your visit with a stroll on the handsome promenade along the **River Arno.** Take a late train back to Florence (the last fast connection departs at 9:30pm).

Days 11 & 12: Venice ★★★

Set out early the next morning for Venice, where you'll spend the next 4 nights. For the first 2 days, follow the itinerary suggested in "Rome, Florence & Venice in 1 Week," p. 10.

Day 13: Padua & Its Giotto Frescoes ★

Lying only 40km (25 miles) west of Venice, **Padua** (p. 290) is a fairly relaxed day trip by train. Visit the **Basilica di Sant'Antonio** (p. 292) to see its Donatello bronzes and the **Cappella degli Scrovegni** (p. 291) for its Giotto frescoes—perhaps the most important paintings in the history of pre-Renaissance Italian art. Return to Venice for the night.

Day 14: Verona: City of Lovers & Gladiators ★★★

Although he likely never set foot in the place, Shakespeare placed the world's most famous love story here, "Romeo and Juliet." Wander **Piazza dei Signori** and **Piazza delle Erbe,** before descending on the **Arena di Verona** (p. 293), the world's best-preserved gladiatorial arena: It's still packed out for monumental opera performances on summer evenings. Book ahead for a high-speed train back to Venice—it takes just 1 hour, 10 minutes, compared with over 2 hours for a slower regional train service.

ITALY FOR FAMILIES

Italy is probably the friendliest family vacation destination in all Europe. Logistically, it presents few challenges. If you're traveling by rental car with young children, request safety car seats ahead of time, so the rental company can arrange for a seat which complies with EU regulations. Reduced-price **family fares** are available on much of the high-speed network; ask when you buy your tickets or contact a booking agent. You won't need to hunt for "child-friendly" restaurants or special kids' menus—there is always plenty available for little ones, even dishes not on the grownup menu. If you have a fussy eater, never be afraid to ask—pretty much any request is met with a smile.

Piazza Bra and Verona's Arena.

A few **tips** from parents who've been there: Space museum visits so you get a chance to see the masterpieces but your youngsters don't suffer a meltdown from too many paintings of saints and holy *bambini*. Punctuate every day with a **gelato** stop—Italy makes the world's best ice cream (you'll easily find soya-milk options for the lactose-intolerant). It's a good idea to limit long, tiring day trips out of town, especially by public transportation. And end your trip in Venice—most kids assume it was dreamed up by Walt Disney anyway.

Day 1: Rome's Ancient Ruins ★★★

History is on your side here: The wonders of **Ancient Rome** (p. 95) should appeal as much to kids as to adults. There are plenty of gory tales to tell at the **Colosseum** (p. 98), where the bookshop has a broad selection of city guides aimed at kids. After that, little ones can let off steam wandering the **Roman Forum** and the **Palatine Hill.** (The roadside ruins of the **Imperial Forums** can be viewed at any time.) Cap the afternoon by exploring the **Villa Borghese** (p. 117), a monumental park in the heart of the city; rent bikes or visit the small zoo in the park's northeast section. For dinner, tuck into crispy crusts at an authentic Roman **pizzeria,** such as **Li Rioni** (p. 72).

Day 2: Rome After the Romans ★★★

Head early to **St. Peter's Basilica** (p. 88), before the long lines form. Kids will find it spooky wandering the Vatican grottoes, and relish the opportunity to climb up to Michelangelo's dome. After lunch, begin your assault on the **Vatican Museums** (p. 90) and the **Sistine Chapel** (be sure to book advance tickets; it's worth the 4€ to skip the lines). Even if your kids don't like art museums, they will gawk at the grandeur. Later in the day, head for the iconic **Spanish Steps** (p. 112), then wander over to the

Italy for Families

Days 1–3	Rome
Days 4–5	Florence
Day 6	Pisa
Day 7	Siena
Days 8–10	Venice

Trevi Fountain (p. 116). Give the kids coins to toss into the fountain, which is said to ensure their return to Rome—perhaps when they are older and can better appreciate the city's many more artistic attractions.

Day 3: Rome Underground ★★★

There are, literally, layers of history below the city streets, and kids will love exploring the catacombs of the **Via Appia Antica** (p. 126), the first cemetery of Rome's Christian community, where the devout secretly practiced their faith during periods of persecution. **Context Travel** (www.context travel.com; see p. 129) runs an excellent family tour of the city's subterranean layers (285€ per party). Eat more **pizza** before you leave; Rome's pizzerias are bettered only by those in Naples, to the south . . . and our next recommended stops all lie north.

Days 4 & 5: Florence: City of the Renaissance ★★★

Take the early train to Florence. While it's usually thought of as more of an adult city, there's enough here to fill 2 family days, plus a couple of day trips. (With day trips, you'll be staying 4 nights in Florence, consider taking an apartment rather than a hotel room, to give you space to spread out; see p. 156.) Begin with the city's monumental main square,

Touring the Roman Forum.

Piazza della Signoria, an open-air museum of statues with the **Palazzo Vecchio** (p. 186) dominating one side; you can tour it on special child-friendly itineraries, including a chance to explore its secret passages. Turn your afternoon visit to the **Uffizi** (p. 181; definitely should be pre-booked) into a treasure trail by first visiting the gift shop to buy postcards of key artworks. On the second morning, kids will delight in climbing to the top of Brunelleschi's dome on the **Duomo** (p. 178) for a classic panorama. Book a slot for as early as possible; waiting times often lengthen during the day. If the kids still have energy to burn, climb the 414 steps up to the **Campanile di Giotto** (p. 178), run around in the **Giardino di Boboli** (p. 197), eat some of Italy's best gelato (p. 173), and stroll the **Ponte Vecchio** (p. 188) at dusk.

Day 6: Pisa & Its Leaning Tower ★★

With children seven or under, you may want to skip **Pisa** (p. 214): Eight is the minimum age for the disorienting ascent up the bell tower of Pisa's cathedral, more commonly known as the **Leaning Tower.** Older kids will appreciate the hyperreal monuments of the **Campo dei Miracoli** and learning about the city's Galileo links: He was born here, and supposedly discovered his law of pendulum motion while watching a swinging lamp inside the **Duomo.** Before returning to Florence, sample a local specialty, *cecina*—a pizzalike flatbread made of garbanzo-bean flour—at **Il Montino.** Rail connections between Florence and Pisa are frequent, fast (60–80 min.), and affordable (under 9€ each way).

Day 7: Gothic Siena ★★★

Count yourself lucky if you can visit **Siena** (p. 211) around July 2 or August 16 for the famous 4-day **Palio** celebrations, when horses race around **Piazza del Campo.** Year-round, however, a couple of epic climbs will thrill the kids. The **Torre del Mangia**—the bell tower of the **Palazzo Pubblico**—yields a dramatic view of the city and countryside. Through the **Museo dell'Opera Metropolitana,** they can scale the "Facciatone" for a dizzying view down into the Campo. At **Santa Maria della Scala,** they will find **Bambimus,** the art museum for kids, with paintings hung at child-friendly heights. The zebra-striped **Duomo** is jazzy enough to pique their curiosity, and Siena's bakeries are famed for their sweet treats. Take the bus back to Florence after an early dinner. (***Note:*** Bus service is much reduced on Sun.)

Days 8, 9 & 10: Venice, City on the Lagoon ★★★

Leave Florence early for Venice, the most kid-pleasing city in Italy. The fun begins the moment you arrive and take a *vaporetto* ride along the **Grand Canal.** Head straight for **Piazza San Marco** (p. 267), where kids delight in an elevator ride up the great **Campanile.** Catch the sparkly mosaics inside the **Basilica di San Marco;** at the **Palazzo Ducale,** walk over the infamous **Bridge of Sighs** after checking out the pint-size knights' armor. Make time for priority art: Visit the **Gallerie dell'Accademia** (p. 270) and **San Rocco** (p. 276), where kids can "read" the Tintoretto paintings like a picture book or graphic novel. For a modern break, the **Peggy Guggenheim Collection** (p. 272) has pop art, an open courtyard, and a rooftop cafe. In summer, save time for the beach at the **Lido** (p. 282). And yes, splurge on a storybook ride on Venice's canals from the seat of a **gondola** (p. 275).

Feeding the pigeons in Piazza San Marco.

ITALY IN CONTEXT

By Donald Strachan

M any of the stereotypes you have heard about this charming country are accurate. Children are fussed over wherever they go; food and soccer are treated like religion; the north–south divide is alive and well; and (alas) bureaucracy is a frustrating feature of daily life for families and businesses. Some stereotypes, however, are wide of the mark: Not every Italian you meet will be open and effusive. Occasionally they do taciturn pretty well, too.

The most important fact to remember is that, for a land so steeped in history—3 millennia and counting—Italy has only a short history *as a country*. As recently as 2011 it celebrated its 150th birthday. Prior to 1861, the map of the peninsula was in constant flux. War, alliance, invasion, and disputed successions caused that map to change color as often as a chameleon crossing a field of wildflowers. Republics, mini-monarchies, client states, Papal states, and city-states, as well as Islamic emirates, colonies, dukedoms, and Christian theocracies, roll onto and out of the pages of Italian history with regularity. In some regions, you'll hear languages and dialects other than Italian. It all combines to form an identity that's often more regional than it is national.

This confusing history explains why your Italian experience will differ wildly if you visit, say, Rome rather than Venice. (And why you should visit both, if you can.) The architecture is different; the food is different; the legends and historical figures are different, as are many of the local issues of the day. And the people are different: While the north–south schism is most often written about, cities as close together as Florence and Siena can feel very dissimilar. This chapter tries to help you understand why.

ITALY TODAY

The big news for many North American travelers to Italy is the recent unfavorable movement in exchange rates. Last year's edition of this guide listed the U.S. dollar/euro exchange rate at $1.06. At time of writing, it's hovering around $1.23. The euro has strengthened quickly and significantly, and this change makes everything in Italy a little more expensive for U.S. visitors. (Canadians have seen a similar movement, from $1.39 to $1.55 in the same period.) Still, currency rates remain better for North Americans than they were 4 or 5 years ago. Mercifully, price inflation in Italy has also remained low during this time, largely due to a stubbornly slow recovery from the global financial crisis, known here as the *Crisi*. It had a disastrous effect on Italy's economy, causing the deepest recession since World War II. Public debt grew to alarming levels and is still around 135% of GDP. In addition, 2011 and 2012 saw Italy pitched into the center of a European banking crisis which almost brought about the collapse of the euro currency. Concerns about major Italian banks rumbled on through 2018, even after the 2017 rescue of giant Monte dei Paschi di Siena (the world's oldest bank).

Light is appearing at the end of Italy's dark economic tunnel—a little, at least—with modest 2017 growth forecasted to be replicated in 2018 and 2019. Yet Italy has, in effect, experienced almost no GDP growth in well over a decade.

Just as in many Western democracies, populism has become a feature of national politics. A party formed by comedian Beppe Grillo—the *MoVimento 5 Stelle* (M5S; 5 Star Movement)—polled around a quarter of the vote in 2013 elections. In 2014, Matteo Renzi swapped his job as *Partito Democratico* (PD; Democratic Party) mayor of Florence to become Italy's youngest prime minister, age 39, heading a center-left coalition. He resigned in late 2016, after defeat in a referendum on wide-ranging electoral reform. The PD remained in power, however, with Paolo Gentiloni taking over as prime minister.

Not everything has been plain sailing for M5S, either: Their candidate, Virginia Raggi, was elected Rome's first female mayor, but her administration has encountered multiple problems since she took office in 2016. She has stated she will not run for reelection in 2021. At the national level, however, M5S with its young new leader, Luigi Di Maio, is on a roll. To a backdrop of discontent over unemployment, wages and pensions, and the pace of immigration, Italians went to the polls in March 2018. M5S and the far-right League gained the most seats in Italy's parliament. But the two parties struggled for months to form a government, until finally installing Giuseppe Conte as prime minister. Whether the coalition will hold remains to be seen.

Italy's population is aging, and a youth vacuum is being filled by immigrants, especially those from Eastern Europe, notably Romania (whose language is similar to Italian) and Albania, as well as from North Africa. In several high-profile tragedies, overloaded boats from Africa have sunk in the Mediterranean Sea, with appalling loss of life. Unlike Britain and France, Italy had scant colonial experience—nor does it have the "melting pot" history of the New World. Tensions were inevitable, and discrimination is a daily fact of life for many minorities. Change is coming—but too slowly for some. The plight of migrant refugees arriving from North Africa and Syria through 2018 adds yet another layer of complexity to Italy's relationship with *stranieri*

THE ESSENTIALS OF italian FOOD

Italians know how to cook—just ask one. But beware: Once Italians start talking food, they don't often pause for breath. Italy doesn't really have a unified national cuisine; it's a loose grouping of delicious regional cuisines that share a few staples, notably pasta, bread, tomatoes, and pig meat cured in endlessly creative ways.

Rome can be the best place to introduce yourself to Italian food, because it has restaurants from every region. There are some authentic Roman specialties, however, such as *saltimbocca alla romana* (literally "jump-in-your-mouth"—thin slices of veal with sage, cured ham, and cheese), *carciofi alla romana* (tender artichokes cooked with herbs), and the ubiquitous *spaghetti alla carbonara*—pasta coated in a silky yellow-white sauce of cured pork cheek, egg, and *Pecorino Romano* (sheep's milk cheese). For historical reasons, a strong current of Jewish cooking also runs through Roman cuisine.

To the north, in **Florence and Tuscany,** you'll find seasonal ingredients served simply. The main ingredient for almost any savory dish is the local olive oil, feted for its low acidity. The typical Tuscan pasta is wide, flat *pappardelle*, generally tossed with a game sauce such as *lepre* (hare) or *cinghiale* (boar). Tuscans are fond of their local pecorino, a strong ewe's-milk cheese made in Pienza. The classic main course is a *bistecca alla fiorentina*, a T-bone-like slab

Fresh seafood and alfresco dining in Italy.

of meat, cut from the white Chianina breed of cattle. Sweet treats are also good here, particularly Siena's *panforte* (a dense, sticky cake) and *biscotti di Prato* (hard, almond-flour biscuits for dipping in dessert wine).

While **Venice** is rarely celebrated for its cuisine, fresh seafood is usually excellent here. Grilled fish is often served with red radicchio, a bitter lettuce that grows best around nearby Treviso. Two classic nonfish dishes are *fegato alla veneziana* (liver and onions) and *risi e bisi* (rice and fresh peas). The traditional carbohydrate up here isn't pasta but *risotto* (rice), delectably flavored with seasonal vegetables or seafood.

(foreigners); events have left immigration centers bursting at the seams and any xenophobic sentiment ripe for exploitation by extremist politicians and marginal parties.

More optimistic signs of Italy's changing society include the 2016 legalization of same-sex civil unions. And prospects for everyone will improve if and when Italy puts the worst of its economic turmoil behind it. From top to toe, highlands to islands, fingers are firmly crossed that the good times are coming around again.

THE MAKING OF ITALY
Etruscans & Villanovans: Prehistory to the Rise of Rome

Of all the early inhabitants of Italy, the most significant legacy was left by the **Etruscans.** No one knows exactly where they came from (though some evidence points to origins in what is now Turkey), and the inscriptions they left behind (often on tombs in necropoli) are too bland to be of much help. Whatever their origins, within 2 centuries of appearing on the peninsula around 800 B.C., they had subjugated the lands now known as **Tuscany** (to which they leave their name), northern Lazio, and Campania, along with the so-called **"Villanovan"** tribes that lived there. They also made Rome the governmental seat of Latium. "Roma" is an Etruscan name, and the mythical ancient kings of Rome had Etruscan names: Numa, Ancus, even Romulus.

The Etruscans ruled until the **Roman Revolt** around 510 B.C., and by 250 B.C. the Romans and their allies had vanquished or assimilated the Etruscans, wiping out their language and religion. However, many of their manners and beliefs remained, and are integral to what we now call "Roman culture."

Rome's **Museo Nazionale Etrusco** (p. 119) and the Etruscan collection in Rome's **Vatican Museums** (p. 90) are a logical starting point if you want to see remnants of Etruscan civilization. Florence's **Museo Archeologico** (p. 194) houses one of the greatest Etruscan bronzes unearthed, the "Arezzo Chimera."

The Roman Republic: ca. 510–27 B.C.

After the Republic was established around 510 B.C.—it's impossible to be precise—the Romans continued to increase their power by conquering neighboring communities in the highlands and forming alliances with other Latins in the lowlands. They gave to their allies, and then to conquered peoples, partial or complete Roman citizenship, with a corresponding obligation of military service. This further increased Rome's power and reach. Citizen colonies were set up as settlements of Roman farmers or veterans, including both **Florence** and **Siena.** The all-powerful Senate presided as Rome defeated rival powers one after another and came to rule the Mediterranean.

No figure was more towering during the late Republic, or more instrumental in its transformation into Empire (see below), than **Julius Caesar,** the charismatic conqueror of Gaul—"the wife of every husband and the husband of every wife," according to scurrilous rumors reported by 1st-century historian Suetonius. After defeating the last resistance of the Pompeiians in 45 B.C., he came to Rome and was made dictator and consul for 10 years. Conspirators, led by Brutus, stabbed him to death at the Theater of Pompey on March 15, 44 B.C., the "Ides of March." The site (now Largo di Torre Argentina) is best known these days as the home of a photogenic feral cat colony.

The conspirators' motivation was to restore the power of the Republic and topple dictatorship. But they failed: **Mark Antony,** a Roman general, assumed control. He made peace with Caesar's willed successor, **Octavian,** and after the Treaty of Brundisium dissolved the Republic, found himself married to Octavian's sister, Octavia. This didn't prevent him, however, from also marrying Egyptian queen Cleopatra in 36 B.C. A furious Octavian gathered legions and defeated Antony at the **Battle of Actium** on September 2, 31 B.C. Cleopatra fled to Egypt, followed by Antony, who committed suicide in disgrace a year later. Cleopatra, unable to retain her rule of Egypt, followed suit with the help of an asp.

Many of the standing buildings of Ancient Rome date to later periods, but parts of the **Roman Forum** (p. 100) date from the Republic, including the **Temple of Saturn.** The adjacent **Capitoline Hill** and **Palatine Hill** have been sacred religious and civic places since the earliest days of Rome. Rome's best Republican-era artifacts are inside the **Musei Capitolini** (p. 96).

The Roman Empire in Its Pomp: 27 B.C.–A.D. 395

Born Gaius Octavius in 63 B.C., and later known as Octavian, **Augustus** became the first Roman emperor in 27 B.C. and reigned until A.D. 14. His autocratic rule ushered in the *Pax Romana,* 2 centuries of peace. In Rome you can still see the remains of the **Forum of Augustus** (p. 99) and admire his statue in the **Vatican Museums** (p. 90).

By now, Rome ruled the entire Mediterranean world, either directly or indirectly. All political, commercial, and cultural pathways led straight to Rome, a sprawling city set on seven hills: the Capitoline, Palatine, Aventine, Caelian, Esquiline, Quirinal, and Viminal. It was in this period that **Virgil** wrote his epic poem "The Aeneid," supplying a grandiose founding myth for the city and empire; **Ovid** composed his erotic poetry; and **Horace** wrote his "Odes."

The emperors brought Rome to new heights. Yet without the counterbalance once provided by the Senate and legislatures, success led to corruption. The centuries witnessed a steady decay in the ideals and traditions on which the Empire had been founded. The army became a fifth column of unruly mercenaries, tax collectors became the scourge of the countryside, and for every good emperor (Augustus, Claudius, Trajan, Vespasian, and Hadrian, to name a few) there were also cruel, debased, or simply incompetent tyrants (Caligula, Nero, Caracalla, and many others).

After Augustus died (by poison, perhaps), his widow, **Livia**—a shrewd operator who had divorced her first husband to marry Augustus—set up her son, **Tiberius,** as ruler, via intrigues and poisonings. A series of murders ensued, and Tiberius, who ruled during Pontius Pilate's trial and crucifixion of Christ, was eventually murdered in his late 70s. Murder was so common that a short time later, **Domitian** (ruled A.D. 81–96) became so obsessed with the possibility of assassination, he had the walls of his palace covered in mica so he could see behind him at all times. (He was killed anyway.)

Excesses ruled the day—at least, if you believe surviving tracts written by biased contemporary chroniclers: **Caligula** supposedly committed incest with

10 EARLY ROMAN emperors

Augustus (ruled 27 B.C.–A.D.14): First, "divine" emperor to whom all later emperors aspired

Tiberius (r. A.D. 14–37): Former general whose increasingly unpopular reign was gripped by fear and paranoia

Caligula (r. A.D. 37–41): Young emperor whose reign of cruelty and terror ended when he was assassinated by his Praetorian Guard

Claudius (r. A.D. 41–54): A sickly man who turned out to be a wise and capable emperor, as well as the conqueror of Britain

Nero (r. A.D. 54–68): Last emperor of the Julio-Claudian dynasty, a cruel megalomaniac who killed his own mother and may have started the Great Fire of Rome (A.D. 64)

Vespasian (r. A.D. 69–79): First emperor of the Flavian dynasty, who built the Colosseum and lived as husband-and-wife with a freed slave, Caenis

Domitian (r. A.D. 81–96): Increasingly paranoid populist and authoritarian who became fixated on the idea he would be assassinated—and was proven right

Trajan (r. A.D. 98–117): Virtuous soldier-ruler who presided over the empire at its widest geographical spread, and also rebuilt much of the city

Hadrian (r. A.D. 113–138): Humanist, general, and builder who redesigned the Pantheon and added the Temple of Venus and Roma to the Forum

Marcus Aurelius (r. A.D. 161–180): Philosopher-king, and last of the so-called Five Good Emperors, whose statue is in the Musei Capitolini

Trajan's Column, Rome.

his sister Drusilla; appointed his horse to the Senate; and proclaimed himself a god. Caligula's successor, his uncle **Claudius,** was poisoned by his final wife—his niece Agrippina the Younger—to secure the succession of **Nero,** her son by a previous marriage. Nero's thanks were later to murder not only his mother but also his wife (Claudius's daughter) and his rival, Claudius's 13-year-old son Britannicus. An enthusiastic persecutor of Christians, Nero supposedly committed suicide with the cry, "What an artist I destroy!"

By the 3rd century A.D., corruption and rivalry had become so prevalent that there were 23 emperors in 73 years. Few, however, were as twisted as **Caracalla,** who, to secure control, had his brother Geta slashed to pieces while Geta was in the arms of their mother, former empress Julia Domna.

Constantine the Great, who became emperor in A.D. 306, made Constantinople (or Byzantium) the new capital of the Empire in 330, moving administrative functions away from Rome altogether, partly because of the growing menace of barbarian attacks in the west. Constantine was the first Christian emperor, allegedly converting after he saw the True Cross in a dream, accompanied by the words, IN THIS SIGN SHALL YOU CONQUER. He defeated rival emperor Maxentius and his followers at the **Battle of the Milivan Bridge** (A.D. 312), a victory commemorated by Rome's triumphal **Arco di Costantino** (p. 95). Constantine formally ended the persecution of Christians with the **Edict of Milan** (A.D. 313).

It was during the Imperial period that Rome flourished in architecture. **Classical orders** were simplified into forms of column capitals: **Doric** (a plain capital), **Ionic** (a capital with a scroll), and **Corinthian** (a capital with flowering acanthus leaves). Much of this development was enabled by the discovery of a type of concrete, and the fine-tuning of the arch, which was used with a logic, rhythm, and ease never before seen. Many of these monumental buildings still stand in Rome, notably **Trajan's Column** (p. 100), the **Colosseum** (p. 98), and Hadrian's **Pantheon** (p. 109). Elsewhere in Italy, Verona's **Arena** (p. 293) bears witness to the kinds of crowds the brutal sport of gladiatorial combat could draw. Three **Roman cities** have been preserved, with street plans and, in some cases, even buildings intact: doomed **Pompeii** (p. 141) and its neighbor **Herculaneum,** both buried by Vesuvius's massive A.D. 79 eruption; and Rome's ancient seaport, **Ostia Antica** (p. 137). At Herculaneum, one of Rome's greatest writers, **Pliny the Elder** (A.D. 23–79), perished. It's thanks to him; his nephew, **Pliny the Younger;** the historians **Tacitus, Suetonius, Cassius Dio,** and **Livy;** and satirist **Juvenal** that much knowledge of ancient Roman life and history was not lost.

Surviving Roman **art** had a major influence on the painters and sculptors of the Renaissance (p. 31). In Rome itself, look for the marble *bas-reliefs* (sculptures projecting slightly from a flat surface) on the **Arco di Costantino** (p. 95); the sculpture and mosaic collections at the **Palazzo Massimo alle Terme** (p. 121); and the gilded equestrian statue of Marcus Aurelius at the **Musei Capitolini** (p. 96). The Florentine Medici were avid collectors of Roman statuary, some now at the **Uffizi** (p. 181).

The Fall of the Empire Through the "Dark Ages"

The Eastern and Western sections of the Roman Empire split in A.D. 395, leaving the Italian peninsula without the support it once received from east of the Adriatic. When the **Goths** moved toward Rome in the early 5th century, citizens in the provinces, who had grown to hate the bureaucracy set up by **Diocletian,** welcomed the invaders. And then the pillage began.

Rome was first sacked by **Alaric I,** king of the Visigoths, in 410. The populace made no attempt to defend their city (other than trying vainly to buy him off, a tactic that had worked 3 years earlier); most people fled into the hills.

ALL ABOUT VINO (and birra, too)

Italy is the largest **wine**-producing country in the world; as far back as 800 B.C., the Etruscans were vintners. However, it wasn't until 1965 that laws were enacted to guarantee consistency in winemaking. Quality wines are labeled **"DOC"** (Denominazione di Origine Controllata). If you see **"DOCG"** on a label (the "G" stands for *Garantita*), it denotes an even higher quality wine region (in theory, at least). **"IGT"** (Indicazione Geografica Tipica) indicates a more general wine zone—for example, Umbria—but still with mandatory quality control.

Below we cite a few of the best Italian wines around Venice, Rome, and Florence, but rest assured there are hundreds more—have some fun sampling to find your own favorites. Even a pitcher of a local *vino della casa* (house wine) can be a delight.

Tuscany: Tuscan red wines rank with some of the world's finest. **Sangiovese** is the king of grapes here, and **Chianti** from the hills south of Florence is the most widely known sangiovese wine. The premium zone is **Chianti Classico,** where a lively ruby-red wine has a bouquet of violets. The Tuscan south houses two even finer DOCGs: mighty, robust **Brunello di Montalcino,** a garnet red ideal for roasts and game; and almost purple **Vino Nobile di Montepulciano,** with its rich, velvet body. End a meal with the Tuscan dessert wine **vin santo,** often accompanied by hard *biscotti* to dunk in your glass.

The Veneto: Reds around Venice vary from light and lunchtime-friendly **Bardolino** to **Valpolicella,** which can be particularly intense if grapes are partially dried before fermentation to make an **Amarone.** White, garganega-based **Soave** has a pale amber color and a peachlike flavor. **Lugana** at its best has a sparkle of gold and a rich but dry structure. **Prosecco** is the classic Italian sparkling white, the base for both a Bellini and a Spritz (joints that use Champagne are doing it wrong).

Latium: Many of Rome's local wines come from the Castelli Romani, the hill towns around the capital. These wines are best drunk when young and are most often white, mellow, and dry. The golden wines of **Frascati** are the most famous.

Italy's drink isn't all about wine, however. Especially among the young, there's a boom in popularity for artisanal **beer.** Although supermarket shelves are still stacked with mainstream brands Peroni and Moretti, smaller stores and bars increasingly offer craft microbrews. Italy had fewer than 50 breweries in 2000; the count was over 1,000 by 2018 and is still rising. Craft-beer consumption has more than tripled since 2012, according to brewers' association, Unionbirrai.

The feeble Western emperor **Honorius** hid out in **Ravenna,** which in 402 he had made capital of the Western Roman Empire.

More than 40 troubled years passed. Then **Attila the Hun** invaded Italy to besiege Rome. Attila was dissuaded from attacking, thanks largely to a peace mission headed by Pope Leo I in 452. Yet relief was short-lived: In 455, **Gaiseric,** king of the **Vandals,** carried out a 2-week sack unparalleled in its savagery. The empire of the West lasted for only another 20 years; finally, in 476, the sacks and chaos ended the once-mighty city, and Rome itself was left to the popes, though ruled nominally from Ravenna.

Although little detailed history of Italy in the immediate post-Roman period is known—and few buildings survive—it's certain the spread of **Christianity** was gradually creating a new society. The religion was probably founded in Rome about a decade after the death of Jesus, and gradually gained strength despite Roman persecution. To relive the early Christian era, visit Rome's Appian Way and its Catacombs, along the **Via Appia Antica** (p. 126), just outside Rome's ancient walls. A church on the Appian Way marks the spot where the disciple Peter, fleeing persecution, is said to have had a pivotal vision of Christ; nearby, the **Catacombs** (p. 126), the first cemeteries of Rome's Christian community, house the remains of early popes and martyrs.

We have Christianity, along with the influence of Byzantium, to thank for the appearance of Italy's next great artistic style: the **Byzantine.** Painting and mosaic work in this era was stylized and static, but also ornate and ethereal. Churches in the Byzantine style include Venice's **Basilica di San Marco** (p. 261) and Rome's **Basilica di San Clemente** (p. 104).

The Middle Ages: 9th–14th Centuries

A ravaged Rome entered the Middle Ages, its population scattered. A modest number of residents continued to live in the swamps of the **Campus Martius.** The seven hills—now without water because the aqueducts were cut—stood abandoned and crumbling.

The Pope turned toward Europe, where he found a powerful ally in **Charlemagne,** king of the Franks. In 800, Pope Leo III crowned him emperor. Although Charlemagne pledged allegiance to the church and made the pope the final arbiter in most religious and cultural matters, he also set Western Europe on a course of bitter opposition to papal meddling in affairs of state.

Outside Rome's city walls, early Christians secretly worshipped—and buried their dead—in the Catacombs.

The successor to Charlemagne's empire was a political entity known as the **Holy Roman Empire** (962–1806). The new Empire defined the end of the Dark Ages but ushered in a long period of bloody warfare. Magyars from Hungary invaded Lombardy and, in turn, were defeated by an increasingly powerful **Venice,** which, having defeated its naval rival Genoa in the 1380 Battle of Chioggia, reigned over most of the eastern Mediterranean. Venetian merchants ruled a republic that lasted for a millennium and built a city full of imposing architecture like the **Doge's Palace** (p. 265).

While Venice flourished, **Rome** during the Middle Ages was a quaint backwater. Narrow lanes with overhanging buildings filled areas that had once been showcases of imperial power. The forums, markets, temples, and theaters of the Imperial era slowly disintegrated. It remained the seat of the Roman Catholic Church, a state almost completely controlled by priests, who aggressively expanded church influence and acquisitions. The result was an endless series of power struggles.

In the mid–14th century, the **Black Death** ravaged Europe, killing perhaps a third of Italy's population; the preservation of Tuscan towns like **San Gimignano** (p. 217) and **Siena** (p. 211) owes much to the fact that they never fully recovered from the devastations of the 1348–49 plague. Despite such setbacks, Italian city-states grew wealthy from Crusades booty, trade, and banking. The **Florin,** a gold coin minted in Florence, became the first truly international currency for centuries, dominating trade all over the continent.

The medieval period marks the beginning of building in stone on a mass scale. Flourishing from 800 to 1300, **Romanesque architecture** took its inspiration and rounded arches from Ancient Rome. Its architects concentrated on building large churches with wide aisles to accommodate the masses. Pisa's **Campo dei Miracoli** (p. 216) is typical of the Pisan-Romanesque style, with stacked arcades of mismatched columns in the cathedral facade (and wrapped around the **Leaning Tower of Pisa**), and blind arcading set with diamond-shaped lozenges. The influence of Arab architecture is obvious—Pisa was a city of seafaring merchants.

Romanesque sculpture was often wonderfully childlike in its narrative simplicity, frequently mixing biblical scenes with the myths and motifs of local pagan traditions. Among Italy's greatest surviving examples of Romanesque sculpture are the 48 relief panels on the bronze doors of the **Basilica di San Zeno Maggiore** in Verona (p. 294).

As the appeal of Romanesque and Byzantine faded, the **Gothic** style flourished between the 13th and 15th centuries. In architecture, Gothic was characterized by flying buttresses, pointed arches, and delicate stained-glass windows. These engineering developments freed architecture from the heavy, thick walls of the Romanesque and allowed ceilings to soar, walls to thin, and windows to proliferate. Many secular Gothic buildings arose, including palaces designed to show off the prestige of various ruling families, like Siena's **Palazzo Pubblico** (p. 213) and many of the great buildings of **Venice** (see chapter 9). **San Gimignano** (p. 217) has a remarkably preserved Gothic center.

Detail of the Baptistery of St. John in Piazza dei Miracoli, Pisa.

Painters such as **Cimabue** (1251–1302) and **Giotto** (1266–1337) in Florence, **Pietro Cavallini** (1259–ca. 1330) in Rome, and **Duccio di Buoninsegna** (ca. 1255–1319) in Siena began to lift art from Byzantine rigidity and set it on the road to realism. Giotto's finest work is his fresco cycle at Padua's **Cappella degli Scrovegni** (p. 291); he was the harbinger of the oncoming Renaissance, which would forever change art and architecture. Duccio's "Maestà," now in Siena's **Museo dell'Opera del Duomo** (p. 213), influenced Sienese painters for centuries. Ambrogio Lorenzetti painted the greatest civic frescoes of the Middle Ages—his "Allegories of Good and Bad Government" in Siena's **Palazzo Pubblico** (p. 213)—before he succumbed to the Black Death, along with almost every significant Sienese artist of his generation.

The medieval period also saw the birth of literature in the Italian language, a written version of the **Tuscan dialect**—primarily because the great writers of the age were Tuscans. Florentine **Dante Alighieri** wrote his "Divine Comedy" in the 1310s, and Boccaccio's "Decameron"—a kind of Florentine "Canterbury Tales"—appeared in the 1350s.

Renaissance & Baroque Italy: 1400s–1700s

The story of Italy from the dawn of the Renaissance in the early 15th century to the Age of Enlightenment in the 17th and 18th centuries is as fascinating and complicated as that of the rise and fall of the Roman Empire.

During this period, **Rome** underwent major physical changes. The old centers of culture reverted to pastures, and new churches and palaces were built using the recycled stones of Ancient Rome. This construction boom did more damage to the temples of the Caesars than any barbarian sack had ever done. Rare marbles were stripped from Imperial-era baths and used as altarpieces or sent to limekilns. So enthusiastic was various popes' destruction of Imperial Rome, it's a miracle anything is left.

This era is best remembered because of its art, and around 1400 the most significant power in Italy was the city where the Renaissance began: **Florence** (see chapter 6). The **Medici** family rose to become the most powerful of the city's ruling oligarchy, gradually usurping the powers of trade guilds and republicans. They reformed law and commerce, expanded the city's power by taking control of neighbors such as **Pisa,** and financed a "renaissance," or rebirth, in painting, sculpture, and architecture. Christopher Hibbert's *The Rise and Fall of the House of Medici* is the most readable historical account of the era.

A lion holds Florence's coat of arms, Museo Nazionale del Bargello.

Netflix's *Medici: Masters of Florence* serves up a fictionalized, sensationalized, but fun "history" of power-plays in the Renaissance city.

Under the patronage of the Medici and other rich Florentine families, innovative painters and sculptors pursued more expressiveness and naturalism. **Donatello** (1386–1466) cast the first free-standing nude since antiquity (now in Florence's **Museo Nazionale del Bargello;** see p. 183). **Lorenzo Ghiberti** (1378–1455) labored for 50 years on two sets of doors for Florence's **Baptistery** (p. 175), the most famous of which were dubbed the "Gates of Paradise." **Masaccio** (1401–28) produced the first painting that realistically portrayed linear perspective, on the nave wall of **Santa Maria Novella** (p. 192).

Next followed a brief period that's become known as the **High Renaissance.** The epitome of the Renaissance man, Florentine **Leonardo da Vinci** (1452–1519) painted his "Last Supper," in Milan, and an "Annunciation" now hanging in Florence's **Uffizi** (p. 181), alongside countless Renaissance masterpieces from such great painters as Paolo Uccello, Sandro Botticelli, Piero della Francesca, and others. **Raphael** (1483–1520) produced a sublime body of work in his 37 years. Skilled in sculpture, painting, and architecture, **Michelangelo** (1475–1564) and his career mark the apogee of the Renaissance. His giant "David" at the **Galleria dell'Accademia** (p. 193) in Florence

RENAISSANCE reading

Whole libraries have been written on the Renaissance—and it's certainly worth acquainting yourself with some of the themes and styles before you visit. The most accessible introductions include Peter and Linda Murray's *The Art of the Renaissance* (1963), Michael Levey's *Early Renaissance* (1967), Evelyn Welch's *Art in Renaissance Italy 1350–1500* (2000), and Peter Murray's *The Architecture of the Italian Renaissance* (1969). Giorgio Vasari's *Lives of the Artists,* first published in 1550, remains the definitive work on Renaissance artists, written by one who knew some of them personally; it's still a good read. In *The Stones of Florence* (1956), Mary McCarthy mixes architectural insight with no-holds-barred opinion.

is the world's most famous statue, and his **Sistine Chapel** frescoes have lured millions to the **Vatican Museums** (p. 90) in Rome.

The father of Venice's High Renaissance was **Titian** (1485–1576), known for his mastery of color and tone. Venice (see chapter 8) offers a rich trove of Titian's work, along with works by earlier Venetian masters **Gentile Bellini** (1429–1507), **Giorgione** (1477–1510), and **Vittore Carpaccio** (1465–1525).

As in painting, Renaissance **architecture** stressed proportion, order, and classical inspiration. In the early 1400s, **Filippo Brunelleschi** (1377–1446) grasped the mathematics of "perspective" and provided artists with ground rules for creating an illusion of three dimensions on a flat surface. (Read Ross

"Annunciation" by Leonardo da Vinci in the Galleria degli Uffizi, Florence.

King's "Brunelleschi's Dome" for the story of his greatest achievement, the crowning of Florence's cathedral with its iconic ochre dome.) Even **Michelangelo** took up architecture late in life, designing the Laurentian Library and New Sacristy at the **Medici Chapels** in Florence (p. 190), then moving to complete his crowning glory, the soaring dome of Rome's **St. Peter's Basilica** (p. 88). The third great Renaissance architect—and most influential of them all—**Andrea Palladio** (1508–80) worked in a classical mode of columns, porticoes, pediments, and other ancient-temple-inspired features. Perhaps his masterpiece is the elegant **Il Redentore** church (p. 279) in Venice.

In time, the High Renaissance evolved into the **baroque.** Stuccoes, sculptures, and paintings were carefully designed to complement each other—and the space itself—to create a unified whole. The baroque movement's spiritual home was Rome, and its towering figure was **Gian Lorenzo Bernini** (1598–1680), the greatest baroque sculptor, a fantastic architect, and a more-than-decent painter. Among many fine sculptures, you'll find his best in Rome's **Galleria Borghese** (p. 118) and **Santa Maria della Vittoria** (p. 121).

In **music,** the most famous baroque composer was Venetian **Antonio Vivaldi** (1678–1741), whose "Four Seasons" is among the most often performed classical compositions of all time. In **painting,** baroque often mixed a kind of super-realism—using peasants as models, exaggerating light and shadow with a technique called *chiaroscuro*—with complex composition and dynamic explosions of movement and color. The period produced many fine painters, most notably **Caravaggio** (1571–1610). Among his masterpieces are a "St. Matthew" cycle in Rome's **San Luigi dei Francesi** (p. 109). The baroque also had an outstanding female painter: **Artemisia Gentileschi** (1593–1652), whose brutal "Judith Slaying Holofernes" hangs in Florence's **Uffizi** (p. 181).

Frothy and ornate, **rococo** art was the baroque taken to flamboyant extremes, and had few serious proponents in Italy. **Giambattista Tiepolo** (1696–1770), arguably the best of the rococo painters, specialized in ceiling frescoes and canvases with cloud-filled heavens of light, as in Venice's **Scuola Grande dei Carmini** (p. 275). For rococo building—more a decorative than an architectural movement—look no further than Rome's **Spanish Steps** (p. 115) or the **Trevi Fountain** (p. 116).

At Last, a United Italy: The 1800s

By the 1800s, the glories of the Renaissance were a fading memory. Chunks of Italy had changed hands many, many times—between the Austrians, the Spanish, and the French, among autocratic thugs and enlightened princes, between the noble and the merchant classes. The 19th century witnessed the final collapse of many Renaissance city-states. The last of the Medici, Gian Gastone, died in 1737, leaving Tuscany in the hands of foreign Lorraine and Habsburg princes. In 1797 French emperor **Napoleon** brought an end to a millennium of republican government in **Venice,** installing puppet rulers across the Italian peninsula. After a British/Prussian/Dutch alliance defeated

Rome's Trevi Fountain.

Napoleon, the **Congress of Vienna** (1814–15) parceled out various parts of Italy once again.

Political unrest became a fact of Italian life, spurred by insurrectionaries like **Giuseppe Mazzini.** Europe's year of revolutions, **1848,** rocked Italy with violent uprisings. After decades of political intrigue, thanks to the efforts of statesman **Camillo Cavour** and rebel general **Giuseppe Garibaldi,** the Kingdom of Italy was proclaimed in 1861, with **Victor Emmanuel (Vittorio Emanuele) II** of Savoy as its first monarch. The kingdom's first capital was **Turin** (1861–65), followed by **Florence** (1865–71).

The establishment of the kingdom, however, didn't signal a complete unification of Italy, because Latium (including Rome) was still under papal control and Venetia was held by Austria. This was partially resolved in 1866, when Venetia joined the rest of Italy after the **Seven Weeks' War** between Austria and Prussia. On September 20, 1870, Rome was taken—present-day **Via XX Settembre** is the very street up which patriots advanced after breaching the city gates—and it became the capital in 1871. The **Risorgimento**—the "resurgence," Italian unification—was complete.

Political heights in Italy seemed to correspond to creative depths in art and architecture. Among the few notable practitioners of this era was Venetian **Antonio Canova** (1757–1822), Italy's major neoclassical sculptor, who became notorious for painting both Napoleon and his sister Pauline as nudes. His best work is in Rome's **Galleria Borghese** (p. 118).

Music, however, was experiencing its Italian golden age, and it's **opera** for which the 19th century will largely be remembered. *Bel canto* composer **Gioachino Rossini** (1792–1868) found success with his 1816 "The Barber of Seville," and the fame of Bergamo native **Gaetano Donizetti** (1797–1848) was assured when his "Anna Bolena" premiered in 1830. Both were later overshadowed by **Giuseppe Verdi** (1813–1901), whose works such as "Rigoletto" and "La Traviata" assumed profound nationalist symbolism. At the turn of the century, the Romantic movement that had dominated music gave way to the *verismo* ("realism") of **Giacomo Puccini** (1858–1924), whose operas "La Bohème," "Tosca," "Madama Butterfly," and the unfinished "Turandot" still pack houses worldwide.

The 20th Century: Two World Wars & One Duce

Statue of Giuseppe Verdi in his home town of Bussetto, just outside Parma, Italy.

In 1915, Italy entered **World War I** on the side of the Allies, joining Britain, Russia, and France to help defeat Germany and the traditional enemy to the north—the Austro-Hungarian Empire—and so to "reclaim" Trentino and Trieste. (Mark Thompson's *The White War* [2008] tells the story of Italy's catastrophic, though victorious, campaign.) In the aftermath of war's carnage, Italians suffered further with rising unemployment and horrendous inflation. As in Germany, political crisis led to the emergence of a dictator.

On October 28, 1922, **Benito Mussolini,** who had started his Fascist Party in 1919, gathered 30,000 Black Shirts for his **March on Rome.** Inflation was soaring and workers had just called a general strike, so rather than recognize a state under siege, **King Victor Emmanuel III** (1900–46) proclaimed Mussolini the new government leader. In 1929, Il Duce—a moniker Mussolini began using from 1925—defined the divisions between the Italian government and pope by signing the Lateran Treaty, which granted political, territorial, and fiscal autonomy to the microstate of **Vatican City.** During the Spanish Civil War (1936–39), Mussolini's support for General Franco's Fascists, who had staged a coup against the elected government of Spain, helped seal the Axis alliance between Italy and Nazi Germany. Italy was inexorably and disastrously sucked into **World War II.**

Deeply unpleasant though their politics were, the Fascist regime did sponsor some remarkable **rationalist architecture,** such as Florence's **Santa Maria Novella station.** (Today a plaque at the station commemorates Jews who were sent from the terminus to their deaths in Nazi Germany.)

After defeat in World War II, Italy voted to establish the **First Republic**—overwhelmingly so in northern and central Italy, which outvoted a southern majority that wanted to keep the monarchy. Italy quickly succeeded in rebuilding its economy, in part because of U.S. aid under the **Marshall Plan** (1948–52). By the 1960s, as a member of the European Economic Community (founded by the **Treaty of Rome** in 1957), Italy had become one of the world's leading industrialized nations, prominent in the manufacture of automobiles and office equipment. Fiat (from Turin), Ferrari (from Emilia-Romagna), and Olivetti (from northern Piedmont) were known around the world.

The postwar Italian **film industry** gained notice for its innovative directors. **Federico Fellini** (1920–93) burst onto the scene with his highly individual style, starting with *La Strada* (1954) and going on to such classics as *The City of Women* (1980). His *La Dolce Vita* (1961) defined an era in Rome. The gritty "neorealism" of controversial **Pier Paolo Pasolini** (1922–75) is conveyed most vividly in *Accattone* (1961), which he wrote and directed.

The country continued to be plagued, however, by economic inequality between the prosperous industrial north and a depressed south. During the late 1970s and early 1980s, it was rocked by domestic terrorism: These were the so-called **Anni di Piombo (Years of Lead),** when extremists of the left and right bombed and assassinated with impunity. Conspiracy theories became the Italian staple diet; everyone from a shadow state to Masonic lodges to the CIA was accused of involvement in what became in effect an undeclared civil war. The most notorious incident of the Anni di Piombo was the kidnap and murder of Prime Minister **Aldo Moro** in 1978. You'll find a succinct account of these murky years in Tobias Jones's *The Dark Heart of Italy* (2003).

Resonant events in recent Italian history have centered on religion. As much of the world watched and prayed, **Pope John Paul II** died in April 2005, at the age of 84, ending a reign of 26 years. Doctrinal hardliner **Pope Benedict XVI** next took the papal throne; in 2013, he became the first pope since the 1400s to resign the office, and was succeeded by the surprisingly liberal **Pope Francis.**

WHEN TO GO

The best months for traveling in most of Italy are from **April to June** and **mid-September to October:** Temperatures are usually comfortable, rural colors are rich, and crowds aren't too intense (except around Easter). From

July through early September the country's holiday spots teem with visitors. **Easter, May,** and **June** usually see the highest hotel prices in Rome and Florence.

August is the worst month in many places: Not only does it get uncomfortably hot and muggy, but seemingly the entire country goes on vacation for at least 2 weeks (some Italians take off the entire month). Many family-run hotels, restaurants, and shops are closed (except at the spas, beaches, and islands, where most Italians head). Paradoxically, Florence in August can seem emptied of locals, and hotels there (and in Rome) were once heavily discounted (alas, now less so). Just be aware that many fashionable restaurants and nightspots are closed for the whole month.

From **late October to Easter,** many attractions operate on shorter (sometimes *much* shorter) winter hours, and some hotels are closed for renovation or redecoration, although that's less likely to be a problem in cities. Many family-run restaurants take a week or three off sometime between **November and February;** beach destinations become padlocked ghost towns. Deals are often available then, if you avoid Christmas and New Year.

Weather

It's warm all over Italy in summer; it can be very hot in the south, and almost anywhere inland—landlocked cities on the northern plains and in Tuscany can be stifling during a July or August hot spell. The higher temperatures (measured in Italy in degrees Celsius) usually begin in May, often lasting until early October. Winters in the north of Italy are cold, with rain and snow, and a biting wind whistles over the mountains into Venice and, less often, Florence. In Rome and farther south, the weather is mostly warm (or at least, warm-ish) all year, averaging 10°C (50°F) in winter. Even here chilly snaps are possible, as freezing temperatures and heavy snow in winters of both 2017 and 2018 proved. The rainiest months are October and November.

Public Holidays

Offices, government buildings (though not usually tourist information centers), and shops in Italy generally close on: January 1 (*Capodanno,* or New Year); January 6 (*La Befana,* or Epiphany); Easter Sunday *(Pasqua)*; Easter Monday *(Pasquetta)*; April 25 (Liberation Day); May 1 (*Festa del Lavoro,* or

Italy's Average Daily High Temperature & Monthly Rainfall

		JAN	FEB	MAR	APR	MAY	JUNE	JULY	AUG	SEPT	OCT	NOV	DEC
ROME	Temp. (°F)	55	56	59	63	71	77	83	83	79	71	62	57
	Temp. (°C)	12	13	15	17	21	25	28	28	26	21	16	13
	Rainfall (in.)	3.2	2.8	2.7	2.6	2	1.3	.6	1	2.7	4.5	4.4	3.8
FLORENCE	Temp. (°F)	49	53	60	68	75	84	89	88	81	69	58	50
	Temp. (°C)	9	11	15	20	23	28	31	31	27	20	14	10
	Rainfall (in.)	1.9	2.1	2.7	2.9	3	2.7	1.5	1.9	3.3	4	3.9	2.8
VENICE	Temp. (°F)	42	47	54	61	70	77	81	81	75	65	53	44
	Temp. (°C)	6	8	12	16	21	25	27	27	24	18	11	7
	Rainfall (in.)	2.3	2.1	2.2	2.5	2.7	3	2.5	3.3	2.6	2.7	3.4	2.1

Labor Day); June 2 (*Festa della Repubblica,* or Republic Day); August 15 (*Ferragosto,* or the Assumption of the Virgin); November 1 (All Saints' Day); December 8 (*L'Immacolata,* or the Immaculate Conception); December 25 (*Natale,* Christmas Day); and December 26 (*Santo Stefano,* or St. Stephen's Day). You'll often find businesses closed for any annual celebration dedicated to the local patron saint (for example, Jan 31 in San Gimignano, Tuscany).

Italy Calendar of Events

FEBRUARY

Carnevale, Venice. At this riotous time, theatrical presentations and masked balls take place across Venice and on islands in its lagoon. Balls are by invitation only (except the Doge's Ball), but street events and fireworks are open to everyone. www.carnevale. venezia.it. Two weeks before Ash Wednesday.

MARCH

Festa di San Giuseppe, Trionfale Quarter, Rome. A decorated statue of St. Joseph graces a fair with food stalls, concerts, and sporting events. Usually March 19.

APRIL

Holy Week, nationwide. Processions and ceremonies are staged—some dating to the Middle Ages. The most notable procession is led by the pope, passing the Colosseum and Roman Forum; a torch-lit parade caps the observance. Beginning 4 days before Easter Sunday.

Easter Sunday (Pasqua), Piazza San Pietro, Rome. In an event broadcast around the world, the pope gives his blessing from the balcony of St. Peter's.

Scoppio del Carro (Explosion of the Cart), Florence. A cart laden with flowers and fireworks is drawn by three white oxen to the Duomo, where at the 11am Mass a mechanical dove detonates it. Easter Sunday.

MAY

Maggio Musicale Fiorentino (Florentine Musical May), Florence. Italy's oldest and most prestigious music festival emphasizes music from the 14th to the 20th centuries, including ballet and opera. www.maggio fiorentino.it. Late April to June.

Concorso Ippico Internazionale (International Horse Show), Piazza di Siena, Rome.

Top-flight international show jumping at the Villa Borghese. www.piazzadisiena.it. Late May.

JUNE

Festa di San Ranieri, Pisa. The city honors its patron saint with candlelit parades, followed the next day by eight-rower teams competing in 16th-century costumes. June 16 and 17.

Calcio Storico (Historic Football), Florence. A revival of a raucous 15th-century form of football, pitting four teams in medieval costumes against one another. Matches usually culminate June 24, feast day of St. John the Baptist. www.calciostoricofiorentino.it. Late June.

Gioco del Ponte, Pisa. Teams in Renaissance costume take part in a long-contested tug-of-war on the Ponte di Mezzo, which spans the Arno. www.giocodelpontedipisa. it. Last weekend in June.

La Biennale di Venezia, Venice. One of the most famous recurring contemporary art events in the world takes place in alternate odd-numbered years. www.labiennale.org. June to November.

JULY

Il Palio, Piazza del Campo, Siena. Palio fever grips this Tuscan hilltown for a wild and exciting horse race from the Middle Ages. Pageantry, costumes, and celebrations in the victorious *contrada* (sort of a neighborhood social club) mark the spectacle. It's a "no rules" event: Even a horse without a rider can win the race. July 2 and August 16.

Festa del Redentore (Feast of the Redeemer), Venice. This festival marks the lifting of the plague in 1576, with fireworks, pilgrimages, and boating. www.redentor evenezia.it. Third Saturday and Sunday in July.

AUGUST

Venice International Film Festival, Venice. Ranking after Cannes, this festival brings together stars, directors, producers, and filmmakers from all over the world to the Palazzo del Cinema on the Lido. www.labiennale.org. Late August to early September.

SEPTEMBER

Regata Storica, Grand Canal, Venice. A maritime spectacular: Many gondolas participate in the canal procession, although gondolas don't race in the regatta itself. www.regatastoricavenezia.it. First Sunday in September.

DECEMBER

Christmas Blessing of the Pope, Piazza San Pietro, Rome. Delivered at noon from the balcony of St. Peter's Basilica, the pope's words are broadcast to the faithful around the globe. December 25.

ROME

By Elizabeth Heath

As the one-time ruler of the Western World, Rome wears its ancient heritage proudly. Even the partial, scattered ruins of that empire inspire awe—the Roman Forum, the Colosseum, the Pantheon, the Appian Way—far more than just piles of sunbaked crumbling stone, they stand as humbling evidence of a once-great civilization that no longer exists. As a visitor to Rome, you will be constantly reminded of this city's extraordinary past. But there is far more to the Eternal City than just a dusty history lesson.

Take time to get away from the crowds to explore the intimate piazzas and lesser basilicas in the back streets of Trastevere and the *centro storico*. Indulge in eno-gastronomic pursuits at coffee bars, trattorias, enotecas and gelaterias. Have a picnic in Villa Borghese or climb to the top of the Gianicolo for million-dollar views. Rome is so compact that without planning too much, you'll end up stumbling across its monuments and its simpler pleasures.

Walk the streets of Rome, and the city will be yours.

STRATEGIES FOR SEEING ROME

With so many sights to see in Rome and so many people trying to see them, you need to plan your days efficiently if you want to save time, avoid long lines, and get the most for your money. These insider strategies will help you enrich your time and travels in Rome.

o **Bypass the lines.** Advance tickets are sold online for the Colosseum and the Vatican Museums and are required for the Galleria Borghese. Absolutely buy ahead. That means picking your exact date and even time slot for entry, but that won't feel so onerous when you skip past the long queues of tourists who didn't plan ahead. Also, while some city passes aren't worth the money, the Roma Pass remains a worthwhile deal if you plan to visit a lot of state-run attractions (Vatican properties are not included) and use public transportation. See p. 44 and individual attraction listings for more info. Alas, unless you book a private tour, there's no way to jump the line to enter St. Peter's Basilica; arrive early in the morning, before the basilica opens, or late in the afternoon for the shortest wait (see p. 88).

o **Avoid ancient overload.** Even though they're all included on the same ticket, the ruins of the Colosseum, Roman Forum, and Palatine Hill are a lot to take in on a single day, particularly in the heat of the Roman summer. Take advantage of the 2-day window your ticket allows, and see the Forum and Palatine on your first day, then hit the Colosseum right when it opens on day 2, before the crowds pile in. If you didn't do an advance purchase, buy your ticket and enter at the Palatine Hill, where there's never a line.

o **Pick a less popular time slot.** If you buy a timed ticket to the Vatican Museums, Galleria Borghese, or elsewhere, pick a lunchtime or late afternoon slot, when you're likely to encounter fewer crowds. For a much more intimate experience, consider seeing the Vatican Museums on a Friday night or on an early-bird tour, which includes breakfast. See p. 90.

o **Streamline your Vatican visit.** Before you visit the Vatican Museums, buy the very useful *Guide to the Vatican Museums and City* book (14€) sold at the Vatican Tourist Office, on the left side of Piazza San Pietro. Review the galleries map and decide which collections or works of art are a priority, so you don't get overwhelmed by the sheer volume of great art here. Once inside, if your priority is to see the Sistine Chapel, follow signs for the "Percorso Breve" (short route) to the Cappella Sistina.

o **Walk the side streets.** On a day when Rome is packed with tourists, Via del Corso and the narrow arteries linking the Pantheon and Trevi Fountain are the last places you want to be—they're crowded with slow-moving tour groups, unlicensed vendors, and, alas, pickpockets. You can cover the same ground in a much more pleasant manner if you wander the side streets and alleys that all more or less take you to the same place. Just keep your map handy.

o **Plan around Sunday closures.** The Vatican Museums and the catacombs of the Appian Way are closed on Sundays. St. Peter's remains open, but the Pope's noontime blessing on St. Peter's Square means dense crowds—so unless you want to participate in that brief service, steer clear. The Campo de' Fiori market and other fresh produce markets are closed on Sundays as well.

o **Don't dine in the shadow of monuments.** With few exceptions, dining with a view of Piazza Navona, the Pantheon, or Campo de'Fiori means unforgettable photo ops and overpriced, absolutely forgettable cuisine. Instead, spend your money in one of the many hidden *trattorie* of Rome's charming, cobbled side streets. When in doubt, follow an Italian—they always seem to know where to eat well!

ESSENTIALS

Arriving

BY PLANE Most flights arrive at Rome's **Leonardo da Vinci International Airport** (www.adr.it; 𝄋 **06/65951**), popularly known as **Fiumicino,**

30km (19 miles) from the city center. (If you're arriving from other European cities, you might land at Ciampino Airport, discussed below). After you leave Passport Control, you'll see a **tourist information desk,** staffed Monday through Saturday from 8:15am to 7pm. A *cambio* (money exchange) operates daily from 7:30am to 11pm, but it's just as easy, and possibly less expensive, to withdraw cash from an ATM *(bancomat)* in the airport. See p. 304 for tips on using Italian ATMs.

Follow signs marked TRENI to find the **airport train station,** where you can catch the delightfully named **Leonardo Express** for a 31-minute shuttle ride) to Rome's main station, **Stazione Termini.** The shuttle runs every 15 minutes (every 30 min. at off-peak hours) from 6:23am to 11:23pm for 14€ one-way (free for kids 12 and under). On the way to the train, you'll pass a yellow machine dispensing tickets (cash or credit), or you can buy them at the Trenitalia window near the tracks. When you arrive at Termini, get out of the train quickly and try to grab a baggage cart. Do watch out for pickpockets at Termini.

A **taxi** from da Vinci airport to the city costs a flat-rate 48€ for the 45-minute to 1-hour trip, depending on traffic (hotels tend to charge 50€–60€ for pickup service). Note that the flat rate is applicable from the airport to central Rome and vice-versa, but only if your central Rome location is inside the Aurelian Walls (most hotels are). Otherwise, standard metered rates apply, which can bump the fare to 75€ or higher. There are also surcharges for large luggage, Sunday and holiday rides, and more than 4 passengers.

If you arrive at **Ciampino Airport** (www.adr.it/ciampino; ✆ **06/65951**), you can take a Terravision bus (www.terravision.eu; ✆ **06/4880086;** first bus at 8:15am, last bus at 12:15am) to Stazione Termini. This takes about 45 minutes and costs 5€. A **taxi** from Ciampino costs a flat rate of 30€, provided you're going to a destination within the old Aurelian Walls.

From either airport, ride-sharing service **Uber** is available—sort of. Because of licensing laws (and strong resistance from Rome's taxi drivers), only Uber Black or Uber Van service is offered, and it's much more expensive than a taxi. If you want Uber-like convenience and in-app payments, consider the **MyTaxi** app, available for iPhones or Androids.

BY TRAIN OR BUS   Trains and buses (including trains from the airport) arrive in the center of old Rome at **Stazione Termini,** Piazza dei Cinquecento. This is the train, bus, and transportation hub for all of Rome, and it is surrounded by many hotels, especially budget ones.

The station is filled with services. A money exchange window is located close to the end of platform 14, and an ATM is at the end of platform 24. **Informazioni Ferroviarie** (in the outer hall) dispenses info on rail travel to other parts of Italy. There is also a **tourist information booth,** plus baggage services, newsstands, clean public toilets, and snack bars. *Tip:* Be wary of young men/women lingering around ticket machines offering to help you. They will expect a tip. At worst, they will be distracting you so that an accomplice can pick your pocket.

To get from Termini to your final destination in Rome, you have several options. If you're taking the **Metropolitana** (subway), follow the illuminated red-and-white M signs. To catch a city bus, go straight through the outer hall and enter the sprawling bus lot of **Piazza dei Cinquecento.** See p. 47 for more information about getting around Rome by public transportation.

You will also find a line of **taxis** parked out front. Note that taxis now charge a 2€ supplement for any fares originating at Termini, plus 1€ for each bag in the trunk. Use the official taxi queue right in front of the station; don't go with a driver who approaches you or get into any cab where the meter is "broken."

BY CAR   From the north or south, the main access route is the **Autostrada A1.** This highway runs from Milan to Naples via Bologna, Florence, and Rome. At 754km (469 miles), it is the longest Italian autostrada and is the "spinal cord" of Italy's road network. All the autostrade join with the **Grande Raccordo Anulare,** a ring road encircling Rome, channeling traffic into the congested city. *Tip:* Long before you reach this road, you should study your route carefully to see what part of Rome you plan to enter. Route signs along the ring road tend to be confusing.

roma PASSES

If you plan to do serious sightseeing in Rome (and why else would you be here?), the **Roma Pass** (www.romapass.it) is worth considering. For 38.50€ per card, valid for 3 days, you get free entry to the first two museums or archaeological sites you visit; "express" entry to the Colosseum; discounted entry to all other museums and sites; free use of the city's public transport network (bus, Metro, tram, and railway lines; airport transfers not included); a free map; and free access to a special smartphone app with audioguides and interactive maps. *Note:* The Vatican Museums are not part of the pass plan.

If your stay in Rome is shorter, you may want to opt for the **Roma Pass 48 Hours** (28€), which offers the same benefits as the 3-day pass, except that only the first museum you visit is free and the ticket is valid for just 48 hours.

The free transportation perk with the Roma Pass is not insignificant, if only because it saves you the hassle of buying paper tickets. In any case, do some

quick math; one major museum or attraction entrance is 12€–15€, and each ride on public transportation is 1.50€. Discounts to other sites range from 20–50%. If you plan to visit a lot of sites and dash around the city on public transport, it's probably worth the money.

You can buy Roma passes online (www.romapass.it) and pick them up at one of the city's Tourist Information Points (INFOPOINTS); you can also order in advance by phone, with a credit card, at ☏ **06/060608.** Roma Passes are also sold directly at Tourist Information Point offices (see p. 45) or at participating museums and ATAC subway ticket offices.

Finally, you should note that the Colosseum, Roman Forum, and Palatine Hill are included under one ticket for 12€, good for 2 days and available for purchase online (plus small fee) or at the sites. Likewise, the four museums of the Museo Nazionale Romano offer a combo ticket good for 3 days that costs 12€.

Trastevere neighborhood and Basilica di Santa Maria in Rome.

Warning: If you must drive a car into Rome, return your rental car immediately on arrival, or at least get yourself to your hotel, park your car, and leave it there until you leave the city. Seriously think twice before driving in Rome—the traffic, as well as the parking options, are nightmarish. Plus most of central Rome is a **ZTL (Zona Traffico Limitato),** off-limits to nonresidents and rigorously enforced by cameras. You will almost certainly be fined; the ticket might arrive at your home address months after your trip.

Visitor Information

Information, online access, maps, and the Roma Pass (p. 44) are available at **Tourist Information Points** maintained by **Roma Capitale** (www.turismoroma.it) around the city. They're staffed daily from 9:30am to 7pm, except the one at Termini (daily 8am–6:45pm), which is located in "Centro Diagnostico" hall (Building F) next to platform 24; there's often a long line at this one. Additional offices are at **Via Nazionale 183,** near the Palazzo delle Esposizioni; on **Piazza delle Cinque Lune,** near Piazza Navona; on **Via dei Fori Imperiali** (for the Forum); on **Via Marco Minghetti,** at the corner of Via del Corso, at **Castel Sant'Angelo** (Piazza Pia), and in Trastevere on **Piazza Sidney Sonnino.** There are also information points at Fiumicino and Ciampino airports.

City Layout

The bulk of what you'll want to visit—ancient, Renaissance, and baroque Rome (as well as the train station)—lies on the east side of the **Tiber River (Fiume Tevere),** which curls through the city. However, several important landmarks are on the other side: **St. Peter's Basilica** and the **Vatican, Castel Sant'Angelo,** and the colorful **Trastevere** neighborhood. Even if those last sights are slightly farther afield, Rome has one of the most compact and walkable city centers in Europe.

That doesn't mean you won't get lost from time to time (most newcomers do). Arm yourself with a detailed street map of Rome (or a smartphone with a hefty data plan). Most hotels hand out a pretty good version of a city map.

Rome's Neighborhoods in Brief

Much of the historic core of Rome does not fall under easy or distinct neighborhood classifications. Instead, when describing a location, the frame of reference is the name of the nearest large monument or square, like St. Peter's or Piazza di Spagna. Street numbers usually run consecutively, with odd numbers on one side of the street, evens on the other. However, in centro, the numbers sometimes run up one side and then run back down on the other side (so #50 could be potentially opposite #308).

Vatican City & Prati Vatican City is technically a sovereign state, although in practice it is just another part of Rome. The **Vatican Museums, St. Peter's,** and the **Vatican Gardens** take up most of the land area; the popes have lived here for 6 centuries. If you plan to spend most of your time exploring Vatican City sights, or if you just want to stay outside the city center, **Prati,** a middle-class neighborhood east of the Vatican, has a smattering of affordable hotels and shopping streets, as well as some excellent places to eat.

Centro Storico & The Pantheon One of the most desirable (and busiest) areas of Rome, the **Centro Storico** ("Historic Center") is a maze of narrow streets and cobbled alleys dating from the Middle Ages and filled with churches and palaces built during the Renaissance and baroque eras, as well as countless hotels and AirBnB rentals. The only way to explore it is by foot. Its heart is **Piazza Navona,** bustling with sidewalk cafes, *palazzi*, street artists…and pickpockets. Nearby, the area around the ancient Roman **Pantheon** is abuzz with crowds, a cafe scene, and nightlife. South of Corso Vittorio Emanuele is the lively square of **Campo de' Fiori,** home to the famous produce market. West of Via Arenula lies the old Jewish **Ghetto,** where restaurants far outnumber hotels.

Ancient Rome, Monti & Celio Although no longer the heart of the city, this is where Rome began, with the **Colosseum, Palatine Hill, Roman Forum, Imperial Forums,** and **Circus Maximus.** This area offers only a few hotels; its restaurants are mostly tour-bus traps. Just beyond the Circus Maximus, the **Aventine Hill** is now a posh residential quarter with great city views. For more of a neighborhood feel, stay in **Monti** (Rome's oldest *rione*, or quarter) or **Celio,** respectively located north and south of the Colosseum. Both also have good dining, and Monti especially has plenty of nightlife.

Tridente & The Spanish Steps The most upscale part of Rome, full of expensive hotels, designer boutiques, and chic restaurants, lies north of Rome's center. It's often called the Tridente, because Via di Ripetta, Via del Corso, and Via del Babuino form a trident leading down from **Piazza del Popolo.** The star here is unquestionably **Piazza di Spagna,** which attracts Romans and tourists alike (though mostly the latter) to linger at its celebrated **Spanish Steps.** Some of Rome's most high-end shopping streets fan out from here, including **Via Condotti.**

Via Veneto & Piazza Barberini In the 1950s and early 1960s, the tree-lined boulevard **Via Veneto** was the swinging place to be, the haunt of la Dolce Vita celebrities and paparazzi. Luxury hotels, cafes, and restaurants still cluster here, although the restaurants are mostly overpriced tourist traps. To the south, Via Veneto ends at **Piazza**

Barberini and the magnificent **Palazzo Barberini,** begun in 1623 by Carlo Maderno and later completed by Bernini and Borromini.

Villa Borghese & Parioli **Parioli** is Rome's most elegant residential section, a setting for excellent restaurants, hotels, museums, and public parks. Bordered by the green spaces of the **Villa Borghese** to the south and the **Villa Glori** and **Villa Ada** to the north, Parioli (and just to its south, Pinciano) is one of the city's safest districts, but it's not exactly central. It's not the best base if you plan to depend on public transportation.

Around Stazione Termini For many visitors, their first glimpse of Rome is the main train station and adjoining **Piazza della Repubblica.** There are a lot of affordable hotels in this area; while they may lack charm, the location is convenient, near the city's transportation hub, and not far from ancient Rome. Hotels on the Via Marsala side often occupy floors of a *palazzo* (palace), with clean and decent, sometimes even charming, rooms. Traffic and noise are worse on the streets to the left of the station. The once-seedy neighborhoods on either side of Termini (Esquilino and Tiburtino) have slowly been cleaning up, but caution is always advisable.

Trastevere In a Roman shift of the Latin *Trans Tiber,* Trastevere means "across the Tiber." Since the 1970s, when expats and other bohemians discovered it, this once-medieval working-class district has been gentrified and is now most definitely on the tourist map. Yet Trastevere retains its colorful appeal, with dance clubs, offbeat shops, pubs, and little *trattorie* and wine bars. Trastavere has places to stay—mostly rather quaint rentals and Airbnb's—and excellent restaurants and bars, too. The area centers on the ancient churches of **Santa Cecilia** and **Santa Maria in Trastevere.**

Testaccio & Southern Rome Once home to slaughterhouses and Rome's port on the Tiber, the working-class neighborhood of **Testaccio** was built around one strange feature: a huge compacted mound of broken amphorae and terracotta roof tiles, begun under Emperor Nero in A.D. 55 and added to over the centuries. Houses were built around the mound; caves were dug into its mass to store wine and foodstuffs. Now known for its authentic Roman restaurants, Testaccio is also one of Rome's liveliest areas after dark. Stay here if you want a taste of a real Roman neighborhood, but bear in mind that you're a bus, tram or subway ride from most touristic sights.

The Appian Way Farther south and east, the 2,300-year-old **Via Appia Antica** road once extended from Rome to Brindisi on the southeast coast. This is one of the most historically rich areas of Rome, great for a day trip, but not a convenient place to stay. Its most famous sights are the **Catacombs,** the graveyards of early Christians and patrician families.

Getting Around Rome

Central Rome is perfect for exploring on foot, with sites of interest often clustered together. Much of the inner core is traffic-free, so you will need to walk whether you like it or not. *Tip:* Plan ahead and wear sturdy, comfortable walking shoes. In the most tourist-trod parts of the city, walking can be challenging, due to crowds, uneven cobblestones, heavy traffic, and narrow (if any) sidewalks.

BY SUBWAY The **Metropolitana** (**Metro;** www.romametropolitane.it; © **06/454640100**) operates daily from 5:30am to 11:30pm (until 12:30am on Sat). A big red м indicates the entrance to the subway. If your destination is close to a Metro stop, hop on, as your journey will be much faster than by

Rome at a Glance

National Etruscan Museum

PRATI

Lepanto Ⓜ

Ottaviano Ⓜ

Cipro-Musei Vaticani Ⓜ

Vatican Museums

VATICAN CITY

St. Peter's

Piazza S. Pietro

Castel Sant'Angelo

Flaminio Ⓜ Piazzale Flaminio

Pincio

PIAZZA DEL POPOLO

Mausoleum of Augustus

Pzzo. di Montecitorio

PIAZZA NAVONA

Pantheon

CAMPO D. FIORI

JANICULUM HILL

Palazzo Farnese

Palazzo Spada

JEWISH GHETTO

Tiber Island

VILLA DORIA PAMPHILJ

Piazza S. Maria in Trastevere

TRASTEVERE

Villa Sciarra

Information ⓘ
City Walls
Metro Ⓐ Ⓜ
Metro Ⓑ Ⓜ
Metro Ⓒ Ⓜ
(under construction)
Railway

TESTACCIO

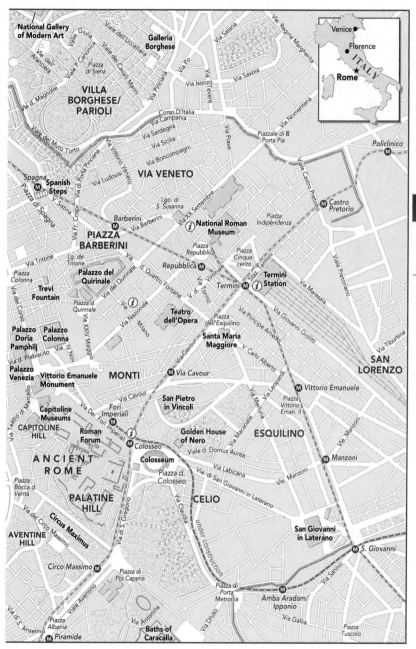

National Gallery
of Modern Art

Galleria
Borghese

Via dell'Uccelliera

Viale Giulia

Viale P. Canonica

Viale dei Cavalli Marini

Piazza
di Siena

Via Pinciana

Via Salaria

Via Po

Via Isonzo

Via Savoia

Vle d.' Magnolie

Viale della Arancera

Via delle Magnolie

VILLA
BORGHESE/
PARIOLI

Viale del Muro Torto

Via Vittorio Pinciana

Via di Porta Pinciana

Corso D'Italia

Via Campania

Via Sardegna

Via Siclia

Via Boncompagni

Via Piave

Via Nomentana

Piazzale di
Porta Pia

Viale Castro Pretorio

Policlinico

Spagna
Spanish
Steps

V. Sistina

Piazza di Spagna

Via Fr. Crispi

Via Ludovisi

VIA VENETO

Lgo. di
S. Susanna

Via XX Settembre

Piazza
Indipendenza

Castro
Pretorio

Barberini

Via Barberini

National Roman
Museum

Piazza
Cinque-
cento

Viale Pretoriano

PIAZZA
BARBERINI

Piazza
Repubblica

Viale Pretoriano

Via Tritone

Lg. de
Tritone

Via d. Quattro Fontane

Repubblica

Piazza
Colonna

Palazzo del
Quirinale

Viminale

Termini

Termini
Station

Via Marsala

Via del Corso

Trevi
Fountain

Piazza d.
Quirinale

Via Nazionale

Via d. Torino

Via Milano

Teatro
dell'Opera

Piazza
dell'Esquilino

Via Giovanni Giolitti

Palazzo
Doria
Pamphilj

Palazzo
Colonna

Via IV Nov.

Via XXIV Maggio

Via Cavour

Santa Maria
Maggiore

Via Principe Amedo

V. Carlo Alberto

Via Tiburtina

SAN
LORENZO

Palazzo
Venezia

Via d. Plebiscito

Vittorio Emanuele
Monument

MONTI

Via Cavour

Via Cavour

Via Leopardi

Vittorio Emanuele

Piazza
Vittorio
Eman. II

Via Merulana

Vle. Manzoni

Capitoline
Museums

Via Dei Fori Imperiali

Fori
Imperiali

San Pietro
in Vincoli

Via Macanate

ESQUILINO

Vle. Manzoni

CAPITOLINE
HILL

Via Teatro di Marcello

Roman
Forum

Colosseo

Golden House
of Nero

Viale d. Domus Aurea

Manzoni

ANCIENT
ROME

Colosseum

Piazza d.
Colosseo

Via di San Giovanni in Laterano

Via Labicana

Piazza
Bocca d.
Verità

PALATINE
HILL

Via di S. Gregorio

CELIO

Via Claudia

under construction

San Giovanni
in Laterano

Circus Maximus

Via del Circo Massimo

AVENTINE
HILL

Viale Aventino

Circo Massimo

Piazza di
Pta.Capena

S. Giovanni

Via Sannio

Via di S. Anselmo

Piazza
Albania

Piramide

Via Antonina

Baths of
Caracalla

Via Druso

Piazza di
Porta
Metronia

Amba Aradam/
Ipponio

Via Gallia

Piazza
Tuscolo

Venice

Florence

ITALY

Rome

4

ROME | Essentials

49

The Pantheon lies at the heart of the Centro Storico, or historic center.

taking surface transportation. There are currently three lines: **Line A** (orange) runs southeast to northwest via Termini, Barberini, Spagna, and several stations in Prati near the Vatican; **Line B** (blue) runs north to south via Termini and stops in Ancient Rome; and a third, **Line C** (green), which is currently under construction and should be completed by 2022, will ultimately run from Monte Compatri in the southeast to Clodio/Mazzini (just beyond the Ottaviano stop on Line A).

Tickets are 1.50€ and are available from *tabacchi* (tobacco shops), many newsstands, and vending machines at all stations. Booklets of tickets are available at newsstands, *tabacchi* and in some terminals. You can also buy a **pass** on either a daily or a weekly basis (see "By Bus & Tram," below). To open the subway barrier, insert your ticket. If you have a **Roma Pass** (p. 44), touch it against the yellow dot and the gates will open. See the Metro map on the tear-out map in this guide.

BY BUS & TRAM   Roman buses and trams are operated by **ATAC** (Agenzia del Trasporto Autoferrotranviario del Comune di Roma; www.atac.roma. it; ✆ **06/57003**). For 1.50€ you can ride to most parts of Rome on buses or trams, although it can be slow going in all that traffic, and the buses are often very crowded. A ticket is valid for 100 minutes, and you can get on many buses and trams (plus one journey on the Metro) during that time by using the same ticket. Tickets are sold in *tabacchi,* at newsstands, and at bus stops, but there are seldom ticket-issuing machines on the vehicles themselves. Note that if you switch from a bus or tram to Metro within your 100-minute ticket time, you must revalidate your ticket before boarding the subway.

You can buy **special timed passes:** A 24-hour (ROMA 24H) ticket is 7€; a 48-hour ticket is 12.50€; a 72-hour ticket costs 18€; and a 7-day ticket is 24€. If you plan to ride public transportation a lot—and if you are skipping between the *centro storico,* Roman ruins, and Vatican, you likely will—these passes save time and hassle over buying a new ticket every time you ride. Purchase the appropriate pass for your length of stay in Rome. All the passes allow you to ride on the ATAC network, and are also valid on the Metro (subway). On the first bus you board, place your ticket in a small (typically yellow) machine, which prints the day and hour you boarded, and then withdraw it. The machine will also print your ticket's time of expiration (*"scad."*—short for scadenza). One-day and weekly tickets are also available at *tabacchi,* many newsstands, and at vending machines at all stations. If you plan to do a lot of sightseeing, however, the **Roma Pass** (p. 44) is a smarter choice.

Buses and trams stop at areas marked *fermata.* Signs will display the numbers of the buses that stop there and a list of all the stops along each bus's route, making it easier to scope out your destination. Digital displays at most stops show how soon the next bus or tram will arrive. Generally, buses run daily from 5am to midnight. From midnight until dawn, you can ride on special night buses (look for the "N" in front of the bus number), which run only on main routes. It's best to take a taxi in the wee hours—if you can find one. Call for one (see "By Taxi," below) in a pinch. **Bus information booths** at Piazza dei Cinquecento, in front of Stazione Termini, offer advice on routes.

BY TAXI   If you've reached your walking limit, don't feel like waiting for a bus, or need to get someplace in a hurry, taking a taxi in Rome is reasonably affordable compared to other major world cities. Just don't count on hailing a taxi on the street. Instead, have your hotel call one, or if you're at a restaurant, ask the waiter or cashier to dial for you. If you want to phone for yourself, try the **city taxi service** at ✆ **06/0609** (Italian only), or one of these **radio taxi numbers,** which may or may not have English-speaking operators on duty: ✆ **06/6645,** 06/3570, or 06/4994. You can also text a taxi at ✆ **366/6730000** by typing the message "Roma [address]" (assuming you know the address in Italian). Taxis on call incur a surcharge of 3.50€. Larger taxi stands are at Piazza Venezia (east side), Piazza di Spagna (Spanish Steps), the Colosseum,

---

Walk or Ride?

Rome is such a walkable city, one where getting there (on foot) is half the fun. And public transportation doesn't necessarily save that much time. (For example, walking from Piazza Venezia to Piazza di Santa Maria in Trastevere takes about 25 min. at a leisurely pace; it takes 12 min. via bus and tram, but that doesn't include potential time spent waiting for the bus or tram to show up.) My take? On a nice day and for relatively short distances, enjoy the stroll. On the other hand, if you want to save your steps (maybe for a marathon tour of the Vatican Museums), then head to the nearest Metro, tram, or bus stop.

First, know that any map of the Roman bus system will likely be outdated before it's printed. There's always talk of renumbering the whole system, so be aware that the route numbers we've listed might have changed by the time you travel. Second, take extreme caution when riding Rome's overcrowded buses—pickpockets abound! This is particularly true on bus no. 64, a favorite of visitors because of its route through the historic districts and thus also a favorite of Rome's pickpocketing community. This bus has earned various nicknames, including the "Pickpocket Express" and "Wallet Eater."

Although routes may change, a few reliable bus routes have remained valid for years in Rome:

- **40 (Express):** Stazione Termini to the Vatican via Via Nazionale, Piazza Venezia and Piazza Pia, by the Castel Sant'Angelo
- **64:** The "tourist route" from Termini, along Via Nazionale and through Piazza Venezia and along Via Argentina to Piazza San Pietro in the Vatican
- **75:** Stazione Termini to the Colosseum
- **H:** Stazione Termini via Piazza Venezia and the Ghetto to Trastevere via Ponte Garibaldi

Corso Rinascimento (Piazza Navona), Largo Argentina, the Pantheon, Piazza del Popolo, Piazza Risorgimento (near St. Peter's), and Piazza Belli (Trastevere).

Many taxis accept credit cards, but it's best to check first, before getting on. Between 6am and 10pm, the meter begins at 3€ (4.50€ Sat–Sun) for the first 3km (1¾ miles) and then rises 1.10€ per kilometer. From 10pm to 6am every day, the meter starts at 6.50€. Trips from Termini incur a 2€ surcharge. The first suitcase is free; every additional piece of luggage costs 1€. *Note:* Italians don't tip taxi drivers like Americans do and, at most, will simply round up to the nearest euro. If the driver is really friendly or helpful, a tip of 1€ to 2€ is sufficient.

As in the rest of the world, taxi apps have caught on in Rome. The main app for official city taxis is **it Taxi** (www.ittaxi.it), which is run by Rome's largest taxi company, **3570** (www.3570.it). It allows users to pay directly from the app using a credit card or PayPal. Popular throughout Europe, the **MyTaxi** app offers Uber-like convenience for ordering and prepaying a cab. **Uber** is currently available in Rome in a limited capacity only.

BY CAR   All roads might lead to Rome, but you probably won't want to drive once you get here. If you do drive into the city, call or email ahead to your hotel to find out the best route into Rome from wherever you are starting out. You will want to get rid of your rental car as soon as possible, or park it in a garage and leave it there until you depart Rome.

If you want to rent a car to explore the countryside around Rome or drive to another city, you will save money if you reserve before leaving home (see p. 298 in chapter 10). If you decide to book a car here, most major car rental companies have desks inside Stazione Termini.

Note that rental cars in Italy may be smaller than what you are used to, including in terms of trunk space. Make sure you consider both luggage size and the number of people when booking your vehicle.

[FastFACTS] ROME

Banks In general, banks are open Monday to Friday 8:30am to 1:30pm and 2:30 or 2:45 to 4pm. Note that many banks do not offer currency exchange.

Business Hours Most Roman shops open at 10am and close at 7pm from Monday to Saturday. Smaller shops close for 1 or 2 hours at lunch and may remain closed Monday morning and Saturday afternoon. Most restaurants are closed for *riposo* (rest) 1 day per week, usually Sunday or Monday.

Dentists **American Dental Arts Rome,** Via del Governo Vecchio 73 (near Piazza Navona; www.adadentists rome.com; ℂ **06/6832613**), uses the latest technology.

Doctors Call the U.S. Embassy at ℂ **06/46741** for a list of English-speaking doctors. You'll find English-speaking doctors at the privately run **Salvator Mundi International Hospital,** Viale delle Mura Gianicolensi 67 (in the Gianicolo neighborhood; www.salvatormundi.it;

ℂ **06/588961**); or at the **Rome American Hospital,** Via Emilio Longoni 69 (www. hcitalia.it/romeamericanhospital; ℂ **06/22551**), located well east of central Rome. The **International Medical Center** is on 24-hour duty at Via Firenze 47 (near Piazza della Repubblica; www.imc84.com; ℂ **06/4882371**). **Medi-Call Italia,** Via Cremera 8 (www. medi-call.it; ℂ **06/8840113**), can arrange for a qualified doctor to make a house call at your hotel or anywhere in Rome.

Emergencies To call the police, dial ℂ **113;** for an ambulance ℂ **118;** for a fire ℂ **115.**

Newspapers & Magazines The English-language expat magazine *Wanted in Rome* (www. wantedinrome.com) comes out every 2 weeks and lists current events and shows. *Time Out* also has a Rome edition.

Pharmacies *Farmacie,* recognizable by their neon

green or red cross signs, are generally open 8:30am–1pm and 4–7:30pm, though some stay open later. **Farmacia Piram** at Via Nazionale 228 is open 24 hours. All closed pharmacies have signs in their windows indicating any open pharmacies nearby.

Police Dial ℂ **113.**

Safety Violent crime is virtually nonexistent in Rome's touristed areas, though pickpocketing is common. Purse snatching happens on occasion, by young men speeding by on scooters; keep your purse on the wall side of your body with the strap across your chest. Sadly, *Romani,* or *Roma* gypsies, often enlist children to beg desperately for money, and many are trained to pick pockets. Other pickpockets dress like typical business-people, so always be suspicious of anyone who tries to "befriend" you in a tourist area. Walking alone at night is usually fine anywhere in the *centro storico.*

WHERE TO STAY IN ROME

Hotels in Rome's *centro storico* are notoriously overpriced, and all too often the grand exteriors and lobbies of historic buildings give way to bland modern rooms. Our selections here made the cut because they offer unique experiences, highly personalized service, or extreme value—and in many cases all of the above.

Room rates vary wildly depending on the season, and last-minute deals are common. For example, a room at a hotel we classify as "expensive" might be had for as low as 99€ if said hotel has empty beds to fill. Always book directly with the hotel—you'll usually get a better rate and the chance to build some rapport with reception staff.

Breakfast in all but the highest echelon of hotels is often a buffet with coffee, fruit, rolls, and cheese. It's not always included in the rate, so check the reservation options carefully. If you are budgeting and breakfast is a payable extra, skip it and go to a nearby cafe-bar, where a caffè and *cornetto* will likely be much cheaper.

Most hotels are heated in the winter, but not all are air-conditioned in summer, which can be vitally important during a stifling July or August. Be sure to check before you book if it's important to you.

Self-Catering Apartments

Rental apartments have some great virtues: They're often cheaper than standard facilities, and they let you save money by preparing at least some of your own meals.

Nearly every vacation rental in Rome—and there are tens of thousands of them—is owned and maintained by a third party (that is, not the rental agency). That means that the decor and flavor of the apartments, even in the same price range and neighborhood, can vary widely. Every reputable agency, however, puts multiple photos of each property they handle on its website, so you'll have a sense of what you're getting into. The photos should be accompanied by a list of amenities. Goliath booking sites **www.airbnb.com**, **Homeaway.com**, and **vrbo.com**, platforms that allow individuals to rent their own apartments to guests, have thousands of listings in Rome. These will often be cheaper than apartments rented through local agencies, but they won't be vetted, and sometimes you're on your own if something goes wrong.

If you decide to rent through one of the agencies below, know that its standard practice for them to collect 30% of the total rental amount upfront to secure a booking. When you get to Rome and check in, the balance of your rental fee is often payable in cash only. Upon booking, the agency should provide you with detailed "check-in" procedures. *Tip:* Make sure you ask for a few numbers to call in case of an emergency. Otherwise, most apartments come with information sheets that list neighborhood shops and services.

RECOMMENDED AGENCIES

Cross Pollinate (www.cross-pollinate.com; ✆ 06/99369799), a multi-destination agency with a roster of apartments and B&Bs in Rome, was created by the American owners of the Beehive Hotel in Rome. Each property is inspected before it gets listed. **GowithOh** (www.gowithoh.com; ✆ 800/567-2927 in the U.S.) is a hip rental agency that covers 12 European cities, Rome among them. **Eats & Sheets** (www.eatsandsheets.com; ✆ 06/83515971) is a small boutique collective comprising two B&Bs (near the Vatican and Colosseum) and a handful of beautiful apartments for rent, most in the *centro storico*. **Roman Reference** (www.romanreference.com; ✆ 06/48903612) offers no-surprises property descriptions (with helpful and diplomatic tags like "better for young people") and even includes the "eco-footprint" for each apartment. You can expect transparency and responsiveness from the plain-dealing staff. **Rental in Rome** (www.rentalinrome.com; ✆ 06/3220068) has an alluring website—with video clips of the apartments—and the widest selection of midrange and luxury apartments in the *centro storico* zone (there are less expensive ones, too).

MONASTERIES & CONVENTS

Staying in a convent or a monastery can be a great bargain. But remember, these are religious houses, which means the decor is most often stark and the rules extensive. Cohabitating is almost always frowned upon—though marriage licenses are rarely required—and unruly behavior is not tolerated (so, no staggering in after too much *limoncello* at dinner). Plus, there's usually a curfew. Most rooms in convents and monasteries do not have private bathrooms, but ask when making your reservation in case some are available. However, if you're planning a mellow, "contemplative" trip to Rome, and you can live with these parameters, convents and monasteries are an affordable and fascinating option. The place to start is **www.monasterystays.com**, which lays out all your monastic options for the Eternal City.

Hotels by Price

EXPENSIVE

Babuino 181 ★★, p. 62
Capo d'Africa ★★, p. 58
Del Sole al Pantheon ★, p. 60
Deko Rome ★★★, p. 62
The Inn at the Roman Forum ★★★, p. 58
The Inn at the Spanish Steps ★★★, p. 62
Portrait Roma ★★★, p. 63
Raphael ★★★, p. 60
Residenza Paolo VI ★★, p. 56
Villa Laetitia ★★★, p. 56
Villa Spalletti Trivelli ★★★, p. 63

MODERATE

Daphne Trevi ★★, p. 64
Duca d'Alba ★★, p. 59
Fontanella Borghese ★, p. 60
Hotel Adriano ★★★, p. 60
Hotel Condotti ★, p. 60
Hotel Mediterraneo ★★★, p. 65
La Lumière ★, p. 64
Lancelot ★, p. 59
La Residenza ★, p. 64
Nicolas Inn ★, p. 59
QuodLibet ★★★, p. 57
Residenza Canali ai Coronari ★, p. 61
Residenza Cellini ★★, p. 65
Residenza in Farnese ★★, p. 61
Rome Armony Suites ★★★, p. 57
Santa Maria ★★, p. 67
Seven Kings Relais ★★, p. 66
Teatro di Pompeo ★★, p. 61

INEXPENSIVE

Arco del Lauro ★★, p. 67
Beehive ★★★, p. 66
Euro Quiris ★, p. 66
Giuliana ★★, p. 66
Hotel San Francesco ★★, p. 67
Mimosa ★, p. 61
Panda ★, p. 64
Parlamento ★, p. 65

Around Vatican City & Prati

For many, this is a rather dull area to be based in. It's well removed from the ancient sites, and though Prati has some good restaurants, the area overall is not geared to nightlife. But if the main purpose of your visit centers on the Vatican, you'll be fine here, and you will be joined by thousands of other pilgrims, nuns, and priests. For hotel locations, see map p. 85.

EXPENSIVE

Residenza Paolo VI ★★ Literally across the street from Vatican City limits, Residenza Paolo can legitimately claim it's "steps from St. Peter's." Taking breakfast on the rooftop terrace is a special treat, as this narrow strip overlooks St. Peter's Square—if your timing's right, you'll see the Pope blessing crowds on Sunday. (There's bar service on the terrace from 4pm onwards.) Old-worldly rooms feature tile or hardwood floors, heavy drapes, Oriental rugs, and quality beds, though square footage is at a premium in many of the standard guest rooms.

Via Paolo VI 29. www.residenzapaolovi.com. ⓒ **06/684870.** 35 units. 151€–400€ double. Rates include breakfast. Metro: Ottaviano. Bus: 64. **Amenities:** Bar; room service.

Villa Laetitia ★★★ This elegant hotel overlooking the River Tiber is the work of Anna Fendi of the Roman fashion dynasty. Thanks to her design aesthetic, the rooms are anything but traditional, despite the 1911 villa setting surrounded by tranquil gardens. The decor features bold patterns on the beds and floors and modern art on the walls. Splurge for the black and white Giulio Cesare suite, with a round leather bed and blissful garden views. Standard rooms are on the snug side, but most have kitchenettes. Look for great last-minute rates on the hotel website. While we love everything about this place, do note that it's well north of centro and perhaps not the best choice for first-timers to Rome. **Enoteca la Torre** is the villa's Michelin-starred restaurant.

Villa Laetitia hotel.

Lungotevere delle Armi 22–23. www.villalaetitia.com. ⓒ **06/3226776.** 20 units. 139€–340€ double. Rates include breakfast. Metro: Lepanto. **Amenities:** Restaurant; bar; babysitting; bike rentals; fitness room; room service; Wi-Fi (free).

Guest room at QuodLibet.

MODERATE

QuodLibet ★★★   The name is Latin for "what pleases," and we'll be frank: Everything pleases us here. This upscale B&B boasts spacious, colorful rooms, gorgeous artwork and furnishings, and generous breakfasts (served on the roof terrace, which offers evening bar service). All the rooms are set on the fourth floor of an elegant building (with elevator and A/C), so it's quieter than many places. It's located just a 10-minute walk from the Vatican Museums, and a block from the Metro. Charming, conscientious hosts possess a deep knowledge of Rome and what will interest visitors. A top pick!

Via Barletta 29. www.quodlibetroma.com. ✆ **06/1222642.** 4 units. 70€–200€ double. Rates include breakfast. Metro: Ottaviano. **Amenities:** Wi-Fi (free).

Rome Armony Suites ★★★   A warning: Rome Armony Suites is almost always booked up months in advance, so if you're interested, book early. Why so popular? The answer starts with service; owner Luca is a charming, sensitive host, especially helpful with first-time visitors to Rome. Rooms are big, plush, clean, and modern, with minimalist decor, tea and coffee facilities, and a fridge in each unit. Final, major perk: free loaner smartphones loaded with maps and tourist info, to help guests get the most out of their visit; calls to the U.S. and Canada included, too.

Via Orazio 3. www.romearmonysuites.com. ✆ **348/3305419.** 6 units. 65€–150€ double. Rates include breakfast. Metro: Ottaviano. **Amenities:** Wi-Fi (free).

Ancient Rome, Monti & Celio

There aren't many hotel rooms on earth with a view of a 2,000-year-old amphitheater, so there's a definite "only in Rome" feeling to lodging on the edge of the ancient city. The negative to staying in this area—and it's a big minus—is that the streets adjacent to those ancient monuments have little life outside tourism. There's a lot more going on in **Monti,** Rome's oldest "suburb" (only 5 min. from the Forum), which is especially lively after dark. **Celio** has more of a neighborhood vibe, a local, gentrified life quite separate from tourism. For hotel locations, see map p. 97.

EXPENSIVE

Capo d'Africa ★★   Twin palm trees guard the entrance to this elegant boutique hotel, located in the heart of Imperial Rome and set in an early-20th-century *palazzo*. Guests are welcomed as if they were in a relaxed and unpretentious Roman home, albeit one with sweeping vistas from the manicured roof terrace (where you eat breakfast), chic design, and an upscale vibe. Light-filled rooms are spacious, smart, and modern, with cherrywood furniture, touches of glass and chrome, incredibly comfy beds, marble bathrooms, and lots of cupboard space. For a truly unforgettable stay, book a studio suite, which comes with a welcome bottle of wine and a private terrace with ethereal views of the Colosseum.

Via Capo d'Africa 54. www.hotelcapodafrica.com. ⓒ **06/772801.** 65 units. 185€–325€ double. Rates include breakfast. Bus: 53, 85, 87. Tram: 3. **Amenities:** Restaurant; bar; exercise room; loaner bikes; room service; Wi-Fi (free).

The Inn at the Roman Forum ★★★   This small hotel is tucked down a medieval lane, on the edge of Monti, with the forums of several Roman emperors as neighbors. Rooms are tastefully luxurious, with ethnic silks, soothing tones, and spacious bathrooms. The posh fifth-floor Master Garden Rooms have private patios surrounded by flowers and greenery, ochre walls,

Executive room at the Inn at the Roman Forum.

and busts of emperors, and a plush apartment with a kitchen sleeps up to six people. The hotel's **roof lounge** has views of the Campidoglio, and for archaeology buffs there's an ancient Roman *cryptoporticus* behind the lobby. The inn isn't cheap, but the views alone more than make up for it.

Via degli Ibernesi 30. www.theinnattheromanforum.com. © **06/69190970.** 20 units. 190€–790€ double. Rates include breakfast. Metro: Cavour. **Amenities:** Bar; concierge; room service; Wi-Fi (free).

MODERATE

Duca d'Alba ★★ Located on one of the main drags of hip Monti, with all the nightlife and authentic dining you'll need, Duca d'Alba strikes a fine balance between old-world gentility and 21st-century amenities. Rooms in the main building are snug and contemporary, with modern furniture and gadgetry but tiny bathrooms. If you want to spring for slightly higher rates, the spacious annex rooms next door have a *palazzo* character, with terracotta floors, oak and cherry furniture, and soundproofed street-facing rooms. Second-floor rooms are the brightest.

Via Leonina 14. www.hotelducadalba.com. © **06/484471.** 27 units. 90€–205€ double. Rates include breakfast. Metro: Cavour. **Amenities:** Bar; bike rentals; Wi-Fi (free).

Lancelot ★ Expect warmth and hospitality from the minute you walk in the door. The staff, all of whom have been here for years, are the heart and soul of Lancelot, and the reason why the hotel has so many repeat guests. The room decor is simple, and most of the units are spacious, immaculately kept, and light-filled, thanks to large windows. Sixth-floor rooms have private terraces overlooking Ancient Rome—well worth springing for. What makes this place truly remarkable are the genteel, chandelier-lit common areas for meeting other travelers, *Room with a View*–style. Unusual for Rome, Lancelot also has private parking, for which you'll need to book ahead.

Via Capo d'Africa 47. www.lancelothotel.com. © **06/70450615.** 60 units. 100€–200€ double; 280€–330€ suite. Rates include breakfast. Bus: 53, 85, 87. Tram: 3. **Amenities:** Restaurant; bar; Wi-Fi (free).

Nicolas Inn ★ This tiny B&B, run by a welcoming American–Lebanese couple, makes a convenient base for those who want to concentrate on Rome's ancient sights—the Colosseum and the Forum are both just blocks away. Rooms are a good size and decorated with wrought-iron beds, cool tiled floors, and heavy wooden furniture. Best of all, light floods in through large windows. Guests take breakfast at a local cafe—with unlimited espresso. Downers: no children under 5, and no credit cards accepted.

Via Cavour 295. www.nicolasinn.com. © **06/97618483.** 4 units. 100€–180€ double. Rates includes breakfast at nearby cafe. Metro: Cavour or Colosseo. **Amenities:** Concierge; Wi-Fi (free).

The Centro Storico & Pantheon

There's nothing like an immersion in the atmosphere of Rome's lively Renaissance heart, though you'll pay for *location, location, location.* Expect to do a lot of walking, but that's a reason many visitors come here in the first place—to wander and discover the glory that was and is Rome. Many restaurants and cafes are an easy walk from the hotels here. For hotel locations, see map p. 108.

EXPENSIVE

Del Sole al Pantheon ★ For history and atmosphere, it's hard to beat a place that's been hosting wayfarers since 1467, with past guests including Jean-Paul Sartre and Simone de Beauvoir, as well as at least one Hapsburg king. Rooms are decorated in a lavish period decor, with lots of brocade drapery, fine fabrics, and classic furniture. Each room comes equipped with air-conditioning and satellite TV, and some feature views of the Pantheon. Suites offer separate bedrooms and Jacuzzi tubs.

Piazza della Rotonda 63. www.hotelsolealpantheon.com. ✆ **06/6780441.** 32 units. 190€–400€ double. Rates include breakfast. **Amenities:** Bar; bike rentals; concierge; garden; Wi-Fi (free).

Raphael ★★★ Planning on proposing? This ivy-covered palace, just off Piazza Navona, is an ideal choice for a special-occasion stay, with luxurious rooms, enthusiastic staff, and a roof terrace with spectacular views across Rome. It's a gorgeous hotel, highlighted by 20th-century artwork inside, including Picasso ceramics and paintings by Mirò, Morandi, and De Chirico scattered across the property. The standard rooms are all decorated in Victorian style, with antique furnishings and hardwood floors. Some prefer staying in the quirky Richard Meier–designed executive suites, which blend modern and Asian design and feature oak paneling, contemporary art, and Carrara marble. A haute organic, vegetarian restaurant will leave even diehard carnivores sated.

Largo Febo 2, Piazza Navona. www.raphaelhotel.com. ✆ **06/682831.** 50 units. 300€–450€ double. Rates include breakfast. **Amenities:** Restaurant; bar; babysitting; concierge; room service; Wi-Fi (free).

MODERATE

Fontanella Borghese ★ Occupying two floors of a palazzo that once belonged to the Borghese family, this is a noble address (equidistant from the Pantheon, Spanish Steps, and Piazza del Popolo) at sort-of plebeian prices. It's not a fancy place, but the classically decorated, family-friendly rooms are bright and spacious, with high ceilings, parquet or marble inlaid floors, and well-organized, if unremarkable, bathrooms.

Largo Fontanella Borghese 84. www.fontanellaborghese.com; ✆ **06/68809504.** 24 units. 85€–250€ double. Rates include breakfast. Metro: Spagna. **Amenities:** Bar; Wi-Fi (free).

Hotel Adriano ★★★ Just 5 minutes from the Pantheon, this stylish retreat occupies an elegant 17th-century *palazzo.* Rooms boast an incredibly chic and modern vibe, with designer furniture carefully chosen for each room. A few deluxe rooms and suites have terraces with views of the Roman rooftops. In a crowded hotel market, Adriano stands out for its plush, well-designed common areas, including **The Gin Corner,** a trendy cocktail bar specializing in…you guessed it. Rooms in the nearby "Domus Adriani" are more akin to self-catering apartments. *Tip:* Email the hotel directly for the lowest rates.

Via di Pallacorda 2. www.hoteladriano.com. © **06/68802451.** 80 units. 100€–300€ double. Rates include breakfast. Bus: C3, 70, 81, 87. **Amenities:** Bar; babysitting; bikes; concierge; gym; Wi-Fi (free).

Residenza Canali ai Coronari ★ This cozy little guesthouse (in a meticulously restored historic building) is on a blink-and-you'll-miss-it pedestrian alleyway in Rome's antiques district. Furnishings are warm and classic, and rooms are bright and surprisingly spacious. The Honeymoon Suite has a private terrace overlooking the terracotta rooftops near Piazza Navona. There are no surprises here, just clean, up-to-date facilities, good prices, and amiable staff. Online rates are quoted with or without breakfast; it's only a few euro more so worth the difference.

Via dei Tre Archi 13. www.residenzacanali.com; © 06/68309541. 10 units. 110€–260€ doubles; online specials often much lower. Some rates include breakfast. Amenities: Wi-Fi (free).

Residenza in Farnese ★★ This little gem is tucked away in a 15th-century mansion across the street from the Palazzo Farnese, within stumbling distance of Campo de' Fiori but still reasonably quiet. Most rooms are spacious and artsy, with tiled floors and a vaguely Renaissance theme. Standard rooms are on the small side but come with free minibars, and prices are usually on the low end of the range shown here. The complimentary breakfast spread is downright generous. *Tip:* Last-minute rates are often much lower than those shown below.

Via del Mascherone 59. www.residenzafarneseroma.it. © **06/68210980.** 31 units. 115€–220€ double. Rates include breakfast. **Amenities:** Airport transfer (free with min. 4-night stay); bar; concierge; room service; Wi-Fi (free).

Teatro di Pompeo ★★ History buffs will appreciate this small hotel, built atop the ruins of the 1st-century Theatre of Pompey, where on the Ides of March Julius Caesar was stabbed to death (p. 24). The atmospheric breakfast area is actually part of the old theater's arcades, with original Roman walls. The large rooms have an authentic feel, with wood-beam ceilings, cherrywood furniture, and terracotta-tiled floors. Some rooms overlook the internal courtyard, others face the small square; all are quiet, though, despite the Campo de' Fiori crowds right behind the hotel. Staff members are extremely helpful. *Tip:* Avoid the Trattoria Der Pallaro restaurant next door; it's a tourist trap.

Largo del Pallaro 8. www.hotelteatrodipompeo.it. © **06/68300170.** 13 units. 110€–220€ double. Rates include breakfast. **Amenities:** Bar; babysitting; room service; Wi-Fi (free).

INEXPENSIVE

Mimosa ★ This budget stalwart in the heart of the *centro storico* enjoys great word of mouth, so book early. Decor is hodgepodge at best, but the straightforward modern rooms are bright and air-conditioned (not a given at this price point); larger units are suitable for families with small children. A location this close to the Pantheon at these prices is hard to beat. Mention Frommer's for a 10% discount.

Via di Santa Chiara 61. www.hotelmimosa.net; ℰ **06/68801753.** 11 units. 69€–150€ double. Rates include breakfast. **Amenities:** Wi-Fi (free).

Tridente, the Spanish Steps & Via Veneto

The heart of the city is a great place to stay if you're a serious shopper or enjoy the romantic, somewhat nostalgic locales of the Spanish Steps and Trevi Fountain. But expect to part with a lot of extra euro for the privilege. This is one of the most elegant areas in Rome; we've found you a few bargains (and some worthy splurges). For hotel locations, see map p. 113.

EXPENSIVE

Babuino 181 ★★ Leave Renaissance and baroque Italy far behind at this sleek, contemporary hotel, with relatively spacious rooms and apartment-size suites outfitted with Frette linens, iPod docks, and Nespresso machines. Bathrooms are heavy on the marble and mosaics, and shuttered windows with hefty curtains provide a quiet and perfectly blacked-out environment for light sleepers. A surcharged breakfast buffet is served on the rooftop terrace, which doubles as a cocktail bar at night.

Via del Babuino 181. www.romeluxurysuites.com/babuino. ℰ **06/32295295.** 24 units. 160€–430€ double. Metro: Flaminio or Spagna. **Amenities:** Bar; babysitting; concierge; room service; Wi-Fi (free).

Deko Rome ★★★ Exceptionally warm and welcoming, this is a true boutique hotel (just nine rooms), occupying the second floor of an early-20th-century *palazzo*. The chic interior blends antiques, vintage '60s pieces, and modern design in a way that's happily retro and quite comfortable; each room comes with an iPad and flatscreen TV. Add the friendly, fun owners (Marco and Serena) and excellent location near Via Veneto, and Deko is understandably hugely popular. Reservations must be made months in advance, though you can find the occasional last-minute bargain.

Via Toscana 1. www.dekorome.com. ℰ **06/42020032.** 9 units. 140€–230€. Rates include breakfast. Metro: Barberini. Bus: 910 (from Termini). **Amenities:** Bar; babysitting; Wi-Fi (free).

The Inn at the Spanish Steps ★★★ Set in one of Rome's most desirable locations on the famed Via dei Condotti shopping street, this hotel is the epitome of luxe. Rooms are fantasias of design and comfort, some with parquet floors and cherubim frescoes on the ceiling, others decked out with wispy fabrics draping canopied beds; upgraded units have swoon-worthy views of Piazza di Spagna. Swank standard perks include flatscreen TVs, iPod docks, Jacuzzi tubs, double marble sinks, pet amenities, and so forth. Rooms located in the annex tend to be larger than those in the main building. The perfectly manicured rooftop garden provides beautiful views, to be enjoyed at breakfast—with its generous buffet spread—or at sunset, with complimentary happy-hour snacks.

Balcony at the Inn at the Spanish Steps, overlooking the Steps themselves.

Via dei Condotti 85. www.atspanishsteps.com. ℃ **06/69925657.** 24 units. 190€–550€ double. Rates include breakfast. Metro: Spagna. **Amenities:** Bar; babysitting; concierge; room service; Wi-Fi (free).

Portrait Roma ★★★ Fashionistas with money to spare, look no further than this boutique all-suites hotel run by the Ferragamo-owned Lungarno hotel group. Sleek and uncluttered are the keywords here, but there's plenty of amusing Italian flair in the ultra-stylish pink and grey suites, which come with kitchenettes. The roof terrace, with its overstuffed cushions, romantic candlelight, and exclusive company, is the epitome of modern Roman fabulousness.

Via Bocca di Leone 23. www.lungarnohotels.com/portrait-roma. ℃ **06/69380742.** 14 units. Suites from 600€. Rates include breakfast. Metro: Spagna. **Amenities:** Bar; concierge; room service; Wi-Fi (free).

Villa Spalletti Trivelli ★★★ This really is an experience rather than a hotel, an early-20th-century neoclassical villa remodeled into an exclusive 14-room guesthouse, where lodgers mingle in the gardens or the great hall, as if invited by an Italian noble for the weekend. There is no key for the entrance door; ring a bell and a staff member will open it for you, often offering you a glass of complimentary prosecco as a welcome. Onsite is a Turkish bath, a sizeable and modern oasis for those who want extra pampering, while rooms feature elegant antiques and Fiandra damask linen sheets, with sitting areas or separate lounges. And the minibar? All free, all day. A rooftop lounge boasts Jacuzzis and a bar serving light fare.

Via Piacenza 4. www.villaspalletti.it. ℃ **06/48907934.** 14 units. 375€–700€ double. Rates include breakfast. Metro: Barberini. **Amenities:** Restaurant; bar; concierge; exercise room; roof terrace; room service; Jacuzzis; sauna; Wi-Fi (free).

MODERATE

Daphne Trevi ★★ In a neighborhood with a lot of overpriced, underwhelming hotels, this above-average boutique option, in an 18th-century building minutes from Trevi Fountain, is a good value even in the summer. What rooms lack in size they make up for with sleek modern design and spotless bathrooms with mosaic tiles (two rooms share a bathroom). A 5th-floor covered terrace is the setting for an ample breakfast buffet with lots of home-baked goodies, as well as evening cocktails and occasional happy hours. The young owner/managers are happy to help you plan your days in Rome and your onward journey.

Via di San Basilio 55. www.daphne-rome.com. ✆ **06/87450086.** 10 units. 90€–240€ double. Rates include breakfast. Metro: Barberini. **Amenities:** Concierge; Wi-Fi (free).

Hotel Condotti ★ This cozy hotel can be a tremendously good deal depending on when you stay and how far out you book. For your money you'll get a clean, unpretentious room, though the common areas aim higher, with marble floors, antiques, tapestries, and a Venetian-glass chandelier. Standard rooms are tight; you'll get a bit more space and modernity in the nearby annex rooms. Overall it's worth considering for its proximity to the Spanish Steps.

Via Mario de' Fiori 37. www.hotelcondotti.com. ✆ **06/6794661.** 16 units. 130€–240€. Rates include breakfast. Metro: Spagna. **Amenities:** Bar; babysitting; bikes; room service; Wi-Fi (free).

La Lumière ★ You won't be checking in for chic design or innovation—this traditional hotel just off Via dei Condotti smacks of middle-class comforts, from rooms with matchy-matchy color schemes, wood floors, and warm lighting to the glassed-in roof terrace or open-air patio where breakfast and evening libations are served. For all but highest season and holidays, it's a winner on the price/location ratio.

Via Belsiana 72. www.lalumieredipiazzadispagna.com. ✆ **06/69380806.** 10 units. 110€–350€ double. Rates include breakfast. Metro: Spagna. **Amenities:** Bar; Wi-Fi (free).

La Residenza ★ Considering its location just off Via Veneto, this hotel—hosting guests since 1936—is a smart deal. Renovated, modern rooms retain a touch of Art Deco appeal, and are all relatively spacious, with a couple of easy chairs or a small couch in addition to a desk. Families with children are especially catered to, with quad rooms and junior suites on the top floor featuring a separate kids' alcove with two sofa beds, and an outdoor terrace with patio furniture. The excellent breakfast buffet includes quality charcuterie and cheeses, homemade breads, and pastries.

Via Emilia 22–24. www.hotel-la-residenza.com. ✆ **06/4880789.** 29 units. 169€–305€ double. Rates include breakfast. Metro: Barberini. **Amenities:** Bar; babysitting; room service; Wi-Fi (free).

INEXPENSIVE

Panda ★ Panda has long been popular among budget travelers, so it books up quickly. Rooms are spare, but not without some old-fashioned charm, like characteristic Roman *cotto* (terracotta) floor tiles, frescoed ceilings, and exposed beams. Most rooms are a bit cramped, but for these prices in this neighborhood they remain a very, very good deal. Outside your doorstep are several great cafes and wine bars where you can start the day with espresso and end it with a nightcap. *Tip:* With its budget single rooms with shared baths, Panda is a good pick for solo travelers.

Via della Croce 35. www.hotelpanda.it. ✆ **06/6780179.** 28 units (8 with shared bath). 75€–130€ double with bath. Metro: Spagna. **Amenities:** Wi-Fi (free).

Parlamento ★   Set on the top floors of a 17th-century *palazzo,* this is one of the best budget deals in the area. All of its rooms have private bathrooms and are equipped with satellite TVs, desks, exposed beams, and parquet or terracotta floors; renovated "boutique" rooms add modern decor. Breakfast is served on the rooftop terrace—you can also chill up there with a glass of wine in the evening. The Trevi Fountain, Spanish Steps, and Pantheon are all within a 5- to 10-minute walk.

Via delle Convertite 5 (at Via del Corso). www.hotelparlamento.it. ✆ **06/69921000.** 21 units. 85€–160€ double. Rates include breakfast. Metro: Spagna. **Amenities:** Bar; concierge; room service; Wi-Fi (free).

Around Termini

Known for its concentration of cheap hotels, the Termini area (see map p. 122) is about the only part of the center where you can score a high-season double for under 100€. The area has some upscale hotels, but if you have the money to spend on a luxe hotel, choose a prettier neighborhood—streets close to the train station are hardly picturesque, and parts of the neighborhood are downright seedy. Still, it's very convenient to most of Rome's top sights, and a hub for Metro lines, buses, and trams.

MODERATE

Hotel Mediterraneo ★★★   Within sight of Termini station, this surprisingly luxurious hotel offers vintage art deco style, along with a team of long-time employees who warmly evoke the spirit of a bygone era of class and service. Rooms are large and well-equipped, with bathrooms of grand proportions; suites are downright palatial, and 7 top-floor units have terraces with sweeping views. Read about the hotel's interesting WWII-era history as you linger over cocktails in its old-school bar. Sister properties **Atlantico** and **Massimo D'Azeglio,** located next door and across the street, respectively, offer lower room prices and share amenities with Mediterraneo. *Tip:* Check online for off-season or last-minute deals on those top-floor suites.

Via Cavour 15. www.romehotelmediterraneo.it. ✆ **06/4884051.** 245 units. 112€–180€ double, suites from 220€. Rates include breakfast. Metro: Termini. **Amenities:** Babysitting; bar; concierge; gym; restaurant; roof terrace; room service; Wi-Fi (free).

Residenza Cellini ★★   For every rule, there's an exception, and in this case, spending a little more near Termini pays off at Cellini. The feeling of refinement begins the second you walk through the door to find a vase of fresh lilies in the elegant, high-ceilinged hall. Antique-styled rooms are proudly 19th century, with thick walls (so no noise from your neighbors), solid furnishings, and handsome parquet floors, yet also offer modern comforts like memory-foam mattresses and A/C. Bathrooms come with Jacuzzi tubs or jetted showers. Service is topnotch and wonderfully personal.

Via Modena 5. www.residenzacellini.it. © **06/47825204.** 18 units. 89€–210€ double. Metro: Repubblica. **Amenities:** Concierge; room service; Wi-Fi (free).

Seven Kings Relais ★★ This unfussy hotel has a slightly retro feel, kitted out with dark wooden furniture, chocolate-brown bedspreads, and modern tiled floors. Despite its location right on one of Rome's busiest thoroughfares, street noise is minimal—an external courtyard and modern soundproofing see to that. Breakfast is a 24-hour self-service bar with tea, coffee, and biscuits, and the area has plenty of inexpensive dining options. Management has several other nearby properties as well, run through **Roma Termini Suites** (www.romaterminisuites.com).

Via XX Settembre 58A. www.sevenkingsrelais.com. © **06/42917784.** 13 units. 50€–200€ double. Metro: Repubblica. **Amenities:** Babysitting; Wi-Fi (free).

INEXPENSIVE

Beehive ★★★ Conceived as part hostel and part hotel, the Beehive is an utterly cheerful lodging experience, run by eco-minded American owners and offering rooms for a variety of budgets. Some have private bathrooms, others have shared facilities or are six-bed dorms—but all are decorated with flair, adorned with artwork or flea-market treasures. The garden with trees and secluded reading/relaxing spaces is the biggest plus. A buzzy cafe offers breakfast a la carte, as well as occasional, budget-friendly vegan/vegetarian meals; there's also a concerted effort to maintain eco-conscious practices. The Beehive's "Other Honey"—Clover and Cacaia guesthouses—is a smart option for a group of traveling friends, offering private rooms and shared bathrooms; it's a 10-minute walk from the original B&B.

Via Marghera 8. www.the-beehive.com. © **06/44704553.** 20 units. 60€–100€ double; 20€–35€ dorm beds. Metro: Termini or Castro Pretorio. **Amenities:** Restaurant; garden; lounge; Wi-Fi (free).

Euro Quiris ★ There's not a frill in sight at this one-star a couple of blocks north of the station. Rooms are on the 5th floor and simply decorated with functional furniture, but they are spotless, and mattresses are a lot more comfortable than you should expect in this price bracket. Bathrooms are en suite, too. The friendly reception staff dispenses sound local knowledge, including tips on where to have breakfast in cafes nearby. No credit cards are accepted, and you'll pay extra for A/C.

Via dei Mille 64. www.euroquirishotel.com. © **06/491279.** 9 units. 40€–160€ double. Metro: Termini. **Amenities:** Wi-Fi (free).

Giuliana ★★ The Santacroce family and their staff bend over backwards to make guests feel welcome at this moderate-priced inn near the station and

Santa Maria Maggiore. Basic but comfy rooms, most done up in crimson and buttercream, come with surprisingly large bathrooms. Breakfast is a simple affair, but all in all, this is a good value for this side of the (train) tracks.

Via Agostino Depretis 70. www.hotelgiuliana.com. ✆ **06/4880795.** 11 units. 50€–160€ double, includes breakfast (with most rates). Metro: Termini or Repubblica. **Amenities:** Bike rentals; concierge; Wi-Fi (free).

Trastevere

This was once an "undiscovered" neighborhood—but no longer. Being based here does give some degree of escape from the busy (and pricey) *centro storico,* however. And there are bars, shops, and restaurants galore among its narrow cobblestone lanes (see map p. 124).

MODERATE

Santa Maria ★★ Hidden behind an ivy-covered wall, the lovely Santa Maria is built around a 16th-century cloister, now a relaxing courtyard fragrant with orange trees. Cheerful rooms, some with exposed brick walls and beamed ceilings, are mostly on the ground floor. Free breakfast and loaner bikes, a roof garden, and a cocktail bar all make this charmer a stand-out in hotel-deprived Trastevere. *Tip:* Several spacious, multi-bed rooms make this a fine option for families.

Vicolo del Piede 2. www.htlsantamaria.com. ✆ **06/5894626.** 20 units. 89€–260€ double. Rates include breakfast. Tram: 8. Bus: 23, 280, 780 or H. **Amenities:** Bar; bikes; Wi-Fi (free).

INEXPENSIVE

Arco del Lauro ★★ Hidden in Trastevere's snaking alleyways, this serene little B&B occupies the ground floor of a shuttered pink *palazzo.* Bright rooms have parquet floors, plush beds, and simple decor, with a mix of modern and period furnishings. Rooms can't be defined as large, but they all feel spacious thanks to lofty wood ceilings. Breakfast is taken at a nearby cafe; there's also coffee and snacks laid out around the clock. No credit cards.

Via Arco de' Tolomei 29. www.arcodellauro.it. ✆ **06/97840350.** 6 units. 85€–145€ double. Rates include breakfast at nearby cafe. Bus: 23, 280, 780, or H. Tram: 8. **Amenities:** Wi-Fi (free).

Hotel San Francesco ★★ Lying at the edge of Trastevere, close to the Porta Portese gate in an area that hasn't (yet) been gentrified, this hotel still has a local feel that has disappeared from much of the neighborhood. All rooms are bright, with color-washed walls and modern tiling. Doubles are fairly small, but the bathrooms are palatial. The grand piano in the lobby adds a touch of old-time charm; a top-floor garden with a cocktail bar overlooks terracotta rooftops and pealing church bell towers. *Tip:* Book a "charity room," and the hotel will match your 2€ donation to help Rome's shelter dogs.

Via Jacopa de' Settesoli 7. www.hotelsanfrancesco.net. ✆ **06/48300051.** 24 units. 69€–199€ double. Bus: H, 44 or 75. Tram: 3 or 8. **Amenities:** Bar; babysitting; Wi-Fi (free).

WHERE TO EAT IN ROME

Rome remains a top destination for food lovers and today offers more dining diversity than ever. Though many of its *trattorie* haven't changed their menus in a quarter of a century (for better or worse), the city has an increasing number of creative spots with chefs willing to revisit tradition.

Restaurants generally serve lunch between 12:30 and 2:30pm, and dinner between 7:30 and 10:30pm. At all other times, most restaurants are closed—though a new generation is moving toward all-day dining, with a limited service at the "in-between" time of mid-afternoon.

If you have your heart set on any of these places below, we seriously recommend *reserving ahead of arrival.* Hot tables go quickly, especially on high-season weekends—often twice: once for the early-dining tourists, and then again by locals, who dine later, typically around 9pm.

A *servizio* (tip or service charge) is almost always added to your bill or included in the price. Sometimes it is marked on the menu as *coperto e servizio* or *pane e coperto* (bread, cover charge, and service). You can leave extra if you wish—a couple of euros as a token. If you have any questions about an item on your bill, don't hesitate to ask for an explanation.

Restaurants by Cuisine

Near Vatican City

For restaurant locations, see map p. 85. If you just want a quick, tasty sandwich before or after your Vatican safari, **Duecento Gradi ★★**, is a topnotch panino joint with lots of yummy choices, right across from the Vatican walls at Piazza Risorgimento 3 (www.duecentogradi.it; ✆ **06/39754239;** Sun–Thurs 10am–2am; Fri–Sat 11am–5am).

EXPENSIVE

Taverna Angelica ★★ MODERN ITALIAN/SEAFOOD   In a sea of overpriced, touristy restaurants near St. Peter's, Angelica serves up surprisingly good and justly priced (though not cheap) fare. Specialties include spaghetti with crunchy bacon and leeks, *fettuccine* with king prawns and

Mussels at Taverna Angelica.

eggplant, turbot with crushed almonds, and a black-bread-encrusted lamb with potato flan. Seafood is fresh and simply cooked, from octopus carpaccio to sea bream with rosemary. Save room for the delicious, non-run-of-the-mill dessert options. Reservations are required.

Piazza A. Capponi 6. www.tavernaangelica.it. $\textit{C}$ **06/6874514.** Main courses 10€–23€; tasting menus 40€ and 45€. Daily 6pm–midnight; also Sun noon–3:30pm. Closed 10 days in Aug. Metro: Ottaviano.

MODERATE

Bonci Pizzarium ★★★ PIZZA Celebrity chef Gabriele Bonci has always had a cult following in the Eternal City. And since he's been featured on TV shows overseas and written up by influential bloggers, you can expect long lines at his pizzeria. No matter—it's worth waiting (and walking 10 minutes west of the Vatican Museums) for some of the best pizza you'll ever taste, sold by the slice or by weight. His ingredients are fresh and organic, the crust is perfect, and the toppings often experimental (try the mortadella and crumbled pistachio). There's also a good choice of Italian craft IPAs and wheat beers, and wines by the glass. There are only a handful of stand-up tables inside and benches outside for seating, and reservations aren't taken. Bonci also has a counter at Termini's Mercato Centrale (see p. 78).

Via della Meloria 43. www.bonci.it. $\textit{C}$ **06/39745416.** Pizza 12€–40€ per kilo, depending on toppings. Mon–Sat 11am–10pm; Sundays noon–10pm. Metro: Cipro.

Su e Giù ★★ ROMAN Italian for "up and down," the name refers to both the dumbwaiter the staff uses for receiving dishes from the basement kitchen, and to the upstairs and downstairs seating from the main dining room. Traditional Roman dishes, such as *cacio e pepe,* spaghetti *alla carbonara,* and sweetbread-centered secondi (for example, *trippa all romana*) headline the menu, but seasonal dishes such as risotto *al radicchio* offer regulars (of which there are many) a break from the mainstays of *la cucina romana.* "Accogliente" (cozy, friendly) is not a typical characteristic of these streets between Vatican City and Castel Sant'Angelo, but it is how we would describe Su e Giù's family-friendly atmosphere.

Via Tacito 42. http://suegiucucinaromana.blogspot.it. $\textit{C}$ **06/3265-0352.** Main courses 9€–18€. Mon–Sat 12:30–5pm and 7:30–11pm. Metro: Lepanto.

Ancient Rome, Monti & Celio

For restaurant locations, see map p. 97. For a cappuccino, a quick bite, or aperitivo snacking, head to the epicenter of Monti, **La Bottega del Caffè** ★★ ($\textit{C}$ **06/4741578**) on lively Piazza Madonna dei Monti, open from 8am to the wee hours. When we hanker for something other than Italian food, we head to **Maharajah** ★★, an elegant Northern Indian eatery at Via dei Serpenti 124 (www.maharajah.it; $\textit{C}$ **06/4747144**).

EXPENSIVE

L'Asino d'Oro ★★ MODERN UMBRIAN/ROMAN This isn't your typical Roman eatery. Helmed by Lucio Sforza, a renowned chef from

Orvieto, L'Asino d'Oro offers a seriously refined take on the flavors of central Italy without a checked tablecloth in sight; instead, the setting is contemporary with a Scandinavian feel thanks to the light-wood interior. As for the food, it's marked by creativity and flair, in both flavor and presentation. Expect highly polished takes on hearty Umbrian standards, such as *baccala* (salted cod) with onions, raisins, and chestnut cream. or handmade *lombrichelli* pasta with black truffles and anchovies.

Via del Boschetto 73. ⓒ **06/48913832.** Main courses 18€–27€. Tues–Sat 12:30–2:30pm, 7:30–11pm. Closed last 2 weeks in Aug. Metro: Cavour.

MODERATE

Caffè Propaganda ★ MODERN ITALIAN   This stylish eatery—part lively Parisian bistro, part cocktail bar—is your best bet for scoring a good meal within eyeshot of the Colosseum. Diners lounge on caramel-colored leather banquettes and choose from a diverse menu that mixes Roman classics such as *carbonara* (pasta with cured pork, egg, and cheese) with inventive Continental fare or more familiar dishes—like an 18€ hamburger. Desserts are Instagram-worthy affairs. After dark, confident bartenders shake up Propaganda's signature cocktails. Service is relaxed by North American standards, so only eat here if you have time to linger.

Via Claudia 15. www.caffepropaganda.it. ⓒ **06/94534255.** Main courses 14€–22€. Mon–Fri 12:30–3:30pm and 7:30pm–2am; Sat–Sun noon–2am. Metro: Colosseo. Bus: C3, 75, 81, 118. Tram: 3 or 8.

InRoma al Campidoglio ★ ITALIAN   Once a club for Rome's film industry, InRoma sits on a cobbled lane opposite the Palatine Hill. Though the place rests heavily on its cinematic laurels, it still serves up authentic Roman and regional cuisine. Meals might start with *caprese di bufala affumicata* (salad of tomatoes and smoked buffalo mozzarella) followed by classic Roman pastas like *all'amatriciana* (cured pork, tomato, and pecorino) or a main course of *tagliata* (beef strip steak) with a red wine reduction. The ambience inside is fairly generic; we recommend the terrace for a table to remember.

Via dei Fienili 56. www.inroma.eu. ⓒ **06/69191024.** Main courses 10€–20€. Daily 11:45am–4pm and 6:30–11:30pm. Bus: C3, H, 81, 83, 160, 170, 628.

La Barrique ★★ MODERN ROMAN   This cozy, contemporary *enoteca* (wine bar with food) has a kitchen that knocks out fresh farm-to-table fare that complements the well-chosen wine list. The atmosphere is lively and informal, with rustic place settings and friendly service—as any proper *enoteca* should be. The menu offers creative takes on familiar Italian dishes, such as *bocconcini di baccalà* (salt-cod morsels), crispy on the outside and served with a rich tomato dipping sauce; or *crostone* (a giant crostino) topped with grilled burrata cheese, chicory, and cherry tomatoes.

Via del Boschetto 41B. ⓒ **06/47825953.** Main courses 10€–16€. Mon–Fri 1–3pm and 7–11:30pm, Sat 7–11:30pm. Metro: Cavour.

Terre e Domus della Provincia Romana ★★ MODERN ROMAN
Located in the stunning Palazzo Valentini (see p. 105), opposite Trajan's Column, this sleek, modern *enoteca* has floor-to-ceiling windows overlooking the Vittoriano and Trajan Markets. The menu showcases the best in local wines and foods, using produce grown at the Rebibbia prison in Rome. It's also a training ground for apprentice chefs and servers. Expect traditional Roman classics plus seasonal, vegetable-driven dishes—a welcome break from the pizza, pasta, and pork circuit.

Foro di Traiano 82–84. www.palazzovalentini.it. © **06/69940273.** Main courses 10€– 15€. Daily 7:30am–12:30am. Metro: Cavour. Bus: 80, 85, 87, 175.

INEXPENSIVE

Li Rioni ★★ PIZZA   This fab neighborhood pizzeria is close enough to the Colosseum to be convenient, but just distant enough to avoid the dreaded "touristy" label that applies to so much dining in this part of town. Roman-style pizzas baked in the wood-stoked oven are among the best in town, with perfect crisp crusts. There's also a bruschetta list (from around 4€) and a range of salads. Outside tables can be cramped, but there's plenty of room inside. If you want to eat late, booking is essential or you'll be fighting with hungry locals for a table. *Tip:* After visiting the Colosseum or the Basilica of San Clemente, stop for an aperitivo, then head here at 7 for an early (and cheap) pizza dinner.

Via SS. Quattro 24. www.lirioni.it. © **06/70450605.** Pizzas 6€–9€. Wed–Mon 7pm–mid-night. Metro: Colosseo. Bus: C3, 51, 85, 87. Tram: 3 or 8.

Centro Storico & the Pantheon

For restaurant locations, see map p. 108. Vegetarians looking for massive salads (or anyone who just wants a break from all those heavy meats and starches) can find great food at the neighborhood branch of **L'Insalata Ricca,** Largo dei Chiavari 85 (www.linsalataricca.it; © **06/68803656;** daily noon–midnight).

EXPENSIVE

Osteria dell'Antiquario ★ MODERN ITALIAN/ROMAN   This cozy *osteria* ticks off all the boxes: candlelit tables, a romantic setting on a quiet terrace overlooking Palazzo Lancillotti, and traditional Roman fare with some inventive detours, such as swordfish carpaccio, or linguini with asparagus, pistachios, and a citrus infusion. Fresh fish here is especially good, and lobster features prominently. This is a good spot to consider the budget-blowing full monty of *antipasto, primo,* and *secondo.*

Piazzetta di S. Simeone 26–27, Via dei Coronari. www.osteriadellantiquario.it. © **06/6879694.** Main courses 18€–26€. Thurs–Tues noon–11pm (no midday closure); Closed July and Aug. Bus: 30, 70, 81, 87, 492 or 628.

Pipero ★★★ CONTEMPORARY ROMAN   Once an outpost of fine dining near Termini, the former Pipero al Rex is now just Pipero, and has moved to much-expanded quarters not far from Campo de' Fiori. Sommelier and consummate host Alessandro Pipero works the front of the Michelin-starred dining room, while Chef Luciano Monosilio runs the kitchen. Service is impeccable and never intrusive, and the menu follows the haute trend of just listing key ingredients ("salmon, quinoa, camomile, radishes"; or "egg, potatoes, tea, hazelnuts") to clue diners in on the carefully curated plates that come out of the kitchen. A la carte or tasting menus are available.

Corso Vittorio Emanuele II, 250. www.piperoroma.it/en. ℂ **06/68139022.** Main courses 30€ and way up; tasting menus 110€–140€. Mon–Sat 12:30–2:30pm and 7–10:30pm. Bus: 40. 46, 62, 64.

MODERATE

Antica Hostaria Romanesca ★ ROMAN   It's very easy to eat badly on Campo de'Fiori, which makes this authentic spot with ringside seats on the piazza such a pleasant surprise. Romanesca does dependable, old-school Roman fare at low prices, including a gloriously juicy *pollo e peperoni* (stewed chicken with peppers) and *abbacchio scottadito,* lamb chops hot off the grill. Locals snatch up the tables after 9pm, so a reservation is advised.

Campo de' Fiori 40 (east side of square). ℂ **06/6864024.** Main courses 9€–15€. Daily noon–3pm and 7–11pm. Bus: 30, 40, 46, 62, 64, 70, 81, 87, 492. Tram: 8.

Armando al Pantheon ★★ ROMAN/VEGETARIAN   You know you're sure of your place in the Roman culinary pantheon (sorry, couldn't resist) when you opt to take Saturday nights and Sundays off. Despite the odd hours and a location just a few steps from the *actual* Pantheon, this family-run trattoria serves as many locals as tourists. Chef Armando Gargioli took over the place in 1961, and his sons now run the business. Roman favorites to look out for include *cacio e pepe,* marinated artichokes, and the Jewish-influenced *aliciotti all'indivia* (endive and roasted anchovies; Tues and Fri only). A Roman rarity: Vegetarians get their own, fairly extensive, menu.

Salita dei Crescenzi 31. www.armandoalpantheon.it. ℂ **06/68803034.** Main courses 10€–25€. Mon–Fri 12:30–3pm and 7–11pm; Sat 12:30–3pm. Closed Sat night, Sun, all of Aug. Bus: 30, 70, 81, 87, 492, 628. Tram: 8.

La Campana ★★ ROMAN/TRADITIONAL ITALIAN   Family atmosphere and a classic Roman elegance permeate the spacious, well-lit rooms of this venerable address, Rome's oldest restaurant (feeding guests since 1518!). The atmosphere is convivial yet refined, with a lovely mixture of regulars and locals. The broad selection of *antipasti* is displayed on a long table at the entrance, and the daily menu features authentic *cucina romana* classics like pasta with oxtail ragout, tripe, gnocchi, *cacio e pepe,* and myriad vegetarian choices. The wine list includes interesting local labels, and the staff and service are impeccable.

Vicolo della Campana 18. www.ristorantelacampana.com. ℂ **06/6875273.** Main courses 10€–22€. Tues–Sun 12:30–3pm and 7:30–11pm. Metro: Spagna. Bus: 70, 81, 87, 280, 492, 628.

Nonna Betta ★★ ROMAN/JEWISH   Though not strictly kosher, this is the only restaurant in Rome's old Jewish quarter historically owned and managed by Roman Jews. Traditional dishes include delicious *carciofi alla giudia:* deep-fried artichokes served with small morsels like battered cod filet, stuffed and fried zucchini flowers, carrot sticks, and whatever vegetable is in season. Don't forego the *baccalà* with onions and tomato or the tagliolini with chicory and mullet roe. Middle Eastern specialties such as falafel and couscous are on the menu, and all desserts are homemade, including a stellar cake with pine nuts.

Via del Portico d'Ottavia 16. www.nonnabetta.it. ℭ **06/68806263.** Main courses 10€–20€. Wed–Mon 11am–5pm and 6–11pm. Bus: H, 23, 63, 280, 780. Tram 8.

Retrobottega ★★ ROMAN   Fresh, modern, and progressive, the somewhat misnamed Retrobottega is a nice contrast to the well-worn streets of the touristy heart of town. This culinary laboratory, founded by four young, accomplished chefs, is an intimate but convivial choice. Most seats surround the open kitchen and customers interact directly with the chefs—there is no waitstaff. The day's offerings focus on local, seasonal, responsibly sourced ingredients and unexpected pairings, like asparagus and fennel, or pasta with octopus ragu.

Via della Stelletta 4. www.retro-bottega.com. ℭ **06/68136310.** Main courses 12€–22€. Tues–Sun noon–11:30pm, Sat 7–11:30pm. Bus: 30, 70, 81, 87, 492, 628.

INEXPENSIVE

Alfredo e Ada ★★ ROMAN   No menus here, just the waiter—and it's usually owner Sergio explaining, in Italian, what the kitchen is preparing that day. Look for Roman trattoria classics like eggplant parmigiana, artichoke lasagna, excellent carbonara, or tripe. The whole place oozes character, with shared tables, scribbled walls festooned with drawings, and the house wine poured into carafes from a tap in the wall. There are only five tables, so it's best to make a reservation or get here early. This sort of place is becoming rare in Rome—enjoy it while you can.

Via dei Banchi Nuovi 14. ℭ **06/6878842.** Main courses 8€–10€. Tues–Sat noon–3pm and 7–10:30pm. Closed Aug. Bus: 40, 46, 62, 64, 916.

Antico Forno Roscioli ★★ BAKERY   The Rosciolis have been running this celebrated bakery for three generations since the 1970s, though bread has been made here since at least 1824. Today it's the home of the finest crusty sourdough in Rome, assorted cakes, and addictive pastries and biscotti, as well as exceptional Roman-style *pizza bianca* and *pizza rossa* sold by weight. This is largely a takeout joint, with limited seating—and the wider range of pizza toppings is only available from noon to 2:30pm. Around the corner is the wonderful **Roscioli restaurant and** *salumeria* **deli** at Via dei Giubbonari 21 and, at Via Cairoli 16, **Roscioli Caffè**, the latest outpost of the family empire, which offers breakfast treats, cappuccini, and palate-pleasing panini.

Via dei Chiavari 34. www.anticofornoroscioli.it. ℭ **06/6864045.** Pizza from 5€ (sold by weight). Mon–Sat 7am–7:30pm. Tram: 8.

La Montecarlo ★★ PIZZA   Dirt-cheap and immensely popular with locals, Montecarlo feels like a big party: Efficient, flirtatious servers sling piping-hot, thin-crusted pies, and the wine and beer flow freely. Sure, they serve other fare, but seriously, come for the pizza. Montecarlo's longtime rival, the equally recommendable **Baffetto** ★★ (www.pizzeriabaffetto.it), is just around the corner on Via del Governo Vecchio. Lines at both joints are long, but move quickly.

Vicolo Savelli 11 (at Corso Vittorio Emanuele II). www.lamontecarlo.it. © **06/6861877.** Pizzas 6€–10€. Tues–Sun noon–1am. Bus: 40, 46, 62, 64, 916.

Tridente, the Spanish Steps & Via Veneto

For restaurant locations, see map p. 113. The historic cafes near the Spanish Steps are saturated with history but, sadly, tend to be overpriced tourist traps, where mediocre slices of cake or even a cup of coffee or tea will cost 5€. Nevertheless, you may want to pop inside the two most celebrated institutions: **Babington's Tea Rooms** (www.babingtons.com; © **06/6786027;** daily 10am–9:30pm), established in 1893 at the foot of the Spanish Steps by a couple of English *signore,* and **Caffè Greco,** Via dei Condotti 86 (www.anticocaffegreco.eu; © **06/6791700;** daily 9am–8pm), Rome's oldest bar, which opened in 1760 and has hosted Keats, Ibsen, Goethe, and many other historical *cognoscenti.*

EXPENSIVE

Al Ceppo ★★ MARCHIGIANA/ROMAN   The setting of this Parioli dining institution is an elegant 19th-century parlor, with dark wood furnishings, chandeliers, fresh flowers, family portraits on the walls, and an open kitchen with a wood-stoked hearth. The menu features regional dishes from the owners' home, the Le Marche region northeast of Rome: *marchigiana*-style rabbit, fish stews, fresh seafood, and grilled meats, all artfully prepared and presented, along with pastas both hearty and delicate. It's reason enough to head north to explore Parioli's many charms.

Via Panama 2 (near Piazza Ungheria). www.ristorantealceppo.it. © **06/8419696.** Main courses 17€–30€. Tues–Sun 12:30–3pm and 7:30–11pm. Mon 7:30pm-11pm. Closed last 2 weeks in Aug. Bus: 52, 53, 223 or 910. Tram: 3 or 19.

Imàgo ★★★ INTERNATIONAL   The views of Rome from this 6th-floor hotel restaurant are jaw-dropping, the old city laid out before you, glowing pink as the sun goes down. The food is equally special, as chef Francesco Apreda reinterprets Italian cuisine, borrowing heavily from Indian and Japanese culinary traditions. The Michelin-star menu changes seasonally, but may include risotto with red chicory, cheese, and coriander; sake-glazed black cod; or even tandoori duck. Reservations are essential; jackets required for the gentlemen.

In Hotel Hassler, Piazza della Trinità dei Monti 6. www.imagorestaurant.com. © **06/69934726.** Main courses 33€–50€; tasting menus 120€–160€. Daily 7–10:30pm. Metro: Spagna.

Metamorfosi ★★★ MODERN ITALIAN   For our money, this is the place to have your blow-the-vacation-budget meal in Rome. This prestigious

Views of Rome from chef Francesco Apreda's Imàgo restaurant (see p. 75).

Michelin-starred restaurant is a feast for the eyes and the taste buds, with minimalistic decor and astonishingly inventive cooking. Chef Roy Caceres, a native of Colombia, likes to tell a story with each beautifully crafted dish, from exquisite risotto and pasta preparations to elegant meat and fish interpretations. Be prepared for memorable items like fish soup ravioli, "encased" risotto with mushrooms and hazelnut, or lamb with red mole sauce and chia seeds. Tasting menus are full of delightful surprises, and the artistry of the presentations is jaw-dropping.

Via Giovanni Antonelli 30/32. www.metamorfosiroma.it. ℗ **06/8076839.** Main courses 38€–45€, tasting menus 100€–130€. Mon–Fri 12:30–2:30pm and 8–10:30pm; Sat 8–10:30pm. Bus: 52, 168, 910.

MODERATE

Al Vero Girarrosto Toscano ★★ TUSCAN   This classic *dolce vita* hangout has been popular with celebrities and gourmands since it opened in the 1960s. Over time, its praised Roman cuisine has been replaced by acclaimed Tuscan recipes, drawing the same VIP crowds. The décor is as elegant as the menu, with wood paneling, sleek finishings, and a cozy fireplace that doubles as open-hearth grill. Go for classic Tuscan hors d'oeuvres, like liver crostini and assorted bruschettas, but also focus your attention on the hearty soups, like pasta e fagioli with borlotti beans, and droolsome *ribollita* (a minestrone with kale, cannellini beans, and bread). Grilled meats (*girarrosto,* as in the restaurant's name) are center stage, featuring the classic *fiorentina* (2-lb. T-bone) as well as succulent tenderloin, beef filet, and a platter of mixed grilled ribs, chops, and sausages.

Via Campagna 29. www.alverogirarrostotoscano.it. ℗ **06/482-1899.** Main courses 18€–35€. Daily 12:30–3pm and 7:30–midnight. Bus: 52, 53, 217, 360, 910.

Canova Tadolini ★★ ROMAN   Few restaurants are as steeped in history as this place. Antonio Canova's sculpture studio was kept as a workshop by the descendants of his pupil Adamo Tadolini until 1967, and even today it's littered with tools and sculptures in bronze, plaster, and marble. The whole thing really does seem like a museum, with tables squeezed between models, casts, drapes, and bas-reliefs. The pasta menu features interesting riffs on gnocchi and traditional *alla carbonara,* while entrees might include seabass with a salt crust or steak salad with arugula and cherry tomatoes.

Via del Babuino 150A–B. www.canovatadolini.com. ✆ **06/32110702.** Main courses 14€–26€. Daily noon–11pm (bar/cafe from 8am). Metro: Spagna.

Colline Emiliane ★★ EMILIANA-ROMAGNOLA   This family-owned restaurant tucked in an alley beside the Trevi Fountain has been serving traditional dishes from Emilia-Romagna since 1931. Service is excellent and so is the food: Classics include *tortelli di zucca* (pumpkin ravioli in butter sauce) and magnificent *tagliatelle alla Bolognese,* the mother of all Italian comfort foods. A menu of *secondi* is heavy on beef. Save room for the walnut-and-caramel cake or lemon meringue pie. Reservations are essential.

Via degli Avignonesi 22 (off Piazza Barberini). www.collineemiliane.com. ✆06/4817538. Main courses 14€–22€. Tues–Sun 12:45–2:45pm; Tues–Sat 7:30–10:45pm. Closed Aug. Metro: Barberini.

Il Bacaro ★ MODERN ITALIAN   Romantic and low-key, Il Bacaro's setting on a hidden backstreet near the Pantheon offers respite from the traffic and tourist crush. Insanely delicious *primi* and *secondi* (like rich *panzerotti* pasta with chestnuts and red wine sauce, or beef filet with gorgonzola and walnuts) are a welcome departure from the usual Roman fare. Desserts revolve around mousses paired with Bavarian chocolate, hazelnuts, caramel,

Sculptures in Canova Tadolini.

and pistachio. The 600-label wine list features well-priced varietals from all over Italy. Try to get a prized sidewalk table on a balmy summer evening.

Via degli Spagnoli 27 (near Piazza delle Coppelle). No website. ℗ **06/6872554.** Main courses 14€–26€. Daily noon–midnight. Bus: 30, 70, 81, 87, 492, 628.

Around Termini

For restaurant locations, see map p. 122. Mostly catering to dazed travelers toting wheeled suitcases and crumpled maps, restaurants around Termini don't have to be good in order to bring in business. The following are some of our favorite exceptions to that norm.

MODERATE

Trattoria Monti ★★ REGIONAL/MARCHE   Word is definitely out on this cozy, plain-Jane trattoria near Termini station. But that just means you need to reserve in advance to sample outstanding, hearty pastas and meat dishes from the Marche region. You will remember the *tortello al rosso d'uovo*—a large, delicate ravioli filled with spinach, ricotta, and egg yolk— for the rest of your life. You also may discover a few new favorites among the territory's underappreciated wines. Vegetarians take heart: There are always 4 or 5 non-meat entrees available.

Via di San Vito 13A (at Via Merulana). ℗ **06/4466573.** Main courses 12€–22€. Tues–Sat 1–2:45pm and 8–10:45pm; Sun lunch only. Metro: Cavour or Vittorio Emanuele. Bus: 50, 71, 105, 360, 590, 649. Tram: 5 or 14.

Trimani Il Wine Bar ★ MODERN ITALIAN   This small bistro and well-stocked wine bar (with a 20-page wine list!) attracts white collars and wine lovers in a modern, relaxed ambience, accompanied by smooth jazz. The refined entrees might include rabbit stuffed with asparagus or Luganega sausage with a zucchini puree. The wines-by-the-glass list changes daily. If you just want a snack to accompany your vino, cheese and salami platters range from 9€ to 14€. The selection at Trimani's vast wine shop next door boggles the oenophilic mind.

Via Cernaia 37B. www.trimani.com. ℗ **06/4469630.** Main courses 12€–24€. Mon–Sat 11:30am–3pm and 5:30pm–midnight. Closed 2 weeks in mid-Aug. Metro: Repubblica or Castro Pretorio.

INEXPENSIVE

Mercato Centrale Roma ★★ GOURMET MARKET   This ambitious, three-story gourmet dining hall and street food hub is the only place worth dining in Termini Station, with top-notch purveyors of everything from gourmet pizza to chocolate to truffles, plus a wine bar and a high-end restaurant. The space is inviting, if a little chaotic. Even if you don't have a train to catch, it's worth having lunch or a quick snack here. *Tip:* Walk through the hall and check out all the offerings, then snag a table and have members of your party take turns going to order their food.

Via Giovanni Giolitti 36 (in Termini Station). www.mercatocentrale.it/roma. ℗ **06/46202900.** Daily 7am–midnight. Metro: Termini.

Pinsere ★★ PIZZA *Pinsa* is an ancient Roman preparation: an oval focaccia made with a blend of four organic flours and olive oil that's left to rise for 2 to 3 days. The result is a crispy yet feather-light single-portion snack perfect for a light lunch. This friendly small bakery always has an assortment of pies ready to pop in the oven. Favorites come with pureed pumpkin, smoked cheese, and pancetta; classic tomato, basil, and *bufala;* or the surprising combo of ricotta, fresh figs, raisins, pine nuts, and honey. Food to go only, or to eat standing up at one of the few small inside or outside counters. *Note:* closed Saturday and Sunday.

Via Flavia 98. www.pinsaromana.info. ℰ **06/42020924.** Pinsa 3.50€–5.50€. Mon–Fri 9am–8pm. Metro: Castro Pretorio. Bus: 60-62, 66, 82, 492, 590, 910.

Trastevere

For restaurant locations, see map p. 124. Popular craft-beer bar **Bir and Fud** ★ (p. 135) also serves pizzas and traditional snacks like *supplì* (fried, stuffed rice croquettes) to hungry drinkers. It serves dinner daily and lunch Thursday through Sunday. Hearts and taste buds soar at **Biscottificio Artigiano Innocenti** ★★ (Via della Luce 21; ℰ **06/5803926**), where Stefania and her family have been turning out delicate handmade cookies and cakes since the 1920s.

EXPENSIVE

Antico Arco ★★★ CREATIVE ITALIAN This well-known address for new Italian cuisine consistently delivers exquisite dishes made with the finest local and seasonal ingredients—creative dishes like tiger shrimp tortelli with sautéed endive, or duck breast with wild carrots, ginger, and raspberries, accompanied by excellent wine and topnotch service. A full meal here makes for a special night out (reservations are essential), but you can also just come to the restaurant's wine bar for vino and some finger food—it pairs nicely with the rapturous *centro storico* views from the nearby terraces of the Janiculum Hill. *Tip:* It's a 15-minute walk uphill from Trastevere, but the climb is gradual and pleasant.

Piazzale Aurelio 7 (at Via San Pancrazio). www.anticoarco.it. ℰ **06/5815274.** Main courses 16€–30€. Daily noon–midnight. Bus: 115, 710, 870.

Glass ★★ MODERN ROMAN In an industrial-chic setting of exposed brick, stark white walls, and polished floors, Michelin-starred chef Cristina Bowerman and partner Fabio Spada serve refined food using high-quality ingredients. The menu changes seasonally, but expect carefully prepared shellfish, aromatic dishes such as foie gras–stuffed ravioli, or lamb cooked with dark beer and Stilton cheese. A vegetarian menu is available. Glass remains one of Rome's hottest tables—reservations are essential.

Vicolo del Cinque 58. www.glass-restaurant.it. ℰ **06/58335903.** Main courses 26€–55€; fixed-price menus 85€–150€. Tues–Sun 7:30–11pm. Closed 2 weeks in Jan, 2 weeks in July. Bus: 23 or 280.

Spirito DiVino ★★ ROMAN/SLOW FOOD In a medieval synagogue on a 2nd-century street (which you can visit on a cellar tour), the Catalani family does exceptional modern plates (like an appetizer salad of raisins, walnuts, pomegranate, and marinated duck) as well as ancient Roman cuisine (like *maiale alla mazio,* a favorite pork dish of Julius Caesar's), food as warm and comforting as the ambience. Finish with the delicately perfumed lavender panna cotta, a cream-based dessert.

Via dei Genovesi 31 (at Vicolo dell'Atleta). www.ristorantespiritodivino.com. ℂ **06/ 5896689.** Main courses 12€–26€. Mon–Sat 7–11:30pm. Bus: H, 23, 44, 280. Tram: 8.

MODERATE

Cacio e Pepe ★ ROMAN   This ultra-traditional trattoria, complete with paper tablecloths, a TV showing the game, the owner chatting up the ladies, and a bustling crowd of patrons waiting to be seated, is a Trastevere neighborhood stalwart. Start with cheapo plates of fried tidbits, from rice *suppli* to cod to vegetables, then move on to the namesake pasta *cacio e pepe* or other classic Roman pasta dishes—and be ready for hearty portions. For *secondo*—if you have room left—consider *polpette* (stewed meatballs), *saltimbocca alla romana* (veal cutlets with sage and ham), or grilled meats, all sold reasonably priced. They even have pizza for the kids.

Vicolo del Cinque 15. www.osteriacacioepepe.it. ℂ **06/89572853.** Main courses 9€–19€. Mon–Fri 7pm–midnight; Sat–Sun 1pm–midnight. Bus: 23, 280. Tram: 8.

Da Enzo ★★ ROMAN   For traditional Roman cuisine, try this down-homey, non-touristy, family-run trattoria. *Cucina romana,* including classic carbonara, *amatriciana,* and *cacio e pepe,* win the gold, as do meat-heavy *secondi* like stewed tripe, or meatballs braised in tomato sauce. Local wines can be ordered by the jug or glass, and desserts (try the mascarpone with wild strawberries) come served in either full or half portions (a good thing, considering Enzo's hefty servings). A few outdoor tables look out on some of Trastevere's characteristic alleyways.

Via dei Vascellari 29. www.daenzoal29.com. ℂ **06/5812260.** Main courses 9€–15€. Mon–Sat 12:30–3pm and 7:30–11:00pm. Bus: 23. 44, 280. Tram: 8.

Osteria La Gensola ★★★ SEAFOOD/ROMAN   Considered one of the best seafood destinations in Rome, this warm and welcoming family-run restaurant feels like a true Trastevere home; decor is cozy, with soft lighting and a life-size wood-carved tree in the middle of the main dining room. Fish-lovers come for heavenly spaghetti with fresh clams, *polpettine* (meatballs) made with tuna, and other traditional Roman cuisine with a marine twist. The grill churns out succulent beefsteaks, among non-fish dishes. Reservations are a must on weekends.

Piazza della Gensola 15. www.osterialagensola.it. ℂ **06/58332758.** Main courses 13–16€. Daily 12:30–3pm and 7:30–11:30pm. Bus: H, 23, 280, 780. Tram: 8.

INEXPENSIVE

Dar Poeta ★ PIZZA   Ranking among the best pizzerias in Rome, "the poet" is a fine place to enjoy a classic Roman pizza margherita (tomato sauce, mozzarella, and fresh basil) or a more creative combo like the *patataccia* (potatoes, creamed zucchini, and *speck* [a smoked prosciutto]). The lines are long to eat in, but you can also order takeout. The decadent dessert calzone is filled with fresh ricotta and Nutella.

Vicolo del Bologna 45. www.darpoeta.com. ✆**06/5880516.** Pizzas 5€–9€. Daily noon–midnight. Bus: 23, 280.

Testaccio

The slaughterhouses of Rome's old meatpacking district (see map on p. 124) have been transformed into art venues, markets, and the museum **MACRO** (p. 125), but restaurants here still specialize in (though are not limited to) meats from the *quinto quarto* (the "fifth quarter")—the leftover parts of an animal after slaughter, typically offal like sweetbreads, tripe, tails, and other goodies you won't find on most American menus. This is an area to eat *cucina romana*—either in the restaurants below or from street-food stalls in the **Nuovo Mercato di Testaccio** (p. 132). Food-themed tours of Rome invariably end up here.

EXPENSIVE

Checchino dal 1887 ★★ ROMAN   Often mischaracterized as an offal-only joint, this establishment, opened in 1887 across from Rome's now-defunct abattoir, is a special-night-out type of place, serving wonderful *bucatini all'amatriciana* and veal saltimbocca—as well as hearty plates of spleens, lungs, and livers. Checchino is a pricier choice than most of the other restaurants in this area, but Romans from all over the city keep coming back when they want the real thing. Despite its meat-centric leanings, Checchino also has a decent vegetarian menu.

Via di Monte Testaccio 30 (at Via Galvani). www.checchino-dal-1887.com. ✆ **06/5746316.** Main course 12€–27€. Set menus 40€–65€. Tues–Sat 12:30–3pm and 8–11:45pm. Sun 12:30–3pm. Closed Aug and last week in Dec. Metro: Piramide. Bus: 83, 673, 719. Tram: 3.

Cannolis make a sweet end to a food tour of Rome.

MODERATE

Flavio al Velavevodetto ★★ ROMAN   Flavio's plain dining room is burrowed out of the side of Rome's most unusual "hill": a large mound made from amphorae discarded during the Roman era (see p. 47). Food-lovers, however, come here for classic Roman pastas like *cacio e pepe* and *amatriciana*, plus *quinto quarto* (nose-to-tail) entrees at fair prices. Hearty dishes like *polpette al sugo* (meatballs in red sauce), *coda alla vaccinara* (oxtail), and *involtini* (stuffed rolled veal) are good for sharing.

Via di Monte Testaccio 97–99. www.ristorantevelavevodetto.it. ℗ **06/5744194.** Main courses 9€–20€. Daily 12:30–3pm and 7:45–11pm. Metro: Piramide. Bus: 83, 673, 719. Tram: 3.

Osteria degli Amici ★★ MODERN ROMAN   On the corner of nightclub central and the hill of broken amphorae, this intimate and friendly *osteria* serves both traditional Roman classics and creative iterations thereof. Claudio and Alessandro base their menu on produce from the nearby market and their combined experience in famous kitchens around the world. Signature musts include fish- and seafood-based pastas and mains, golden-fried mozzarella *in carrozza*, and a range of pastas from classic *carbonara* to *paccheri* tubes with shrimp, mint, and zucchini. Leave room for the apple tartlet with cinnamon gelato.

Via Nicola Zabaglia 25. www.osteriadegliamiciroma.it. ℗ **06/5781466.** Main courses 10€–20€. Wed–Mon 12:30–3pm and 8pm–midnight. Metro: Piramide. Bus: 83, 673, 719. Tram: 3.

Porto Fluviale ★ MODERN ITALIAN   This multifunctional restaurant—part trattoria, part street-food stall, part pizzeria—can accommodate pretty much whatever you fancy. The decor is vaguely industrial, with a daytime clientele made up of families and white collars—the vibe gets younger after dark. From the various menus, best bets are the 30 or so *cicchetti*, small plates that allow you to taste the kitchen's range. Both the locale and the menus are highly kid-friendly.

Ultramodern décor pairs well with creative noshes at Romeo Chef and Baker.

Via del Porto Fluviale 22. www.portofluviale.com. ℗ **06/5743199.** Cicchetti (tapas) 3€–5€, main courses 7€–19€. Daily 10:30am–2am (Fri and Sat to 3am). Metro: Piramide. Bus: 23, 673, 715, 716.

Romeo Chef & Baker ★★ MODERN ITALIAN/PIZZA   In a cavernous former car showroom at the foot of the Avetine Hill, this ambitious venture from dynamic duo Cristina Bowerman and Fabio Spada of **Glass** (p. 79) marries French bistro, street food, craft cocktail, old-school pizzeria, and gourmet gelateria. The ultramodern space has seating for 500(!), plus standing noshing/cocktail space

GETTING YOUR FILL OF gelato

Don't leave town without trying one (or several) of Rome's outstanding **ice-cream parlors.** However, choose your gelato carefully: Don't buy close to the tourist-packed piazzas, and don't be dazzled by vats of brightly (and artificially) colored, air-pumped gelato. The best gelato is made only from natural ingredients, which impart a natural color—if the pistachio gelato is bright green, move on. Take your cone *(cono)* or small cup *(coppetta)* and stroll as you eat—sitting down on the premises is usually more expensive. The recommended spots below are generally open mid-morning to late, sometimes after midnight on summer weekends. Cones and small cups cost between 2.50€ and 4€.

Near Campo de' Fiori, one of Rome's oldest artisan gelato makers, **Gelateria Alberto Pica** ★★★ (Via della Seggiola 12; ⏱ **06/6868405;** Bus H, 63 or 780; Tram 8) produces top-quality gelato churned with local ingredients, including wild strawberries grown on the family's countryside estate. In the Monti area, fabulous (and gluten-free) **Fatamorgana** ★★★ (Piazza degli Zingari 5; www.gelateriafatamorgana.it; ⏱ **06/86391589;** Metro Cavour) is the place to try inventive flavors like delicate lavender and chamomile, or zingy avocado, lime, and white wine.

Two exceptions to the rule about avoiding gelato in touristy areas: venerable **Old Bridge Gelateria** ★ (Viale Bastioni di Michelangelo; ⏱ **328/411-9478;** gelateriaoldbridge.com), which delights customers lined up for the Vatican Museums; and, near Piazza Navona, **Frigidarium** ★★★ (Via del Governo Vecchio 112; www.frigidarium-gelateria.com; ⏱ **334/995-1184**), whose intense and creamy flavors will make you weep with joy (have a copetta of mango and coconut for me!).

In the Termini area, tiny but sleek **Come il Latte** ★★★ (Via Silvio Spaventa 24; www.comeillatte.it; ⏱ **06/42903882;** Metro Repubblica or Castro Pretorio) turns out artisan gelatos in flavors ranging from salted caramel (yes please!), to mascarpone and crumbled cookies; fruit flavors change according to season.

Trastevere's best artisan gelato, **Fior di Luna** ★★★ (Via della Lungaretta 96; www.fiordiluna.com; ⏱ **06/64561314;** Bus H or 780; Tram 8), is made with natural and Fair Trade produce. Star flavors are the incredibly rich chocolates, spiked with fig or orange, and an absolutely perfect pistachio.

for hundreds more. It's a real experience, offering the chance to sample Bowerman's creations—she's a Michelin-starred chef—at everyday prices.

Piazza dell'Emporio 28. www.romeo.roma.it. ⏱ **06/32110120.** Main courses 13€–20€. Metro: Piramide. Bus: 23, 75, 280, 716. Tram: 3.

Trattoria Perilli ★★ ROMAN Dine elbow to elbow with locals and enjoy the old-school atmosphere at this beloved institution of Roman *ristorazione*. With zero pretense, Perilli's formally attired waitstaff serve unadulterated renditions of Roman classics. The dishes are reliable, from pasta standbys like *carbonara* and *cacio e pepe* to grilled meats to that most English of Italian desserts, *zuppa inglese* (literally "English soup," or trifle). It's a fun and reasonably affordable place to go for a real four-course meal of *antipasto, primo, secondo,* and *dolce.* Reservations recommended.

Via Marmorata 39 (at Via Galvani). No website. ⓒ **06/5742415.** Entrees 11€–18€. Thurs–Tues 12:30–3pm and 7:30–11pm. Metro: Piramide. Bus: 23, 75, 280, 716. Tram: 3.

INEXPENSIVE

Da Remo ★★ PIZZA   Mentioning "Testaccio" and "pizza" in the same sentence elicits one typical response from locals: Da Remo, a Roman institution. In the summer especially, come early or be prepared to wait for a table. Every crisp-crusted, perfectly foldable pizza is made for all to see behind open counters. The most basic ones (margherita and marinara) start at around 7€. If it's too crowded on a summer evening, order your pizza for takeout and eat it in the park across the street.

Piazza Santa Maria Liberatrice 44. No website. ⓒ **06/5746270.** Most pizzas 6€–8€. Mon–Sat 7pm–1am. Bus: 83, 673, 719.

EXPLORING ROME

Rome's ancient monuments are a constant reminder that this was one of the greatest centers of Western civilization. In the heyday of the Empire, all roads led to Rome, with good reason. It was one of the first cosmopolitan cities, importing food, textiles, slaves, gladiators, great art, and even citizens from the far corners of the world. Despite its brutality and corruption, Rome left a legacy of law, a heritage of art, architecture, and engineering, and a canny lesson in how to conquer enemies by absorbing their cultures.

Bypassing the Lines

The endless lines outside Italian museums and attractions are a fact of life. But reservation services can help you avoid the wait, at least for some of the major museums.

Buying a **Roma Pass** (p. 44) is a good start; holders can use a special entrance at the Colosseum and skip the long ticket-buying line (you'll still have to line up for a security check).

Coopculture (www.coopculture.it) operates an online ticket office, which allows you to skip the line at many sites, including the Colosseum and the Forum, with a 1.50€ booking fee and a 2€ charge to print tickets.

For the **Vatican Museums,** buy an advance ticket at **http://biglietteria musei.vatican.va**; you'll pay an extra 4€ but you'll skip the entrance line (which can be very, very long). From late April to late October, the museum offers special access every **Friday night** from 7 to 11pm (last entry 9:30pm) for the same price as regular daytime admission. Given the greatly reduced crowds, you'll feel like you have the galleries to yourself.

Unfortunately, **St. Peter's** has no skip-the-line perk: The only way to jump the line there is to book a private or group tour (p. 88).

Vatican City & Prati

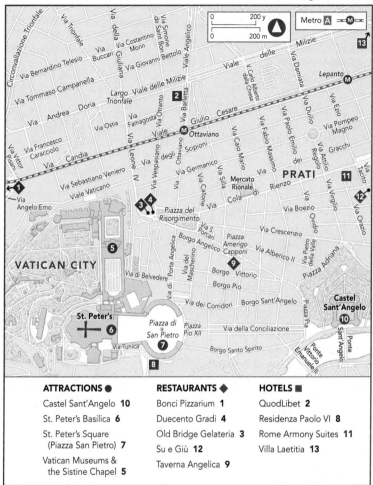

ATTRACTIONS ●	RESTAURANTS ◆	HOTELS ■
Castel Sant'Angelo **10**	Bonci Pizzarium **1**	QuodLibet **2**
St. Peter's Basilica **6**	Duecento Gradi **4**	Residenza Paolo VI **8**
St. Peter's Square	Old Bridge Gelateria **3**	Rome Armony Suites **11**
(Piazza San Pietro) **7**	Su e Giù **12**	Villa Laetitia **13**
Vatican Museums &	Taverna Angelica **9**	
the Sistine Chapel **5**		

But ancient Rome is only part of the spectacle. The Vatican has had a tremendous influence on making the city a tourism center. Although Vatican architects stripped down much of the city's ancient glory during the Renaissance, looting ruins (the Forum especially) for their precious marble, they created more treasures and occasionally incorporated the old into the new—as Michelangelo did when turning Diocletian's Baths complex into a church. And in the years that followed, Bernini adorned the city with baroque wonders, especially his glorious fountains.

Index of Attractions & Sights

St. Peter's & the Vatican

VATICAN CITY

The world's smallest sovereign state, **Vatican City** is a truly tiny territory, comprising little more than St. Peter's Basilica and the walled headquarters of the Roman Catholic Church. There are no border controls, though the city-state's 800 inhabitants (essentially clergymen and Swiss Guards) have their own radio station, daily newspaper, tax-free pharmacy and petrol pumps, postal service, and head of state—the Pope. The Pope had always exercised a high degree of political independence from the rest of Italy, formalized by the 1929 Lateran Treaty between Pope Pius XI and the Italian government to create the Vatican. The city is still protected by the flamboyantly uniformed (designed by Michelangelo) Swiss Guards, a tradition dating from when the Swiss, known as brave soldiers, were often hired out as mercenaries for foreign armies. Today the Vatican remains the center of the Roman Catholic world, the home of the Pope—and the resting place of St. Peter. **St. Peter's Basilica** is obviously one of the highlights, but the only part of the Apostolic Palace itself that you can visit independently is the **Vatican Museums,** the world's biggest and richest museum complex.

On the left side of Piazza San Pietro, the **Vatican Tourist Office** (www.vatican.va; ⓒ **06/ 69882019;** Mon–Sat 8:30am– 7:30pm) sells maps and guides that will help you make sense of the treasures in the museums; it also accepts reservations for tours of the Vatican Gardens. Adjacent to the information office, the **Vatican Post Office** sells special Vatican postage stamps (Mon–Fri 8:30am–7pm, Sat 8:30am–6pm).

The only entrance to St. Peter's for tourists is through one of the glories of the Western world: Bernini's 17th-century **St. Peter's Square (Piazza San Pietro).** As you stand in the huge

Statue of St. Peter in St. Peter's Square, Vatican City.

St. Peter's has a hard-and-fast dress code that makes no exceptions: **Men and women in shorts, above-the-knee skirts, or bare shoulders** are not admitted to the basilica, period, and **hats should be off.** I've occasionally seen guards handing out disposable cloaks for the scantily clad, but don't count on that: Cover up or bring a shawl. The same holds for the Roman Necropolis and the Vatican Museums.

piazza, you are in the arms of an ellipse partly enclosed by a majestic **Doric-pillared colonnade.** Stand in the marked marble discs embedded in the pavement near the fountains to see all the columns lined up in a striking optical/geometrical play. Straight ahead is the facade of St. Peter's itself, and to the right, above the colonnade, are the dark brown buildings of the **papal apartments** and the Vatican Museums. In the center of the square stands a 4,000-year-old **Egyptian obelisk,** created in the ancient city of Heliopolis on the Nile delta and appropriated by the Romans under Emperor Augustus. Flanking the obelisk are two 17th-century **fountains.** The one on the right (facing the basilica), by Carlo Maderno, who designed the facade of St. Peter's, was placed here by Bernini himself; the other is by Carlo Fontana.

St. Peter's Basilica ★★★ CHURCH   The Basilica di San Pietro, or simply **St. Peter's,** is the holiest shrine of the Catholic Church, built on the site of St. Peter's tomb by the greatest Italian artists of the 16th and 17th centuries. One of the lines on the right side of the piazza funnels you into the basilica, while the other two lead to the underground grottoes or the dome. Whichever you opt for first, you must be **properly dressed**—a rule that is very strictly enforced.

In Roman times, the Circus of Nero, where St. Peter is said to have been crucified, was just to the left of where the basilica is today. Peter was allegedly buried here in A.D. 64, and in A.D. 324 Emperor Constantine commissioned a church to be built over Peter's tomb. That structure stood for more than 1,000 years. The present basilica, mostly completed in the 1500s and 1600s, is predominantly High Renaissance and baroque. Inside, the massive scale is almost too much to absorb, showcasing some of Italy's greatest artists: Bramante, Raphael and Michelangelo. In a church of such grandeur—overwhelming in its detail of gilt, marble, and mosaic—you can't expect much subtlety. It is meant to be overpowering.

Going straight into the basilica, the first thing you see on the right side of the nave—the longest nave in the world, as clearly marked in the floor along with other cathedral measurements—is the chapel containing Michelangelo's graceful **"Pietà"** ★★★. Created in the 1490s when the master was still in his 20s, it clearly shows his genius for capturing the human form. (The sculpture has been kept behind reinforced glass since an act of vandalism in the 1970s.) Note the lifelike folds of Mary's robes and her youthful features; although she would've been middle-aged at the time of the Crucifixion, Michelangelo portrayed her as a young woman to convey her purity.

Further inside the nave, Michelangelo's dome is a mesmerizing space, rising high above the supposed site of St. Peter's tomb. With a diameter of 41.5m (136 ft.), the dome is Rome's largest, supported by four bulky piers decorated with reliefs depicting the basilica's key holy relics: St. Veronica's handkerchief (used to wipe the face of Christ); the lance of St. Longinus, which pierced Christ's side; and a piece of the True Cross.

Under the dome is the twisty-columned **baldacchino ★★**, by Bernini, sheltering the papal altar. The ornate 29m-high (96-ft.) canopy was created in part, so it is said, from bronze stripped from the Pantheon. Bernini sculpted the face of a woman on the base of each pillar; starting with the face on the left pillar (with your back to the entrance), circle the entire altar to see the progress of expressions from the agony of childbirth through to the fourth pillar, where the woman's face is replaced with that of her newborn baby.

Just before reaching the dome, on the right, the devout stop to kiss the foot of the 13th-century **bronze of St. Peter ★**, attributed to Arnolfo di Cambio. Elsewhere the church is decorated by more of Bernini's lavish sculptures, including his monument to Pope Alexander VII in the south transept, its winged skeleton writhing under the heavy marble drapes.

An entrance off the nave leads to the Sacristy and the **Historical Museum (Museo Storico)** or **treasury ★**, which is chock-full of richly jeweled chalices, reliquaries, and copes, as well as the late-15th-century bronze tomb of Pope Sixtus IV by Pollaiuolo.

You can also head downstairs to the **Vatican grottoes ★★**, with their tombs of the popes, both ancient and modern (Pope John XXIII got the most

papal AUDIENCES

When the pope is in Rome, he gives a public audience every Wednesday beginning at 10:30am (sometimes 10am in summer). If you want a good seat near the front, arrive early and prepare to wait—security begins to admit visitors between 8 and 8:30am but the line starts much earlier. Audiences are held in the Paul VI Hall of Audiences, although sometimes in summer they move to St. Peter's Square.

To attend, you must obtain a **free ticket.** Visit www.papalaudience.org to download a request form, which must be submitted via fax (yes, really) to the **Prefecture of the Papal Household** at ✆ **06/69885863.** Tickets can be picked up at an office just inside the Bronze Doors (located just after security at St. Peter's) from 3 to 7pm on the preceding day, or 7 to 10am on the morning of the audience. If you don't have a reservation, you can try the Swiss Guards by the Bronze Doors (8am–8pm in summer and 8am–7pm in winter). You can obtain tickets here up to 3 days in advance, subject to availability.

At noon on Sundays, the Pope appears briefly at his study window to give a blessing to the crowd gathered in St. Peter's Square. (No tickets are required for this.) To verify the Pope's whereabouts and appearances, go to the Vatican website, vatican.va.

adulation until the interment of **Pope John Paul II** in 2005). Behind a wall of glass is what is considered to be the tomb of St. Peter.

After you leave the grottoes, you find yourself in a courtyard and ticket line for the grandest sight in the basilica: the climb to **Michelangelo's dome ★★★**, about 114m (375 ft.) high. You can walk all the way up or take the elevator as far as it goes. The elevator saves you 171 steps, but you *still* have 320 to go after getting off. After you've made it to the top, you'll have a scintillating view over the rooftops of Rome and even the Vatican Gardens and papal apartments.

Visits to the **Necropolis Vaticana ★★** and St. Peter's tomb itself are restricted to 250 persons per day on guided tours (90 min.) You must send a fax or e-mail 3 weeks beforehand, or apply in advance in person at the Ufficio Scavi (②/fax **06/69873017;** e-mail: scavi@fsp.va; Mon–Fri 9am–6pm, Sat 9am–5pm), which is located through the arch to the left of the stairs up from the basilica. For details, check **www.vatican.va**. Children 14 and under are not admitted to the Necropolis.

Piazza San Pietro. www.vatican.va. ② **06/69881662.** Basilica (including grottoes) free. Necropolis Vaticana (St. Peter's tomb) 13€. Stairs to the dome 6€; elevator (part-way) to the dome 8€; sacristy (with Historical Museum) 5€ adults, 3€ 12 and under. **Basilica** Oct–Mar daily 7am–6:30pm, Apr–Sep daily 7am–7pm. **Dome** Oct–Mar daily 8am–4:45pm, Apr–Sept daily 8am–6pm. **Sacristry/museum** 9am–6:15pm Apr–Sep, to 5:15pm Oct–Mar. **Grottoes** 7am–6pm Apr–Sep, to 5pm Oct–Mar. Metro: Ottaviano/San Pietro, then a 10 min walk; or take bus 40, 46, or 62 to Piazza Pia/Traspontina, then about a 10 min walk.

Vatican Museums & the Sistine Chapel ★★★ MUSEUM

Nothing else in Rome quite lives up to the awe-inspiring collections of the **Vatican Museums,** a 15-minute walk from St. Peter's out of the north side of Piazza San Pietro. It's a vast treasure store of art from antiquity and the Renaissance gathered by the Roman Catholic Church through the centuries, filling a series of ornate Papal palaces, apartments, and galleries leading to one of the world's most beautiful interiors, the justly celebrated **Sistine Chapel.**

Note that the Vatican dress code also applies to its museums (no sleeveless blouses, no miniskirts, no shorts, no hats allowed), though it tends to be less rigorously enforced than at St. Peter's.

Obviously, one trip will not be enough to see everything here. To have an even deeper experience, consider a breakfast or after hours visit (p. 129), or book a private tour of the collections, available only online at **https://big lietteriamusei.vatican.va/musei/tickets**.

Below are previews of the main highlights, showstoppers, and masterpieces on display (in alphabetical order).

APPARTAMENTO BORGIA (BORGIA APARTMENTS) ★ Created for Pope Alexander VI (the infamous Borgia pope) between 1492 and 1494, these rooms were frescoed with biblical and allegorical scenes by Umbrian painter Pinturicchio and his assistants. Look for what is thought to be the earliest European depiction of Native Americans, painted little more than a year after Columbus returned from the New World and Alexander had "divided" the globe between Spain and Portugal.

COLLEZIONE D'ARTE CONTEMPORANEA (COLLECTION OF MODERN RELIGIOUS ART) ★   Spanning 55 rooms of almost 800 works, these galleries contain the Vatican's concession to modern art. There are some big names here and the quality is high, and themes usually have a spiritual and religious component: Van Gogh's "Pietà, after Delacroix" is here, along with Francis Bacon's eerie "Study for a Pope II." You will also see works by Paul Klee ("City with Gothic Cathedral"), Siqueiros ("Mutilated Christ No. 467"), Otto Dix ("Road to Calvary"), Gauguin ("Religious Panel"), Chagall ("Red Pietà"), and a whole room dedicated to Georges Rouault.

MUSEI DI ANTICHITÀ CLASSICHE (CLASSICAL ANTIQUITIES MUSEUMS) ★★★   The Vatican maintains four classical antiquities museums, the most important being the **Museo Pio Clementino** ★★★, crammed with Greek and Roman sculptures in the small Belvedere Palace of Innocent VIII. At the heart of the complex lies the Octagonal Court, where highlights include the sculpture of the Trojan priest **"Laocoön"** ★★★ and his two sons locked in a struggle with sea serpents, dating from around 40 B.C., and the exceptional **"Belvedere Apollo"** ★★★ (a 2nd-c. Roman reproduction of an authentic Greek work from the 4th c. B.C.), the symbol of classic male beauty and a possible inspiration for Michelangelo's "David." Look out also for the impressive gilded bronze statue of **"Hercules"** in the Rotonda, from the late 2nd century A.D., and the **Hall of the Chariot,** containing a magnificent sculpture of a chariot combining Roman originals and 18th-century work by Antonio Franzoni.

The **Museo Chiaramonti** ★ occupies the long loggia that links the Belvedere Palace to the main Vatican palaces, jam-packed on both sides with more than 800 Greco-Roman works, including statues, reliefs, and sarcophagi. In the **Braccio Nuovo** ★ ("New Wing"), a handsome Neoclassical extension of the Chiaramonti sumptuously lined with colored marble, lies the colossal statue of the **"Nile"** ★, the ancient river portrayed as an old man with his 16 children, most likely a reproduction of a long-lost Alexandrian Greek original.

The **Museo Gregoriano Profano** ★★, built in 1970, houses more Greek sculptures looted by the Romans (some from the Parthenon), mostly funerary steles and votive reliefs, as well as some choice Roman pieces, notably the restored mosaics from the floors of the public libraries in the **Baths of Caracalla** (p. 95).

MUSEO ETNOLOGICO (ETHNOLOGICAL MUSEUM) ★★   Founded in 1926, this astounding assemblage of artifacts and artwork is from cultures around the world, from ancient Chinese coins and notes, to plaster sculptures of Native Americans and ceremonial art from Papua New Guinea.

MUSEO GREGORIANO EGIZIO ★★   Nine rooms are packed with plunder from Ancient Egypt, including sarcophagi, mummies, pharaonic statuary, votive bronzes, jewelry, cuneiform tablets from Mesopotamia, inscriptions from Assyrian palaces, and Egyptian hieroglyphics.

MUSEO GREGORIANO ETRUSCO ★★ The core of this collection is a cache of rare Etruscan art treasures dug up in the 19th century, dating from between the 9th and the 1st centuries B.C. The Romans learned a lot from the Etruscans, as the highly crafted ceramics, bronzes, silver, and gold on display attest. Don't miss the **Regolini-Galassi tomb** (7th c. B.C.), unearthed at Cerveteri. The museum is housed within the *palazzettos* of Innocent VIII (reigned 1484–92) and Pius IV (reigned 1559–65), the latter adorned with frescoes by Federico Barocci and Federico Zuccari.

PINACOTECA (ART GALLERY) ★★★ The great painting collections of the Popes are displayed in the Pinacoteca, including work from all the big names in Italian art, from Giotto and Fra' Angelico to Perugino, Raphael, Veronese, and Crespi. Early medieval work occupies Room 1, with the most intriguing piece a keyhole-shaped wood panel of the "Last Judgment" by Nicolò e Giovanni, dated to the late 12th century. **Giotto** takes center stage in Room 2, with the "Stefaneschi Triptych" (six panels) painted for the old St. Peter's basilica between 1315 and 1320. **Fra' Angelico** dominates Room 3, his "Stories of St. Nicholas of Bari" and "Virgin with Child" justly praised (check out the Virgin's microscopic eyes in the latter piece). Carlo Crivelli features in Room 6, while decent works by Perugino and Pinturicchio grace Room 7, though most visitors press on to the **Raphael salon ★★★** (Room 8), where you can view five paintings by the Renaissance master. The best are the "Coronation of the Virgin," the "Madonna of Foligno," and the vast "Transfiguration" (completed shortly before his death). Room 9 boasts Leonardo da Vinci's **"St. Jerome with the Lion" ★★**, as well as Giovanni Bellini's "Pietà." Room 10 is dedicated to Renaissance Venice, with Titian's "Madonna of St. Nicholas of the Frari" and Veronese's "Vision of St. Helen" being paramount. Don't skip the remaining galleries: Room 11 contains Barocci's "Annunciation," while Room 12 is really all about one of the masterpieces of the baroque, Caravaggio's **"Deposition from the Cross" ★★**.

STANZE DI RAFFAELLO (RAPHAEL ROOMS) ★★★ In the early 16th century, Pope Julius II hired the young Raphael and his workshop to decorate his personal apartments, on the second floor of the Pontifical Palace. Completed between 1508 and 1524, the **Raphael Rooms** now represent one of the great artistic spectacles inside the Vatican.

The **Stanza dell'Incendio** served as the Pope's high court room and later, under Leo X, a dining room. Most of its lavish frescoes have been attributed to Raphael's pupils. Leo X commissioned much of the work here, which explains the themes (past Popes with the name Leo). Note the intricate ceiling, painted by Umbrian maestro Perugino, who was Raphael's first teacher.

Raphael is the main focus in the **Stanza della Segnatura,** originally used as a Papal library and private office and home to the awe-inspiring **"School of Athens" ★★★** fresco, depicting primarily Greek classical philosophers such as Aristotle, Plato, and Socrates. Many of the figures are thought to be based on portraits of Renaissance artists, including Bramante (on the right as Euclid, drawing on a chalkboard), Leonardo da Vinci (as Plato, the bearded man in the center), and even Raphael himself (in the lower-right corner with a black hat). On the wall opposite stands the equally magnificent "Disputa del Sacramento," where Raphael used a similar technique; Dante Alighieri stands behind the pontiff on the right, and Fra' Angelico poses as a monk (which in fact, he was) on the far left.

The **Stanza d'Eliodoro** was used for the private audiences of the Pope and was painted by Raphael immediately after he did the Segnatura. His aim here was to flatter his papal patron, Julius II: The depiction of the pope driving Attila from Rome was meant to symbolize the contemporary mission of Julius II to drive the French out of Italy. Finally, the **Sala di Costantino,** used for Papal receptions and official ceremonies, was completed by Raphael's students after the master's death, but based on his designs and drawings. It's a jaw-dropping space, commemorating four major episodes in the life of Emperor Constantine.

SISTINE CHAPEL ★★★ Michelangelo labored for 4 years (1508–12) to paint the ceiling of the Sistine Chapel; it is said he spent the entire time on his feet, paint dripping into his eyes. But what a result! Thanks to a massive restoration effort in the 1990s, the world's most famous fresco is today as vibrantly colorful and filled with roiling life as it was in 1512. And the chapel is still of central importance to the Catholic Church: This is where the Papal Conclave meets to elect new popes.

The "Creation of Adam," at the center of the ceiling, is one of the best known and most reproduced images in history, the outstretched hands of God and Adam—not quite touching—an iconic symbol of not just the Renaissance but the Enlightenment that followed. Nevertheless, it is somewhat ironic that this is Michelangelo's best-known work: The artist always regarded himself as a sculptor first and foremost.

Tip: The ceiling **frescoes** are obviously the main showstoppers, though staring at them tends to take a heavy toll on the neck. To relieve your neck (and your tired feet), make your way to one of the benches that line both long sides of the gallery. As soon as someone gets up, grab a seat so you can gaze upward in relative comfort.

Commissioned by Pope Julius II in 1508 and completed in 1512, the ceiling frescoes primarily depict nine scenes from the Book of Genesis (including the famed "Creation of Adam"), from the "Separation of Light and Darkness" at the altar end to the "Great Flood" and "Drunkenness of Noah." Surrounding these main frescoes are paintings of 12 people who prophesied the coming of Christ, from Jonah and Isaiah to the Delphic Sibyl. Once you have admired the ceiling, turn your attention to the altar wall. At the age of 60, Michelangelo was summoned to finish the chapel decor 23 years after he finished the ceiling work. Apparently saddened by leaving Florence and depressed by the morally bankrupt state of Rome at that time, he painted these dark moods in his "Last Judgment," where he included his own self-portrait on a sagging human hide held by St. Bartholomew (who was martyred by being flayed alive).

Yet the Sistine Chapel isn't all Michelangelo. The southern wall is covered by a series of astonishing paintings completed in the 1480s: "Moses Leaving to Egypt" by Perugino, the "Trials of Moses" by Botticelli, "The Crossing of the Red Sea" by Cosimo Rosselli (or Domenico Ghirlandaio), "Descent from Mount Sinai" by Cosimo Rosselli (or Piero di Cosimo), Botticelli's "Punishment of the Rebels," and Signorelli's "Testament and Death of Moses."

On the right-hand northern wall are Perugino's "The Baptism of Christ," Botticelli's "The Temptations of Christ," Ghirlandaio's "Vocation of the Apostles," Perugino's "Delivery of the Keys," Cosimo Rosselli's "The Sermon on the Mount" and "Last Supper." On the eastern wall, originals by Ghirlandaio and Signorelli were painted over by Hendrik van den Broeck's "The Resurrection" and Matteo da Lecce's "Disputation over Moses" in the 1570s.

Vatican City, Viale Vaticano (a long walk around the Vatican walls from St. Peter's Sq.). www.museivaticani.va. ℂ **06/69884676.** 17€ adults, 8€ children 6–13, free for children 5 and under; 2-hr. tours of Vatican Gardens 33€ (no tours Wed or Sun). Mon–Sat 9am–6pm (ticket office closes at 4pm). Also open Fri 7–11pm (late Apr to late Sept) per online booking. Also open last Sun of every month 9am–2pm (free admission). Closed Jan 1 and 6, Feb 11, Mar 19, Easter, May 1, June 29, Aug 14–15, Nov 1, and Dec 25–26. Advance tickets (reservation fee 4€) and guided tours (33€ per person) through https://biglietteriamusei.vatican.va. Metro: Ottaviano or Cipro–Musei Vaticani; bus 46 stops in front of the entrance.

Castel Sant'Angelo ★★ CASTLE/PALACE   Over the years, this bulky cylindrical fortress on the Vatican side of the Tiber has had many lives: as the mausoleum tomb of Emperor Hadrian in A.D. 138; as a papal residence in the 14th century; as a castle, where in 1527 Pope Clement VII hid from the looting troops of Charles V; and as a military prison from the 17th century on. Consider renting an audio guide at the entrance to fully appreciate its various manifestations.

From the entrance a stone ramp *(rampa elicoidale)* winds to the upper terraces, where you can see amazing views of the city and enjoy a coffee at the outdoor cafe. The sixth floor features the **Terrazza dell'Angelo,** crowned by

---

Seeing the Vatican at Night . . . or for Breakfast

Vatican Museum visitors now have an extraordinary opportunity to stroll through the galleries after sunset, at least on Friday nights from 7pm to 11pm (last entrance at 9:30) during the high tourist season, from the last Friday in April through July and the first Friday in September through the end of October. These **twilight visits** allow access to important collections, including the Pio-Clementine Museum, the Egyptian Museum, the Upper Galleries (candelabra, tapestries, and maps), the Raphael Rooms, the Borgia Apartments, the Collection of Modern Religious Art, and the Sistine Chapel.

Early birds should consider booking a **breakfast tour** of the museums. Starting at 7:15am (before the official opening time), breakfast visits cost 68€, including a buffet breakfast and access to all galleries. It's a far more tranquil visitor experience that daytime visits.

a florid 18th-century statue of the Archangel Michael. It's famous to opera fans—the last act of Puccini's "Tosca" is set here. From here you can walk back down through five floors. On levels 3 to 5 you'll see the Renaissance apartments used by some of Rome's most infamous Popes, including Alexander VI, the Borgia pope. The art collection displayed throughout is fairly mediocre by Rome standards, although there are a few works by Carlo Crivelli and Luca Signorelli, notably a "Madonna and Child with Saints" from Signorelli. Below the apartments are the grisly dungeons (**"Le Prigioni"**) used as torture chambers in the medieval period (Cesare Borgia made great use of them). The castle is connected to St. Peter's Basilica by **Il Passetto di Borgo,** a walled passage built in 1277 by Pope Nicholas III, used by popes who needed to make a quick escape to the fortress in times of danger.

Note that the dungeons, Il Passetto, and the apartments of Clement VII are usually open by guided tour only (English tours Tues–Sun at 10am and 4pm, 5€), with occasional late-night openings in the summer. Classical music and jazz concerts are also held in and around the castle in summertime.

Lungotevere Castello 50. www.castelsantangelo.com. © **06/6819111.** 10€. Tues–Sun 9am–7:30pm. Bus: 23, 40, 62, 271, 280, 982 (to Piazza Pia).

The Colosseum, Forum & Ancient Rome
THE MAJOR SIGHTS OF ANCIENT ROME

Your sightseeing experience will be enhanced if you know a little about the history and rulers of Ancient Rome: See p. 26 for a brief rundown.

Arch of Constantine (Arco di Costantino) ★★ MONUMENT The photogenic triumphal arch next to the Colosseum was erected by the Senate in A.D. 315 to honor Constantine's defeat of the pagan Maxentius at the Battle of the Milvian Bridge (A.D. 312). Many of the reliefs have nothing whatsoever to do with Constantine or his works, but they tell of the victories of earlier Antonine rulers (lifted from other, long-forgotten memorials).The arch marks a period of great change in the history of Rome. Converted to Christianity by a vision on the eve of battle, Constantine ended the centuries-long persecution of the Christians, during which many followers of the new religion had been put to death in a gruesome manner. Although Constantine didn't ban paganism (which survived officially for another half century or so), he espoused Christianity himself and began the process that ended in the conquest of Rome by the Christian religion.

Btw. Colosseum and Palatine Hill. Metro: Colosseo.

Baths of Caracalla (Terme di Caracalla) ★★ RUINS Named for Emperor Caracalla, a particularly unpleasant individual, the baths were completed in A.D. 217 after his death. The richness of decoration has faded, but the massive brick ruins and the mosaic fragments that remain give modern visitors an idea of its scale and grandeur. In their heyday, the baths sprawled across 11 ha (27 acres) and included hot, cold, and tepid pools, as well as a *palestra* (gym) and changing rooms. A museum in the tunnels below the complex—built over an even more ancient *mithraem,* a worship site of an eastern cult—explores the hydraulic and heating systems (and slave power) needed to serve 8,000 or so Romans per day. Summer operatic performances here are an ethereal treat (see p. 134).

Via delle Terme di Caracalla 52. www.coopculture.it/en. ℭ **06/39967700.** 8€ (10€ online). For combined ticket with Tomb of Caecilia Metella see p. 126. Oct–Mar 15 Mon 9am–2pm, Tues–Sun 9am–4:30pm (Oct until 6:30pm, Feb 16–Mar 15 until 5pm). Mar 16–Sept Mon 8:30am–2pm, Tues–Sun 9am–7pm. Last entry 1 hr. before closing. Bus: 118 or 628.

Capitoline Museums (Musei Capitolini) ★★ MUSEUM   The masterpieces here are considered Rome's most valuable (recall that the Vatican Museums are *not* technically in Rome). They certainly were collected early: This is the oldest public museum *in the world.* So try and schedule adequate time, as there's much to see.

First stop is the courtyard of the **Palazzo dei Conservatori** (the building on the right of the piazza designed by Michelangelo, if you enter via the ramp from Piazza Venezia). It's scattered with gargantuan stone body parts—the remnants of a massive 12m (39-ft.) statue of the emperor Constantine, including his colossal head, hand, and foot. It's nearly impossible to resist snapping a selfie next to the giant finger. On the palazzo's **ground floor,** the unmissable works are in the first series of rooms. These include "Lo Spinario" **(Room III),** a lifelike bronze of a young boy digging a splinter out of his foot that was widely copied during the Renaissance; and the "Lupa Capitolina" **(Room IV),** a bronze statue from 500 B.C. of the famous she-wolf that suckled Romulus and Remus, the mythical founders of Rome. The twins were not on the original Etruscan statue, but added in the 15th century. **Room V** has Bernini's famously pained portrait of "Medusa," even more compelling when you see its writhing serpent hairdo in person. Before heading upstairs, go toward the new wing at the rear, which houses the original equestrian **statue of Marcus Aurelius** ★★★, dating to around A.D. 180—the piazza outside, where it stood from 1538 until 2005, now has a copy. There's a giant bronze head from a statue of Constantine (ca. A.D. 337) and the foundations of the original Temple of Jupiter that stood on the Capitoline Hill since its inauguration in 509 B.C. The **second-floor picture gallery** ★ is strong on baroque oil paintings. Masterpieces include Caravaggio's "John the Baptist" and "The Fortune Teller" (1595) and Guido Reni's "St. Sebastian" (1615).

A tunnel takes you under the piazza to the other part of the Capitoline Museums, the **Palazzo Nuovo,** via the **Tabularium** ★★. This was built in 78 B.C. to house ancient Rome's city records, and was later used as a salt mine and then as a prison. Here, the moody *galleria lapidaria* houses a well-executed exhibit of ancient portrait tombstones and sarcophagi, many of their poignant epitaphs translated into English, and provides access to one of the best balcony **views** ★★★ in Rome: along the length of the Forum toward the Palatine Hill.

Much of the Palazzo Nuovo is dedicated to statues that were excavated from the forums below and brought in from outlying areas like Hadrian's Villa

Ancient Rome, Monti & Celio

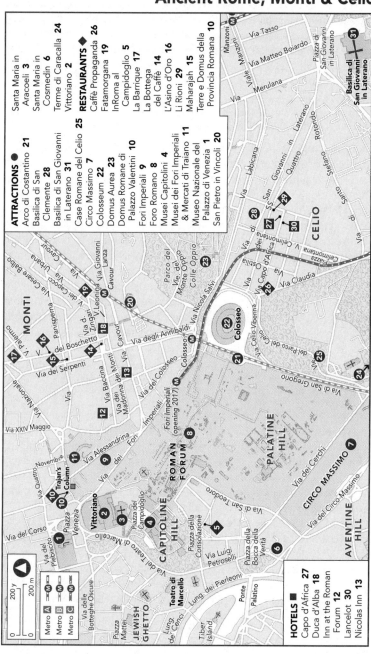

ATTRACTIONS ●

Arco di Costantino **21**
Basilica di San
  Clemente **28**
Basilica di San Giovanni
  in Laterano **31**
Case Romane del Celio **25**
Circo Massimo **7**
Colosseum **22**
Domus Aurea **23**
Domus Romane di
  Palazzo Valentini **10**
Fori Imperiali **9**
Foro Romano **8**
Musei Capitolini **4**
Musei dei Fori Imperiali
  & Mercati di Traiano **11**
Museo Nazionale del
  Palazzo di Venezia **1**
San Pietro in Vincoli **20**

Santa Maria in
  Aracoeli **3**
Santa Maria in
  Cosmedin **6**
Terme di Caracalla **24**
Vittoriano **2**

RESTAURANTS ◆

Caffè Propaganda **26**
Fatamorgana **19**
InRoma al
  Campidoglio **5**
La Barrique **17**
La Bottega
  del Caffè **14**
L'Asino d'Oro **16**
Li Rioni **29**
Maharajah **15**
Terre e Domus della
  Provincia Romana **10**

HOTELS ■

Capo d'Africa **27**
Duca d'Alba **18**
Inn at the Roman
  Forum **12**
Lancelot **30**
Nicolas Inn **13**

4

ROME | Exploring Rome

97

in Tivoli (p. 139). If you're running short on time at this point, head straight for the 1st-century **"Capitoline Venus"** ★★, in Room III—a modest girl covering up after a bath—and in Rooms IV and V, a chronologically arranged row of distinct, expressive busts of Roman emperors and their families. Another favorite is the beyond handsome **"Dying Gaul"** ★★, a Roman copy of a lost ancient Greek work. Lord Byron considered the statue so lifelike and moving that he mentioned it in his poem "Childe Harold's Pilgrimage."

Piazza del Campidoglio 1. www.museicapitolini.org. ☏ **06/0608.** 15€. Daily 9:30am–7:30pm. Last entry 1 hr. before closing. Bus: 40, 44, 60, 63, 64, 70, 118, 160, 170, 628, 716 or any bus that stops at Piazza Venezia.

Circus Maximus (Circo Massimo) ★ HISTORIC SITE

Today mostly an oval-shaped field, the once-grand circus was pilfered by medieval and Renaissance builders in search of marble and stone—it's a far cry from its *Ben-Hur*–esque heyday. What the Romans called a "circus" was a large arena ringed by tiers of seats and used for sports or spectacles. At one time, 300,000 Romans could assemble here, while the emperor observed the games from his box high on the Palatine Hill. The last games were held in A.D. 549 on the orders of Totilla the Goth, who had seized Rome twice. Afterwards, the Circus Maximus was never used again, and the demand for building materials reduced it, like so much of Rome, to a great dusty field, now used mostly for big-name rock concerts. An archaeological area at its eastern end (closest to the Metro station) offers insights into how the space once functioned. *Tip:* If you're crunched for time, bypass the Circus Maximus and instead take in the emperor's-eye views of the arena from atop the Palatine Hill.

Btw. Via dei Cerchi and Via del Circo Massimo. http://mobile.060608.it/en. ☏ **06/0608.** Archaeological area, 5€. Sat–Sun 10am–4pm, or by guided tour only Tues–Fri. Metro: Circo Massimo. Bus: 81, 118, 160.

Colosseum (Colosseo) ★★★ ICON

No matter how many pictures you've seen, your first view of the Flavian Amphitheater (the Colosseum's original name) is likely to amaze you with its sheer size and ruined grandeur. While you're still outside its massive walls, it's important to walk completely around its 500m (1,640-ft.) circumference. It doesn't matter where you start, but do the circle. Look at the various stages of ruin; note the different column styles on each level. Mere photos could never convey its physical impact.

Vespasian ordered the construction of the elliptical bowl in A.D. 72; it was inaugurated by Titus in A.D. 80. Built for gladiator contests and wild animal fights, the stadium could hold as many as 87,000 spectators by some counts; seats were sectioned on three levels, dividing the people by social rank and gender. Some 80 entrances allowed the massive crowds to be seated within a few minutes, historians say. When the Roman Empire fell, however, the abandoned arena was eventually overgrown. Much of the travertine that once sheathed its outside was used for palaces like the nearby Palazzo Venezia and Palazzo Cancelleria near the Campo de' Fiori.

An ongoing conservation effort, funded by the Italian design house Tod's, helped eliminate nearly 2,000 years of soot from the monument's exterior; restoration efforts have now shifted to its underground vaults and passageways. Access to the **Colosseum Underground** and **Belvedere** (upper tier) is by guided tour only, ticketed separately from admission to the Colosseum (and *not* included with the Roma Pass). The process for purchasing tickets online can be baffling, but essentially you can reserve a tour of the underground OR the belvedere OR both areas, up to one month in advance. These tours sell out very quickly. A combined tour costs 17€, in addition to the admission fee. Remember that the same ticket you buy for the Colosseum includes admission to the Forum and Palatine Hill, and is valid for 2 days. Your prepurchased Colosseum ticket (or Roma Pass) allows you to skip the long line to enter, but you still must go through security screening, which can take up to an hour on busy days.

Piazzale del Colosseo. www.coopculture.it/en/colosseo-e-shop.cfm. ✆ **06/39967700.** 12€; 14€ if purchased online (recommended). Includes Roman Forum & Palatine Hill). Nov–Feb 15 daily 8:30am–4:30pm; Feb 16–Mar 15 daily 8:30am–5pm; Mar 16–31 daily 8:30am–5:30pm; Apr–Aug daily 8:30am–7:15pm; Sept daily 8:30am–7pm; Oct daily 8:30am–6:30pm. Last entry 1 hr. before closing. Guided tours (45 min.) in English 5€; see website for times. Metro: Colosseo. Bus: 51, 75, 85, 87, 118. Tram: 3, 8.

Imperial Forums (Fori Imperiali) ★ RUINS   Begun by Julius Caesar to relieve overcrowding in Rome's older forums, the Imperial Forums were, at the time of their construction, flashier, bolder, and more impressive than anything that had come before them in Rome. They conveyed the unquestioned authority of the emperors at the height of their absolute power. Alas, Mussolini felt his regime was more important than the ancient one and issued the controversial orders to cut through centuries of debris and buildings to carve out Via dei Fori Imperiali, linking the Colosseum to the 19th-century monuments of Piazza Venezia. Excavations under his Fascist regime uncovered countless archaeological treasures. Most ruins more recent than imperial Rome were destroyed—*argh!*

The best view of the Forums is from the railings on the north side of Via dei Fori Imperiali; begin where Via Cavour joins the boulevard. (Visitors are not permitted down into the ruins.) Closest to the junction are the remains of the **Forum of Nerva,** built by the emperor whose 2-year reign (A.D. 96–98) followed the assassination of the paranoid Domitian. You'll be struck by how much the ground level has risen in 19 centuries. The only really recognizable remnant is a wall of the Temple of Minerva with two fine Corinthian columns. The next along is the **Forum of Augustus ★★,** built to commemorate Emperor Augustus's victory over Julius Caesar's assassins, Cassius and Brutus, in the Battle of Philippi (42 B.C.). Continuing along the railing, you'll see the vast, multilevel semicircle of **Trajan's Markets ★★,** essentially an ancient shopping mall whose arcades were once stocked with merchandise from the far corners of the Roman world. You can visit the part that has been transformed into the **Museo dei Fori Imperiali & Mercati di Traiano** (p. 104).

THREE free views TO SAVOR FOR A LIFETIME

The Forum from the Campidoglio
Standing on Piazza del Campidoglio, outside the Musei Capitolini (p. 96), walk around the right or left side of the Palazzo Senatorio to terraces overlooking the best panoramas of the Roman Forum, with the Palatine Hill and Colosseum as a backdrop. At night, the ruins look even more haunting when the Forum is dramatically floodlit.

The Whole City from the Janiculum Hill From many vantage points in the Eternal City, the views are panoramic. But one of the best spots for a memorable vista is the Janiculum Hill (Gianicolo), above Trastevere. Laid out before you are Rome's rooftops, peppered with domes ancient and modern. From up here, you will understand why Romans complain about the materials used to build the 19th-century Vittoriano (p. 106)—it's a white shock in a sea of rose- and honey-colored stone. Walk 50 yards north of the famous balcony (favored by tour buses) for a slightly better angle, from the Belvedere 9 Febbraio 1849. Views from the 1612 Fontana dell'Acqua Paola are also splendid, especially at night.

The Aventine Hill & the Priori dei Cavalieri di Malta The mythical site of Remus's original settlement, the Aventine (Aventino) is now a leafy, upscale residential neighborhood—but also blessed with some magical views. From Via del Circo Massimo walk through the gardens along Via di Valle Murcia, and keep walking in a straight line. Along your right side, gardens offer views over the dome of St. Peter's. When you reach Piazza dei Cavalieri di Malta, look through the keyhole of the Priory gate (on the right) for a "secret" view of the Vatican.

In front of the Markets, the **Forum of Trajan ★★** was built between A.D. 107 and 113, designed by Greek architect Apollodorus of Damascus (who also laid out the adjoining market building). Many statue fragments and pedestals bear still-legible inscriptions, but more interesting is the great Basilica Ulpia, whose gray marble columns rise roofless into the sky. This forum was once regarded as one of the architectural wonders of the world. Beyond the Basilica Ulpia is **Trajan's Column ★★★**, in magnificent condition, with an intricate bas-relief sculpture depicting Trajan's victorious campaign.

The **Forum of Julius Caesar ★★**, the first of the Imperial Forums to be built, lies on the opposite side of Via dei Fori Imperiali, adjacent to the Roman Forum. This was the site of the stock exchange as well as the Temple of Venus.

Along Via dei Fori Imperiali. Metro: Colosseo. Bus: 51, 75, 85, 87, 118.

Roman Forum (Foro Romano) & Palatine Hill (Palatino) ★★★

RUINS   Traversed by the **Via Sacra (Sacred Way) ★**, the main thoroughfare of ancient Rome, the Roman Forum flourished as the center of religious, social, and commercial life in the days of the Republic, before it gradually lost prestige (but never spiritual draw) to the Imperial Forums (see above).

You'll see ruins and fragments, some partially intact columns, and an arch or two, but you can still feel the rush of history here. That any semblance of the Forum remains today is miraculous: It was used for years as a quarry (as was the Colosseum). Eventually it reverted to a *campo vaccino* (cow pasture). Excavations in the 19th century and later in the 1930s began to bring to light one of the world's most historic spots.

You can spend at least a morning wandering the ruins of the Forum. Enter via the gate on Via dei Fori Imperiali, at Via della Salara Vecchia. Turn right at the bottom of the entrance slope to walk west along the old Via Sacra toward the arch. Just before it on your right is the large brick **Curia ★★**, the main seat of the Roman Senate, built by Julius Caesar, rebuilt by Diocletian, and consecrated as a church in A.D. 630.

The triumphal **Arch of Septimius Severus ★★** (A.D. 203), is the next important sight, displaying time-bitten reliefs of the emperor's victories in what are now Iran and Iraq. During the Middle Ages, Rome became a provincial backwater, and frequent flooding of the Tiber helped bury (and thus preserve) most of the Forum. Some bits did still stick out aboveground, including the top half of this arch, which was used to shelter a barbershop!

Just to the left of the arch, you can make out the remains of a cylindrical lump of rock with some marble steps curving off it. That round stone was the **Umbilicus Urbus,** considered the center of Rome and of the entire Roman Empire; the curving steps are those of the **Imperial Rostra ★**, where great orators and legislators stood to speak and the people gathered to listen. Nearby, a much-photographed trio of fluted columns with Corinthian capitals supports a bit of architrave from the corner of the **Temple of Vespasian and Titus ★★** (emperors were routinely turned into gods upon dying).

Arch of Emperor Septimus Severus in the Roman Forum.

Start heading to your left toward the eight Ionic columns marking the front of the **Temple of Saturn ★★** (rebuilt in 42 B.C.), which housed the first treasury of Republican Rome. It was also the site of one of the Roman year's biggest annual blowout festivals, the December 17 feast of Saturnalia, which, after a bit of tweaking, Christians now celebrate as Christmas. Turn left to start heading back east, past the worn steps and stumps of brick pillars outlining the enormous **Basilica Julia ★★**, built by Julius Caesar. Farther along, on the right, are the three Corinthian columns of the **Temple of the Dioscuri ★★★**, dedicated to the Gemini twins, Castor and Pollux. Forming one of the most photogenic sights of the Roman Forum, a trio of columns supports an architrave fragment. The founding of this temple dates from the 5th century B.C.

Beyond the bit of curving wall that marks the site of the little round **Temple of Vesta** (rebuilt several times after fires started by the sacred flame within), you'll find the reconstructed **House of the Vestal Virgins** (A.D. 3rd–4th c.). The temple was the home of the consecrated young women who tended the sacred flame in the Temple of Vesta. Vestals were girls chosen from patrician families to serve a 30-year-long priesthood. During their tenure, they were among Rome's most venerated citizens, with unique powers such as the ability to pardon condemned criminals. The cult was quite serious about the "virgin" part of the job description—if one of Vesta's earthly servants was found to have "misplaced" her virginity, the miscreant Vestal was buried alive, because it was forbidden to shed a Vestal's blood. (Her amorous accomplice was merely flogged to death.) The overgrown rectangle of their gardens is lined with broken, heavily worn statues of senior Vestals on pedestals.

The path dovetails back to Via Sacra. Turn right, walk past the so-called "Temple of Romulus," and then left to enter the massive brick remains of the 4th-century **Basilica of Constantine and Maxentius ★★** (Basilica di Massenzio). These were Rome's public law courts, and their architectural style was adopted by early Christians for their houses of worship (the reason so many ancient churches are called "basilicas").

Return to the path and continue toward the Colosseum. Veer right to the Forum's second great triumphal arch, the extensively rebuilt **Arch of Titus ★★** (A.D. 81), on which one relief depicts the carrying off of treasures from Jerusalem's temple. Look closely and you'll see a menorah among the booty. The war that this arch glorifies ended with the expulsion of Jews from the colonized Judea, signaling the beginning of the Jewish Diaspora throughout Europe. You can exit behind the Arch to continue on to the Colosseum, or head up to the Palatine Hill.

Access the **Palatine Hill ★★** (Palatino)—where Romulus, after eliminating his twin brother Remus, founded Rome around 753 B.C.—via the **Imperial Ramp.** A secret passageway built by Emperor Domitian in the 1st century A.D., the 11m-tall (36 ft.) switchback ramp allowed the assassination-paranoid ruler to go back and forth undetected between his palace and the forum below. (He was murdered in the passageway anyway.) Later, emperors and other ancient bigwigs built their palaces and private entertainment facilities up here.

NERO'S golden HOUSE ★★★

After the Great Fire of 64 A.D., charismatic, despotic Emperor Nero staged a land grab to facilitate construction of his *Domus Aurea*, or Golden House, a massive, gilded villa complex covering all or parts of the Palatine, Esquiline, and Caelian hills and displaying a level of ostentation and excessiveness unheard of even among past emperors. After his death by noble suicide in 68 A.D., a campaign to erase all traces of Nero from the imperial city ensured that the palace was stripped of its gold, marble, jewels, mosaics, and statuary, then intentionally buried under millions of tons of rubble. It remained buried until the Renaissance, when young artists, including Raphael, descended into its "grottos" (actually the vaulted ceilings) to study the fanciful frescoes—the term grotesque (*grottoesque*) was coined here. Later excavations, both haphazard and scientific, revealed the scale and richness of the villa, but also subjected it to catastrophic moisture damage. After a years-long closure for restoration and restabalization, the Domus Aurea is once again open for tours—but only if you time your trip well and plan ahead. Guided tours (16€; www.coopculture.it/en) of the scaffolded underground site (hardhats required) are offered on **Saturdays and Sundays only,** and with advance reservations. The tour includes a spectacular virtual reality experience that in itself is worth the visit.

Upon exiting at the top of the ramp, visitors are presented with a sprawling, mostly crowd-free archaeological garden, with plenty of shady spots for cooling off in summer.

The Palatine was where the first settlers built their huts under the direction of Romulus. In later years, the hill became a patrician residential district that attracted such citizens as Cicero. In time, however, the area was gobbled up by imperial palaces and drew an infamous roster of tenants, such as Livia (some of the frescoes in the House of Livia are in miraculous condition), Tiberius, Caligula (murdered here by members of his Praetorian Guard), Nero, and Domitian. A museum houses some of the most important finds from hill excavations. The elaborately decorated **houses of Livia and Augustus ★★** are occasionally open for tours, which must be booked in advance through www.coopculture.it.

Only the ruins of the Palatine's grandeur remain today, but it's worth the climb for the panoramic views of both the Roman and the Imperial Forums, as well as the Capitoline Hill, the Colosseum and Circus Maximus. You can also enter from here and do the entire tour in reverse.

Forum entrance at Via della Salara Vecchia 5/6. Palatine Hill entrance at Via di San Gregorio 30 (south of the Colosseum). www.coopculture.it/en/heritage.cfm?id=4. ℂ **06/39967700.** 12€ (includes Colosseum; 14€ prepurchased). Nov–Feb 15 daily 8:30am–4:30pm; Feb 16–Mar 15 daily 8:30am–5pm; Mar 16–31 daily 8:30am–5:30pm; Apr–Aug daily 8:30am–7:15pm; Sept daily 8:30am–7pm; Oct daily 8:30am–6:30pm. Last entry 1 hr. before closing. Metro: Colosseo. Bus: 51, 75, 85, 87, 118. Tram: 3, 8 (for Palatine Hill).

Museum of the Imperial Forums (Museo dei Fori Imperiali & Mercati di Traiano) & Trajan's Markets ★★RUINS/MUSEUM   Built on three levels, Emperor Trajan's Market housed 150 shops and commercial offices—think of it as the world's first shopping mall. Grooves still evident in the thresholds allowed merchants to slide doors shut and lock up for the night. You're likely to have the covered, tunnel-like market halls mostly to yourself—making the ancient past feel all the more present in this overlooked site. The Museum of the Imperial Forums occupies a converted section of the market and has excellent visual displays that help you imagine what these grand public squares and temples used to look like. All in all, it's home to 172 marble fragments from the Fori Imperiali; here are also original remnants from the Forum of Augustus and Forum of Nerva.

Via IV Novembre 94. www.mercatiditraiano.it. ✆ **06/0608.** 15€. Daily 9:30am–7:30pm. Last admission 1 hr. before closing. Bus: 40, 60, 64, 70, 170.

OTHER ATTRACTIONS NEAR ANCIENT ROME

Basilica di San Clemente ★★ CHURCH   A perfect example of how layers of history overlap in Rome, this 12-century Norman church, full of beautiful Byzantine mosaics, hides much more. Down in its eerie grottos (which you explore on your own) you'll find frescoes and mosaic floors from its previous incarnations as a 4th-century Christian church and a temple dedicated to the pagan deity Mithras—and below that, the foundations of a Roman house from the 1st century A.D., where early Christians worshipped in secret.

Via San Giovanni in Laterano (at Piazza San Clemente). www.basilicasanclemente.com. ✆ **06/7740021.** Basilica free; excavations 10€. Mon–Sat 9am–12:30pm and 3–6pm; Sun 12:15–6pm. Last entry 30 min before closing. Metro: Colosseo. Bus: 51, 85, 87, 117. Tram: 3.

Basilica di San Giovanni in Laterano ★ CHURCH   This church, not St. Peter's, is officially the cathedral of the diocese of Rome; the Pope celebrates Mass here on certain holidays. Though it was built in A.D. 314 by Constantine, only parts of the original baptistery remain; what you see today is an 18th-century facade by Alessandro Galilei (note signs of damage from a 1993 terrorist bomb) and an interior by Borromini, built for Pope Innocent X. In a misguided redecoration long ago, frescoes by Giotto were apparently destroyed; remains attributed to Giotto, discovered in 1952, are displayed against the first inner column on the right.

Across the street is the **Santuario della Scala Santa (Palace of the Holy Steps),** Piazza San Giovanni in Laterano 14 (✆ **06/7726641**), a set of 28 marble steps supposedly brought from Jerusalem by Constantine's mother, Helen. Though some historians say the stairs might date only from the 4th century, legend claims these were the stairs Christ climbed at Pontius Pilate's villa the day he was sentenced to death. Today pilgrims from all over the world come here to climb the steps on their knees.

Piazza San Giovanni in Laterano 4. ✆ **06/69886433.** Free admission. Daily 7am–6:30pm. Metro: San Giovanni.

Case Romane del Celio ★ RUINS Beneath the 5th-century Basilica of SS. Giovanni e Paolo lies a fascinating archeological site: a complex of Roman houses of different periods—a wealthy family's townhouse from the 2nd century A.D. and a 3rd-century-A.D. apartment building for artisans. According to tradition, the latter was the home of two Roman officers, John and Paul (not the Apostles), who were beheaded during the reign of Julian the Apostate (361–63) for refusing to serve in a military campaign. They were later made saints, and their bones were said to have been buried here. The two-story construction also contains a small museum with finds from the site and fragmentary 12th-century frescoes.

Piazza Santi Giovanni e Paolo 13 (entrance on Clivo di Scauro). www.caseromane.it. ℰ **06/70454544.** 8€ adults, 6€ ages 12–18. Thurs–Mon 10am–1pm and 3–6pm. Metro: Colosseo or Circo Massimo. Bus: 75, 81, 118. Tram: 3.

Domus Romane di Palazzo Valentini ★★★ RUINS/EXHIBIT All too often in Italy, archaeological sites are presented with little context, and it's difficult for untrained eyes to really understand what they're seeing. Not so at Palazzo Valentini, possibly Rome's best-presented ancient site. Visitors descend underneath a Renaissance palazzo and peer through a glass floor into the remains of several upscale Roman homes. With innovative use of 3-D projections, the walls, ceilings, floors. and fountains of these once-grand houses spring to life, offering a captivating look at lifestyles of the ancient rich and famous. A scale model shows the surrounding area (adjacent to Trajan's Column) as it looked around the time of its completion (113 A.D.).

Via Foro Traiano 85 (near Trajan's Column). www.palazzovalentini.it; ℰ **06/22761280.** 13.50€. Wed–Mon 9:30am–6:30pm. Timed entrance, with guided tours in English several times daily; reservations suggested. Metro: Colosseo. Bus: 40, 63, 70, 81, 83, 87, or any bus to Piazza Venezia. Tram: 8.

Museo Nazionale del Palazzo di Venezia ★ MUSEUM Best remembered today as Mussolini's Fascist headquarters in Rome, the palace was built in the 1450s as the Rome outpost of the Republic of Venice—hence the name. Today, several of its rooms house an eclectic mix of European paintings and decorative and religious objects spanning the centuries; highlights include Giorgione's enigmatic "Double Portrait" and some early Tuscan altarpieces.

Via del Plebiscito 118. www.museopalazzovenezia.beniculturali.it. ℰ **06/6780131.** 5€. Tues–Sun 8:30am–7:30pm. Bus: 30, 40, 46, 62, 64, 70, 87, or any bus to Piazza Venezia. Tram: 8.

St. Peter in Chains (San Pietro in Vincoli) ★ CHURCH Founded in the 5th century to house the chains that supposedly bound St. Peter in Jerusalem (preserved under glass below the main altar), this lovely church is mainly worth visiting to see one of the world's most famous sculptures: **Michelangelo's "Moses"** ★★, carved for the tomb of Pope Julius II. Michelangelo never completed the 44 magnificent figures planned for the tomb, but this "minor" figure he did complete now numbers among his masterpieces.

Piazza San Pietro in Vincoli 4A.
© **06/97844952.** Free. Spring–summer daily 8:30am–12:30pm and 3:30–7pm (fall–winter to 6pm). Metro: Colosseo or Cavour. Bus: 75.

Santa Maria in Aracoeli ★
CHURCH   According to legend, Augustus once ordered a temple erected on this spot, on the Capitoline Hill, where a sibyl foretold the coming of Christ. The current church, built for the Franciscans in the 13th century, boasts a coffered Renaissance ceiling and the tomb of Giovanni Crivelli (1432) carved by the great Renaissance sculptor Donatello. The **Cappella Bufalini ★** (first chapel on the right) was frescoed by Pinturicchio with scenes of the life and death of St. Bernardino of Siena.

Michelangelo's masterful "Moses" adorns a tomb in the quiet church of San Pietro in Vincoli.

A chapel behind the altar contains the **Santo Bambino,** a devotional wooden figure of the Baby Jesus, which is venerated annually on Christmas Eve. The long flight of stairs leading up to the church was built in 1348 to celebrate the end of the Black Plague.

Scala dell'Arcicapitolina 12. © **06/69763838.** Free. Daily 9am–6:30pm (fall–winter to 5:30pm). Bus: 30, 40, 46, 62, 64, 70, 87, or any bus to Piazza Venezia.

Santa Maria in Cosmedin ★ CHURCH   People line up outside this ancient church with a Romanesque bell tower not for great art treasures, but to see the **"Mouth of Truth,"** a large disk on the wall of the portico. As Gregory Peck demonstrated to Audrey Hepburn in the film *Roman Holiday,* the mouth is supposed to chomp down on the hands of liars. It may have been an ancient drain cover, though one hypothesis says it was a so-called "talking statue," where anonymous notes were left to betray wrongdoers. Our take? Save this hokey photo op until you've seen everything else you want to see in Rome.

Piazza della Bocca della Verità 18. © **06/6787759.** Church free; 2€ fee for photo of the Mouth of Truth. Daily 9:30am–5:50pm; closes 4:50pm in winter. Bus: 23, 81, 118, 160, 280, 715.

Vittoriano (Altare della Patria) ★ MONUMENT   It's impossible to miss the white marble Vittorio Emanuele monument dominating Piazza Venezia. Built in the late 1800s to honor the first king of a united Italy, this flamboyant (and widely disliked) landmark has been compared to everything from a wedding cake to a Victorian typewriter, its harsh white color glaring in a city of honey-gold tones. An eternal flame burns at the Tomb of the Unknown Soldier. For a panoramic city view, take a glass elevator to the **Terrazza delle Quadrighe (Terrace of the Chariots)** ★.

Piazza Venezia. © **06/6780664.** Elevator 7€. Daily 9:30am–6:45pm. Bus: 30, 40, 46, 62, 64, 70, 87, or any bus to Piazza Venezia.

Centro Storico & the Pantheon

Just across the Tiber from the Vatican and Castel Sant'Angelo lies the true heart of Rome, the **Centro Storico,** or "historic center," the triangular wedge of land that bulges into a bend of the river. Although the area lay outside the Roman city, it came into its own during the Renaissance, and today its streets and alleys are crammed with piazzas, elegant churches, and lavish fountains, all buzzing with scooters and people. It's a wonderful area in which to wander and get lost.

PIAZZA NAVONA & NEARBY ATTRACTIONS

Rome's most famous square, **Piazza Navona** ★★★, is a gorgeous baroque gem, lined with cafes and restaurants and often crammed with tourists, street artists, and pigeons. Its long, oval shape follows the contours of the old ruined Roman Stadium of Domitian, where chariot races once took place, made over in the mid–17th century by Pope Innocent X. The twin-towered facade of 17th-century **Sant'Agnese in Agone** lies on the piazza's western side, while the **Fontana dei Quattro Fiumi (Fountain of the Four Rivers)** ★★★ opposite is one of three great fountains in the square, this one a typically exuberant creation by Bernini, topped with an Egyptian obelisk. The four stone personifications below symbolize the world's greatest rivers: the Ganges, Danube, de la Plata, and Nile. It's fun to try to figure out which is which. (**Hint:** The figure with the shroud on its head is the Nile, so represented because the river's source was unknown at the time.) At the south end is Bernini's **Fontana del Moro (Fountain of the Moor)** and the 19th-century **Fontana di Nettuno (Fountain of Neptune).**

Art lovers should make the short walk from the piazza to **Santa Maria della Pace** ★★ on Arco della Pace, a 15th-century church given the usual baroque makeover by Pietro da Cortona in the 1660s. The real gems are inside, beginning with Raphael's **"Four Sibyls"** ★★ fresco, above the arch of the Capella Chigi, and the **Chiostro del Bramante (Bramante cloister)** ★, built between 1500 and 1504 and the Renaissance master's first work in the city. The church is normally open on Monday, Wednesday, and Saturday 9am to noon, while the cloister opens daily 10am to 8pm (to 9pm Sat and Sun). The church is free, but admission to the cloister (www.chiostrodelbramante. it), which hosts temporary art exhibitions, costs 10€ and up, depending on the exhibit.

Tip: Waiters from Piazza Navona's many overpriced restaurants lie in wait, hoping to woo passing tourists. Buyer beware: While the setting is unmatchable, you'll have a far better meal on any of the side streets off the piazza.

Centro Storico

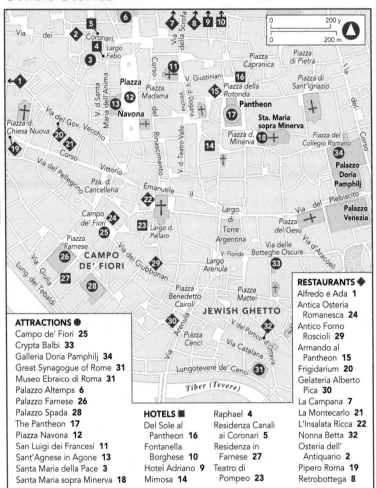

ATTRACTIONS ●
Campo de' Fiori **25**
Crypta Balbi **33**
Galleria Doria Pamphilj **34**
Great Synagogue of Rome **31**
Museo Ebraico di Roma **31**
Palazzo Altemps **6**
Palazzo Farnese **26**
Palazzo Spada **28**
The Pantheon **17**
Piazza Navona **12**
San Luigi dei Francesi **11**
Sant'Agnese in Agone **13**
Santa Maria della Pace **3**
Santa Maria sopra Minerva **18**

HOTELS ■
Del Sole al
   Pantheon **16**
Fontanella
   Borghese **10**
Hotel Adriano **9**
Mimosa **14**
Raphael **4**
Residenza Canali
   ai Coronari **5**
Residenza in
   Farnese **27**
Teatro di
   Pompeo **23**

RESTAURANTS ◆
Alfredo e Ada **1**
Antica Osteria
   Romanesca **24**
Antico Forno
   Roscioli **29**
Armando al
   Pantheon **15**
Frigidarium **20**
Gelateria Alberto
   Pica **30**
La Campana **7**
La Montecarlo **21**
L'Insalata Ricca **22**
Nonna Betta **32**
Osteria dell'
   Antiquario **2**
Pipero Roma **19**
Retrobottega **8**

Palazzo Altemps ★★ MUSEUM Inside this 15th-century *palazzo,* today a branch of the National Museum of Rome, is one of Rome's most charming museums. It's rarely crowded yet houses some of Rome's most famous private and public art collections. Much of it was once part of the famed **Boncompagni Ludovisi Collection,** created by Cardinal Ludovico Ludovisi (1595–1632) and sold at auction in 1901. Among the highlights is the **"Ludovisi Ares"** ★★, a handsome 2nd-century copy of an earlier Greek statue of Mars (Ares to the Greeks). Equally renowned is the **"Ludovisi Gaul"** ★, a marble depiction of a Gaulish warrior plunging a sword into his chest (rather than become a slave of Rome), looking backwards defiantly as he supports a dying woman with his left arm. Also worth a look is the **"Ludovisi Throne,"** a sculpted block of white marble, thought to date from the 5th century B.C., depicting Aphrodite rising from the sea.

Piazza di Sant'Apollinare 46. www.museonazionaleromano.beniculturali.it. ☏ **06/39967700.** 12€ (15€ during special exhibits), valid for 3 days; also includes Palazzo Massimo, Baths of Diocletian, Crypta Balbi. 17 and under free. Tues–Sun 9am–7:45pm. Last entry 1 hr. before closing. Bus: C3, 70, 81, 87, 492, 628.

San Luigi dei Francesi ★★ CHURCH   For a painter of such stratospheric standards as Caravaggio, it is impossible to be definitive in naming his "masterpiece." However, the **"Calling of St. Matthew"** ★★, in the far-left chapel of Rome's French church, must be a candidate. The panel dramatizes the moment Jesus and Peter "called" the customs officer to join them, in Caravaggio's distinct *chiaroscuro* (extreme light and shade) style. Around the same time (1599–1602) Caravaggio also painted the other two St. Matthew panels in the Capella Contarelli—including one depicting the saint's martyrdom. Other highlights inside include Domenichino's masterful "Histories of Saint Cecilia" fresco cycle.

Via di Santa Giovanna d'Arco 5. www.saintlouis-rome.net. ☏ **06/688271.** Free. Mon–Fri 9:30am–12:45pm; Sat 9:30am–12:15pm; Sun 11:30–12:45pm, plus daily 2:30–6:30pm. Bus: C3, 70, 81, 87, 492, 628.

THE PANTHEON & NEARBY ATTRACTIONS

The Pantheon stands on **Piazza della Rotonda,** a lively square with cafes, vendors, and great people-watching.

The Pantheon ★★★ HISTORIC SITE   Stumbling onto Piazza della Rotunda from the dark warren of streets surrounding it will likely leave you agape, marveling at one of ancient Rome's great buildings—the only one that remains intact. The Pantheon ("Temple to All the Gods") was originally built in 27 B.C. by Marcus Agrippa but was entirely reconstructed by Hadrian in the early 2nd century A.D. This remarkable building, 43m (142 ft.) wide and 43m (142 ft.) high (a perfect sphere resting in a cylinder) is among the architectural wonders of the world, even today. Hadrian himself is credited with the basic plan. There are no visible arches or vaults holding up the dome; instead they're sunk into the concrete of the building's walls. The ribbed dome outside is a series of almost weightless cantilevered bricks.

Animals were once sacrificed and burned in the center, with the smoke escaping through the only means of light, the oculus, an opening at the top 5.5m (18 ft.) in diameter. The interior was richly decorated, with white marble statues ringing the central space in its niches. Nowadays, apart from the jaw-dropping size of the space, the main items of interest are the tombs of two Italian kings (Vittorio Emanuele II and his successor, Umberto I) and artist **Raphael** (fans still bring him flowers), with its poignant epitaph. Since the 7th century, the Pantheon has been used as a Catholic church, the **Santa Maria ad Martyres,** informally known as "Santa Maria della Rotonda." Note that at press time, plans were in the works to introduce a 2€ admission fee for non-worshippers, starting in May 2018.

Piazza della Rotonda. www.pantheonroma.com/en. (*) **06/68300230.** Free. Mon–Sat 9am–7:15pm; Sun 9am–5:45pm. Bus: 40, 46, 62, 64, 70, 81, 87, 492, 628 to Largo di Torre Argentina.

Santa Maria sopra Minerva ★★ CHURCH Just one block behind the Pantheon, Santa Maria sopra Minerva is Rome's most significant Dominican church and the only major Gothic church downtown. The facade is in Renaissance style (the church was begun in 1280 but worked on until 1725), but inside, the arched vaulting is pure Gothic. The main art treasures here are the "Statua del Redentore" (1521), a statue of Christ by **Michelangelo** (just to the left of the altar), and a wonderful fresco cycle in the **Cappella Carafa** (on the right before the altar), created by Filippino Lippi between 1488 and 1493 to honor St. Thomas Aquinas. Devout Catholics flock to the tomb of **Saint Catherine of Siena** under the high altar—the room where she died in 1380 was reconstructed by Antonio Barberini in 1637 (far left corner of the church). **Fra' Angelico,** the Dominican friar and painter, also rests here, in the **Cappella Frangipane e Maddaleni-Capiferro.** A delightful elephant statue by **Bernini** holds up a small obelisk in the piazza in front of the church.

Piazza della Minerva 42. www.basilicaminerva.it. (*) **06/69920384.** Free. Mon–Fri 6:55am–7pm; Sat 10am–12:30pm and 3:30–7pm; Sun 8:10am–12:30pm and 3:30–7pm.

Crypta Balbi ★ MUSEUM/RUINS This branch of the National Museum of Rome houses the archaeological remains of the vast portico belonging to the 1st-century-B.C. **Theatre of Lucius Cornelius Balbus,** discovered here in 1981. The ground floor's exhibits chronicle the history of the site through to the medieval period and the construction of the Conservatorio di Santa Caterina della Rosa. The second floor ("Rome from Antiquity to the Middle Ages") explores the transformation of the city between the 5th and 9th centuries, using thousands of ceramic objects, coins, lead seals, bone and ivory implements, precious stones, and tools found on the site. The museum helps decode the complex layers under Rome's streets, but given its comprehensive collections, it's recommended for history buffs.

Via delle Botteghe Oscure 31. www.museonazionaleromano.beniculturali.it. (*) **06/39967700.** 12€ (15€ during special exhibits), valid for 3 days; also includes Palazzo Massimo, Palazzo Altemps, Baths of Diocletian. 17 and under free. Tues–Sun 9am–7:45pm. Last entry 1 hr. before closing. Bus: C3, H, 40, 46, 62, 64, 70, 81, 87, 492, 780. Tram: 8.

Galleria Doria Pamphilj ★★ ART MUSEUM One of the city's finest rococo palaces, the Palazzo Doria Pamphilj is still privately owned by the aristocratic Doria Pamphilj family, but their stupendous art collection is open to the public. The *galleria* winds through the old apartments, their paintings displayed floor-to-ceiling among antique furniture and richly decorated walls. The strong Dutch and Flemish collection includes Pieter Brueghel the Elder's "Battle in the Port of Naples," and his son Jan Brueghel the Elder's "Earthly

Paradise with Original Sin." Among the best Italian works are two Caravaggio paintings, the moving "Repentant Magdalene" and his wonderful "Rest on the Flight into Egypt," hanging near Titian's "Salome with the Head of St. John." There's also Raphael's "Double Portrait," an "Annunciation" by Filippo Lippi, and a "Deposition from the Cross" by Vasari. The gallery's real treasures occupy a special room: Bernini's bust of the Pamphilj **"Pope Innocent X"** ★, and **Velázquez's enigmatic painting** ★★ of the same man. Make sure you grab a free audio guide at the entrance—it's colorfully narrated by Prince Jonathan Doria Pamphilj himself.

Via del Corso 305 (just north of Piazza Venezia). www.doriapamphilj.it. ℂ **06/6797323.** 12€ adults, 8€ students. Daily 9am–7pm, last entry 6pm. Bus: 64 or any to Piazza Venezia.

CAMPO DE' FIORI

The southern section of the Centro Storico, **Campo de' Fiori** is another neighborhood of narrow streets, small piazzas, and ancient churches. Its main focus remains the piazza of **Campo de' Fiori** ★★ itself, where a touristy but delightful open-air market runs Monday through Saturday, selling a dizzyingly colorful array of fruits, vegetables, and spices as well as cheap T-shirts and handbags from early in the morning until midday. (Keep an eye on your purse or wallet here.) From the center of the piazza rises a statue of the severe-looking monk **Giordano Bruno,** a reminder that heretics were occasionally burned at the stake here: Bruno was executed by the Inquisition in 1600. Curiously this is the only piazza in Rome that doesn't have a church in its perimeter.

Built from 1514 to 1589, the **Palazzo Farnese** ★, on Piazza Farnese just to the south of the Campo, was designed by Sangallo and Michelangelo, among others, and was an astronomically expensive project for the time. Its famous residents have included a 16th-century member of the Farnese family, plus Pope Paul III, Cardinal Richelieu, and the former Queen Christina of Sweden, who moved to Rome after abdicating. During the 1630s, when the heirs couldn't afford to maintain the *palazzo,* it was inherited by the Bourbon kings of Naples and was purchased by the French government in 1874; the French Embassy is still located here, so the building is closed to the general public, though small group visits are sometimes offered (9€; www.inventerrome.com).

Palazzo Spada/Galleria Spada ★ MUSEUM   Built around 1540 for Cardinal Gerolamo Capo di Ferro, Palazzo Spada was purchased by the eponymous Cardinal Spada in 1632, who then hired Borromini to restore it—most of what you see today dates from that period. Its richly ornate facade, covered in high-relief stucco decorations in the Mannerist style, is the finest of any building from 16th-century Rome. The State Rooms are closed (the Italian Council of State still meets here), but the richly decorated courtyard and corridor, Borromini's masterful illusion of perspective *(la prospettiva di Borromini),* and the four rooms of the **Galleria Spada** are open to the public. Inside you will find some absorbing paintings, such as the "Portrait of Cardinale Bernardino Spada" by Guido Reni, and Titian's "Portrait of a

Violinist," plus minor works from Caravaggio, Parmigianino, Pietro Testa, and Giambattista Gaulli.

Piazza Capo di Ferro 13. www.galleriaspada.beniculturali.it. © **06/6874893.** 5€. Mon–Sun 8:30am–7:30pm. Bus: H, 23, 63, 280, 780. Tram: 8.

THE JEWISH GHETTO

Across Via Arenula, Campo de' Fiori merges into the old **Jewish Ghetto ★★**, established near the River Tiber by a Papal Bull in 1555, which required that all the Jews in Rome live in one area. Walled in, overcrowded, prone to floods and epidemics, and on some of the worst land in the city, it was an extremely grim place to live. After the Ghetto was abolished in 1882, its walls were finally torn down and the area largely reconstructed. In the waning years of WWII, Nazis sent more than 1,000 Roman Jews to concentration camps; only a handful returned.

The **Via Portico d'Ottavia** forms the heart of a flourishing Jewish Quarter, with Romans flocking here to sample the **Roman-Jewish and Middle Eastern food** for which the area is known.

Museo Ebraico di Roma (Jewish Museum of Rome) & Great Synagogue ★ MUSEUM   On the premises of the Great Synagogue of Rome, this museum chronicles the history of not only Roman Jews but Jews from all over Italy. There are displays of works of 17th- and 18th-century Roman silversmiths, precious textiles from all over Europe, and a number of parchments and marble carvings that were saved when the Ghetto's original synagogues were demolished. Admission to the museum includes a guided English-language tour of the **Great Synagogue of Rome** (Tempio Maggiore), built from 1901 to 1904 in an eclectic style evoking Babylonian and Persian temples. Attacked by terrorists in 1982, the synagogue is now heavily guarded by *carabinieri,* a division of the Italian police armed with machine guns.

Via Catalana. www.museoebraico.roma.it. © **06/6840061.** 11€ adults, 5€ students, free for children 10 and under. Apr–Sept Sun–Thurs 10am–6pm and Fri 10am–4pm; Oct–Mar Sun–Thurs 10am–5pm and Fri 9am–2pm.

The Tridente & the Spanish Steps

The northern half of central Rome is known as the **Tridente,** thanks to the trident shape formed by three roads—Via di Ripetta, Via del Corso, and Via del Babuino—leading down from **Piazza del Popolo.** The area around **Piazza di Spagna** and the **Spanish Steps** was once the artistic quarter of the city, attracting English poets Keats and Shelley, German author Goethe, and film director Federico Fellini (who lived on Via Margutta). Institutions such as Antico Caffè Greco and Babington's Tea Rooms are still here (see p. 75), but between the high rents and the throngs of tourists and shoppers, you're unlikely to see many artists left.

PIAZZA DEL POPOLO

Elegant **Piazza del Popolo ★★** is haunted with memories. Legend has it that the ashes of Nero were enshrined here, until 11th-century residents began complaining to the pope about his imperial ghost. The **Egyptian obelisk** dates

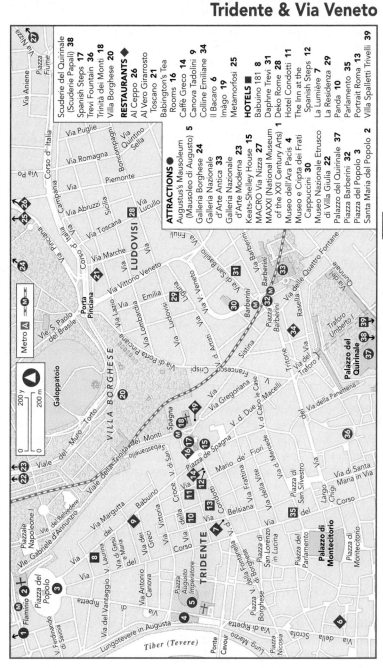

ATTRACTIONS ●

Augustus's Mausoleum
(Mausoleo di Augusto) **5**
Galleria Borghese **24**
Galleria Nazionale
d'Arte Antica **33**
Galleria Nazionale
d'Arte Moderna **23**
Keats-Shelley House **15**
MACRO Via Nizza **27**
MAXXI (National Museum
of the XXI Century Arts) **1**
Museo dell'Ara Pacis **4**
Museo e Cripta dei Frati
Cappuccini **30**
Museo Nazionale Etrusco
di Villa Giulia **22**
Palazzo del Quirinale **37**
Piazza Barberini **32**
Piazza del Popolo **3**
Santa Maria del Popolo **2**

Scuderie del Quirinale
(Scuderie Papali) **38**
Spanish Steps **17**
Trevi Fountain **36**
Trinità dei Monti **18**
Villa Borghese **20**

RESTAURANTS ◆

Al Ceppo **26**
Al Vero Girarrosto
Toscano **21**
Babington's Tea
Rooms **16**
Caffè Greco **14**
Canova Tadolini **9**
Colline Emiliane **34**
Il Bacaro **6**
Imàgo **19**
Metamorfosi **25**

HOTELS ■

Babuino 181 **8**
Daphne Trevi **31**
Deko Rome **28**
Hotel Condotti **11**
The Inn at the
Spanish Steps **12**
La Lumière **7**
La Residenza **29**
Panda **10**
Parlamento **35**
Portrait Roma **13**
Villa Spalletti Trivelli **39**

4

ROME | Exploring Rome

from the 13th century B.C.; it was removed from Heliopolis to Rome during Augustus's reign (it once stood at the Circus Maximus).

The current piazza was designed in the early 19th century by Valadier, Napoleon's architect. Standing astride the three roads that form the "trident" are almost-twin baroque churches, **Santa Maria dei Miracoli** (1681) and **Santa Maria di Montesanto** (1679). The stand-out church, however, is at the piazza's northern curve: the 15th-century **Santa Maria del Popolo ★★**, with its splendid baroque facade modified by Bernini between 1655 and 1660. Inside, look for Raphael's mosaic series the "Creation of the World" adorning the interior dome of the **Capella Chigi** (the second chapel on the left). Pinturicchio decorated the main choir vault with frescoes such as the "Coronation of the Virgin." The **Capella Cerasi** (to the left of the high altar) contains gorgeous examples of baroque art: an altarpiece painting of "The Assumption of Mary" by Carracci, and on either side two great works by Caravaggio, "Conversion on the Road to Damascus" and "The Crucifixion of Saint Peter."

MAXXI (National Museum of the XXI Century Arts) ★ MUSEUM Ten minutes north of Piazza del Popolo by tram, leave the Renaissance far behind at MAXXI, a masterpiece of contemporary architecture with bending and overlapping oblong tubes designed by the late Zaha Hadid. The museum is divided into two sections, MAXXI art and MAXXI architecture, primarily serving as a venue for temporary exhibitions of contemporary work in both fields (although it does have a small permanent collection). The building is worth a visit in its own right.

Via Guido Reni 4a. www.fondazionemaxxi.it. ⓒ **06/3201954.** 12€ 31 and over, 8€ ages 30 and under, 4€ students, free children 13 and under. Tues–Fri and Sun 11am–7pm; Sat 11am–10pm. Metro: Flaminio, then tram 2.

Museo dell'Ara Pacis ★★ MUSEUM Set in a stunning ultra-modern building designed by American architect Richard Meier, the templelike marble "Altar of Peace" was erected in 9 B.C. to honor soon-to-be-Emperor Augustus's success in subduing tribes north of the Alps. For centuries the monument was lost to memory; signs of its existence surfaced in the 16th century, but it wasn't until the 1930s that it was fully excavated, and even so it lay virtually abandoned after World War II, until a true restoration began in the 1980s. The exhibit complex provides context, with interactive displays in English. From here you get great views of the huge, overgrown ruin of **Augustus's Mausoleum (Mausoleo di Augusto),** built in the 1st-century-B.C., where the ashes of emperors Augustus, Caligula, Claudius, Nerva, and Tiberius once rested. Long closed to the public, the tomb is now being restored. On Friday and Saturday evenings, **L'Ara com'era (The Ara as It Was) ★★**, an immersive virtual reality experience, transports visitors to the Ara and its surroundings during their 1st-century heyday (2 entries per evening, adults 12€, no children 12 and under).

Lungotevere in Augusta. www.arapacis.it/en. ⓒ **06/060608.** 10.50€. Daily 9:30am–7:30pm (last entry 6:30pm). Metro: Spagna. Bus: C3, 70, 81, 87, 280, 492, 628, 913.

PIAZZA DI SPAGNA

The undoubted highlight of Tridente is **Piazza di Spagna,** which attracts hordes of tourists to admire its celebrated **Spanish Steps (Scalinata della Trinità dei Monti) ★★,** the widest stairway in Europe. Fresh from a 1.5-million-euro renovation paid for by luxury jeweler Bulgari, the Steps are especially enchanting in early spring, when they are framed by thousands of blooming azaleas. At their foot lies "Fontana della Barcaccia," a fountain shaped like an old boat, the work of Pietro

No Swimming or Picnicking Allowed

In an effort to keep tourists from littering the city's monuments, or soaking their feet and even swimming (yes, it's happened) in its famous fountains, visitors are no longer permitted to picnic (or even eat a gelato) on the Spanish Steps or sit on the edge of the Trevi and other landmark fountains. You can stop long enough for a photo or coin toss, but don't plan on getting comfortable (or taking a dip).

Bernini, father of sculptor and fountain-master Gian Lorenzo Bernini. Built from 1723 to 1725, the monumental 135-step stairway and its square take their names from the Spanish Embassy (once headquartered here), but were actually funded almost entirely by the French. That's because the **Trinità dei Monti** church at the top was under the patronage of the Bourbon kings of France at the time. The stately baroque facade of the 16th-century Trinità dei Monti is perched photogenically at the top of the Steps, behind yet another Roman obelisk, the "Obelisco Sallustiano." It's worth climbing up just for the views.

Keats-Shelley House ★ MUSEUM   At the foot of the Spanish Steps is the 18th-century house where the Romantic English poet John Keats died of

Even at night, crowds congregate on Rome's iconic Spanish Steps.

consumption on February 23, 1821, at age 25. Since 1909, when it was bought by well-intentioned English and American literary types, it has been a working library established in honor of Keats and fellow Romantic Percy Bysshe Shelley, who drowned off the coast of Viareggio with a copy of Keats' works in his pocket. Mementos range from kitsch to extremely moving. The apartment where Keats spent his last months, tended by his close friend Joseph Severn, shelters a death mask of Keats as well as the "deadly sweat" drawing by Severn. Both Keats and Shelley are buried in their beloved Rome, at the Protestant cemetery near the Pyramid of Cestius, in Testaccio.

Piazza di Spagna 26. www.keats-shelley-house.org. ✆ **06/6784235.** 5€. Mon–Sat 10am–1pm and 2–6pm. Metro: Spagna.

Palazzo del Quirinale ★★ HISTORIC SITE   Until the end of World War II, this palace was home to the king of Italy; before the crown resided here, it was the summer residence of the pope. Since 1946 the palace has been the official residence of the President of Italy, but parts of it are open to the public.

Although it can't compare to Rome's major artistic showstoppers (there's little art or furniture in the rooms), the palace's baroque and neoclassical walls and ceilings are quite a spectacle. Few rooms anywhere are as impressive as the richly decorated 17th-century **Salone dei Corazzieri,** the **Sala d'Ercole** (once the apartments of Umberto I but completely rebuilt in 1940), and the tapestry-covered 17th-century **Sala dello Zodiaco.** Despite its Renaissance origins, this *palazzo* is rich in associations with ancient emperors and deities. The colossal statues of the "Dioscuri," Castor and Pollux, which now form part of the fountain in the piazza, were found in the nearby Baths of Constantine; in 1793 Pius VI had an ancient Egyptian obelisk moved here from the Mausoleum of Augustus. The sweeping view of the city from the piazza, which crowns the highest of the seven ancient hills of Rome, is itself worth the trip.

Piazza del Quirinale. palazzo.quirinale.it/palazzo.html. ✆ **06/39-96-7557.** 1.50€ for basic tour; 10€ for extended tour including gardens, carriages, and special collections. Reservations must be made at least 5 days prior to visit. Tues–Wed and Fri–Sun 9:30am–4pm. Closed Aug. Metro: Barberini. Bus: C3, 40, 60, 62-64, 70, 71, 80, 83, 85, 492.

Trevi Fountain (Fontana di Trevi) ★★ MONUMENT   As you elbow your way through the summertime crowds around the **Trevi Fountain,** it's hard to believe that this little piazza was nearly always deserted before 1950, when it began "starring" in films. The first was *Three Coins in the Fountain,* and later it was the setting for an iconic scene in Fellini's 1960 masterpiece *La Dolce Vita.* It was also where Audrey Hepburn gets her signature haircut in *Roman Holiday.* To this day, thousands of euros worth of coins are tossed into the fountain daily. The area is always jam-packed with tourists and selfie-stick hawkers, so keep your eye (and your hands) on your belongings. Completed in 1762, this glorious baroque fountain centers on the triumphant figure of Neptune, standing on a shell chariot drawn by winged steeds and led by a pair of tritons. Two allegorical figures in the side niches represent good health and fertility. On the southwestern corner of the piazza, the unimpressive church of **SS. Vincenzo e Anastasio** has a strange claim to fame: Within it are the relics (hearts and intestines) of several popes.

Piazza di Trevi. Metro: Barberini. Bus: C3, 51, 53, 62, 63, 71, 80, 83, 85, 160, 492.

Villa Borghese & Parioli

Villa Borghese ★★, just northeast of the Tridente, is not actually a villa but one of Europe's most elegant large parks, 6km (3¾ miles) in circumference. Cardinal Scipione Borghese created the park in the 1600s; Umberto I, king of Italy, acquired it in 1902 and presented it to the city of Rome. The greenbelt is crisscrossed by roads, but you can escape from the traffic and seek a shaded area under a tree to enjoy its landscaped vistas. On a sunny weekend, it's a pleasure to stroll here and see Romans at play, relaxing or inline skating. The park has a few casual cafes and food vendors; you can also rent bikes or Segways here. In the northeast part of the park you'll find a **zoo** and the **Galleria Borghese** (see below). The neighborhoods to the north, Parioli and

Rotunda at the Villa Borghese Gardens.

Pinciano, are elegant enclaves for those wishing to stay outside the crowded city center (see p. 47).

Galleria Borghese ★★★ ART MUSEUM   On the far northeastern edge of the Villa Borghese, the Galleria Borghese occupies the former Villa Borghese Pinciana, built between 1609 and 1613 for Cardinal Scipione Borghese, an early patron of Bernini and an astute collector of work by Caravaggio. Today the gallery displays much of his collection and a lot more besides, making this one of Rome's great art treasures. It's also one of Rome's most pleasant sights to tour, thanks to the curators' mandate that only a limited number of people be allowed in at a time.

The ground floor is a **sculpture gallery** par extraordinaire, housing Canova's famously risqué statue of Paolina Borghese, sister of Napoleon and wife of the reigning Prince Camillo Borghese (when asked if she was uncomfortable posing nude, she reportedly replied, "No, the studio was heated"). The genius of Bernini reigns supreme in the following rooms, with his "David" (the face of which is thought to be a self-portrait) and **"Apollo and Daphne"** ★★ both seminal works of baroque sculpture. Look also for Bernini's Mannerist sculpture next door, "The Rape of Persephone." Caravaggio is represented by the "Madonna of the Grooms," the shadowy "St. Jerome," and the frightening **"David Holding the Head of Goliath"** ★★. Upstairs lies a rich collection of paintings, including Raphael's graceful "Deposition" and his sinuous "Lady with a Unicorn." There's also a series of self-portraits by Bernini, and his lifelike busts of Cardinal Scipione and Pope Paul V. One of Titian's best, **"Sacred and Profane Love"** ★, lies in one of the final rooms.

Important information: No more than 360 visitors at a time are allowed on the ground floor, and no more than 90 are allowed on the upper floor, during set 2-hour windows. **Reservations are essential,** so call ✆ **06/32810** (Mon–Fri 9am–6pm; Sat 9am–1pm). You can also make reservations by visiting **www. tosc.it**, or stopping by in person on your first day in Rome to reserve tickets for a later date. English labeling in the museum is minimal. Guided tours of the galleries in English cost an extra 6.50€, but failing that, opt for an audio guide.

Piazzale del Museo Borghese 5 (off Via Pinciana). www.galleriaborghese.it.✆ **06/32810.** 15€ (plus 2€ service charge); 18 and under 2€. Audio guides 5€. Tues–Sun 8:30am–7:30pm. Bus: C3, 53, 61, 89, 160, 490, 495, 590, 910.

MACRO Via Nizza ★ MUSEUM   Rome's contemporary art museum was recently expanded to occupy an entire block of early-1900s industrial buildings, formerly the Peroni beer factory, located near the Porta Pia gate of the Aurelian walls. Designed by French architect Odile Decq, the museum hosts contemporary art exhibits with edgy installations, visuals, and multimedia events. Another branch of the museum is housed in a converted slaughterhouse in Testaccio (p. 125).

Via Nizza 138. www.museomacro.org. ✆ **06/671070400.** 18€ (combined ticket with MACRO Mattatoio–Testaccio). Mon–Sun 9am–9pm. Last entry 7pm. Bus: 38, 60, 62, 66, 80, 82, 88-90. Tram: 3, 19.

Museo Nazionale Etrusco di Villa Giulia (National Etruscan Museum) ★★★ MUSEUM   The great Etruscan civilization was one of Italy's most advanced, although it remains relatively mysterious, in part because of its centuries-long rivalry with Rome. Rome definitively conquered the Etruscans by the 3rd century B.C., and though they adopted certain aspects of Etruscan culture, including religious practices, engineering innovations, and gladiatorial combat, gradual Romanization eclipsed virtually all the Etruscans' achievements. This museum, housed in the handsome Renaissance Villa Giulia, built by Pope Julius III between 1550 and 1555, is the best place in Italy to learn about the Etruscans, thanks to a cache of precious artifacts, sculptures, vases, monuments, tools, weapons, and jewels, the vast majority of it from tombs. Fans of ancient history could spend several hours here, but for those with less time, the most striking attraction is the stunning **Sarcofago degli Sposi (Sarcophagus of the Spouses)** ★★, a late 6th-century-B.C. terracotta funerary monument featuring a life-size bride and groom, supposedly lounging at a banquet in the afterlife (Paris's Louvre has a similar monument). Equally fascinating are the **Pyrgi Tablets,** gold-leaf inscriptions in both Etruscan and Phoenician from the 5th century B.C., and the **Apollo of Veii,** a huge painted terracotta statue of Apollo dating to the 6th century B.C. The **Euphronios Krater** is also here, a renowned and perfectly maintained red-figured Greek vase from the 6th century B.C. that returned home from New York's Metropolitan Museum of Art after a long legal battle.

Piazzale di Villa Giulia 9. www.villagiulia.beniculturali.it. © **06/3226571.** 8€. Tues–Sun 9am–8pm. Bus: C3, 982. Tram: 2, 3, 19.

Galleria Nazionale d'Arte Moderna (National Gallery of Modern Art) ★ ART MUSEUM   Housed in the monumental Bazzani Building constructed in 1911, this "modern" art collection ranges from unfashionable neoclassical and Romantic paintings and sculpture to better 20th-century works. Quality varies, but fans should seek out van Gogh's "Gardener" and "Portrait of Madame Ginoux" in Room 15, the handful of Impressionists in Room 14 (Cézanne, Degas, Monet, and Rodin), and Klimt's harrowing "Three Ages" in Room 16. Surrealist and Expressionist works by Miró, Kandinsky, and Mondrian appear in Room 22, and Pollock's "Undulating Paths" and Calder's "Mobile" hold court in Room 27. One of Warhol's "Hammer and Sickle" series is tucked away in Room 30.

Viale delle Belle Arti 131. www.gnam.beniculturali.it. © **06/322981.** 10€, ages 17 and under free. Tues–Sun 8:30am–7:30pm. Bus: 61, 160, 490, 495. Tram: 3 or 19.

Via Veneto & Piazza Barberini

Piazza Barberini lies at the foot of several streets, among them Via Barberini, Via Sistina, and Via Vittorio Veneto. It would be a far more pleasant spot were it not for the traffic swarming around its principal feature, Bernini's **Fountain of the Triton (Fontana del Tritone)** ★. For more than 3 centuries, the figure sitting in a vast open clam has been blowing water from his triton. To one side of the piazza is the aristocratic facade of the **Palazzo Barberini,** named for one of Rome's powerful families; inside is the **Galleria Nazionale d'Arte Antica** (see p. 120). The Barberini reached their peak when a son was elected pope as Urban VIII; he encouraged Bernini and gave him patronage. As you walk up **Via Vittorio Veneto,** look for the small fountain on the right corner of Piazza Barberini—another Bernini, the **Fountain of the Bees (Fontana delle Api).** At first they look more like flies, but they're the bees of the Barberini, the crest of that powerful family complete with the crossed keys of St. Peter above them. (Keys were always added to a family crest when a son was elected pope.)

Museo e Cripta dei Frati Cappuccini (Museum and Crypt of the Capuchin Friars) ★★ RELIGIOUS SITE/MUSEUM
One of the most mesmerizingly macabre sights in all Christendom, this otherwise restrained museum dedicated to the Capuchin order ends with a series of six chapels in the crypt, adorned with the skulls and bones of more than 3,700 Capuchin brothers, woven into mosaic "works of art." Some of the skeletons are intact, draped with Franciscan habits; others form lamps and ceiling friezes. The tradition of the friars dates to a period when Christians had a richly creative cult of the dead and great spiritual masters meditated and preached with a skull in hand. Whatever you believe, the experience is a mix of spooky and meditative. The entrance is halfway up the first staircase on the right of the church of the Convento dei Frati Cappuccini, completed in 1630 and rebuilt in the early 1930s. *Note:* Because this site is located within a church, it maintains a strict dress code—no short pants or skirts and no bare arms.

Beside the Convento dei Frati Cappuccini, Via Vittorio Veneto 27. www.cappuccinivia veneto.it. © **06/88803695.** 8.50€, 5€ ages 17 and under. Daily 9am–7pm, last entry 6:30pm. Metro: Barberini. Bus: 52, 53, 61, 63, 80, 160.

Galleria Nazionale d'Arte Antica (National Gallery of Ancient Art) ★★ ART MUSEUM
On the southern side of Piazza Barberini, the grand **Palazzo Barberini** houses the Galleria Nazionale d'Arte Antica, which despite the "ancient" in its title is a trove of Italian art mostly from the early Renaissance to late baroque periods. Some of the art on display is wonderful, but the building itself is the main attraction, a baroque masterpiece begun by Carlo Maderno in 1627 and completed in 1633 by Bernini, with additional work by Borromini (notably a whimsical spiral staircase). The **Salone di Pietro da Cortona** in the center is the most captivating space, with a trompe l'oeil ceiling frescoed by Pietro da Cortona, a depiction of "The Triumph of Divine Providence." The museum has intriguing works, including Raphael's "La Fornarina," a baker's daughter thought to have been the artist's lover (look for Raphael's name on her bracelet); paintings by Tintoretto and Titian (Room 15); a portrait of English King Henry VIII by Holbein (Room 16); and a couple of typically unsettling El Grecos in Room 17. Caravaggio dominates room 20 with the justly celebrated "Judith and Holofernes" and **"Narcissus" ★★.**

Via delle Quattro Fontane 13. www.barberinicorsini.org. © **06/4814591**. 12€, valid for 10 days, also includes Palazzo Corsini; 17 and under free. Tues–Sun 8:30am–7pm; last entry 6pm. Metro: Barberini. Bus: 53, 61–63, 80, 81, 83, 160, 492, 590.

Around Stazione Termini

Palazzo Massimo alle Terme ★★ MUSEUM A third of Rome's assortment of ancient art can be found at this branch of the Museo Nazionale Romano; among its treasures are a major coin collection, extensive maps of trade routes (with audio and visual exhibits on the network of traders over the centuries), and a vast sculpture collection that includes portrait busts of emperors and their families, as well as mythical figures like the Minotaur and Athena. But the real draw is on the second floor, where you can see some of the oldest of Rome's **frescoes** ★★; they depict an entire garden, complete with plants and birds, from the Villa di Livia a Prima Porta. (Livia was the wife of Emperor Augustus and was deified after her death in A.D. 29.)

Largo di Villa Peretti. www.museonazionaleromano.beniculturali.it. © **06/39967700**. 12€ (15€ during special exhibits), valid for 3 days, also includes Palazzo Altemps, Baths of Diocletian, Crypta Balbi. 17 and under free. Tues–Sun 9am–7:45pm. Last entry 1 hr. before closing. Metro: Termini or Repubblica. Bus: 40, 64, or any bus that stops at Termini.

Santa Maria della Vittoria ★ CHURCH A visit to this pretty little baroque church is all about one artwork: Gian Lorenzo Bernini's **"Ecstasy of St. Teresa"** ★★★. Crafted from marble between 1644 and 1647, it shows the Spanish saint at the moment of her ecstatic encounter with an angel (the so-called "Transverberation"). Bernini's depiction is deliciously erotic. Look for the Cornaro family, who sponsored the chapel's construction, watching the saint's ecstasy from a balcony on the right.

Via XX Settembre 17 (at Largo S. Susanna). www.chiesasantamariavittoriaroma.it. © **06/42740571**. Free. Mon–Sat 8:30am–noon and 3:30–6pm; Sun 3:30–6pm. Metro: Repubblica. Bus: 60-62, 66, 82, 85, 492, 590, 910.

Santa Maria Maggiore (St. Mary Major) ★★ CHURCH This imposing church, one of Rome's four papal basilicas, was founded by Pope Liberius in A.D. 358 and rebuilt on the orders of Pope Sixtus III from 432 to 440. Its 14th-century **campanile** is the city's loftiest. Don't be put off by the overdone 18th-century façade; there are treasures within, such as the 5th-century Roman mosaics in its nave, and its coffered ceiling, said to have been gilded with gold brought from the New World. The church also contains the **tomb of Bernini,** Italy's most important baroque sculptor–architect. The man who changed the face of Rome is buried in a tomb so simple that it takes a sleuth to track it down (to the right, near the altar).

Piazza di Santa Maria Maggiore. © **06/69886800**. Free. Daily 7am–6:45pm. Metro: Termini or Cavour. Bus: C3, 16, 70, 71, 75, 360, 590, 649, 714.

Terme di Diocleziano (Baths of Diocletian) ★ MUSEUM/RUINS
Originally this spot held the largest of Rome's hedonistic baths (dating back

4

ROME | Exploring Rome

Around Termini

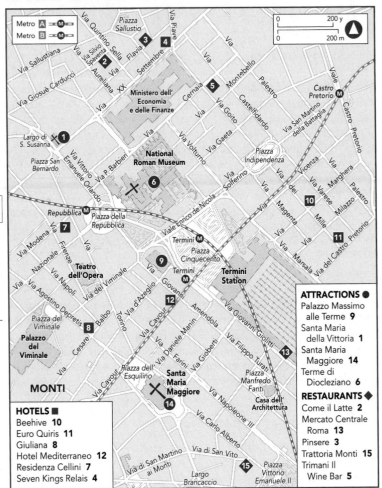

Map Legend:

Metro A ◼M◼
Metro B ◼M◼

0 — 200 y
0 — 200 m

ATTRACTIONS ●
Palazzo Massimo
  alle Terme **9**
Santa Maria
  della Vittoria **1**
Santa Maria
  Maggiore **14**
Terme di
  Diocleziano **6**

RESTAURANTS ◆
Come il Latte **2**
Mercato Centrale
  Roma **13**
Pinsere **3**
Trattoria Monti **15**
Trimani Il
  Wine Bar **5**

HOTELS ◼
Beehive **10**
Euro Quiris **11**
Giuliana **8**
Hotel Mediterraneo **12**
Residenza Cellini **7**
Seven Kings Relais **4**

to A.D. 298 and the reign of Emperor Diocletian); during the Renaissance a church, cloister, and convent were built around the ruins—much of it designed by Michelangelo, no less. Today the entire hodgepodge is part of the Museo Nazionale Romano; it's a compelling museum stop that's usually quieter than the city's blockbusters. Exhibits include statuary and a large collection of inscriptions and other stone carvings from the Roman and pre-Roman eras. Only Aula 10 remains of the vast baths, which once accommodated 3,000 at a time, only to be abandoned in the 6th century after the Goth invasions.

Viale E. di Nicola 78. www.museonazionaleromano.beniculturali.it. ℂ **06/39967700.** 12€ (15€ during special exhibits) valid for 3 days, also includes Palazzo Massimo, Palazzo

Altemps, Crypta Balbi. 17 and under free. Tues–Sun 9am–7:30pm. Last entry 1 hr. before closing. Metro: Termini or Repubblica. Bus: 66, 82, 85, 590, 910 or any bus to Termini.

Trastevere

Galleria Nazionale d'Arte Antica in Palazzo Corsini ★ PALACE/ART MUSEUM   Palazzo Corsini first found fame—or more accurately, notoriety—as the home of Queen Christina of Sweden, a Catholic convert who moved to Rome after abdicating the Swedish throne. (She was famously described as "Queen without a realm, Christian without a faith, and a woman without shame," referring to her open bisexuality.) Several other big names stayed in this beautiful palace, from Michelangelo to Napoleon's mother, Letizia. Today one wing houses a moderately interesting museum, housing a lot of the runoff from Italy's national art collection. Worth a look is Caravaggio's "St. John the Baptist" (1606) and panels by Luca Giordano, Fra' Angelico, and Poussin; otherwise the palace history is more interesting than the museum itself.

Via della Lungara 10. www.barberinicorsini.org. ✆ **06/68802323.** 12€, valid for 10 days, also includes Palazzo Barberini; ages 17 and under free. Wed–Mon 8:30am–7pm. Bus: 23 or 280.

A TRIO OF churches IN TRASTEVERE

Before Trastevere became bohemian and cool, it was a working-class neighborhood, separated by the Tiber from Rome's bustle. Step into the shadowy calm of any of these neighborhood churches to get a glimpse of the old Trastevere. Admission is always free, and they're open daily, though they may close at lunchtime.

On Piazza Santa Maria, the heart of Trastevere, ornate **Santa Maria in Trastevere** ★★ is one of Rome's oldest churches, founded around A.D. 350. The pride of the neighborhood, it's spectacular inside and out, with a Romanesque brick bell tower, colorful frescoes, mosaics, and loads of recycled ancient marbles. Look for Cavallini's 1293 mosaics of the "Life of the Virgin Mary" in the apse.

From there, Via di San Francisco a Ripa angles southeast to the church of **San Francesco d'Assisi a Ripa** ★ (www.sanfrancescoinripa.com), so named because it's built over a convent where

St. Francis stayed in 1219 when he came to Rome to see the pope (his simple cell is preserved inside). A Bernini treasure is tucked into the last chapel on the left: the "Tomb of Beata Ludovica Albertoni" (1675), commemorating a noblewoman who dedicated her life to the city's poor.

From there, follow Via Anicia northeast to **Santa Cecilia in Trastevere** ★ (Piazza Santa Cecilia; www.benedettine santacecilia.it), a still-functioning convent with a peaceful courtyard garden. Tradition holds that the saint herself once lived on this site; the church's altar has an exquisite marble sculpture of her (ca. 1600) carved by Stefano Maderno. On weekday mornings for a small fee (2.50€) you can go under the church to see a set of Roman-era ruins, and then a nun will accompany you to an upstairs room to see the partial remains of a "Last Judgment," by Pietro Cavallini (ca. 1293), a masterpiece of Roman medieval painting.

Trastevere & Testaccio

CAMPO DE' FIORI

JEWISH GHETTO

Tempio Maggiori

Teatro di Marcello

TIBER ISLAND

TRASTEVERE

Piazza Sta. Maria in Trastevere

Piazza in Piscinula

Piazza di Sta. Cecilia

Piazza S. Francesco d'Assisi

Piazza di Porta Portese

Giardino di Sant'Alessio

Parco di San Alessio

RIPA

Piazza dell'Emporio

Piazza di Sta. Maria Liberatrice

TESTACCIO

Monte Testaccio

Cimitero acattolico di Roma (Protestant Cemetery)

ATTRACTIONS ●
Centrale Montemartini **27**
Galleria Nazionale d'Arte Antica in Palazzo Corsini **2**
MACRO Testaccio **23**
San Francesco d'Assisi a Ripa **17**
San Paolo Fuori le Mura **27**
Santa Cecilia in Trastevere **16**
Santa Maria in Trastevere **9**
Villa Farnesina **3**

RESTAURANTS ◆
Antico Arco **1**
Bir & Fud **4**
Biscottificio Artigiano Innocenti **13**
Cacio e Pepe **6**
Checchino dal 1887 **24**
Da Enzo **15**
Da Remo **20**
Dar Poeta **5**
Fior di Luna **10**
Flavio al Velavevodetto **25**
Glass **7**
Osteria degli Amici **22**
Osteria La Gensola **11**
Porto Fluviale **26**
Romeo Chef & Baker **19**
Spirito DiVino **14**
Trattoria Perilli **21**

HOTELS ■
Arco del Lauro **12**
San Francesco **18**
Santa Maria **8**

ROME | Exploring Rome

Villa Farnesina ★ HISTORIC HOME   Originally built for Sienese banker Agostino Chigi in 1511, this elegant villa was acquired by the Farnese family in 1579. With two such wealthy Renaissance patrons, it's hardly surprising that the interior decor is top drawer. Architect Baldassare Peruzzi began the decoration, with frescoes and motifs rich in myth and symbolism. He was later assisted by Sebastiano del Piombo, Sodoma, and, most notably, Raphael. Raphael's **"Loggia of Cupid and Psyche"** ★★ was frescoed to mark Chigi's marriage to Francesca Ordeaschi—though his assistants did much of the work. The ornamental gardens are perfumed and colorful in the spring and summer.

Via della Lungara 230. www.villafarnesina.it. ℂ **06/68077268.** 6€. Mon–Sat 9am–2pm; 2nd Sun of month 9am–5pm. Bus: 23, 280.

Testaccio & Southern Rome

Centrale Montemartini ★★ MUSEUM   The renovated boiler rooms of Rome's first thermoelectric plant now house a grand collection of Roman and Greek statues, creating a unique juxtaposition of classic and industrial archaeology. The 19th-century powerhouse was the first public plant to produce electricity for the city. Striking installations include the vast boiler hall, a 1,000-square-meter (10,764-sq.-ft.) room where classical statues share space with a complex web of pipes, masonry, and metal walkways. Equally striking is the Hall of Machines, where two towering turbines stand opposite the reconstructed pediment of the Temple of Apollo Sosiano, which illustrates a famous Greek battle. Unless you run across a school group, this place is never crowded, and it provides an intimate look at the ancient world, despite the cavernous setting.

Via Ostiense 106. www.centralemontemartini.org. ℂ **06/0608.** 11€. Tues–Sun 9am–7pm. Last entry 30 min. before closing. Metro: Garbatella. Bus: 23 or 792.

MACRO Testaccio ★ MUSEUM   The Testaccio outpost of Rome's contemporary art museum is housed—appropriately for this former meatpacking neighborhood—in a converted slaughterhouse. The edgy programs and exhibits are a mix of installations, visuals, events, and special viewings. Opening times are made for night owls: Make a late visit before going on to Testaccio's bars and restaurants.

Piazza Orazio Giustiniani 4. www.museomacro.org. ℂ **06/671070400.** 6€ (18€ combined ticket with MACRO Via Nizza). Tues–Sun 2–8pm. Last entry 30 min before closing. Metro: Piramide. Bus: 23, 75, 83, 170, 280, 719. Tram: 3, 8.

San Paolo Fuori le Mura (St. Paul Outside the Walls) ★★ CHURCH   The giant Basilica of St. Paul, whose origins date from the time of Constantine, is Rome's fourth great patriarchal church. It was erected over the tomb of St. Paul and is the second-largest church in Rome after St. Peter's. The basilica fell victim to fire in 1823 and was subsequently rebuilt—hence the relatively modern look. Inside, translucent alabaster windows illuminate a forest of single-file columns and mosaic medallions (portraits of the various popes). Its most important treasure is a 12th-century marble candelabrum by Vassalletto, who's also responsible for the remarkable cloisters containing twisted pairs of columns enclosing a rose garden. Miraculously, the baldacchino by Arnolfo di Cambio (1285) wasn't damaged in the fire; it now shelters the tomb of St. Paul the Apostle.

Via Ostiense 190 (at Piazzale San Paolo). www.basilicasanpaolo.org. *C* **06/69880800.** Basilica free; cloisters 4€. Basilica daily 7am–6:30pm. Cloisters daily 8:30am–6pm. Metro: Basilica di San Paolo. Bus: 23.

The Via Appia (Appian Way) & the Catacombs

Of all the roads that led to Rome, **Via Appia Antica** (begun in 312 B.C.) was the most famous. It stretched all the way to the seaport of Brindisi, through which trade with Greece and the East was funneled. (According to Christian tradition, it was along the Appian Way that an escaping Peter encountered the vision of Christ, causing him to go back into the city to face martyrdom.) The road's initial stretch in Rome is lined with the monuments and ancient tombs of patrician Roman families—burials were forbidden within the city walls as early as the 5th century B.C.—and, below ground, miles of tunnels hewn out of the soft *tufa* stone that hardens on exposure to the air. These tunnels, or catacombs, were where early Christians buried their dead. A few are open to the public, so you can wander through musty-smelling tunnels whose walls are gouged out with tens of thousands of now mostly empty burial niches, including small niches made for children. Early Christians referred to each chamber as a *dormitorio*—they believed the bodies were only sleeping, awaiting resurrection (which is why they could not observe the traditional Roman practice of cremation). In some you can still discover the remains of early Christian art. The obligatory guided tours feature occasionally biased history, plus a dash of sermonizing, but the guides are very knowledgeable.

The Appia Antica park is a popular Sunday picnic site for Roman families, following the half-forgotten pagan tradition of dining in the presence of one's ancestors on holy days. The Via Appia Antica is closed to cars on Sundays, left for the picnickers, walkers and bicyclists. See **www.parcoappiaantica.it**

A Noble Survivor

Of all the monuments on the Appian Way itself, the most impressive is the **Tomb of Cecilia Metella ★**, within walking distance of the catacombs. The cylindrical tomb, clad in travertine and topped with a marble frieze, honors the wife of one of Julius Caesar's military commanders from the republican era. Why such an elaborate tomb for a figure of relatively minor historical importance? Other mausoleums may have been even more elaborate, but Cecilia Metella's earned enduring fame simply because her tomb has remained while the others have decayed. Part of the reason is its symbiotic relationship with the early-14th-century **Castle Caetani** attached to the rear. For centuries, the tomb survived being plundered for building materials because of the castle, which was built to guard the road and collect tolls; in later eras, the castle was spared because it was attached to the romantic ruin of the tomb. Admission to the tomb is 5€, or 8€ on a combined ticket with the Baths of Caracalla (p. 95).

for more, including downloadable maps. To reach the catacombs area, take bus no. 218 from the San Giovanni Metro stop or the 118 from Colosseo or Circus Maximus. *Tip:* The 118 runs more frequently than the 218 and deposits you closer to the catacombs, but there's no service on Sundays. If you are in a hurry to accommodate your visit to the catacombs, take a cab (p. 44).

Riding bikes along the Appian Way.

Catacombe di San Callisto (Catacombs of St. Callixtus) ★★ RELIGIOUS SITE/TOUR "The most venerable and most renowned of Rome," said Pope John XXIII of these funerary tunnels. These catacombs are often packed with tour-bus groups, but the tunnels are phenomenal. They're the first cemetery of Christian Rome, burial place of 16 popes in the 3rd century. They bear the name of the deacon St. Callixtus, who served as pope from A.D. 217–22. The network of galleries is on four levels and reaches a depth of about 20m (65 ft.), the deepest in the area. There are many sepulchral chambers and almost half a million tombs of early Christians.

Entering the catacombs, you see the most important crypt, that of nine popes. Some of the original marble tablets of their tombs are preserved. Also commemorated is St. Cecilia, patron of sacred music (her relics were moved to her church in Trastevere during the 9th c.; see p. 123). Farther on are the Cubicles of the Sacraments, with 3rd-century frescoes.

Via Appia Antica 110–26. www.catacombe.roma.it. ✆ **06/5130151.** 8€ adults, 5€ children ages 7–15. Thurs–Tues 9am–noon and 2–5pm. Closed late Jan to late Feb. Bus: 118 or 218.

Catacombe di Domitilla ★★★ RELIGIOUS SITE/TOUR The oldest of the catacombs is the hands-down winner for most enjoyable experience. Groups are relatively small (in part because the site is not directly on the Appian Way), and guides are entertaining and personable. The catacombs—Rome's longest at 17km (11 miles)—were built below land donated by Domitilla, a noblewoman of the Flavian dynasty who was exiled from Rome for practicing Christianity. They were rediscovered in 1593, after a church abandoned in the 9th century collapsed. The visit begins in the sunken church founded in A.D. 380, the year Christianity became Rome's state religion. There are fewer "sights" here than in the other catacombs, but this is the only catacomb where you'll still see bones; the rest have emptied their tombs to rebury the remains in inaccessible lower levels. Elsewhere in the tunnels, 4th-century frescoes contain some of the earliest representations of Saints Peter and Paul. Notice the absence of crosses: It was only later that Christians replaced the traditional fish symbol with the cross. During this period, Christ's crucifixion was a source of shame to the community. He had been killed like a common criminal.

Via delle Sette Chiese 282. www.domitilla.info. ℗ **06/5110342.** 8€ adults, 5€ children ages 6–14. Wed–Mon 9am–noon and 2–5pm. Closed mid-Dec to mid-Jan. Bus: 714 (to Piazza dei Navigatori) or 118 or 218.

Catacombe di San Sebastiano (Catacombs of St. Sebastian) ★
RELIGIOUS SITE/TOUR   Today the tomb and relics of St. Sebastian are in the ground-level basilica, but his original resting place was in the catacombs beneath it. Sebastian was a senior Milanese soldier in the Roman army who converted to Christianity and was martyred during Emperor Diocletian's persecutions, which were especially brutal in the first decade of the 4th century. From the reign of Valerian to that of Constantine, the bodies of Saints Peter and Paul were also hidden in the catacombs, which were dug from the soft volcanic rock *(tufa)*. The church was built in the 4th century and remodeled in the 17th century. In the tunnels and mausoleums are mosaics and graffiti, along with many other pagan and Christian objects, as well as four Roman tombs with their frescoes and stucco fairly intact, found in 1922 after being buried for almost 2,000 years.

Via Appia Antica 136. www.catacombe.org. ℗ **06/7850350.** 8€ adults, 5€ children 6–15. Mon–Sat 10am–4:30pm. Closed Dec. Bus: 118 or 218.

Especially for Kids

There's a real Jekyll and Hyde quality to exploring Rome with kids. On the one hand, it's a capital city, big, busy, and hot, and with dodgy public transportation. On the other, the very best parts of the city for kids—Roman ruins, subterranean worlds, and *gelato*—are aspects you'd want to explore anyway. Seeing Rome with kids doesn't demand an itinerary redesign. And despite what you have heard about its famous seven hills, much of the center is mercifully flat, and pedestrian-friendly. Food is pretty easy too: Roman **pizzas** are some of the best in the world—see "Where to Eat" (p. 68) for our favorites. Ditto the ice cream, or *gelato* (p. 68). Restaurants in any price category will be happy to serve up a simple *pasta al pomodoro* (pasta with tomato sauce), and kids are welcomed virtually everywhere, including late in the evening.

The city is shorter on green spaces than many European cities, but the landscaped gardens of the **Villa Borghese** have plenty of space for kids to let off steam. Pack a picnic or rent some bikes (p. 117). The **Parco Appia Antica** (www.parcoappiaantica.it) is another favorite, especially on a Sunday or holiday when the old cobbled road is closed to traffic. The park's **Catacombs** (p. 126) are eerie enough to satisfy young minds, but also fascinating Christian and historical sites in their own right.

ORGANIZED tours

Forget the flag-waving guides leading a herd of dazed travelers around monuments. A better class of professionally guided tours delivers insider expertise, focused themes, and personal attention, plus perks such as skipping entry lines and visiting after hours.

One of the leading tour operators in Rome, **Context Travel** ★ (www.context travel.com; ⓒ **800/691-6036** in the U.S., or 06/96727371) uses local scholars—historians, art historians, archaeologists—to lead small-group walking tours around Rome's monuments, museums, and historic piazzas, as well as culinary walks and excellent family programs. Custom-designed tours are also available. Tour prices are high, beginning at about 90€ for 2 hours, but most participants consider them a highlight of their trip.

The affable team at **The Roman Guy** (www.theromanguy.com, ⓒ **06/342-8761859**) provides knowledgeable guides who explain thousands of years of history in an engaging, informal way. They offer small-group (most about 10 people) tours of the Colosseum (including dungeons), Vatican Museums, Catacombs, and food tours of Trastevere, among other options. Prices run from 54€ per person to much more for exclusive VIP access and/or private excursions.

Eating Italy (www.eatingitalyfood tours.com) offers in-depth small-group food and wine tours in Rome, particularly of Testaccio and Trastevere. Guides connect Rome's culinary culture to the city's

history and traditions, and guests leave with their curiosity (and hunger) sated. Tours from 59€.

Walks of Italy (www.walksofitaly.com; ⓒ **06/95583331**) also runs excellent guided tours of Rome starting from 39€; more in-depth explorations of the Colosseum, Vatican Museums, and Forum go for 55€ to 125€.

Enjoy Rome (www.enjoyrome.com; ⓒ **06/4451843**) offers a number of "greatest hits" walking tours, plus an early-evening tour of the Jewish Ghetto and Trastevere; their bus excursion to the Catacombs and Appian Way visits an ancient aqueduct that most Romans, let alone tourists, never see. Tours cost 30€ to 60€ per person; entrance fees are included with some, but not all tours.

The team at **Through Eternity** (www. througheternity.com; ⓒ **06/7009336**) are art historians and architects; what sets them apart is their theatrical delivery, helped along by the dramatic scripts that many of the guides follow. It can be a lot of fun, but it's not for everyone. A 5-hour tour of the Vatican is 69€; most other tours range from 39€ to 119€.

For something completely different, artist Kelly Medford runs **Sketching Rome Tours** (www.sketchingrometours. com), 3-hour small group drawing and painting lessons in some of Rome's prettiest corners. Supplies are provided and no artistic talent is required (95€ per person).

Museums, of course, are trickier, though my 6-year-old was recently enthralled by several galleries of gory Renaissance paintings depicting biblical murders and sacrifices. You can probably get kids fired up more easily for the really ancient stuff. Make the bookshop at the **Colosseum** (p. 98) an early stop; it has a good selection of guides aimed at under-12s, themed on gladiators and featuring funny or cartoonish material. The **Musei Capitolini** (p. 96) invites kids to hunt down the collection's treasures highlighted on a free leaflet—it'll buy you a couple of hours to admire the exhibits and perhaps see them from a new and unexpected angle, too. The multiple levels below **San Clemente** (p. 104) and the **Case Romane del Celio** (p. 105) are another draw for small visitors. Aspiring young gladiators may want to spend 2 hours at the **Scuola Gladiatori Roma (Rome Gladiator School),** where they can prepare for a duel in a reasonably authentic way. You can book through **Viator.com.**

Kids will also likely enjoy some of the cheesier city sights—at the very least these will make some good family photos to share on Facebook or Instagram. Build in some time to place your hands in the Bocca della Verità, at **Santa Maria in Cosmedin** (p. 106), to throw a coin in the **Trevi Fountain** (p. 116), and to enjoy watching the feral cats relaxing amid the ruins of **Largo di Torre Argentina.** A cat sanctuary here provides basic healthcare to Rome's many strays.

If you want to delve deeper into the city as a family, check out the tours on **Context Travel**'s family program (see "Organized Tours," p. 129). The 2- to 3-hour tours are pricey (300€–425€ per family) but first-rate, and you will have the docent all to yourselves.

ROME SHOPPING

While Rome's status as a shopping capital is somewhat eclipsed by fashion mecca Milan, it's still a magnet for high-end shoppers, foodies, and lovers of antiques. In our limited space below we've summarized streets and areas known for their shops. Keep in mind that the monthly rent on the famous streets is very high, and those costs are passed on to you. Note that **sales** usually run twice a year, in January and July.

The Top Shopping Streets & Areas

AROUND PIAZZA DI SPAGNA Most of Rome's haute couture and seriously upscale shopping fans out from the bottom of the Spanish Steps. **Via Condotti** is probably Rome's poshest shopping street, where you'll find Prada, Gucci, Bulgari, and the like. A few more down-to-earth stores have opened, but it's still largely a playground for the super-rich. Neighboring **Via Borgognona** is another street where the merchandise is chic and ultra-expensive, but thanks to its pedestrian-only access and handsome baroque and neoclassical facades, it offers a nicer window-browsing experience. Shops are more densely concentrated on **Via Frattina,** the third member of this trio of upscale streets. Chic boutiques for adults and kids rub shoulders with ready-to-wear fashions, high-end chains, and a few tourist tat vendors. It's usually crowded with shoppers who appreciate the lack of motor traffic.

VIA COLA DI RIENZO The commercial heart of the Prati neighborhood, this long, straight street runs from the Tiber to Piazza Risorgimento and is known for stores selling a variety of merchandise at reasonable prices—from jewelry to fashionable clothing, bags, and shoes. Among the most prestigious is the historic Roman perfume store (with products for men and women), **Bertozzini Profumeria dal 1913,** at no. 192 (✆ **06/6874662**). The department store **Coin** is at no. 173 (with a large supermarket in the basement), the largest branch of venerable gourmet food store **Castroni** at no. 196 (www.castroni. it), and the smaller, more selective gourmet grocery **Franchi** at no. 200 (www. franchi.it).

VIA DEL CORSO   With less of a glamour quotient (and less stratospheric prices) than Via Condotti or Via Borgognona, Via del Corso boasts affordable styles aimed at younger consumers. Occasional gems are scattered amid international shops selling jeans and sports equipment. The most interesting stores are toward the Piazza del Popolo end of the street (**Via del Babuino** here has a similar profile). The farther south you walk (towards the Vittoriano monument), the narrower the sidewalks—and generally, the tackier the stores. *Tip:* If you are shopping with young children, it's useful to know that the upper part of Via del Corso (from Piazza Colonna to Piazza del Popolo) is largely car-free, save for taxis.

VIA DEI CORONARI   An antique-lover's souk. If you're shopping, or just window-shopping for antiques or vintage-style souvenir prints, then spend an hour walking the length of this pretty, pedestrian-only street.

CAMPO DE'FIORI   Though the campo itself is now chockablock with restaurants, the streets leading up to it, notably **Via dei Giubbonari** and **Via Dei Baullari,** offer edgy and often one-of-a-kind fashions. Boutiques go in and out of business with dizzying frequency, but something interesting is always popping up.

VIA MARGUTTA   This beautiful, tranquil street is home to numerous art stalls and artists' studios—Federico Fellini used to live here—though all the stores tend to offer the same sort of antiques and mediocre paintings these days. You have to shop hard to find real quality. Highlights include **Bottega del Marmoraro** at no. 53b, the studio of master stonecarver Sandro Fiorentini, and **Saddlers Union** (at no. 11; www.saddlersunion.com) for exquisite handmade leather items.

MONTI   Rome's most fashion-conscious central neighborhood has a pleasing mix of artisan retailers, vintage boutiques, and honest, everyday stores frequented by locals, with not a brand name in sight. Roam the length of **Via del Boschetto** for one-off fashions, designer ateliers, and unique homewares. In fact, you can roam in every direction from the spot where Via del Boschetto meets **Via Panisperna.** Turn on nearby **Via Urbana** or **Via Leonina,** where boutiques jostle for space with cafes that are ideal for a break or light lunch. Via Urbana also hosts the weekend **Mercatomonti** (see "Rome's Best Markets," below).

Rome's Best Markets

Campo de' Fiori ★   Central Rome's food market has been running since at least the 1800s. It's no longer the place to find a produce bargain (though the fruit and veg displays are dazzling and colorful) and it tends to attract more tourists than locals, but it's still a genuine slice of Roman life in one of its most attractive squares. The market runs Monday through Saturday 7am to 1 or 2pm. Campo de' Fiori. No phone. Bus: H, 40, 46, 62-64, 280, 780. Tram: 8.

Eataly ★ Remember how cool the Hard Rock Café was when there was just *one* of them? Now that branches of Eataly, the mega-grocery store devoted to Italian food, have opened around the world, some of the novelty has been lost. For lovers of the brand, this four-floor homage to all things Italiano is a must-see, must-shop experience. Still, for foodie souvenirs to carry home, we prefer to buy from small local shops. *Tip:* Eataly is great for filling a gourmet picnic basket on your way out to Ostia Antica or Tivoli (see p. 139). Piazzale XII Ottobre 1492 (at Ostiense train station). www.roma.eataly.it. ✆ **06/90279201.** Metro: Piramide.

Mercatomonti ★★ Everything from contemporary glass jewelry to vintage cameras, handmade clothes for kids and adults, and one-off designs are sold here in the heart of trendy Monti, in a commandeered parking garage (where else?). The market runs Saturdays and Sundays 10am to 8pm. Via Leonina 46. www.mercatomonti.com. No phone. Metro: Cavour.

Nuovo Mercato di Testaccio (New Testaccio Market) ★★★ Traditional food and produce stalls meet street food central in this modernist, sustainably powered market building. It's not just the best place to go produce shopping, but a terrific stop for a lunch of *suppli* (fried rice balls) and craft beer (at **Food Box** ★★, Box 66), meat and sauce-stuffed panini (at **Mordi e Vai** ★★, Box 15, www.mordievai.it), or an espresso and something sweet from **Chicchi e Lettere** ★ (Box 43). There are also clothes and kitchenware stalls, but the food is the star. The market runs Monday through Saturday 7am to 3:30pm. Btw. Via Luigi Galvani and Via Aldo Manuzio (at Via Benjamin Franklin). www.mercatoditestaccio.it. No phone. Metro: Piramide. Bus: 83, 673, 719.

Porta Portese ★ Trastevere's vast weekly flea market stretches all the way from the Porta Portese gate along Via di Porta Portese to Viale di Trastevere. You have to wade through a lot of junk (and a sea of humanity—hold tight to your belongings), but there are good stalls for vintage housewares, clothing, and collectibles. It runs Sundays from dawn until midafternoon. Via di Porta Portese. No phone. Tram: 8.

ENTERTAINMENT & NIGHTLIFE

Several English-language outlets offer current information about nightlife and cultural events in the Eternal City. *Wanted in Rome* (www.wantedinrome. com) has listings of opera, rock, English-language cinema showings, and such and gives an insider look at expat Rome. **Un Ospite a Roma** (www.unospite-aroma.it) offers comprehensive details on cultural events and kid-friendly pursuits. *Romeing* (www.romeing.it) is worth consulting, especially for contemporary arts and culture.

Unless you're dead set on making the Roman nightclub circuit, try what might be a far livelier and less expensive option—sitting late into the evening

When the sun goes down, Rome's palaces, ruins, fountains, and monuments are bathed in a theatrical white light. During your stay in Rome, be sure to make time for a memorable evening stroll past the solemn pillars of old temples or the cascading torrents of Renaissance fountains glowing under the blue-black sky.

The **Fountain of the Naiads** ("Fontana delle Naiadi") on Piazza della Repubblica, the **Fountain of the Tortoises** ("Fontana della Tartarughe") on Piazza Mattei, the **Fountain of Acqua Paola** ("Fontanone") at the top of the Janiculum Hill, and the **Trevi Fountain** (p. 116) are particularly beautiful at night. The **Capitoline Hill** (or Campidoglio) is magnificently lit after dark, with its Renaissance facades glowing like jewel boxes. The view of the Roman Forum seen from the rear of Piazza del Campidoglio is perhaps the grandest in Rome (see "Three Free Views to Savor for a Lifetime," p. 100). If you're across the Tiber, the Vatican's **Piazza San Pietro** (p. 87) is impressive at night without the crowds. The combination of illuminated architecture, baroque fountains, and sidewalk shows makes **Piazza Navona** (p. 107) even more delightful at night.

on **Piazza della Rotonda** (the Pantheon), **Piazza del Popolo,** or one of Rome's other piazzas, all for the (admittedly inflated) cost of an espresso or a Campari and soda. If you're a clubber who likes it loud and late, jump in a cab to **Monte Testaccio** or **Via del Pigneto** and bar-hop wherever takes your fancy. In Trastevere, there's always a bit of life on **Via Politeana** where it meets **Piazza Trilussa.** In the *centro storico,* a nice *aperitivo-cena* scene unfolds along **Via del Governo Vecchio.**

Performing Arts & Live Music

Rome's music scene doesn't have the same vibrancy as Florence's (p. 206), nor the high-quality opera of Milan's **La Scala** or **La Fenice** in Venice (p. 268). Still, classical music fans are well catered to here. In addition to the major venues featured below, be on the lookout for concerts and one-off events in churches and salons around the city. Check **www.operainroma.com** for a calendar of opera and ballet staged by the Opera in Roma association at enchanting venues across the city. The **Pontificio Instituto di Musica Sacra,** Piazza Sant'Agostino 20A (www.musicasacra.va; ℂ **06/6638792**), and **All Saints' Anglican Church,** Via del Babuino 153 (www.accademiadoperaitaliana.it; ℂ **06/7842702**), both regularly run classical music and operatic evenings.

Alexanderplatz Jazz Club ★ Alexanderplatz has been the home of Rome's jazz scene since the early 1980s. If there's a good act in the city, you will find it here. Via Ostia 9. www.alexanderplatzjazzclub.com. ℂ **06/39742171.** Cover usually 10€. Metro: Ottaviano. Bus: 23, 70, 492, 913, 990.

Auditorium–Parco della Musica ★★ This exciting multipurpose center for the arts, designed by Renzo Piano, brings a refreshing breath of modernity to Rome. The schedule features lots of aging rockers and eclectic

4

ROME | Entertainment & Nightlife

133

singer-songwriter acts, as well as traditional orchestras. Great cafes and a bookstore on-site, too. Viale Pietro de Coubertin 30. www.auditorium.com. ℂ **06/80241281.** Bus: 53, 168, 910, 982. Tram: 2.

Teatro dell'Opera di Roma ★★ Here you'll find marquee operas such as *La Traviata, Carmen,* and *Tosca;* classical concerts from top-rank orchestras; and such ballets as *Giselle, Swan Lake,* and *The Nutcracker.* In summer the action moves outdoors for unforgettable open-air operatic performances at the ruined **Baths of Caracalla** (p. 95). Piazza Beniamino Gigli 1 (at Via del Viminale). www. operaroma.it. ℂ **06/4817003** (box office). Tickets 25€–150€. Metro: Repubblica.

Cafes

Remember: In Rome and everywhere else in Italy, if you just want to drink a quick coffee and bolt, walk up to *il banco* (the bar), order *"un caffè, per favore"* or *"un cappuccino,"* and don't move. They will make it for you to drink on the spot. It will usually cost more (at least double) to sit down to drink it (if you're in high-traffic, touristy areas—which you'll most likely be!), and outdoor table service is the most expensive way to go. Even in the heart of the city center, a short coffee *al banco* should cost no more than 1€; add around .30€ for a *cappuccino.* Expect to pay up to five times that price if you sit outdoors on a marquee piazza. Most cafes in the city serve a decent cup of coffee, but here's a small selection of places worth hunting down.

   Sant'Eustachio il Caffè ★★ (Piazza Sant'Eustachio 82; www.santeustachioilcaffe.it; ℂ **06/68802048**) roasts its own Fair Trade Arabica beans and draws a friendly crowd a few deep at the bar. (Unless you ask, the coffee comes with sugar.) Debate still rages among Romans as to whether the city's best cup of coffee is served at Sant'Eustachio or **Tazza d'Oro ★**, near the Pantheon (Via degli Orfani 84; www.tazzadorocoffeeshop.com; ℂ **06/6789792**). Jacketed baristas work at 100mph at **Spinelli ★** (Via dei Mille 60; ℂ **06/31055552**), a no-nonsense locals' cafe.

Wine Bars, Cocktail Bars & Craft Beer Bars

For Rome's most creative modern cocktails in a casual environment, visit **Caffè Propaganda** (p. 71).

Ai Tre Scalini ★ This little *bottiglieria* (wine bar) is the soul of Monti. There's a traditional menu, as well as a wine list sourced from across Italy. Arrive early or call for a table: This place is usually jammed. Via Panisperna 251. ℂ **06/48907495.** Metro: Cavour.

Bar del Fico ★ With its shabby-chic interior and namesake fig tree backdrop to charming outdoor seating, this is one of Rome's most beloved *aperitivo* spots, with a see-and-be-seen cachet. Piazza del Fico 26. www.bardelfico.com. ℂ **06/6880-8413.** Bus: 30, 40, 46, 62, 64, 70, 916.

Barnum Café ★★ An honest-to-goodness cocktail bar (with wine and crafts beers to boot), Barnum draws a grown-up crowd getting mellowly buzzed—making it a nice alternative to the nighttime antics at Campo de'Fiori. It's also a good morning stop for caffè and cornetti. Via del Pellegrino 87. www.barnumcafe.com. ℓ **06/64760483.** Bus: 40, 46, 62, 64, 916.

Bir and Fud ★ Around 15 beers on tap (most of them Italian craft brews, some as strong as 9%) as well as carb-heavy snacks like pizza and *supplì* (fried rice balls). It's 5€ for a small beer. Via Benedetta 23. www.birandfud.it. ℓ **06/5894016.** Bus: 23, 280.

Cavour 313 ★★ A wine bar that's as traditional and genuine as you will find this close to the ancient ruins serves over 30 wines by the glass (from 3.50€) as well as cold cuts, cheese, and vegetable platters, or excellent carpaccio. Closed Sunday in summer. Via Cavour 313. www.cavour313.it. ℓ **06/6785496.** Metro: Colosseo and Cavour.

Ex Circus ★ This convivial hub for digital nomads, hungry tourists on a budget and aperitivo drinkers seeking an ample spread is just a few blocks from Piazza Navona. They also do a great Sunday brunch. Via della Vetrina 15. ℓ **06/97619258.** Bus: 30, 70, 81, 87, 492, 628.

Freni e Frizioni ★★ Trastevere's "Brakes and Clutches" is a former mechanics garage turned nighttime hot spot, with an ethnic-inflected *aperitivo* spread (think curried risotto). On the adjacent square, an effervescent crowd lounges against stone walls and parked *motorini*. Via del Politeama 4–6 (near Piazza Trilussa). www.freniefrizioni.com. ℓ **06/45497499.** Bus: 23, 280, or H. Tram: 8.

La Bottega del Caffè ★ Beers, wine, cocktails, *aperitivo*—there's a little of everything at one of Monti's busiest neighborhood bars. Piazza Madonna dei Monti 5. ℓ **06/64741578.** Metro: Cavour.

Litro ★★ This wine bar in Monteverde Vecchio (a residential area above Trastevere) serves natural wines, cocktails, and snacks sourced from Lazio-based purveyors of cured meats and cheeses, plus bruschetta and stellar alcoholic sorbets. An entire menu is devoted to mezcal, tequila's smoky cousin. Via Fratelli Bonnet 5. www.vinerialitro.it. ℓ **06/45447639.** Bus: 75, 982.

Aperitivo Culture

The mass social phenomenon of the *aperitivo* (happy hour) can be a great way to meet, or at least observe the particular ways of, real Romans. It started in hard-working northern cities like Milan, where you'd go to a bar after leaving the office and, for the price of one drink, get access to an unlimited buffet of high-quality food—often with cheese, cured meats, bruschetta, and pasta salad. Luckily for Rome, the custom trickled down here, and now the city is filled with casual little places to drop in for a drink (from 6 or 7pm onward) and eat to your heart's content. *Aperitivo* spreads vary in quantity and quality, but generally you'll pay less than 10€ per person for a drink and buffet. All the places listed here are fine for families, too—Italian kids love *aperitivo* (minus the alcohol)! Look for signs in the window and follow your nose. The **Monti** neighborhood is a good place to begin. The **Terre e Domus della Provincia Romana** (p. 72) also does good *aperitivo*.

Open Baladin ★★   If anyone ever tells you "Italians don't do good beer," send them to this bar near the Ghetto. A 40-long row of taps lines the bar, with beers from their own Piedmont brewery and across Italy. Via degli Specchi 5–6. www.openbaladin.com. ℰ **06/6838989.** Tram: 8.

Salotto42 ★★   It's all fancy cocktails and well-chosen wines at this über-hip "bookbar" set opposite the columned facade of 2nd-century Hadrian's Temple (near the Pantheon). This makes for a classy after-dinner stop. It also does shared plates, fresh juices, smoothies, and infused teas. Piazza di Pietra 42 (off Via del Corso). www.salotto42.it. ℰ **06/6785804.** Bus: 51, 62, 63, 80, 83, 85, 117, 160, 492, 628.

Stravinskij Bar ★   An evening at this award-winning cocktail bar inside one of Rome's most famous grand hotels is always a regal affair. Mixology, ingredients, and canapés are all topnotch. Inside Hotel de Russie, Via del Babuino 9. ℰ **06/32888874.** Metro: Spagna.

DAY TRIPS FROM ROME

By Elizabeth Heath

I f you only have 3 days or so, you will probably want to spend them in Rome itself. But if you are here for a week— or on your second visit to Rome—head out of the city to see some of the ruins, old towns, and ancient villas that lie beyond, for a true all-around Roman experience.

OSTIA ANTICA ★★

24km (15 miles) SW of Rome

The ruins of Rome's ancient port are a must-see for anyone who can't make it to Pompeii (see p. 141). It's an easier daytrip on a similar theme: the chance to wander around the preserved ruins of an ancient Roman settlement that has been barely touched since its abandonment.

Ostia, at the mouth of the Tiber, was the port of Rome, serving as the gateway for riches from the far corners of the Empire. Founded in the 4th century B.C., it became a major port and naval base under two later emperors, Claudius and Trajan. A prosperous city developed, full of temples, baths, theaters, and patrician homes.

Ostia flourished between the 1st and 3rd centuries and survived until around the 9th century before it was abandoned. Gradually it became little more than a malaria bed, a buried ghost city that faded into history. A papal-sponsored commission launched a series of digs in the 19th century; however, the major work of unearthing was carried out under Mussolini's orders from 1938 to 1942. The city is only partially dug out today, but it's believed that all the chief monuments have been uncovered. There are quite a few impressive ruins—this is no dusty field like the Circus Maximus.

Note: Ostia is a mostly flat site, but the Roman streets underfoot are all clad in giant basalt cobblestones—wear comfortable walking shoes.

Essentials

ARRIVING   Take the Metro to Piramide, changing lines there for the Lido train to Ostia Antica. (From the platform, take the "Air Terminal" exit and turn right at the top of the steps, where the station name changes to Porta San Paolo.) Departures to Ostia are

5

about every half-hour; the trip takes 25 minutes and is included in the price of a Metro single-journey ticket or Roma Pass (see p. 44). It's just a 5-minute walk to the excavations from the Metro stop: Exit the station, walk ahead and over the footbridge, and then continue straight ahead until you reach the car park. The ticket booth is to the left.

VISITOR INFORMATION   The site opens daily at 8:30am. Closing times vary seasonally, ranging from 7:15pm in high season (Apr–Aug) to 4:30pm off-season (Nov–Feb 15); check at **www.ostiaantica.beniculturali.it** or call ℂ **06/5635-0215.** The ticket office closes 1 hour before the ruins close. Admission costs 10€, free for ages 17 and under and 65 and over. The inexpensive map on sale at the ticket booth is a wise investment.

PARKING   The car park, on Viale dei Romagnoli, costs 2.50€ per day, but it is fairly small. Arrive early if you're driving.

Exploring Ostia Antica

The principal monuments are all labeled. On arrival, visitors first pass the *necropoli* (burial grounds, always outside the city gates in Roman towns and cities). The main route follows the giant cobblestones of the **Decumanus ★** (the main street) into the heart of Ostia. The **Piazzale delle Corporazioni ★★** is like an early version of Wall Street: This square contained nearly 75 corporations, the nature of their businesses identified by the patterns of preserved mosaics. Nearby, Greek dramas were performed at the **Teatro,** built in the early days of the Empire. The theater as it looks today is the result of much rebuilding. Every town the size of Ostia had a **Forum ★**, and the layout is still intact: A well-preserved **Capitolium** (once the largest temple in Ostia) faces the remains of the 1st-century A.D. **Temple of Roma and Augustus.**

Amphitheater and mausoleum in Ostia Antica.

Elsewhere in the grid of streets are the ruins of the **Thermopolium ★★**, which was a bar; its name means "sale of hot drinks." An *insula* (a Roman block of apartments) remains, **Casa Diana ★**, with its rooms arranged around an inner courtyard. The **Terme di Nettuno ★** was a vast baths complex; climb the building at its entrance for an aerial view of its well-preserved mosaics. In addition, in the enclave is a **museum** displaying Roman statuary along with fragmentary frescoes.

Where to Eat

There is no real need to eat by the ruins—a half-day here should suffice, and Ostia is within easy reach of the abundant restaurants of Rome's city center. The obvious alternative is a picnic; the well-stocked foodie magnet **Eataly** (see p. 132) is only a couple of minutes from the Lido platform at Piramide Metro station, making it easy to grab provisions when you make the Metro interchange. There are perfect picnic spots beside fallen columns or old temple walls. If you crave a sit-down meal, trattoria **Allo Sbarco di Enea,** Viale dei Romagnoli 675 (℮ **06/5650034**), is right outside the archaeological park. There's also a snack and coffee bar at the site.

TIVOLI & THE VILLAS ★★

32km (20 miles) E of Rome

Perched high on a hill east of Rome, Tivoli is an ancient town that has always been something of a retreat from the city. In Roman times it was known as Tibur, a retirement town for the wealthy; later during the Renaissance, it again became the playground of the rich, who built their country villas out here. You need a full day to do justice to the gardens and villas that remain—especially if the Villa Adriana is on your list, as indeed it should be—so set out early.

Essentials

ARRIVING Tivoli is 32km (20 miles) east of Rome on Via Tiburtina, about an hour's drive with traffic (the Rome–L'Aquila *autostrada,* A24, is usually faster). If you don't have a car, take Metro Line B to Ponte Mammolo. After exiting the station, transfer to a **Cotral bus** for Tivoli (www.cotralspa.it). Cotral buses depart every 15 to 30 minutes during the day. Villa d'Este is in Tivoli itself, close to the bus stop; to get to Villa Adriana you need to catch a regional bus from town.

Exploring Tivoli & the Villas

Villa Adriana (Hadrian's Villa) ★★★ HISTORIC SITE/RUINS Globe-trotting Emperor Hadrian spent the last 3 years of his life in grand style. Less than 6km (3¾ miles) from Tivoli, between 118 and 134 A.D. he built one of the greatest estates ever conceived, filling acre after acre with architectural wonders he'd seen on his travels. Hadrian erected theaters, baths, temples, fountains, gardens, and canals, filling palaces and temples with sculpture, some of which now rest in the museums of Rome. In later centuries, barbarians, popes, and cardinals, as well as anyone who needed a slab of marble, carted off much that made the villa so spectacular. But enough of the fragmented ruins remain to inspire a real sense of awe.

The most outstanding remnant is the **Canopo ★★★**, a recreation of the Egyptian town of Canopus with its famous Temple of the Serapis. The ruins of a rectangular area, **Piazza d'Oro,** are still surrounded by a double portico. Likewise, the **Edificio con Pilastri Dorici (Doric Pillared Hall) ★** remains, with its pilasters with bases and capitals holding up a Doric architrave. The apse and the ruins of some magnificent vaulting are found at the **Grandi Terme** (Great Baths), while only the north wall remains of the **Pecile ★**, otherwise known as the *Stoà Poikile di Atene* or "Painted Porch," which Hadrian discovered in Athens and had had reproduced here. The best is saved for last—the **Teatro Marittimo ★★★**, a circular maritime theater in ruins, with its central building enveloped by a canal spanned by small swing bridges.

For a closer look at some of the items excavated, you can visit the museum on the premises and a visitor center near the villa parking area.

Largo Marguerite Yourcenar 1, Tivoli. www.villaadriana.beniculturali.it. ✆ **0774/312070.** 8€. Daily 9am–sunset (about 7:30pm in May–Aug, 5pm Nov–Jan, 6pm Feb, 6:30pm Mar and Oct, and 7pm Apr and Sept). Bus: 4 from Tivoli.

Villa d'Este ★★ PARK/GARDEN   Like Hadrian centuries before, Cardinal Ippolito d'Este of Ferrara ordered this villa built on a Tivoli hillside in the mid-16th century. The dank Renaissance structure, with its second-rate paintings, is not that interesting; the big draw for visitors is the **spectacular gardens ★★★**, designed by Pirro Ligorio. As you descend the cypress-studded garden slope you're rewarded with everything from lilies to gargoyles spouting water, torrential streams, and waterfalls. The loveliest fountain is the **Fontana dell Ovato ★★**, by Ligorio. But nearby is the most spectacular engineering achievement: the **Fontana dell'Organo Idraulico (Fountain of the Hydraulic Organ) ★★**, dazzling with its music and water jets in front of a baroque chapel, with four maidens who look tipsy (the fountain "plays" every 2 hr. from 10:30am). The moss-covered **Fontana dei Draghi (Fountain of the Dragons),** also by Ligorio, and the so-called **Fontana di Vetro (Fountain of Glass),** by Bernini, are also worth seeking out, as is the main promenade, lined with 100 spraying fountains. The garden is worth hours of exploration, but it involves a lot of walking, with some steep climbs.

Piazza Trento 5, Tivoli. www.villadestetivoli.info. ✆ **0774/312070.** 8€ Tues–Sun 8:30am to 1 hr. before sunset; Mon from 2pm. Bus: Cotral service from Ponte Mammolo (Roma–Tivoli); the bus stops near the entrance.

Villa Gregoriana ★ PARK/GARDEN   Villa d'Este dazzles with artificial glamour, but the Villa Gregoriana relies more on nature. Originally laid out by Pope Gregory XVI in the 1830s, its main highlight is the panoramic waterfall of Aniene, with the trek to the bottom studded with grottoes and balconies that open onto the chasm. The only problem is that if you do make the full descent, you might need a helicopter to pull you up again (the climb back up is fierce).

From one of the belvederes, there's a view of the **Temple of Vesta** on the hill.

Largo Sant'Angelo, Tivoli. www.visitfai. it/parcovillagregoriana. © **0774-332650.** 7€. Apr–Oct Tues–Sun 10am–6:30pm; Mar Tues–Sun 10am–5pm; Nov–Dec Tues–Sun 10am–4pm. Closed part of Dec and all of Jan–Feb. Bus: Cotral service from Ponte Mammolo (Roma–Tivoli); the bus stops near the entrance.

Where to Eat

Tivoli's gardens make for a pleasant picnic place (see **Eataly,** p. 132), but if you crave a sit-down meal, **Antica Trattoria del Falcone,** Via del Trevio 34 (© **0774/312358**), is a dependable option in Tivoli itself. Just off Largo Garibaldi, it's been open since 1918 and

Villa d'Este's Fountain of the Hydraulic Organ.

specializes in excellent pizza (ask for the pizza menu), Roman pastas, and roast meats. It is open daily for lunch and dinner.

POMPEII ★★★

240km (150 miles) SE of Rome

Italy's most famous archaeological site is the Disneyland of the ancient world. Not that there's anything shallow or ersatz about the extensive excavations of this coastal town on the Bay of Naples, where life stopped so abruptly on August 24, A.D. 79. No other ancient town has been brought to light so completely, providing an opportunity to step into a world locked in an ancient time. The 4–6m (13–20 ft.) of volcanic ash with which Mount Vesuvius buried the city preserved 44 hectares (109 acres) of shops, civic buildings, and private houses. Ever since 1748, archaeologists have worked to painstakingly uncover the town, and the ruins provide the vicarious thrill of sharing space with residents of a lively, ancient Roman port.

How many people were living in Pompeii at the time of the eruption is not known. The city had been rocked by a major earthquake in A.D. 62 that, along with fires caused by toppled oil lamps, destroyed temples, houses, and public works. Repairs were still underway in A.D. 79, though many of the city's 11,000 recorded inhabitants had probably resettled elsewhere. The unfortunate Pompeiians who remained behind are the most haunting presence at the site. The decaying bodies often left a mold inside the ash and lava that buried them. Excavators filled these empty spaces with plaster, and these eerie, life-like casts are perhaps the most affecting objects of the entire site.

By making a long day of it, you can visit the famous ruins from Rome without having to spend the night near Pompeii, where the modern city has little appeal. It's a 3½-hour drive from the capital, and even less by train. Count spending at least 4 or 5 hours wandering the site to do it justice. Pompeii can be crowded in the mornings, especially when tours arrive in force in July and August, but crowds thin out by early afternoon.

Remember also to take plenty of water with you as well as **sunscreen,** because there's not much shade anywhere among the ruins, and you'll be doing a lot of walking: Wear sturdy, comfortable shoes and a hat and/or sunglasses to shield your face/eyes/top of head from Pompeii's typically penetrating sun.

Essentials

ARRIVING   The best option is to take the Trenitalia "Frecciarossa" high-speed **train** from Termini to Naples (1 hr. 10 min.; from 40€ one-way), though InterCity trains are cheaper (around 28€) and take just over 2 hours—still doable if you start early. The first Frecciarossa usually departs around 7am. Once at Napoli Centrale (Naples Central Station), follow the signs to Napoli Piazza Garibaldi station downstairs, where you transfer to the **Campania Express** (www.eavsrl.it; © **800/211388** toll-free in Italy). Note that this railway is separate from Trenitalia, so you won't be able to buy a through ticket to Pompeii from Rome; just get a return to Naples and buy the Pompeii portion on arrival in Naples. Trains depart to Pompeii every half-hour from Piazza Garibaldi, but make sure you get on the train headed toward Sorrento and get off at Pompeii/Scavi (*scavi* means "archaeological dig"). If you get on the "Pompei" train (toward Poggiomarino), you'll end up in the town of Pompei—which is in a totally different place—and will have to double back to get to the ruins. A ticket costs about 3.50€ one-way; trip time is about 40 minutes. The excavations entrance is about 45m (150 ft.) from the station. **Circumvesuviana Express** trains (www.eavsrl.it; © **800/211388** toll-free in Italy) run along the line with service about 8 times a day from mid-March to mid-October, cutting the trip to Pompeii to 30 minutes.

To reach Pompeii by **car** from Rome, take the A1 *autostrada* toward Naples, then the A3 all the way to the signposted turnoff for the ruins just after the tollbooth—a straightforward and usually hassle-free drive.

TOURS   Consider letting someone else take care of the driving and logistics of a Pompeii trip. Plenty of tour operators run guided tours or transport to Pompeii from Rome. **Enjoy Rome** (www.enjoyrome.com; © **06/4451843**) runs a Pompeii shuttle bus on Tuesday, Thursday, and Saturday (Mar–Nov) at 7:30am from its office near the Cavour Metro station, arriving at the ruins at around 11am. You can wander around independently (a guide costs extra) before leaving at 3:30pm, to arrive back in Rome around 7pm). The shuttle costs 68€ (though you may find online specials) and does not include entrance fees. Most of the tour operators listed on p. 129 offer day trips to Pompeii, as does **Dark Rome** (www.darkrome.com), and some include brief stops in Naples or along the Amalfi Coast. Tours start at 138€.

VISITOR INFORMATION   Official infopoints (www.pompeiisites.org; ℂ **081/857-5111**) can be found at the Porta Marina, Piazza Esedra, and Piazza Anfiteatro entrances. Admission is 15€. Every first Sunday of the month, admission is free. The Pompeii excavations are open April through October, daily 9am to 7:30pm; November through March, daily 8:30am to 5:30pm. Last admission is 90 minutes before closing. The ticket office provides free maps and detailed booklets to guide you through the site. Inside the entrance, a **bookstore** sells additional guidebooks (available in English). You can rent an audio guide for 8€, 6.50€ for two people (but sharing is not a particularly good idea), with a kids' version for 5€.

PARKING   There is a parking lot at Pompeii, though it is quite small. If you plan on driving, get there early. The charge is 3€ per hour. *Tip:* Do not leave valuables in your rental car and if you have luggage aboard, keep it out of sight.

Exploring Pompeii

Pompeii covers a large area with a lot to see, so try to be selective. Note that many of the streets run through little more than stone foundations, and even some of the best-known buildings might be temporarily closed without notice. Decades of unchecked tourism traffic have damaged this fragile site, and in the past few years the government has had to halt some operations to compensate.

Enter through the impressive **Porta Marina** gate and head to the **Forum (Foro)** ★, a long, narrow, open space surrounded by the ruins of the **basilica** (the city's largest single structure), the **Temple of Apollo** ★★ (Tempio di Apollo), the **Temple of Jupiter** ★★ (Tempio di Giove), and the **Granai al Foro** ★ (Granary), where several plaster casts of Vesuvius's victims have been preserved.

Walk north along the Via di Mercurio to see some of Pompeii's most famous villas. The **Casa del Poeta Tragico** ★ (House of the Tragic Poet) contains some eye-catching mosaics, notably the CAVE CANEM ("Beware of the Dog") design by its main entrance. The vast **Casa del Fauno** ★★ (House of the Faun) features an amicable *"Ave"* ("welcome") mosaic and the copy of a tiny, bronze faun (the original is in Naples's Archaeological Museum). Nearby, the **Casa dei Vettii** ★★★ was the ultimate bachelor pad of the Vettii brothers, wealthy merchants. Its celebrated murals included an image of Priapus (the fertility god), resting his ludicrously oversized phallus on a pair of scales.

Keep walking beyond the old city walls to the northwest for the **Villa dei Misteri** ★★★, Pompeii's best-preserved villa, a 3rd-century B.C. mansion containing a series of stunning depictions of the Dionysiac initiation rites. The paintings are remarkably clear, bright, and richly colored after all these years.

Fresco in Pompei's Villa dei Misteri.

Walking to the eastern side of Pompeii from the Porta Marina, you'll pass the 5th-century B.C. **Teatro Grande ★**, well-preserved and still used for performances today. Continue west on Via dell'Abbondanza, passing the **Fullonica Stephanus** (a laundry with a large tiered washtub); and the **Casa della Venere in Conchiglia ★★** (House of the Venus in a Shell), named after the curious painting on its back wall. At the far eastern end of the town lies the **Anfiteatro ★★**, Italy's oldest amphitheater, dating from 80 B.C.

Where to Eat in Pompeii

To dine really well around Pompeii, you have to go into (and stay overnight in) Naples or Sorrento. If you're doing Pompeii as a day trip, skip the so-so restaurants around Pompeii itself and pack a picnic before you set off from Rome. If you need a quick bite, Pompeii has a cafeteria inside the archaeological zone that's handy for sandwiches and drinks.

FLORENCE

Florence may be small, but over the centuries it has packed a major punch in European history. Its center—which you can still easily cross on foot—still evokes this illustrious past, packed as it is with monuments from the city's golden age. In the 15th and 16th centuries, Florence's achievements in art and architecture, science, literature, and even banking, were unmatched—and the rest of Europe knew it.

This was the center of the Renaissance movement and the hometown of its leaders, Michelangelo, Brunelleschi, Leonardo da Vinci, Giotto, Galileo and others. Florence built up a store of riches that still dazzles today: the masterpiece-packed **Uffizi Gallery,** the ingenious domed Cathedral, Michelangelo's *David,* and any number of stunningly decorated halls, palaces and chapels. These treasures are still representative of the best humankind can achieve. And because of this, Florence remains a must-visit destination for every first-time traveler to Italy, and a must-return destination for anyone who cares about art and architecture.

STRATEGIES FOR SEEING FLORENCE

You want to make the most of your time in Florence, but also to get the most for your money, know the best ways to get around, and avoid hassles like long lines. The following essential strategies and hard-working tips will help you enrich your time and travels in Florence.

o **Avoid the lines.** If I was to give one single piece of advice to a friend visiting Florence, it would be this: **Book Uffizi and Accademia tickets in advance.** Reserving a timed entrance slot is relatively easy (see p. 146) and gets you into a *much* shorter line. Failing to book at the Uffizi, especially, could cost you a half-day in a queue. No joke. And your best (or only) chance of standing alone in front of a popular artwork is to enter at 8:15am.

o **Save on unnecessary booking fees.** Conversely, apart from the Uffizi, Accademia, and Brunelleschi's dome (where it's required; see p. 180), you won't need a timed admission slot anywhere else. Save the booking money.

o **Discount tickets.** Do you need one? The answer, unfortunately, is "it depends." To decide whether the 72€ **Firenze Card** is for you, see p. 149.

o **Walk.** Florence's tortuous one-way road system makes taxis expensive, and the city has no metro. Pack comfortable shoes and hit the streets on foot. *Note:* The hill up to Piazzale Michelangelo is fairly steep, however. If that sounds daunting, buses 12 and 13 go there.

o **Mondays.** Italian state museums are traditionally closed on Mondays, which means no Uffizi, no Pitti Palace, and no "David." Monday, then, is a good time to visit Florence's other sights, like the Palazzo Vecchio, Santa Maria Novella, and churches including the Duomo complex—all of which are open as usual. One caveat: With the big-hitters closed, other sights will inevitably be busier, so Mondays also make a perfect day-trip day; see chapter 7 for our recommended short trips outside the city.

o **Eat lunch and *aperitivo*; skip dinner.** Unless you have a huge appetite, you likely won't need three big meals a day. To save money, eat a full, late lunch, which is usually cheaper, and swap dinner for an *aperitivo* buffet. These are often generous and appear around 6:30pm at bars all over the city. Buy one drink and you can nosh as much as you like. Florentines even have a name for this: *apericena* (*cena* means "dinner").

o **First Sundays.** Like elsewhere in Italy, the first Sunday of every month is *#domenicalmuseo,* meaning admission to state-owned museums is free (note: this is not the same as *city*-owned). So, you can enter the Uffizi, Bargello, Medici Chapels, Pitti Palace, Boboli Garden, and more without paying a cent. The downside? Queues and crowds, of course—mostly of Italians taking advantage of the promotion. Forget the Uffizi, which is packed, and try your luck at others. The **tourist office** (see p. 148) has a full list. Obviously, if you are here for one day only and it's a first Sunday, do not buy a Firenze Card.

Essential: Reservations for the Uffizi, Accademia & More

As soon as you decide to visit Florence, make advance reservations for the Uffizi and the Accademia museums—it's the best way to avoid spending hours in line. (Buying a cumulative ticket— see "Discount Tickets for Florence," p. 149—is your other smart strategy for getting into the express queue.) Contact **Firenze Musei** (✆ **055/294-883;** Mon–Fri 8:30am–6:30pm, Sat until 12:30pm) at **www.firenzemusei.it**. There's a 4€ fee; you can pay by credit card. Reservations are also possible, but usually not necessary, for the Galleria Palatina in the Pitti Palace, the Bargello, and several others. If you arrive in Florence without reservations, you can also reserve in person at a kiosk in the facade of Orsanmichele, on Via dei Calzaiuoli (Mon–Sat); or at a desk inside the bookshop **Libreria My Accademia,** Via Ricasoli 105R (✆ **055/288-310**), almost opposite the Uffizi (open Tues–Sun). You can reserve, for the Uffizi only, at the Uffizi itself; do so at the teller window inside entrance number 2. The Uffizi's ticket collection point is across the piazza, at entrance number 3.

The Ponte Vecchio, seen from the banks of the River Arno.

ESSENTIALS

Arriving

BY PLANE   Most international travelers will reach Florence via the airports in Rome (see p. 42) or Milan, proceeding on to Florence via train (see below). There are also direct international flights into Pisa's **Galileo Galilei Airport** (see p. 297), 97km (60 miles) west of Florence; several budget airlines offer cheap flights here from other European cities. Around 14 daily **Autostradale** buses (www.airportbusexpress.it; ℰ **02/3008-9000**) connect downtown Florence direct with Pisa Airport in just over 1 hour (14€ adults; 7€ children 2–12). **Sky Bus Lines** (www.caronnatour.com) runs the same route, with the same prices, 6 times daily. Florence is also connected with Bologna Airport, by the **Appennino Shuttle** (www.appenninoshuttle.it; ℰ **055/5001-302**), which runs 10 times each day and takes between 80 and 90 minutes; tickets cost 25€, 10€ ages 5 to 10, free ages 4 and under. Buses arrive at and depart from Piazzale Montelungo, between Florence's Santa Maria Novella rail station and the Fortezza da Basso.

A few European airlines also serve Florence's **Amerigo Vespucci Airport** (www.aeroporto.firenze.it/en; ℰ **055/306-15** switchboard, 055/306-1300 for flight info), also called **Peretola,** just 5km (3 miles) northwest of town. **Busitalia**'s half-hourly **Vola in Bus** shuttles make the 20–30-minute trip between Florence airport and downtown's bus station at Via Santa Caterina da Siena 17 (www.fsbusitalia.it; ℰ **800/373760**), beside the train station; the cost is 6€ one-way, 10€ round-trip. Metered **taxis** line up outside the airport's arrival terminal and charge a flat rate of 22€ for the 15-minute journey to the city center (24€ on holidays, 25.30€ after 10pm; additional 1€ per bag). If you're in a group of three or four, it makes sense to take a cab.

BY TRAIN   Florence is Tuscany's rail hub, with regular connections to all of Italy's major cities. To get here from Rome or Milan, take Trenitalia's high-speed **Frecciarossa** or **Frecciargento** train (1½ hr.; www.trenitalia.com) or rival high-speed trains operated by **Italo** (www.italotreno.it). High-speed trains also run to Venice (2 hr.) via Bologna and Padua.

Most Florence-bound trains roll into **Stazione Santa Maria Novella,** Piazza della Stazione (www.firenzesantamarianovella.it), which you'll see abbreviated as **S.M.N.** The station is an architectural masterpiece, albeit one dating to Italy's Fascist period, rather than the Renaissance. It lies on the northwestern edge of the city's compact historic center, a 10-minute walk from the Duomo and a brisk 15-minute walk from Piazza della Signoria and the Uffizi.

BY CAR   The **A1 autostrada** runs north from Rome past Arezzo to Florence and continues to Bologna, and **unnumbered superhighways** run to and from Siena (the *SI-FI raccordo*) and Pisa (the so-called *FI-PI-LI*). To reach Florence from Venice, take the A13 southbound then switch to the A1 at Bologna.

Driving to Florence is easy; the problems begin once you arrive. Almost all cars are banned from the historic center for most of the day—only residents or merchants with permits are allowed to circulate freely around this large, camera-patrolled *zona a trafico limitato* (the "ZTL"). You can enter the ZTL to drop off baggage at your hotel or go direct to a prebooked parking garage (either can organize a temporary ZTL permit when provided with your license plate). Usual ZTL hours are Monday to Friday 7:30am to 8pm, Saturday 7:30am to 4pm. It's a real hassle, so only rent a car if you're leaving town to visit somewhere off the rail network.

If you do drive here, your best bet for overnight or longer-term parking is one of the city-run garages. The best deal—better than many hotels' garage rates—is at the **Parterre parking lot** under Piazza Libertà at Via Madonna delle Tosse 9 (© **055/5030-2209**). It's open round the clock and costs 2€ per hour, or 10€ for the first 24 hours, 15€ for the second, then 20€ per 24 hours thereafter; it's 70€ for up to a week's parking. Find more info on parking at **www.firenzeparcheggi.it**.

Don't park your car overnight on the street without local knowledge; if you're towed and ticketed, it will set you back substantially—and the headaches to retrieve a car are beyond description. If this happens to you, start by calling the vehicle removal department *(Recupero Veicoli Rimossi)* at © **055/422-4142.** One more reason **you should not drive in Florence.**

Visitor Information

TOURIST OFFICES   The closest office to the train station (© **055-212-245**) is opposite the terminus at Piazza della Stazione 5. With your back to the tracks, take the left exit, cross onto the concrete median, and bear right; it's

It may seem a little odd to label the **Firenze Card** (www.firenzecard.it) a "discount ticket," since it costs a substantial 72€. Is it a good buy? If you are planning a busy, museum-packed break here, the Firenze Card is a good value. If you only expect to see a few highlights, skip it.

For culture vultures out there, the card (valid for 72 hr.) allows one-time entrance to each of 60-plus sites; the list includes a handful that are free anyway, but also the Uffizi, Accademia, Cappella Brancacci, Palazzo Pitti, Brunelleschi's dome, San Marco, and many more. In fact, *everything* we recommend in this chapter is included in the price of the card, as well as some sites in Fiesole (p. 210). It gets you into much shorter lines, taking ticket pre-booking hassles out of the equation—and another saving of 3€ to 4€ for busy museums, above all the Uffizi and Accademia. The **Firenze-Card+** add-on (5€) includes up to 3 days' free bus travel (which you likely won't use) and free public Wi-Fi (which you might).

Don't buy a Firenze Card for anyone ages 17 and under: They can always enter via the express queue with you. Those under 17 gain free admission to civic museums (such as the Palazzo Vecchio) and pay only the "reservation fee" at state-owned museums (it's 4€ at the Uffizi, for example). Private museums and sights have their own payment rules, but it's very unlikely to add up to 72€ per child.

If you don't spring for the Firenze card, you'll need to buy the **Grande Museo del Duomo** ticket to visit any of the sites on the cathedral square. The joint ticket, which costs 18€, 3€ for children ages 6 to 11, and is valid for 72 hours, covers Brunelleschi's dome (including the now **obligatory** booking of a time slot), the Baptistery, Campanile di Giotto, the revamped Museo dell'Opera, and crypt excavations of Santa Reparata (inside the cathedral). In Florence, buy it at the ticket office almost opposite the Baptistery, on the north side of Piazza San Giovanni. See **www.ilgrandemuseodelduomo.it** for more details, to buy online ahead of arrival, and to book a time slot for the dome.

across the busy road junction ahead. Revamped in 2017, this office is usually open Monday through Saturday from 9am to 7pm and Sunday 9am to 2pm.

Another helpful office is under the Loggia del Bigallo on the corner of Piazza San Giovanni and Via dei Calzaiuoli (© **055-288-496**); it's also open Monday through Saturday 9am to 7pm, Sunday 9am to 2pm. Another office at Via Cavour 1R (www.firenzeturismo.it; © **055-290-832**), two blocks north of the Duomo, is open only Monday through Friday 9am to 1pm. There's also a central **phone number for tourist assistance:** © **055-000.** In all offices, the free map is good for navigation purposes; there's no need to upgrade to a paid version, especially if you are also navigating by smartphone.

WEBSITES The official Florence tourism website, **www.firenzeturismo.it**, contains lots of up-to-date city information. On the site's "Useful Information" section, you can download the latest opening hours for major city sights (tourist offices also supply a printout, or visit **http://pubblicazioni.provincia. fi.it/orario_musei/orario_musei.pdf**), as well as official city **apps,** maps, and a monthly events calendar. Most of the best-informed city **blogs** are

The address system in Florence has a split personality. Private homes, some offices, and hotels are numbered in black (or blue), but businesses, shops, and restaurants are numbered independently in red. (That's the theory anyway; in reality, the division between black and red numbers isn't so clear-cut.) The result is that 1, 2, 3 (black) addresses march up the block numerically oblivious to their 1R, 2R, 3R (red) neighbors. You might find the doorways on one side of a street numbered 1R, 2R, 3R, 1, 4R, 2, 3, 5R. The color codes occur only in the *centro storico* and other old sections of town; outlying districts didn't bother with this confusing system.

written in Italian by locals: **Io Amo Firenze** (www.ioamofirenze.it) is handy for reviews of eating and drinking spots. For one-off exhibitions and culture, **Art Trav** (www.arttrav.com) is an essential bookmark and written in English. The city itself maintains a more detailed events portal: **http://eventi.comune.fi.it**. Listings magazines are covered in the "Entertainment & Nightlife" section, p. 206. For updated Florence info, go to **www.frommers.com/destinations/florence**.

City Layout

Florence is a smallish city, sitting on the Arno River and petering out to olive-planted hills rather quickly to the north and south, but extending farther west and east along the Arno valley with suburbs and light industry. It has a compact center that is best negotiated on foot. No two major sights are more than a 25-minute walk apart, and most of the hotels and restaurants in this chapter are in the relatively small *centro storico* **(historic center),** a compact tangle of medieval streets and *piazze* (squares) where visitors spend most of their time. The bulk of Florence, including most of the tourist sights, lies north of the river, with the **Oltrarno,** an old working artisans' neighborhood, hemmed in between the Arno and the hills on the south side.

The Neighborhoods in Brief

The Duomo The area surrounding Florence's cathedral is as central as you can get. The Duomo itself is halfway between the two monastic churches of Santa Maria Novella and Santa Croce, as well as at the midpoint between the Uffizi Gallery and the Ponte Vecchio to the south, and San Marco and the Accademia (home of Michelangelo's "David") to the north. A medieval tangle of streets south of the Duomo head toward **Piazza della Signoria** (see below); southwest of the Duomo, **Piazza della Repubblica** lies in an even older part of town, still laid out in a Roman-era grid, though the piazza itself was heavily "modernized" in the 19th century.

The Duomo neighborhood is one of the most hotel-heavy parts of town, offering a range from luxury inns to student dives, but beware: Many hotels and restaurants here rely on location, rather than quality, for success.

Piazza della Signoria The city's civic heart is also prime territory for museum hounds: The Uffizi Gallery, Palazzo Vecchio, Bargello sculpture collection, and **Ponte Vecchio** are all nearby. A few blocks just north of the

Ponte Vecchio have reasonable shopping, but unappealing modern buildings, due to post-WWII reconstruction. The neighborhood can be stiflingly crowded in peak season—**Via Por Santa Maria** is one street to avoid—but in rare moments when it's empty of tour groups, its narrow medieval lanes remain the romantic heart of pre-Renaissance Florence. As in the Duomo neighborhood, be *very* choosy when picking a restaurant (or even an ice cream shop!) around here.

San Lorenzo & the Mercato Centrale Centered on the Medici's old family church of **San Lorenzo,** this wedge of streets between the train station and the Duomo is market territory. The vast indoor **Mercato Centrale** food market is here, along with the **San Lorenzo street market,** full of stalls hawking leather and other souvenirs. It's a colorful but hardly quiet area, with many budget hotels and good, affordable dining spots.

Piazza Santa Trínita This piazza sits just north of the river at the south end of Florence's shopping mecca, **Via de' Tornabuoni.** It's a quaint, well-to-do, and still medieval neighborhood, and if you're an upscale shopping fiend, there's no better place to be.

Santa Maria Novella Bounding the western edge of the *centro storico,* this neighborhood has two characters: an unattractive zone around the train station, and a nicer area south of it, between the church of Santa Maria Novella and the river. In general, the train station area noisy and lacks medieval atmosphere, but it does have more good budget options than any other quarter, especially along **Via Faenza** and its tributaries. Try to avoid staying on heavily trafficked **Via Nazionale.** The situation improves dramatically as you head south toward the river,

where **Piazza Santa Maria Novella** and its tributary streets have several stylish hotels.

San Marco & Santissima Annunziata On the northern edge of the *centro storico,* these two churches are fronted by *piazze*—**Piazza San Marco,** a busy transport hub, and **Piazza Santissima Annunziata,** the most architecturally unified square in the city. The neighborhood is home to Florence's university, the Accademia, the San Marco paintings of Fra' Angelico, and quiet streets with some hotel gems. It's not a bad walk from the heart of the action, but just far enough to escape tourist crowds.

Santa Croce Few tourists roam east beyond **Piazza Santa Croce,** so if you want to feel like a local, head here. The streets around the **Mercato di Sant'Ambrogio** have an appealing feel, and they get lively after dark, especially. **Via Pietrapiana** and the northern end of **Via de' Macci.** Some of the city's best restaurants and bars are in this area; *aperitivo* time is particularly vibrant along **Via de' Benci.**

The Oltrarno, San Niccolò & San Frediano "Across the Arno" is the artisans' neighborhood, still dotted with workshops. It began as a working-class neighborhood to catch the overflow from the medieval city on the opposite bank, and later became an area for aristocrats to build palaces with countryside views. The largest of these, the **Pitti Palace,** today houses a set of paintings second only to the Uffizi in scope. The Oltrarno's lively tree-shaded center, **Piazza Santo Spirito,** is lined with bars and close to some great restaurants and nightlife. West of here, the neighborhood of **San** Frediano gets ever more fashionable, and **San Niccolò,** at the foot of Florence's southern hills has popular bars. Oltrano's hotel range isn't great—but come here at night to eat and drink better, and at better prices, than in the *centro storico.*

Getting Around Florence

Florence is a **walking** city. You can stroll between the two top sights, Piazza del Duomo and the Uffizi, in 5 minutes or so. The hike from the most northerly major sights, San Marco and the Accademia, to the most southerly, the Pitti Palace across the Arno, should take no more than 30 minutes. From Santa

Maria Novella eastward to Santa Croce is a flat 20- to 30-minute walk. But beware: **Flagstones,** some of them uneven, are everywhere. Wear sensible shoes with good padding and foot support.

BY BUS & TRAM   You'll rarely need to use Florence's efficient **ATAF bus system** (www.ataf.net; ℡ **800/424-500** in Italy), since the city is so compact. Bus tickets cost 1.20€ and are good for 90 minutes, irrespective of how many changes you make. A 24-hour pass costs 5€, a 3-day pass 12€, and a 7-day pass 18€. Tickets are sold at *tabacchi* (tobacconists), automatic machines, some bars, and most newsstands. *Note:* Once on board, validate a paper ticket in the box near the rear door to avoid a steep fine. Since traffic is restricted in most of the center, buses make runs on principal streets only, except for four tiny electric bus lines (*bussini* services C1, C2, C3, and D) that trundle about the *centro storico.* The most useful lines to outlying areas are no. 7 (for Fiesole) and nos. 12 and 13 (for Piazzale Michelangelo). Buses run from 7am until 9 or 9:30pm daily, with a limited night service on a few key routes. **Tram** line T1 (www.gestramvia.com) runs until after midnight, connecting Santa Maria Novella station with the Opera di Firenze, Cascine Park, and Florence's southwestern suburbs. Lines T2 (to the airport) and T3 are under construction.

BY TAXI   Taxis aren't cheap, and with the city so small and the one-way system forcing drivers on convoluted routes, they aren't an economical way to get about. They're most useful to get you and your bags between the train station or airport and a hotel. It's 3.30€ to start the meter (which rises to 5.30€ on Sun; 6.60€ 10pm–6am), plus 1€ per bag or for a fourth passenger in the cab. There are taxi stands outside the train station, on Borgo San Jacopo, and in Piazza Santa Croce; otherwise, call **Radio Taxi SOCOTA** at ℡ **055/4242** or **Radio Taxi COTAFI** at ℡ **055/4390.** For the latest taxi information, see **www.4242.it**.

BY BICYCLE & SCOOTER   Florence is largely flat and increasingly closed to cars, and so is ideal for seeing on two wheels. Many of the bike-rental shops in town are located between San Lorenzo and San Marco. They include **Alinari,** Via San Zanobi 38R (www.alinarirental.com; ℡ **055/280-500**), which rents city bikes (2.50€ per hour; 12€ per day) and mountain bikes (3€ per hour; 18€ per day). It also hires out 125cc scooters (15€ per hour; 55€ per day). Another renter with similar prices is **Florence by Bike,** Via San Zanobi 54R (www.florencebybike.it; ℡ **055/488-992**). Make sure to use a lock (one will be provided with your rental): Bike theft is common. In 2017 global app-powered **bike-sharing** scheme **Mobike** (www.mobike.com) also launched in Florence. When you've downloaded the app, registered, and paid a 1€ deposit, you're free to rent in periods of up to 30 minutes (.50€). All payments are handled inside the app.

BY CAR   Trying to drive in the *centro storico* is a frustrating, useless exercise, and moreover, for most of the time unauthorized cars will be fined if they enter the limited traffic zone (ZTL). You need a permit to do anything beyond dropping off and picking up bags at your hotel. Park your vehicle in one of the underground lots on the center's periphery and pound the pavement. (See "By Car" under "Arriving," p. 147.)

[FastFACTS] FLORENCE

Business Hours Hours mainly follow the Italian norm (see p. 305). In Florence, however, many larger and more central shops stay open through the midday *riposo* or nap (note the sign ORARIO NONSTOP).

Doctors & Dentists Tourist-oriented **Medical Service Firenze** is at Via Roma 4, in the city center (www.medicalservice.firenze. it; ✆ **055/475-411**). It's open for walk-ins Mon–Fri 11am–noon, 1–3pm, and 5–6pm; Sat 11am–noon and 1–3pm. **Dr. Stephen Kerr** has an office at Piazza Mercato Nuovo 1 (www.dr-kerr. com; ✆ **335/836-1682** or 055/288-055), open Mon–Fri 3–5pm without an appointment (appointments are available 9am–3pm). The consultation fee is 60€, or 48€ if you show a student ID card. Prices are similar for the **Medico Subito** service (✆ **055/711-111;** Mon–Fri 10am–6pm), which

lets you call an English-speaking doctor to deal with minor injuries or dental pain.

Hospitals The most central hospital is **Santa Maria Nuova**, a block northeast of the Duomo on Piazza Santa Maria Nuova (www.asf. toscana.it; ✆ **055/69-381**), with an emergency room (*pronto soccorso*) open 24 hours.

Left Luggage At Santa Maria Novella Station, you can leave luggage at **KiPoint** (www.kipoint.it), open daily 6am–11pm; the cost is 6€ per item for the first 5 hours, 1€ per hour thereafter. Even cheaper (1€/hr.; 6€/day) is **Left Luggage Florence,** Via de' Boni 5R (www.leftluggageflorence. com).

Mail Florence's **main post office** (✆ **055/273-6481**) is at Via Pellicceria 3, off the southwest corner of Piazza della Repubblica. It's open Mon–Fri 8:20am–7:05pm, Sat 8:20am–12:35pm.

Pharmacies There is a 24-hour pharmacy (also open Sun and state holidays) in **Stazione Santa Maria Novella** (✆ **055/216-761;** ring the bell opposite taxi rank 11pm–7am). On holidays and at night, look for the sign in any pharmacy window telling you which ones are open locally.

Police To report a crime or passport problems, call the *questura* (police headquarters) at ✆ **055/49-771.** Lost property might find its way to the *Ufficio oggetti ritrovati*: ✆ **055/334802.**

Safety As in any city, pickpockets are a risk in Florence, often light-fingered youngsters (especially around the train station) Otherwise it's a fairly safe city, but steer clear of the Cascine Park after dark, and the area around Piazza Santo Spirito and the backstreets behind Santa Croce in the wee hours when nightlife is finished.

WHERE TO STAY IN FLORENCE

Thanks to a rapidly growing stock of hotel beds, lodging prices in Florence have not increased in recent years, although that doesn't mean they're exactly cheap. It is hard to find a high-season double you'd want to stay in for much less than 100€, and once-attractive August deals have mostly dried up. Florence no longer seems to get much quieter in its hottest month.

On top of that, Florence's government levies an extra .80€ to 2€ per person per night per government-rated hotel star, for the first 10 nights of any stay. It is payable on departure and is not usually included in quoted rates. Children

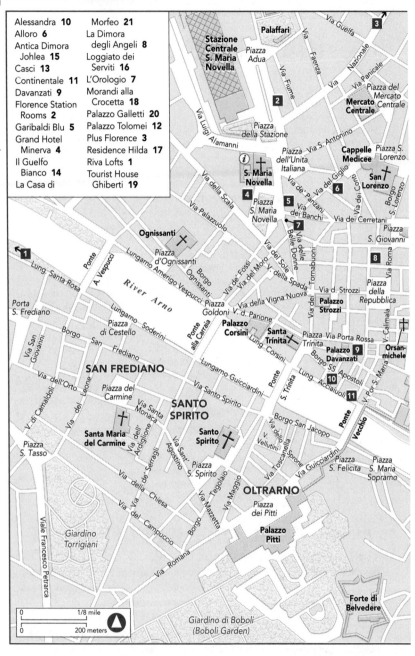

Alessandra **10**
Alloro **6**
Antica Dimora
  Johlea **15**
Casci **13**
Continentale **11**
Davanzati **9**
Florence Station
  Rooms **2**
Garibaldi Blu **5**
Grand Hotel
  Minerva **4**
Il Guelfo
  Bianco **14**
La Casa di

Morfeo **21**
La Dimora
  degli Angeli **8**
Loggiato dei
  Serviti **16**
L'Orologio **7**
Morandi alla
  Crocetta **18**
Palazzo Galletti **20**
Palazzo Tolomei **12**
Plus Florence **3**
Residence Hilda **17**
Riva Lofts **1**
Tourist House
  Ghiberti **19**

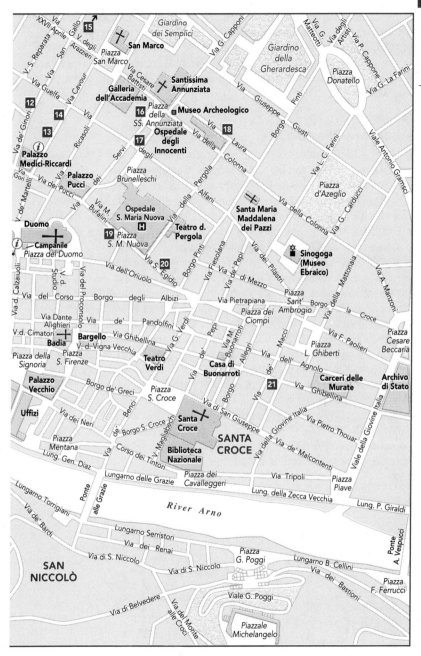

below age 12 are exempt from the tax. Airbnb and other holiday rentals are **not** exempt.

Peak hotel season is Easter through early July, September through early November, and Christmas through January 6. May, June, and September are popular; January and February are the months to grab a bargain—never be shy to haggle if you're coming then. **Booking direct** using phone, e-mail, or the hotel's own website is often the key to unlocking the lowest rates or complimentary extras.

Apartment Rentals & Alternative Accommodations

It's the way of the modern world: Global players in apartment rental have finally overtaken most local specialists in Florence. **HomeAway.com,** TripAdvisor–owned **HolidayLettings.co.uk, Airbnb,** and others are also well stocked with central and suburban apartments. Online agency **Cross Pollinate** ★ (www.cross-pollinate.com; ✆ **800/270-1190** in U.S., 06/9936-9799 in Italy) has built a Florence apartment portfolio over two decades. Apartments are all hand-picked and service is personal from the Rome-based team.

An alternative budget option is to stay in a **religious house** ★. A few monasteries and convents in the center receive guests for a modest fee. Our favorites are the **Suore di Santa Elisabetta,** Viale Michelangiolo 46 (near Piazza Ferrucci; ✆ **055/681-1884**), in a colonial villa just south of the Ponte San Niccolò; and close to Santa Croce, the **Istituto Oblate dell'Assunzione,** Borgo Pinti 15 (✆ **055/2480-582**), which has simple, peaceful rooms in a Medici-era building ranged around a courtyard garden. The easiest way to build a monastery and convent itinerary in Florence and beyond is via agent **MonasteryStays.com** ★. Remember that most religious houses have a curfew, generally 11pm or midnight.

Tip: For basic grocery shopping in the center, try **Conad City,** Via dei Servi 56R (✆ **055-280-110**), or any central branch of **Carrefour Express.** Both the **Mercato Centrale** and **Mercato di Sant'Ambrogio** sell fresh produce (see "Florence's Best Markets," p. 204).

Hotels by Price

EXPENSIVE

MODERATE

INEXPENSIVE

Near the Duomo
MODERATE
La Dimora degli Angeli ★★★

This B&B occupies two levels of a grand apartment building in one of the city's busiest shopping districts. Rooms on the original floor are for romantics; bright wallpaper contrasts pleasingly with iron-framed beds and classic furniture. ("Beatrice" is the largest, with a view of Brunelleschi's dome—just.) The floor below is totally different, with sharp lines and leather or wooden headboards throughout. Breakfast is available at a local cafe—or if you prefer, you can grab a coffee in the B&B and use your token for a light lunch instead.

The Cerere suite at Palazzo Galletti.

Via Brunelleschi 4. www.dimoredeicherubini.it. © **055/288-478.** 12 units. 76€–198€ double. Breakfast (at nearby café) 12€. Parking 26€. Bus: C2. **Amenities:** Wi-Fi (free).

Palazzo Galletti ★★   Not many hotels within a sensible budget give you the chance to live like a Florentine noble. Rooms here have towering ceilings and an uncluttered arrangement of carefully chosen antiques. Most have frescoed or painted-wood showpiece ceilings. Bathrooms, in contrast, have a sharp, contemporary design, decked out in travertine and marble. Aside from two street-facing suites, every room has a small balcony, ideal for a predinner glass of wine. If you're here for a once-in-a-lifetime trip, spring for the "Giove" or (especially) "Cerere"; both are large suites, and the latter has walls covered in original frescoes from the 1800s. Snag a free bottle of their own estate wine when you book direct and show this Frommer's guide. The relaxing **Soulspace** urban spa (www.soulspace.it) is right downstairs.

Via Sant'Egidio 12. www.palazzogalletti.it. © **055/390-5750.** 12 units. 100€–170€ double. Rates include breakfast. Parking 30€–35€. Bus: C1 or C2. **Amenities:** Babysitting; Wi-Fi (free).

Near San Lorenzo & the Mercato Centrale
EXPENSIVE

Palazzo Tolomei ★★★   In its heyday, this palace was close to the heart of Medici power. It even welcomed the painter Raphael as a guest in 1505 (probably in two rooms at the front, now Barocco 1 and 2). Guest rooms are large, with Renaissance wooden ceilings and terracotta floors left untouched. Modern fittings—including leather sofas, soft mattresses, and crystal chandeliers—chime perfectly with a baroque redecoration completed in the 1600s, including ceiling frescoes by Alessandro Gherardini. The lower floor houses opulent public rooms, just as it would have been when it was the *"piano* *nobile"* of the family *palazzo.* These days you'll find a music room, art books, a welcoming host, and probably an open bottle of Tuscan red wine somewhere. Book direct for the best deal: perhaps a free airport transfer, free late checkout, or a discounted room rate.

Via de' Ginori 19. www.palazzotolomei.it. ℰ **055/292-887.** 8 units. 166€–379€ double. Rates include breakfast in nearby café. Bus: C1. **Amenities:** Concierge; Wi-Fi (free).

MODERATE

Il Guelfo Bianco ★★   Decor in this former noble Florentine family home retains its authentic *palazzo* feel, though carpets have been added for comfort and warmth. No two rooms are the same—stone walls this thick cannot just be knocked through—and several have antiques integrated into their individual schemes. Grand rooms at the front (especially 101, 118, and 228) have spectacular Renaissance coffered ceilings and masses of space. Sleep at the back and you'll wake to an unusual sound in Florence: birdsong. Under the same ownership, the adjacent "farm-to-fork"-style bistro **Il Desco** (www.ildescofirenze.it; ℰ **055/288-330**) serves seasonal dishes made with organic ingredients—it's open to guests and nonguests alike.

Via Cavour 29 (near corner of Via Guelfa). www.ilguelfobianco.it. ℰ **055/288-330.** 40 units. 90€–280€ double. Rates include breakfast. Parking 27€–33€. Bus: C1. **Amenities:** Restaurant; bar; babysitting; room service; Wi-Fi (free).

INEXPENSIVE

Alloro ★★   Officially a "bed and breakfast," this feels more like a small hotel, whose modern rooms inside a Renaissance palace overlook a silent inner courtyard—cleverly soundproofing them against a noisy neighborhood. Rooms offer an excellent value for the price and location, with high ceilings, color-washed walls, and air-conditioning. Breakfast is a traditional spread of fresh fruit and pastries. A friendly ghost from the Renaissance era reputedly roams part of the palace; you're unlikely to get a discount if you spot him, but there's no harm in asking.

Via del Giglio 8. www.allorobb.it. ℰ **055/211-685.** 5 units. 70€–202€ double. Rates include breakfast. Bus: C1. **Amenities:** Concierge; Wi-Fi (free).

Casci ★   The front part of the palace now occupied by the Casci was once composer Gioachino Rossini's Florence digs. This affordable, central hotel has long been a Frommer's favorite, and the partial pedestrianization of Via Cavour has made it an even more attractive base. Rooms follow a labyrinthine layout, split between Rossini's old *piano nobile* and a former convent to the rear, where the bigger rooms are located, including a couple of spacious family units. Rooms are simply decorated and some can be a little dark, but a recent modernization installed new, light-toned furniture to counteract that. The welcome from some of Florence's friendliest family hoteliers is an unchanging feature.

Via Cavour 13 (btw. Via dei Ginori and Via Guelfa). www.hotelcasci.com. ℰ **055/211-686.** 25 units. 50€–170€ double. Rates include breakfast (gluten-free on request). Valet parking 25€–27€. Bus: C1. Closed 2 weeks in Dec. **Amenities:** Bar; babysitting; concierge; Wi-Fi (free).

Near the Ponte Vecchio

EXPENSIVE

Continentale ★★★   Everything about the Continentale is cool, and the effect is achieved without a hint of frostiness. Rooms are uncompromisingly modern, decorated in bright white and bathed in natural light. Deluxe units, which are built into a medieval riverside tower, have mighty walls and medieval-sized windows (read: small). Standard rooms are large (for Florence), and there's a 1950s feel to the overall styling. Communal areas are a major hit, too: A relaxation room has a glass wall with a front-row view of the Ponte Vecchio. Top-floor **La Terrazza** (p. 208) mixes Florence's best rooftop cocktails.

Vicolo dell'Oro 6R. www.lungarnocollection.com. *©* **055/27-262.** 43 units. 153€–750€ double. Parking 35€. Bus: C3 or D. **Amenities:** Bar; concierge; spa; Wi-Fi (free).

MODERATE

Alessandra ★   This typical Florentine *pensione* transports you back to the age of the gentleman and lady traveler. Decor has grown organically since the place opened as a hotel in 1950; Alessandra is a place for evolution, not revolution. A pleasing mix of styles is the result: Some rooms have carved headboards, gilt frames, and gold damask; others have eclectic postwar furniture, like something from a midcentury movie set. A couple rooms have views of the Arno, while front-side rooms overlook Borgo SS. Apostoli, one of the center's most atmospheric streets. Added in 2018 in a building across the street, two split-level rooms with mezzanines have contemporary décor.

Borgo SS. Apostoli 17. www.hotelalessandra.com. *©* **055/283-438.** 27 units. 160€–180€ double. Rates include breakfast. Parking 25€. Bus: C3 or D. Closed a few days around Christmas. **Amenities:** Concierge; Wi-Fi (free).

Davanzati ★★   Although installed inside a historic building, the Davanzati never rests on its medieval laurels: There is a laptop and an iPad with cellular data in every room for free guest use around the city, and HD movies can be streamed to your TV. Rooms are simply decorated in the Tuscan style, with color-washed walls and half-canopies over the beds. Room 100 is probably the best family hotel room in Florence, full of nooks, crannies, and split-levels that give the adults and the kids a sense of private space. A free *aperitivo* for guests remains part of the Davanzati's family welcome.

Via Porta Rossa 5 (at Piazza Davanzati). www.hoteldavanzati.it. *©* **055/286-666.** 27 units. 122€–211€ double; 152€–243€ superior (sleeping up to 4). Rates include breakfast. Valet parking 26€. Bus: C2. **Amenities:** Bar; babysitting; concierge; use of nearby gym; Wi-Fi (free).

Near Santa Maria Novella

EXPENSIVE

Grand Hotel Minerva ★★   Poet Henry Wadsworth Longfellow stayed in lodgings on the site of this hotel, on what is now one of Florence's most prestigious square. I doubt the service he experienced was anywhere near the international corporate standards set here. The quietly stylish rooms were mostly revamped in 2016, with cream tones, natural wood, tan leather, and travertine bathrooms. Each one is well soundproofed against neighbors and outdoor noise. A major bonus from May to September: a rooftop pool with panoramic sundeck, bar, and evening *aperitivo* buffet.

Piazza Santa Maria Novella 16. www.grandhotelminerva.com. ℰ **055/27-230.** 100 units. 240€–465€ double. Parking 30€–40€. Bus: C2, 6, 11, or 22. **Amenities:** Restaurant; 2 bars; concierge; outdoor pool; use of nearby gym; Wi-Fi (free).

MODERATE

Florence Station Rooms ★★   The streets outside are busy 24/7, but you'd never know it from the perfume-scented calm of these 4th-floor rooms in a building that once lodged Romantic poet Percy Shelley. Bedrooms are midsized and mix contemporary details—laminate floors and soft, thick mattresses—with baroque flourishes like gilded picture frames and artfully distressed furniture. This is far from the sexiest location in town, but it's much improved in recent years, has unbeatable transportation links, and is only 5 minutes' walk from the Duomo steps. An optional Italian breakfast is served at a café opposite the Medici Chapels.

Piazza della Stazione 2. www.florencestation.it. ℰ **055/230-2623.** 4 units. 105€–140€ double. Bus: C2, 6, 11, or 22. **Amenities:** Concierge; Wi-Fi (free).

Garibaldi Blu ★★   The hotels of Piazza Santa Maria Novella are frequented by fashion models, rock stars, and blue-chip businessfolk. You can get a taste of that, for a fraction of the price, at this boutique hotel with attitude. Each of the mostly midsize rooms is immaculate, and reflects the hotel's "warm denim" palette, with retro 1970s furniture, parquet floors, and marble

Grand Hotel Minerva.

bathrooms. It's well worth paying 30€ extra for a deluxe room at the front: These have much more space and a view over Florence's prettiest church facade, Santa Maria Novella itself. Dotted around the hotel, life-size models of superheroes like Captain America add a touch of fun surrealism.

Piazza Santa Maria Novella 21. www.hotelgaribaldiblu.com. ✆ **055/277-300.** 21 units. 130€–350€ double. Rates include breakfast. Parking 35€–48€. Bus: C2, 6, 11, or 22. **Amenities:** Bar; babysitting; concierge; Wi-Fi (free).

L'Orologio ★ As the name suggests, this hotel is an homage to the clock, with historic timepiece designs scattered artfully about. The remaining color palette is rich, with mahogany wood and natural leather everywhere. The cheapest rooms ("Superior") are not large, but their marble bathrooms are, and library-like, wood-paneled common areas are spacious and comfortable. Staff is superb. This is rapidly becoming Florence's most sought-after accommodation in the neighborhood: It's atmospheric, very close to the train station, and the view from its top-floor breakfast room is a showstopper.

Piazza Santa Maria Novella 24. www.hotelorologioflorence.com. ✆ **055/277-380.** 55 units. 95€–350€ double. Rates include breakfast. Parking 35€–48€. Bus: C2, 6, 11, 22. **Amenities:** Bar; babysitting; concierge; gym; sauna; Wi-Fi (free).

Near Santissima Annunziata

EXPENSIVE

Residence Hilda ★★ These luxe mini-apartments are all bright-white decor and designer furnishings, with natural wood flooring, fiber Wi-Fi, hypoallergenic mattresses, Starck chairs, and modern gadgetry to keep everything running. Each is spacious, cool in summer, and soundproofed against Florence's background noise. Every apartment has a mini-kitchen, equipped for preparing a simple meal—ideal if you have kids in tow. The top-floor Executive unit has a Nespresso machine, yoga mats, and exercise bike. Unusual for apartments, all are bookable by the single night.

Via dei Servi 40 (2 blocks north of the Duomo). www.residencehilda.com. ✆ **055/288-021.** 12 units. 90€–400€ per night for 2-to-4-person apartment. Parking 31€. Bus: C1, 6, 19, 31, or 32. **Amenities:** Airport transfer; babysitting; concierge; room service; Wi-Fi (free).

MODERATE

Loggiato dei Serviti ★★ Stay here to experience Florence as the gentleman and lady visitors of the Grand Tour did. For starters, the building is a genuine Renaissance landmark, built by Sangallo the Elder in the 1520s. There is a sense of faded grandeur and unconventional luxury throughout—no gadgetry or chromotherapy showers, but you will find rooms with writing desks and lots of vintage ambience. No unit is small, but standard rooms lack a view of either Brunelleschi's dome or the perfect piazza outside. Air-conditioning is pretty much the only concession to the 21st century—and you will love it that way. Book direct for the deals.

Piazza Santissima Annunziata 3. www.loggiatodeiservitihotel.it. ✆ **055/289-592.** 37 units. 120€–330€ double. Rates include breakfast. Parking 22€. Bus: C1, 6, 19, 31, or 32. **Amenities:** Babysitting; concierge; Wi-Fi (free).

Morandi alla Crocetta ★★

Like many in Florence, this hotel was built in the shell of a former convent. Morandi alla Crocetta has retained the original convent layout, meaning some rooms are snug. But what you lose in size, you more than gain in character: Every single one oozes *tipico fiorentino*—even the "new" breakfast room makes you feel like you're on the Grand Tour. Rooms have parquet flooring thrown with rugs and dressed with antique wooden furniture. Original Zocchi prints of Florence, from 1744, are scattered around the place. Superior rooms have more space and either a private courtyard terrace or, in one, original

Loggiato dei Serviti (see p. 161).

frescoes decorating the entrance to the former convent chapel, though the chapel itself is permanently sealed off. The hotel is set on a quiet street.

Via Laura 50 (1 block east of Piazza Santissima Annunziata). www.hotelmorandi.it. ✆ **055/234-4747.** 12 units. 90€–177€ double. Rates include breakfast. Parking 25€. Bus: 6, 19, 31, or 32. **Amenities:** Bar; babysitting; concierge; Wi-Fi (free).

Tourist House Ghiberti ★

A pleasing mix of the traditional and the modern prevails at this backstreet guesthouse named after a famous former resident: The creator of the Baptistery's "Gates of Paradise" had workshops on the top floor of the *palazzo*. Rooms have plenty of space, with herringbone terracotta floors, whitewashed walls, and high, painted wood ceilings in a vaguely Renaissance style. There is a sauna and Jacuzzi for communal use, so you can soak away the aches and pains of a day's sightseeing; memory-foam mattresses should help with that, too. E-mail direct if you want to bag the best room rate.

Via M. Bufalini 1. www.touristhouseghiberti.com. ✆ **055/284-858.** 6 units. 64€–179€ double. Rates include breakfast. Parking 20€–30€. Bus: C1. **Amenities:** Jacuzzi; sauna; Wi-Fi (free).

Near Santa Croce
MODERATE

La Casa di Morfeo ★

For a cheery, affordable room in the lively eastern part of the center, look no further than this small hotel on the second floor of a grand, shuttered palace. There is no huge difference in quality among the guest rooms: All are midsize, with modern gadgetry, and painted in bright contemporary colors, each individual scheme corresponding to a flower after which the room is named. Our favorite is Mimosa, painted in light mustard, with a ceiling fresco and a view over Via Ghibellina. Colored lighting brings a bit of fun, too.

Via Ghibellina 51. www.lacasadimorfeo.it. ℂ **055/241-193.** 9 units. 79€–189€ double. Rates include breakfast. Parking 25€. Bus: C2 or C3. **Amenities:** Wi-Fi (free).

North of the Center
MODERATE
Antica Dimora Johlea ★   There is a real neighborhood feel to the streets around this *dimora* (traditional Florentine home) guesthouse, which means evenings are lively and Sundays are silent (although it's under a 10-min. walk to San Lorenzo). Standard-size rooms are snug; upgrade to a deluxe if you need more space, but there is no difference in the decor, a mix of Florentine and earthy boho styling. Help yourself to coffee, a soft drink, or a glass of wine from the honesty bar and head up to a roof terrace for knockout views over the terracotta rooftops to the center and hills beyond. It is pure magic at dusk. No credit cards.

Via San Gallo 80. www.antichedimorefiorentine.it. ℂ **055/463-3292.** 6 units. 90€–220€ double. Rates include breakfast. No credit cards. Parking 25€. Bus: C1, 1, 6, 11, 14, 17, or 23. **Amenities:** Honesty bar; Wi-Fi (free).

INEXPENSIVE
Plus Florence ★★   There's simply nowhere in Florence with as many services for your buck—including seasonal indoor and outdoor swimming pools—all in a price bracket where you're often fortunate to get an en suite bathroom (and Plus has those, too). The best rooms in this large, well-equipped hostel are in the rear wing, which has private rooms only. Units here are dressed in taupe and brown, with subtle uplighting and space (in some) for up to four beds. The only minuses: an un-picturesque building and the location, between two busy roads. Light sleepers should request a room facing the internal courtyard.

Via Santa Caterina d'Alessandria 15. www.plushostels.com/plusflorence. ℂ **055/628-6347.** 240 units. 35€–125€ double. Bus: 20. **Amenities:** Restaurant; bar; concierge; gym; 2 swimming pools; sauna (winter only); Wi-Fi (free).

West of the Center
MODERATE
Riva Lofts ★★   The traditional Florentine alarm call—a morning mix of traffic and tourism—is replaced by birdsong when you awake in one of the stylish rooms here, on the banks of the River Arno. A former stone-built artisan workshop, Riva has had a refit to match its "loft" label: mellow color schemes, laminate flooring, floating staircases, marble bathrooms with rainfall showers, and clever integration of natural materials in such features as original wooden workshop ceilings. Noon checkouts are standard—a traveler-friendly touch. The center is a 30-minute walk, or jump on one of Riva's vintage-style bikes and cycle to the Uffizi along the Arno banks. Another standout feature in this price bracket: a shaded garden with outdoor plunge pool.

Via Baccio Bandinelli 98. www.rivalofts.com. ℂ **055/713-0272.** 10 units. 165€–255€ double. Rates include breakfast. Parking 20€. Bus: 6/Tram: T1 (3 stops from central station). **Amenities:** Bar; bike rental (free); honesty bar; outdoor pool; Wi-Fi (free).

WHERE TO EAT IN FLORENCE

Florentine cuisine is increasingly cosmopolitan, but flavors are often Tuscan at heart. Even in fine restaurants, meals might kick off with country concoctions like *ribollita* (seasonal vegetable stew) before moving onto the chargrilled delights of a *bistecca alla fiorentina* (Florentine beefsteak on the bone), washed down with a fine **Chianti Classico.** At lunchtime, a plate of cold cuts and Pecorino cheese makes a classic light lunch, or for the adventurous, *lampredotto alla fiorentina,* a sandwich of cow's stomach stewed in tomatoes and garlic.

Florence is well-supplied with restaurants, though in the most touristy areas (around the Duomo, Piazza della Signoria, Piazza della Repubblica, and the Ponte Vecchio), you must choose carefully—many eateries are of below-average quality or charge high prices, sometimes both. The highest concentrations of excellent *ristoranti* and *trattorie* are around **Santa Croce** and across the river in the **Oltrarno** and **San Frediano.** There's also an increasing buzz around **San Lorenzo,** particularly the top floor of the Mercato Centrale (see p. 170), with its wealth of counters selling delicious street food. Bear in mind that menus at restaurants in Tuscany can change weekly or even (at some of the very best places) daily. The city has also become much more **gluten-savvy.** If you have any sort of food intolerance, don't be afraid to ask. **Vegan** food is also widely available.

Reservations are strongly recommended if you have your heart set on eating anywhere in particular, especially at dinner on weekends.

Restaurants by Cuisine

CAFES
Caffetteria delle Oblate ★, p. 207
Ditta Artigianale Oltrarno ★★, p. 207
La Menagere ★, p. 207
La Terrazza ★, p. 208
Procacci ★, p. 208
Rivoire ★, p. 208

CONTEMPORARY ITALIAN
A Crudo ★★, p. 172
Fishing Lab Alle Murate ★★, p. 165
Il Santo Bevitore ★, p. 173
Mercato Centrale ★★★, p. 170
Vagalume ★★, p. 171

CONTEMPORARY TUSCAN
iO: Osteria Personale ★★, p. 172
Ora d'Aria ★★, p. 168
Osteria di Giovanni ★★, p. 169

FLORENTINE
Bondi ★★, p. 170
Da Tito ★, p. 171

Il Magazzino ★, p. 172
La Gratella ★★, p. 169
Mario ★, p. 170

GELATO
Amorino ★, p. 174
Gelateria della Passera ★★, p. 174
Gelateria de' Medici ★★, p. 174
Gelateria de' Neri ★, p. 174
La Carraia ★★, p. 174

GRILL
La Gratella ★★, p. 169

JAPANESE
Koto Ramen ★, p. 171

LIGHT FARE
Bondi ★★, p. 170
I Due Fratellini ★, p. 168
Pugi ★, p. 171
Sandwichic ★★, p. 170

PIZZA
Da Gherardo ★★, p. 173
Mercato Centrale ★★★, p. 170

RAW FOOD
A Crudo ★★, p. 172
Fishing Lab Alle Murate ★★, p. 165

SEAFOOD
Fishing Lab Alle Murate ★★, p. 165
Mercato Centrale ★★★, p. 170

TRADITIONAL TUSCAN
Coquinarius ★★, p. 165
Da Tito ★, p. 171
Osteria del Porcellino ★, p. 169

VEGETARIAN/VEGAN
Brac ★★★, p. 171
Konnubio ★, p. 169

Near the Duomo
MODERATE

Coquinarius ★★ TUSCAN   There is a regular menu here—pasta, mains such as beef cheek in red wine or Chianina tartare, main-size salads, traditional desserts. But the real pleasure is tucking into a couple of sharing plates and quaffing from the excellent wine list. Go for something from an extensive carpaccio list (beef, boar, octopus, swordfish) or pair a *misto di salumi e formaggi* (mixed Tuscan salami and cheeses) with a full-bodied red wine, to cut through the strong flavors of the deliciously fatty and salty pork and Tuscan sheep's milk cheese, pecorino.

Via delle Oche 11R. www.coquinarius.com. ✆ **055/230-2153.** Main courses 15€–20€. Daily 12:30–3:30pm and 6:30–10:30pm. Bus: C1 or C2.

Fishing Lab Alle Murate ★★ SEAFOOD   This temple to seafood serves fish any way you like (almost). The range is largely safe—shrimp, tuna, bream, bass, and salmon dominate—but fish are carefully sourced and preparation is refreshingly modern. Tartare and carpaccio are both super-fresh and dressed delicately with citrus fruit. Hot mains include grilled fillets, fishy pastas, and *fritto misto* (a mixed fry of baby squid, shrimp, and sardines served

A plate of mixed appetizers at Coquinarius.

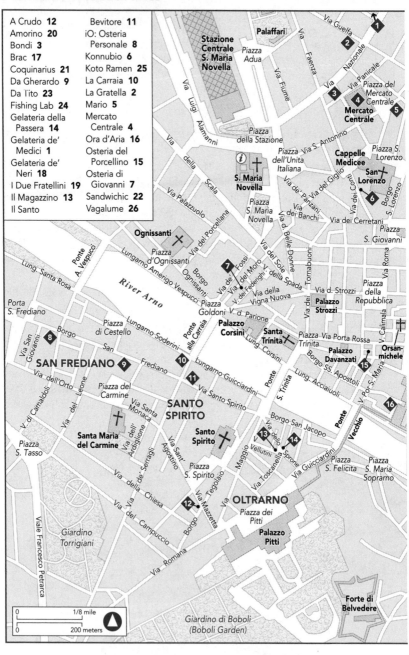

A Crudo **12**
Amorino **20**
Bondi **3**
Brac **17**
Coquinarius **21**
Da Gherardo **9**
Da Tito **23**
Fishing Lab **24**
Gelateria della
    Passera **14**
Gelateria de'
    Medici **1**
Gelateria de'
    Neri **18**
I Due Fratellini **19**
Il Magazzino **13**
Il Santo

Bevitore **11**
iO: Osteria
    Personale **8**
Konnubio **6**
Koto Ramen **25**
La Carraia **10**
La Gratella **2**
Mario **5**
Mercato
    Centrale **4**
Ora d'Aria **16**
Osteria del
    Porcellino **15**
Osteria di
    Giovanni **7**
Sandwichic **22**
Vagalume **26**

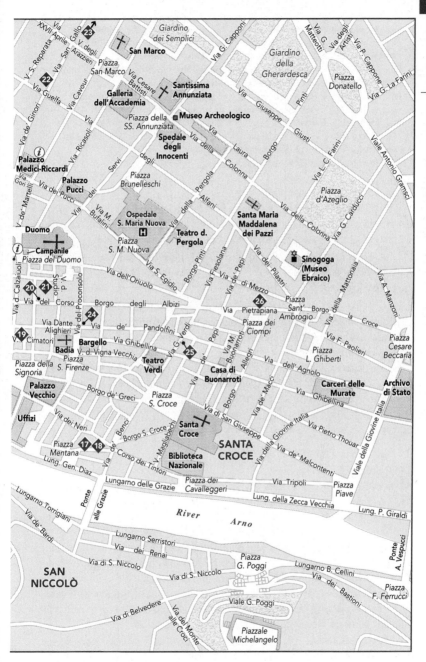

in a skillet). A young and lively menu is mood-matched with the clientele, urban decor, and staff. Service is brisk. Half-portions are available at lunch; they also do takeout (even fish and chips). Reservations highly recommended.

Via del Proconsolo 16R. www.fishinglab.it. ℭ **055-240-618.** Main courses 10€–14€. Daily 11am–11pm. Bus: C1 or C2.

INEXPENSIVE
I Due Fratellini ★ LIGHT FARE   This hole-in-the-wall has been serving food to go since 1875. The drill is simple: Choose a filling, pick a drink, then eat your roll on the curb opposite or find a nearby piazza perch. There are around 30 fillings to choose from, including the usual Tuscan meats and cheeses—salami, pecorino, cured ham—and more flamboyant combos such as goat cheese and Calabrian spicy salami or *bresaola* (air-dried beef) and wild arugula. A glass of wine costs from 2€. Lunchtime lines can be long.

Via dei Cimatori 38R (at Via Calzaiuoli). www.iduefratellini.it. ℭ **055/239-6096.** Sandwiches 4€. No credit cards. Daily 10am–7pm (Jul–Aug often closed Sun). Bus: C2.

Near the Ponte Vecchio
EXPENSIVE
Ora d'Aria ★★ CONTEMPORARY TUSCAN   If you want to see what the latest generation of Tuscan chefs can do in a kitchen, this place should top your list. The mood is modern and elegant, but never stuffy. Dishes are subtle and creative, combining traditional ingredients in original ways. The menu changes daily—expect the likes of *pappardelle* pasta with snail ragù and mint, or slow-roasted suckling pig and turnip greens with a garlic and lavender cream. If you can't stretch the budget for dinner, book a table at lunch to taste simpler, cheaper (13€–18€) dishes such as caramelized tomato with cauliflower puree, orange oil, and a spiced crumble, served in full-size or half-price "tapas" portions. Reservations are essential.

Via dei Georgofili 11–13R (off Via Lambertesca). www.oradariaristorante.com. ℭ **055/200-1699.** Main courses 38€–45€ at dinner; tasting menus 60€–150€. Tues–Sat 12:30–2:30pm; Mon–Sat 7:30–10pm. Closed 3 weeks in Aug. Bus: C3 or D.

MODERATE

Osteria del Porcellino ★ TUSCAN   So many characterful restaurants of "old Florence" have dropped standards in the age of mass tourism, but not this place. Traditional Tuscan is what they do best, and pasta dishes such as *pappardelle* with wild boar sauce are always tasty. Follow that with a *tagliata* (sliced steak) with arugula and Parmigiano or a filet of *Cinta Senese* pork (a local breed), to savor the city's carnivorous traditions. Lighter options include sublime "flan": a potato cake with cured ham, Vin Santo wine, and a *stracchino* cheese sauce. All-day dining means you (or the kids) can eat when you like.

Via Val di Lamona 7R. www.osteriadelporcellino.com. ② **055/264-148.** Main courses 15€–20€. Daily 11:30am–midnight. Bus: C2.

Near Santa Trinita
MODERATE

Osteria di Giovanni ★★ MODERN TUSCAN   If only every Tuscan restaurant in town was this good. Family-run Osteria di Giovanni is a standout in this category and therefore always buzzing: You should reserve even in low season. Meat is a specialty, both traditional (the *bistecca alla fiorentina* is legendary) and modern interpretations like *faraona all'arancia* (guinea hen stewed in slightly sweet orange). Only the very brave should attempt a *primo/secondo/dolce* route: Portions are large. A seemingly steep cover charge (4€) is actually a good deal, because it includes a couple of tasty snacks and all the mineral water you can drink.

Via del Moro 22. www.osteriadigiovanni.com. ② **055/284-897.** Main courses 18€–28€. Sat–Sun 12:30–2:30pm; daily 7–10:30pm. Bus: 6, 11.

Near San Lorenzo & the Mercato Centrale
MODERATE

Konnubio ★ CREATIVE TUSCAN/VEGAN   There's a warm glow (candles and low-watt lighting) about this place—it makes you instantly happy, and the cooking keeps you there. Ingredients are largely Tuscan, but combined creatively, such as in warm guinea hen salad with cream of roasted tomatoes, or a risotto of peas and cuttlefish. There's an extensive vegan menu, too, like curried cream of yellow squash with crispy tofu and mango. Under brick vaults and a covered courtyard, it could work for a romantic dinner; but you won't be out of place in a family group either. Dishes are simpler at lunch.

Via dei Conti 8R. www.konnubio.it. ② **055/238-1189.** Main courses 16€–32€; tasting menus 55€–85€. Daily noon–3pm and 7–11pm. Bus: C1.

La Gratella ★★ FLORENTINE/GRILL   It doesn't look much—a workers' canteen on a nondescript side street—but looks don't matter much when you can source and cook meat like they do here. Star of the show is the *bistecca alla fiorentina,* a large T-bone-like cut grilled on the bone and brought to the table over coals. It is sold by weight and made for sharing; expect to pay about 50€. Pair this or any market-fresh meat on the menu with simple Tuscan sides like *fagioli al fiasco* (beans stewed in olive oil). They cater to celiacs, too.

Via Guelfa 81R. www.trattorialagratella.com. ℂ **055/211-292.** Main courses 9€–22€. Daily noon–3pm and 7:30–9pm. Bus: 1, 6, 11, 14, 17, or 23.

INEXPENSIVE

Bondi ★ FLORENTINE/LIGHT FARE   To label this place opposite the Mercato Centrale a mere sandwich shop is like describing the Super Bowl as "a football game." Bondi is an institution, specializing in *piadine* (flatbread sandwich) in the Florentine style. Choose from a long list of traditional and unusual combinations, then order at the bar and take a seat on rustic wooden benches to await the arrival of your *piadine* (toasted or cold) filled with any number of combos, including radicchio and mozzarella, salt cod with tomato and pink peppercorns, or eggplant Parmigiana. Wash it down with a glass of Chianti at 2€ a pop.

Via dell'Ariento 85. ℂ **055/287-390.** Sandwiches 2.50€–4.50€. No credit cards. Daily 11am–11pm. Bus: C1.

Mario ★ FLORENTINE   There is no doubt that this market workers' trattoria is now firmly on the tourist trail. But Mario's clings to the same traditions and ethos as when it first fired up the kitchen burners 60 years ago. Food is simple, hearty, and served at communal tables—"check in" on arrival and you will be offered seats together wherever they come free. Think *passata di fagioli* (bean puree soup) followed by Tuscan beef stew, *peposo,* or *coniglio arrosto* (roast rabbit).

Via Rosina 2R (north side of Piazza Mercato Centrale). www.trattoriamario.com. ℂ **055/218-550.** Main courses 8.50€–14€. No credit cards. Mon–Sat noon–3:30pm. Closed Aug. Bus: C1.

Mercato Centrale ★★★ MODERN ITALIAN   In 2014 the upper floor of Florence's produce market reopened as a bustling shrine to Italian street food. Counters sell dishes from all over the country: pasta, authentic Neapolitan pizza, vegetarian and vegan fare, cold cuts and cheeses, fresh fish dishes, *Chianina* burgers and meatballs, and lots more. It works perfectly for families who can't agree on a dinner choice. Or just stop by for a drink and soak up the buzz: There's a beer bar (disappointing) and enoteca (superb), plus soccer games on the big screen.

Piazza Mercato Centrale. www.mercatocentrale.it. ℂ **055/239-9798.** Dishes 5€–20€. Daily 10am–midnight. Bus: C1.

Sandwichic ★★ LIGHT FARE   Perhaps Florence's best sandwich bar, Sandwichic succeeds because it keeps things simple, with freshly baked bread and expertly sourced ingredients including Tuscan cured meats and savory preserves. Try the likes of *finocchiona* (salami spiked with fennel), pecorino cheese, and *crema di porri* (a creamy leek relish). Located inside a former haberdashery, it's a tight squeeze: Go for takeout.

Via San Gallo 3R. www.sandwichic.it. ℂ **055/281-157.** Sandwiches 4€–5€. Daily 11am–9pm. Bus: C1.

Near San Marco

San Marco is the place to head for *schiacciata,* olive-oil flatbread loaded with savory toppings. The best in the center is from **Pugi ★**, Piazza San Marco 9B (www.fornopugi.it; © **055/280-981**), open 7:45am to 8pm Monday to Saturday. It's closed most of August.

MODERATE

Da Tito ★★ TUSCAN/FLORENTINE Sure, they ham it up a little for the tourists, but every night feels like party night at one of central Florence's rare genuine neighborhood trattorias. (And for that reason, it's usually packed— reserve ahead.) The welcome and the dishes are authentically Florentine, with a few modern Italian curveballs: Start, perhaps, with a seasonal *risotto* (fresh artichokes in spring; peas and cured pork cheek in early summer) before proceeding to a traditional grill such as *lombatina di vitella* (veal chop steak). The neighborhood location, a 10-minute walk north of San Lorenzo, and a mixed clientele keep the quality consistent.

Via San Gallo 112R. www.trattoriadatito.it. © **055/472-475.** Main courses 10€–18€. Mon–Sat 12:30–3pm and 7–11pm. Bus: C1, 1, 7, 20, or 25.

Near Santa Croce
MODERATE

Brac ★★★ VEGETARIAN An artsy cafe-bookshop for most of the day, at lunch and dinner this place turns into Florence's best spot for vegetarian and vegan food. There are seasonal salads and creative pasta dishes, but a *piatto unico* works out best for hungry diners: one combo plate loaded with three dishes from the menu, perhaps pear carpaccio with Grana Padana cheese and a balsamic reduction; *tagliatelle* with broccoli, pecorino, and lemon; and a fried *pane carasau* (Sardinian flatbread) stuffed with creamed beet and fennel. The back room's courtyard atmosphere is intimate and romantic, yet singletons won't feel out of place eating at the counter out front. Booking at dinner is a must.

Via dei Vagellai 18R. www.libreriabrac.net. © **055-094-4877.** Main courses 10€–15€. Daily noon–midnight. Bus: C1, C3, or 23.

Koto Ramen ★ JAPANESE Ramen's march to world domination continues, in a city whose culinary traditions could hardly be further from Tokyo. The cooking here is authentic, however, with each item on the short menu based on a deep, rich broth that's homemade (as are the noodles). The "tantan" ramen, with chopped pork, sesame pesto, and Japanese hot pepper, is a spicy treat. Sides are also traditional, including edamame, filled gyoza, and *kara-age* (fried marinated chicken thighs); there's a strong sake list, too. No reservations.

Via Verdi 42R. www.kotoramen.it. © **055/247-9477.** Main courses 11€–16€. Wed–Mon 7pm–midnight. No reservations. Closed Aug. Bus: C3.

Vagalume ★ MODERN ITALIAN The style here is *"tapas fiorentine"*— there are no "courses," and you compile a dinner from a range of good-size dishes in any order you please. Dishes are all seasonal and change daily, but may include a soufflé of zucchini and sundried tomatoes with a taleggio cheese cream; rabbit stewed in Vernaccia wine with olives; a *"tarte tatin"* of beetroot and burrata cheese; or tagliolini with a clam and fava bean pesto. The decor is stripped-back, and jazz-funk is played on an old vinyl turntable. The wine list is short but carefully chosen.

Via Pietrapiana 40R. www.facebook.com/vagalume.firenze. ℭ **055/246-6740.** Dishes 7€–16€. Daily 6pm–2am. Bus: C2 or C3.

In the Oltrarno, San Niccolò & San Frediano

EXPENSIVE

iO: Osteria Personale ★★ CONTEMPORARY TUSCAN
There's a definite hipster atmosphere, with whitewashed brick, banquettes, minimalist decor, and a young waitstaff. The food ethos here is cutting edge, too. Ingredients are usually familiar to Tuscan cooking but are often combined in ways you may not have seen before. The menu always has a good range of seafood, meat, and vegetarian dishes: perhaps tempura artichoke flowers stuffed with taleggio cheese and marjoram followed by guinea-hen ravioli, then roasted octopus with garbanzo-bean cream, lime, and cumin. Reservations are recommended.

Borgo San Frediano 167R (at Piazza di Verzaia). www.io-osteriapersonale.it. ℭ **055/933-1341.** Main courses 15€–22€; tasting menus 40€ for 4 dishes, 55€ for 6 dishes. Mon–Sat 7:30–10pm. Closed 10 days in Jan and all Aug. Bus: D or 6.

MODERATE

A Crudo ★★ CONTEMPORARY ITALIAN/RAW FOOD
The name means "raw," which provides a clue to the strengths of this inventive spot. A short carpaccio list might include the likes of venison with bitter citrus and pink peppercorn vinaigrette. But the real star is the meat tartare, done in traditional style as well as in such creative combos as Kathmandù (with lime and avocado) and Marinata (with gin and parsley). There's also vegetarian raw food tartare. A Crudo is a perfect example of modern Florence doing what it does best: tapping into food traditions and letting them breathe some 21st-century air.

Via Mazzetta 5R. www.acrudo.com. ℭ **055/265-7483.** Main courses 8€–16€. Wed–Mon 12:30–3pm and 7pm–midnight. Bus: C3, D, 11, 36, or 37.

Il Magazzino ★ FLORENTINE
A traditional *osteria* that specializes in the flavors of old Florence, it looks the part, too, with its terracotta tiled floor and barrel vault, chunky wooden furniture, and hanging lamps. If you dare, this is a place to try tripe or *lampredotto* (intestines), the traditional food of working Florentines, prepared expertly here in ravioli or meatballs, boiled, or *alla fiorentina* (stewed with tomatoes and garlic). The rest of the menu is carnivore-friendly, too: Follow *tagliatelle al ragù bianco* (pasta ribbons with a "white" meat sauce made with milk instead of tomatoes) with *guancia di vitello in agrodolce* (veal cheek stewed with baby onions in a sticky-sweet sauce).

Piazza della Passera 3. ℭ **055/215-969.** Main courses 10€–18€. Daily noon–3pm and 7:30–11pm. Bus: C3 or D.

Il Santo Bevitore ★ CONTEMPORARY ITALIAN   Sure, this place has lost its original in-the-know, local buzz. But the commitment to top produce served simply, and a trademark take on Tuscan ingredients, is unwavering—and reservations are still a must. Carefully sourced cold cuts make an ideal sharing antipasto: *prosciutto crudo* from Umbria, *pecorino* cheese from Pienza in southern Tuscany. Mains are eclectic, seasonal, and come in all appetite sizes, from a whole *burrata* (fresh cheese) served with spinach to lamb knuckle with scallions and pear puree or stuffed squid with artichokes. There is a long, expertly compiled wine list, with about 10 offered by the glass, plus craft beers.

Via Santo Spirito 66R (at Piazza N. Sauro). www.ilsantobevitore.com. ℂ **055/211-264.** Main courses 11€–25€. Mon–Sat 12:30–2:30pm; daily 7:30–11pm. Closed 10 days in mid-Aug. Bus: C3, D, 6, 11, 36, or 37.

INEXPENSIVE

Da Gherardo ★★ PIZZA   This informal, cavelike restaurant is packed tight with tables for a reason: It's always busy. Pizzas arrive quickly from a wood-fired oven, in Naples style. But toppings go well beyond Neapolitan tradition—with *'nduja* (soft, spicy salami), four cheese, and zucchini on the menu—though the marinara (tomato, garlic, oregano, basil) is hard to beat. Reservations are strongly advised, but if you forget, they do takeout, which you can munch around the corner in Piazza del Carmine. No credit cards.

Borgo San Frediano 57R. www.gherardopizzeria.com. ℂ **055/282-921.** Pizzas 4.50€–11€. Daily 7:30pm–1am. Bus: D or 6.

Gelato

Having a fair claim to being the birthplace of gelato, Florence has some of the world's best *gelaterie*—but many, many poor imitations, too. Steer clear of spots around the major attractions, where air-fluffed mountains of ice cream are so full of artificial colors and flavors they practically glow in the dark. If you can see the Ponte Vecchio or Piazza della Signoria from the front door of the gelateria, you may want to move on. You might only have to walk a block, or duck down a side street, to find a genuine artisan in the gelato kitchen. Trust

The dining room at iO: Osteria Personale.

us, you'll taste the difference. Opening hours tend to be discretionary: When it's warm, many places stay open until 11pm or beyond.

Amorino ★   Expensive, small portions but exquisite flavor from all-natural ingredients, plus a convenient location near the sights. *Dulce de leche* is memorable.

Via del Corso 46R. www.amorino.com. *℡* **055/267-0016.** Cone from 2.90€. Bus: C2.

Gelateria della Passera ★★   Milk-free water ices here are among the most intensely flavored in the city, and relatively low in sugary sweetness. Try the likes of pink grapefruit or jasmine tea gelato.

Via Toscanella 15R (at Piazza della Passera). www.gelaterialapassera.wordpress.com. *℡* **055/291-882.** Cone from 2€. Bus: C3 or D.

Gelateria de' Medici ★★   Ice-cream obsessives should make a pilgrimage to this place just outside the center, considered by many to be the city's best. The sublime chocolate orange is liberally studded with candied peel.

Via dello Statuto 5R. www.gelateriademedici.com. *℡* **055/475-156.** Cone from 1.80€. Bus: 4, 8, 20, or 28. Also at Piazza Beccaria 7R (*℡* **055-386-0008**).

Gelateria de' Neri ★   There's a large range of fruit, *crema* (yellow-white egg cream), and chocolate flavors here, but nothing overly elaborate. If the ricotta and fig is available, you're in luck.

Via dei Neri 9R. *℡* **055/210-034.** Cone from 1.80€. Bus: C1, C3, or 23.

La Carraia ★★   It's packed with locals late into the evening on summer weekends—for good reason. The range is vast, the quality high. Signature flavor *Sinfonia Carraia* combines *crema,* dark chocolate, and orange.

Piazza N. Sauro 25R. www.lacarraiagroup.eu. *℡* **055/280-695.** Cone from 2€. Bus: C3, D, 6, 11, 36, or 37. Also at Via de' Benci 24R (*℡* 329/363-0069).

EXPLORING FLORENCE

Many museums in Florence still accept cash only at the door. Staff is usually happy to direct you to the nearest ATM *(un bancomat).* **Precise opening times can change** without notice, especially at city churches (for example, the Baptistery often remains open until 11pm in summer). The tourist office maintains an up-to-date list of hours, also available for download at www. firenzeturismo.it. Note, too, that the last admission to the museums and monuments listed is usually between 30 and 45 minutes before final closing time.

Index of Attractions & Sights

Piazza del Duomo

The cathedral square is always crowded—filled with tourists and caricature artists during the day, strolling crowds in the early evening, and students strumming guitars on the Duomo's steps at night. The piazza's vivacity amid the glittering facades of the cathedral and the Baptistery doors keep it an eternal Florentine sight.

Battistero (Baptistery) ★★★ CHURCH   In choosing a date to mark the beginning of the Renaissance, art historians often seize on 1401, the year Florence's powerful wool merchants' guild held a contest to decide who would receive the commission to design the **North Doors** ★★ of the Baptistery to match its Gothic **South Doors,** cast 65 years earlier by Andrea Pisano. The era's foremost Tuscan sculptors each cast a bas-relief bronze panel depicting their own vision of the "Sacrifice of Isaac." Twenty-two-year-old Lorenzo Ghiberti, competing against Donatello, Jacopo della Quercia, and Filippo Brunelleschi, won. He spent the next 21 years casting 28 bronze panels and building his doors. The restored originals are now inside the **Museo dell'Opera del Duomo** (see p. 179).

The result so impressed the merchants' guild—not to mention the public and Ghiberti's fellow artists—that they asked him in 1425 to do the **East Doors** ★★★, facing the Duomo, this time giving him the artistic freedom to realize his Renaissance ambitions. Twenty-seven years later, just before his death, Ghiberti finished 10 dramatic Old Testament scenes in gilded bronze, each a masterpiece of Renaissance sculpture and some of the finest examples of low-relief perspective in Italian art. Each illustrates episodes in the stories of Noah (second down on left), Moses (second up on left), Solomon (bottom

Florence Attractions

Battistero **4**
Biblioteca delle
  Oblate **24**
Campanile di Giotto **27**
Cappelle Medicee **2**
Cenacolo di
  Sant'Appollonia **29**
Chiostro dello Scalzo **30**
Duomo **26**
Galleria degli Uffizi **21**
Galleria dell'
  Accademia **32**
Giardino Bardini **17**
Giardino di Boboli **16**
Museo Archeologico **34**
Museo Marino Marini
  & Cappella Rucellai **9**
Museo Nazionale
  del Bargello **23**
Museo Novecento **5**
Museo dell'Opera
  del Duomo **25**
Museo Zoologia
  "La Specola" **12**
Orsanmichele **6**
Palazzo Davanzati **7**
Palazzo Medici-
  Riccardi **28**
Palazzo Pitti **13**
Palazzo Strozzi **8**
Palazzo Vecchio **22**

Piazzale
  Michelangelo **19**
Ponte Vecchio **14**
San Lorenzo **3**
San Marco **31**
San Miniato
  al Monte **18**
Santa Croce **20**
Santa Felicita **15**
Santa Maria del
  Carmine **10**
Santa Maria
  Novella **1**
Santissima
  Annunziata **33**
Santo Spirito **11**
Spedale degli
  Innocenti **35**

Giardino
dei Semplici

30

31 **San Marco**

Piazza
San Marco

29

Via XXVII Aprile

Via degli Arazzieri

Via S. Reparata

Via San Gallo

Via v. degli

Via Cavour

Via Guelfa

Via de' Ginori

Via Cesare Battisti

Giardino
della
Gherardesca

Piazza
Donatello

Via G. Capponi

Via G. Matteotti

Via degli Artisti

Via P. Capone

Via G. La Farini

**Santissima
Annunziata**

33

32

**Galleria dell'
Accademia**

Piazza della
SS. Annunziata

35

**Spedale
degli Innocenti**

34 **Museo Archeologico**

Via della Laura

Via degli Servi

Via Giuseppe

Via Borgo Pinti

Via Giusti

Via L. C. Farini

Piazza
d'Azeglio

Viale Antonio Gramsci

Via Ricasoli

Via della Colonna

28

Via de' Martelli

Via de' Pucci

Via Gori

**Palazzo
Pucci**

Piazza
Brunelleschi

Via M. Bufalini

Via della Pergola

Via degli Alfani

**Ospedale
S. Maria Nuova**

**Santa Maria
Maddalena
dei Pazzi**

Via della Colonna

Via G. Carducci

26 **Duomo**

27

25

Piazza
S. M. Nuova

**Teatro d.
Pergola**

Via della Pergola

Via de' Pepi

Via A. Marzoni

Piazza del Duomo

Via d. Calzaiuoli

V. d. Studio

Via de' Proconsolo

Via S. Egidio

24

Via dell'Oriuolo

Via Fiesolana

Via de' di Mezzo

**Sinogoga
(Museo
Ebraico)**

Via dei Pilastri

Via della Mattonaia

Via del Corso

Borgo degli Albizi

Via Pietrapiana

Piazza
Sant'
Ambrogio

Borgo la Croce

Via Dante Alighieri

Via de' Pandolfini

Piazza dei
Ciompi

Via G. Verdi

Via M. Buonarroti

Piazza
C. Beccaria

V. Cimatori

Badia

Bargello Via Ghibellina

V. d. Vigna Vecchia

Via de' Pepi

Via dell'Agnolo

Via F. Paolieri

23

Piazza
S. Firenze

**Teatro
Verdi**

**Casa di
Buonarroti**

Piazza
L. Ghiberti

Piazza della
Signoria

22 **Palazzo
Vecchio**

Borgo de' Greci

Piazza
S. Croce

Via de' Macci

Via dell'Agnolo

**Carceri delle
Murate**

**Archivio
di Stato**

21

Uffizi

Via dei Neri

Borgo S. Croce

Via de' Benci

20

**Santa
Croce**

**SANTA
CROCE**

Via di San Giuseppe

Via Borgo Allegri

Via della Giovine Italia

Via Ghibellina

Via Pietro Thouar

Viale della Giovine Italia

Piazza
Mentana

Lung. Gen. Diaz

**Biblioteca
Nazionale**

Via de' Corso dei Tintori

Via Magliabechi

Piazza dei
Cavalleggeri

Via Tripoli

Via de' Malcontenti

Piazza
Piave

Lungarno delle Grazie

Lung. della Zecca Vecchia

Lungarno Torrigiani

Ponte alle Grazie

River Arno

Lung. P. Giraldi

Via de' Bardi

Lungarno Serristori

Via dei Renai

Piazza
G. Poggi

Lungarno B. Cellini

Ponte A. Vespucci

17 **SAN
NICCOLÒ**

Via di S. Niccolo

Via di S. Niccolo

Via dei Bastioni

Piazza
F. Ferrucci

Via di Belvedere

Via del Monte alle Croci

Viale G. Poggi

19

18

Piazzale
Michelangelo

right), and others. The panels mounted here are also copies, with the originals in the **Museo dell'Opera del Duomo.** Years later, Michelangelo was standing before these doors and someone asked his opinion. His response sums up Ghiberti's accomplishment as no art historian could: "They are so beautiful that they would grace the entrance to Paradise." They've been nicknamed the Gates of Paradise ever since.

Its marble cladding now gleaming after a thorough clean, the building itself is ancient, first mentioned in city records in the 9th century and probably already 300 years old by then. Its interior is ringed with columns pilfered from ancient Roman buildings, with a riot of mosaic-work above and below. The floor was inlaid in 1209, and between 1225 and the early 1300s the ceiling was covered with glittering **mosaics ★★** most of them crafted by Venetian or Byzantine-style workshops working off designs by the era's best artists. Coppo di Marcovaldo drew sketches for an over 7.8m-high (26-ft.) "Christ in Judgment" and a "Last Judgment" that fills over a third of the ceiling. Bring binoculars if you want a closer look.

Piazza San Giovanni. www.ilgrandemuseodelduomo.it. ⓒ **055/230-2885.** 18€. Grande Museo del Duomo ticket; see box p. 149. Mon–Sat 8:15–10:15am and 11:15am–7:30pm; Sun (and 1st Sat of month) 8:15am–1:30pm. Bus: C2.

Campanile di Giotto (Giotto's Bell Tower) ★★ ARCHITECTURE

In 1334, Giotto started the cathedral bell tower but completed only the first two levels before his death in 1337. He was out of his league with the engineering aspects of architecture, and the tower was saved from falling by Andrea Pisano, who doubled the thickness of the walls. Pisano also changed the design to add statue niches—he even carved a few statues himself—before quitting the project in 1348. Francesco Talenti finished the job between 1350 and 1359. The **reliefs** and **statues** in the lower levels—by Andrea Pisano, Donatello, Luca della Robbia, and others—are all copies; the weatherworn originals are housed in the Museo dell'Opera del Duomo. We recommend climbing the 414 steps to the top; the **view ★★** is memorable as you ascend and offers the city's best close-up of Brunelleschi's dome.

Brunelleschi's dome, seen from the top of Giotto's bell tower.

Piazza del Duomo. www.ilgrandemuseodelduomo. it. ⓒ **055-230-2885.** 18€ Grande Museo del Duomo ticket; see above. Daily 8:15am–7pm. Bus: C2.

Duomo (Cattedrale di Santa Maria del Fiore) ★★★ CATHEDRAL

By the late 13th century, Florence was feeling peevish: Its archrivals Siena and Pisa sported flamboyant new cathedrals while it was saddled with the tiny 5th- or 6th-century cathedral of Santa Reparata. So, in 1296, the city hired Arnolfo di Cambio to design a new Duomo, and he raised the facade and the first few bays before his death (around 1310). Work continued under the auspices of the wool guild and architects Giotto di Bondone (who concentrated on the bell tower) and Francesco Talenti (who expanded the planned size and finished as far as the drum of the dome). The facade we see today is a neo-Gothic composite designed by Emilio de Fabris and built from 1871 to 1887.

The Duomo's most distinctive feature, however, is its enormous **dome** ★★★ (or *cupola*), which dominates the skyline and is a symbol of Florence itself. The raising of this dome, the largest in the world in its time, was no mean

Interior of the Duomo.

architectural feat, tackled by Filippo Brunelleschi between 1420 and 1436 (see "A Man & His Dome," p. 180). You can climb up between its two shells for one of the classic panoramas across the city—something not recommended for claustrophobes or anyone with no head for heights. Booking a time slot to climb the dome is now **compulsory:** Queues can be long anyway, but your best shot at a short wait comes with the first or last slots of the day.

The cathedral is rather Spartan inside, though check out an optical-illusion equestrian "statue" of English mercenary soldier Sir John Hawkwood on the north wall, painted in 1436 by Paolo Uccello. The remains of old **Santa Reparata** ★ are in the crypt, with mosaic floors revamped in 2018.

Piazza del Duomo. www.ilgrandemuseodelduomo.it. ⓒ **055/230-2885.** Church free; Santa Reparata and cupola with 18€ Grande Museo del Duomo ticket. Church Mon–Wed and Fri 10am–5pm; Thurs 10am–4pm; Sat 10am–4:30pm; Sun 1:30–4:45pm. Cupola Mon–Fri 8:30am–7pm; Sat 8:30am–5pm; Sun 1–4pm. Bus: C1 or C2.

Museo dell'Opera del Duomo (Cathedral Museum) ★★ ART MUSEUM

Florence's Cathedral Museum reopened to huge acclaim in 2015, a major overhaul doubling the space to show off Italy's second-largest collection of devotional art after the Vatican Museums (p. 90). The site itself is significant: It once housed the workshop where Michelangelo sculpted his statue of "David." Today the museum's prize exhibit is the original **Gates of Paradise** ★★★ cast by Lorenzo Ghiberti in the early 1400s (see "Baptistery," p. 175), displayed as the centerpiece of a life-size re-creation of the early 1400s piazza, complete with a re-imagined version of what the cathedral's Gothic-era façade might have looked like. Ghiberti's Baptistery **North**

A MAN & HIS dome

Filippo Brunelleschi, a diminutive man whose ego was as big as his talent, managed in his arrogant, quixotic, and brilliant way to invent Renaissance architecture. Having been beaten by Lorenzo Ghiberti in the contest to cast the **Baptistery** doors (see above), Brunelleschi resolved that he would rather be the top architect than the second-best sculptor and took off for Rome to study the buildings of the ancients. On returning to Florence, he combined subdued gray *pietra serena* stone with smooth white plaster to create airy arches, vaults, and arcades of perfect classical proportions, in his own variant on the ancient Roman orders of architecture. He designed **Santo Spirito,** the elegant **Ospedale degli Innocenti,** a chapel at **Santa Croce,** and a new sacristy for **San Lorenzo,** but his greatest achievement was erecting the dome over Florence's cathedral.

The Duomo—at that time the world's largest church—had already been built, but nobody had figured out how to cover the daunting space over its center without spending a fortune. No one was even sure if they could create a dome that would hold up under its own weight. Brunelleschi insisted he knew how, and once granted the commission, revealed his ingenious plan, which may have been inspired by close study of Rome's **Pantheon** (p. 109).

He built the dome in two shells, the inner one thicker than the outer, both shells thinning as they neared the top, thus leaving the center hollow and removing a good deal of weight. He also planned to construct the dome from giant vaults with ribs crossing them, and dovetailed the stones making up the actual fabric of the dome. In this way, the walls of the dome would support themselves as they were erected. In the process of building, Brunelleschi found himself as much an engineer as architect, constantly designing winches and hoists to carry the materials (plus food and drink) faster and more efficiently up to the level of the workmen.

His finished work speaks for itself, 45m (148 ft.) wide at the base and 90m (295 ft.) high from drum to lantern. For his achievement, Brunelleschi was accorded the honor of a burial inside Florence's cathedral.

Doors ★★ have also been moved inside (and will be joined soon by Pisano's **South Doors**).

Also here is a Michelangelo **"Pietà"** ★★ that nearly wasn't. Early in the process he had told students that he wanted this "Pietà" to stand at his tomb, but when he found an imperfection in the marble, he began attacking it with a hammer (look at Christ's left arm). The master never returned to the work, but his students later repaired the damage. The figure of Nicodemus was untouched—legend has it, because it was a self-portrait of the artist—a Michelangelo myth that, for once, is probably true. Elsewhere are works by Donatello—including his restored **"Magdalen"** ★—Andrea del Verrocchio, Luca della Robbia, and others. In 2017, a restored early Giotto **"Madonna"** ★ damaged in the 1993 Uffizi car bomb became the museum's newest star turn.

Piazza del Duomo 9 (behind cathedral). www.ilgrandemuseodelduomo.it. ⓒ **055/230-2885.** 18€ Grande Museo del Duomo ticket. Daily 9am–7pm. Closed 1st Tues of month. Bus: C1.

Around Piazza della Signoria & Santa Trínita

Galleria degli Uffizi (Uffizi Gallery) ★★★ ART MUSEUM There is no collection of Renaissance art on the planet that can match the Uffizi. Period. For all its crowds and other inconveniences, the Uffizi remains a must-see. And what will you see? Some 60-plus rooms and marble corridors—built in the 16th century as the Medici's private offices, or *uffici*—all packed with famous paintings, among them Giotto's "Ognissanti Madonna," Botticelli's "Birth of Venus," Leonardo da Vinci's "Annunciation," Michelangelo's "Holy Family," and many, many more.

Start with **Room 2** for a look at the pre-Renaissance, Gothic style of painting born in the Middle Ages. Compare teacher and student with Cimabue's "Santa Trínita Maestà," painted around 1280, and Giotto's **"Ognissanti Madonna"** ★★★ done in 1310. The similar subject and setting for both paintings shows how Giotto transformed Cimabue's iconlike Byzantine style into something more human. Giotto's Madonna looks like she's sitting on a throne, her clothes emphasizing the curves of her body, whereas Cimabue's Madonna and angels float in space, like portraits on coins, with stiff positioning. Also worth a look-see: Duccio's **"Rucellai Madonna"** ★ (1285), a founding work of the ethereal Sienese School of painting.

Room 3 showcases the Sienese School at its peak, with Simone Martini's dazzling **"Annunciation"** ★★ (1333) and Ambrogio Lorenzetti's "Presentation at the Temple" (1342). The Black Death of 1348 wiped out this entire generation of Sienese painters, and most of that city's population along with them. **Room 7** shows Florentine painting at its most decorative, in a style known as "International Gothic." The iconic work is Gentile da Fabriano's **"Procession of the Magi"** ★★★ (1423). The line to see the newborn Jesus is full of decorative and comic elements and is even longer than the one waiting outside the Uffizi.

Galleria degli Uffizi, interior.

shamelessly stolen by Leonardo da Vinci 40 years later for his "Mona Lisa." Lippi's work was also a celebrity scandal. The woman who modeled for Mary was said to be Filippo's lover—a would-be nun called Lucrezia Buti whom he had spirited away from a convent before she took vows—and the child looking toward the viewer the product of their union. That son, Filippino Lippi, became a painter in his own right, and some of his works hang in the same room. However, it was Filippo's student (who would, in turn, become Filippino's teacher) who would go on to become one of the most famous artists of the 15th century. His name was Botticelli.

A renovation completed in late 2016 split **Rooms 10 to 14** into two separate spaces (despite the numbering, this had been a single room since 1978). The area remains devoted to the works of Sandro Filipepi, better known by his nickname "Little Barrels," or Botticelli. Botticelli's 1485 **"Birth of Venus"** ★★ hangs like a billboard you have seen a thousand times. Venus's pose is taken from classical statues, while the winds Zephyr and Aura blowing her to shore, and the muse welcoming her are from Ovid's "Metamorphosis." Botticelli's 1478 **"Primavera"** ★★★, its dark, bold colors a stark contrast to filmy, pastel "Venus," defies definitive interpretation. Again, it features Venus (center), alongside Mercury, with the winged boots, the Three Graces, and the goddess Flora. In **Room 15,** Botticelli's "Adoration of the Magi" contains a self-portrait of the artist. He's the one in yellow on the far right. A monumental "Adoration" by Flemish painter Hugo Van Der Groes is almost contemporaneous (ca. 1475).

As soon as you cross to the Uffizi's west wing—past picture windows with views of the Arno River to one side and the perfect, Renaissance perspective of the Uffizi piazza to the other—you're walloped with another line of masterpieces. Among the highlights of this "second half" is Michelangelo's 1505–08 **"Holy Family"** ★ **(Room 35).** The twisting shapes of Mary, Joseph, and Jesus recall those in the Sistine Chapel in Rome for their sculpted nature and the bright colors. The torsion and tensions of the painting (and other Michelangelo works) inspired the next generation of Florentine painters, known as the **Mannerists.** Andrea Del Sarto, Rosso Fiorentino, and Pontormo are all represented in the revamped **Sale Rosse (Red Rooms, 57–61)** downstairs. Here too, the Uffizi has several Raphaels, including his often-copied **"Madonna of the Goldfinch"** ★★ (Room 66), with a background landscape lifted from Leonardo and Botticelli.

A few rooms farther on, you'll find Leonardo da Vinci's restored but unfinished **"Adoration of the Magi"** ★★ and **"Annunciation"** ★★★, which are now neighbors. In the latter, completed in the early 1470s while Leonardo was still a student in Verrocchio's workshop, da Vinci's ability to orchestrate the viewer's focus is already masterful: The line down the middle of the brick corner of the house draws your glance to Mary's delicate fingers, which themselves point along the top of a stone wall to the angel's two raised fingers. Those, in turn, draw attention to the mountain in the center of the two parallel trees dividing Mary from the angel, representing the gulf between the worldly and the spiritual. Its unusual perspective was painted to be viewed from the lower right.

Titian's reclining nude **"Venus of Urbino" ★★** (Room 83) is another highlight of the later works. It's no coincidence that the edge of the curtain, the angle of her hand and leg, and the line splitting floor and bed all intersect at the forbidden part of her body. Mark Twain, on a visit to the Uffizi, declared Titian's Venus obscene.

Opened in 2018, the new **Sale Seicento (1600s Rooms)** showcase paintings by Caravaggio, notably his crazed **"Medusa" ★** self-portrait and an enigmatic **"Bacchus" ★**. These new rooms also explore the 17th-century *caravaggieschi* artists who aped his *chiaroscuro* (bright light and dark shadows) style. Greatest among them was Artemisia Gentileschi, a rare female painter from this period. Her **"Judith Slaying Holofernes" ★** (ca. 1612), is one of the bloodiest paintings in the gallery.

Also refreshed in 2018, **Rooms 46 to 55** showcase the works of foreign painters in the Uffizi. The best among the so-called **Sale Blu (Blue Rooms)** is the Spanish gallery, with works by Goya, El Greco's "Sts. John the Evangelist and Francis" (1600), and Velázquez's **"Self-Portrait" ★**. **Room 49** displays some of Rembrandt's most familiar portraits and self-portraits.

If you find yourself flagging at any point (it happens to us all), there is a **coffee shop** at the far end of the west wing. Prices are in line with the piazza below, plus you get a great close-up of the Palazzo Vecchio's facade from the terrace. Fully refreshed, you can return to discover works by the many great artists we haven't space to cover here: Cranach and Dürer; Giorgione, Bellini, and Mantegna; and Uccello, Masaccio, Bronzino, and Veronese. There are original Roman statues and friezes, too, notably in a room dedicated to the Medici garden at San Marco. In short, there is nowhere like the Uffizi anywhere in Italy, or the world.

Piazzale degli Uffizi 6 (off Piazza della Signoria). www.uffizi.it. Reserve tickets at www. firenzemusei.it or ✆ **055/294-883.** Mar–Oct 20€, Nov–Feb 12€. Tues–Sun 8:15am– 6:50pm. Bus: C1 or C2.

Museo Nazionale del Bargello (Bargello Museum) ★★ MUSEUM

This is the most important museum anywhere for Renaissance **sculpture**— and often inexplicably quieter than other museums in the city. In a far cry from its original use as the city's prison, torture chamber, and execution site, the Bargello now stands as a three-story art museum containing some of the best works of Michelangelo, Donatello, and Ghiberti, as well as of their most successful Mannerist successor, Giambologna.

In the ground-level Michelangelo room, you'll witness the variety of his craft, from a whimsical 1497 **"Bacchus" ★★** to a severe, unfinished "Brutus" of 1539. "Bacchus," created when Michelangelo was just 22, genuinely looks drunk, leaning back a little too far, his head off kilter, with a cupid about to bump him over. Nearby is Giambologna's twisting **"Mercury" ★**, poised to take off, propelled by the breath of Zephyr.

PIAZZA DELLA signoria

When the medieval Guelph party finally came out on top after a long political struggle with the Ghibellines, they razed part of the old center to build a new palace for civic government. It's said the Guelphs ordered architect Arnolfo di Cambio to build what we now call the **Palazzo Vecchio** (see p. 186) in a corner of this space, but to be sure that not 1 inch of his building sat on cursed former Ghibelline land. This odd legend was probably fabricated to explain Arnolfo's quirky off-kilter architecture.

The space around the *palazzo* became the new civic center of town, L-shaped **Piazza della Signoria ★★**, named after the oligarchic ruling body of the medieval city (the "Signoria"). Today, it's an outdoor sculpture gallery, teeming with tourists, postcard stands, horses and buggies, and expensive outdoor cafes. If you want to catch the square at its serene best, come by 8am.

The statuary on the piazza is particularly beautiful, starting on the far left (as you're facing the Palazzo Vecchio) with Giambologna's equestrian statue of "Grand Duke Cosimo I" (1594). To its right is one of Florence's favorite sculptures to hate, the **"Fontana del Nettuno"** ("Neptune Fountain"; 1560–75), created by Bartolomeo Ammannati as a tribute to Cosimo I's naval ambitions but nicknamed by the Florentines "Il Biancone," or "Big Whitey." Its two-year restoration, paid for by the Ferragamo fashion house, is due for completion by 2019. The **porphyry plaque** set in the ground in front of the fountain marks the site where puritanical monk Savonarola held the Bonfire of the Vanities: With his fiery apocalyptic preaching, he whipped the Florentines into a frenzy, and hundreds filed into this piazza, arms loaded with paintings, clothing, and other effects that represented their "decadence." They threw it all onto the flames.

To the right of Neptune is a long, raised platform fronting the Palazzo Vecchio known as the *arringheria*, from which soapbox speakers would lecture to crowds (we get our word "harangue" from this). On its far left corner is a copy (original in the Bargello) of Donatello's **"Marzocco,"** symbol of the city, with a Florentine lion resting his raised paw on a shield emblazoned with the city's emblem, the *giglio* (lily). To its right is another Donatello replica, **"Judith Beheading Holofernes."** Farther down is a man who needs little introduction, Michelangelo's **"David,"** a 19th-century copy of the original now in the Accademia. Near enough to David to look truly ugly in comparison is Baccio Bandinelli's **"Hercules and Cacus"** (1534). Poor Bandinelli was trying to copy Michelangelo's muscular male form but ended up making his Hercules merely lumpy.

At the piazza's south end is one of the square's earliest and prettiest embellishments, the **Loggia dei Lanzi ★★** (1376–82), named after the Swiss guard of lancers *(lanzi)* whom Cosimo de' Medici stationed here. The airy loggia was probably built on a design by Andrea Orcagna, spawning another of its many names, the Loggia di Orcagna (yet another is the Loggia della Signoria). At the front left stands Benvenuto Cellini's masterpiece in bronze, **"Perseus" ★★★** (1545), holding out the severed head of Medusa. On the far right is Giambologna's **"Rape of the Sabines" ★★**, one of the most successful Mannerist sculptures in existence, and a piece you must walk all the way around to appreciate, catching the action and artistry of its spiral design from different angles. Talk about moving it indoors, safe from the elements, continues . . . but for now, it's still here.

Fountain of Neptune in the Piazza della Signoria.

Upstairs an enormous vaulted hall is filled with some of Donatello's most accomplished sculptures, including his original "Marzocco" (from outside the Palazzo Vecchio; p. 186), and **"St. George"** ★ from a niche on the exterior of Orsanmichele. Notable among them is his bronze **"David"** ★★ (which some think might actually be the god Mercury), done in 1440, the first freestanding nude sculpture since Roman times. The classical detail of these sculptures, as well as their naturalistic poses and reflective mood, is the essence of the Renaissance style.

Side by side on the back wall are the contest entries submitted by Ghiberti and Brunelleschi for the commission to do the Baptistery doors in 1401. With the "Sacrifice of Isaac" as their biblical theme, both displayed innovative use of perspective. Ghiberti won the contest, perhaps because his scene is more thematically unified. Brunelleschi could have ended up a footnote in the art history books, but instead he turned his attentions to architecture instead, which turned out to be a wise move (see "A Man & His Dome," p. 180).

Via del Proconsolo 4. ✆ **055/238-8606.** 8€ (9€ during temporary exhibitions; free 1st Sun of month). Mon–Fri 8:15am–1:50pm, Sat–Sun 8:15am–4:50pm. Closed 1st, 3rd, and 5th Mon, and 2nd and 4th Sun of each month. Bus: C1 or C2.

Orsanmichele ★★ CHURCH/ARCHITECTURE   This bulky structure halfway down Via dei Calzaiuoli looks more like a Gothic warehouse than a church—which is exactly what it was, built as a granary and grain market in 1337. After a miraculous image of the Madonna appeared on a column inside, its lower level was turned into a shrine and chapel. The city's merchant guilds each undertook the task of decorating one of the exterior Gothic tabernacles with a statue of their guild's patron saint. Masters such as Ghiberti, Donatello, Verrocchio, and Giambologna all cast or carved masterpieces to set here (those remaining are mostly copies, including Donatello's "St. George").

In the dark interior, an elaborate Gothic stone **Tabernacle** ★ (1349–59) by Andrea Orcagna protects a luminous 1348 "Madonna and Child" painted by Giotto's student Bernardo Daddi, to which miracles were ascribed during the Black Death of 1348–50.

Tip: On Mondays (10am–4:50pm) and Saturdays (10am–12:30pm) only, you can access the upper floors, which house many original sculptures that once adorned Orsanmichele's exterior niches. Among the treasures of this so-called **Museo di Orsanmichele** ★ are a trio of bronzes: Ghiberti's "St. John the Baptist" (1412–16), the first life-size bronze of the Renaissance; Verrocchio's "Incredulity of St. Thomas" (1483); and Giambologna's "St. Luke" (1602). Climb up one floor further, to the top, for an unforgettable 360° **panorama** ★★ of the city.

Via Arte della Lana 1. ℂ **055/238-8610.** Free, donations accepted. Daily 10am–5pm. Bus: C2.

Palazzo Davanzati ★★ PALACE/MUSEUM   One of the best-preserved 14th-century palaces in the city shines a light on domestic life during the medieval and Renaissance period. It was originally built for the Davizzi family in the mid-1300s, then bought by the Davanzati clan; the latter's family tree, dating back to the 1100s, is emblazoned on the wall of a ground-floor courtyard. The palace's painted wooden ceilings and murals have aged well (even surviving World War II damage), but the emphasis remains not on the decor, but on providing visitors with insights into medieval life for a noble Florentine family: feasts and festivities in the **Sala Madornale;** a private, internal well to secure water supply when things in Florence got sticky; and magnificent bedchamber frescoes from the 1350s, which recount, comic-strip style, "The Chatelaine of Vergy," a 13th-century morality tale. An interesting footnote: In 1916, a New York auction of furnishings from this very palace launched a "Florentine style" trend in U.S. interior design circles.

Via Porta Rossa 13. ℂ **055/238-8610.** 6€. Mon–Fri 8:15am–1:50pm, Sat–Sun 1:15–6:50pm. Closed 2nd and 4th Sun, and 1st, 3rd, and 5th Mon of each month. Bus: C2.

Palazzo Vecchio ★★ PALACE   The core of Florence's fortresslike town hall was built from 1299 to 1302 to the designs of Arnolfo di Cambio, Gothic master builder. The palace was home to the various Florentine governments (and is today to the city government). When Duke Cosimo I and his Medici family moved to the *palazzo* in 1540, they redecorated: Michelozzo's 1453 **courtyard** ★ was left architecturally intact but frescoed by Vasari with scenes of Austrian cities, to celebrate the 1565 marriage of Francesco de' Medici and Joanna of Austria.

A grand staircase leads up to the **Sala dei Cinquecento** ★, named for the 500-man assembly that met here in the pre-Medici days of the Florentine Republic. It's also the site of the greatest fresco cycle that ever wasn't. Leonardo da Vinci was commissioned in 1503–05 to paint one long wall with a battle scene celebrating Florence's victory at the 1440 Battle of Anghiari. Always trying new methods and materials, he decided to mix wax into his pigments. Leonardo had finished painting part of the wall, but it wasn't drying fast enough, so he brought in braziers stoked with hot coals to try to hurry the process. As onlookers watched in horror, the wax in the fresco melted under the heat and colors ran down the walls to a puddle on the floor. The search for remains of his work continues; some hope was provided in 2012 with the discovery of pigments used by Leonardo in a cavity behind the current wall.

Michelangelo was supposed to paint a fresco on the opposite wall, but he never got past the preparatory drawings before Pope Julius II called him to Rome to paint the Sistine Chapel. Vasari and his assistants covered the bare walls from 1563 to 1565 with subservient frescoes exalting Cosimo I and the military victories of his regime, against Pisa (on the near wall) and Siena (far wall). Opposite the door you enter is Michelangelo's statue of **"Victory"** ★, carved from 1533 to 1534 for Pope Julius II's tomb but later donated to the Medici.

The first series of rooms on the upper floor is the **Quartiere degli Elementi,** frescoed with allegories and mythological characters again by Vasari. Crossing the balcony overlooking the Sala dei Cinquecento, you enter the **Apartments of Eleonora di Toledo ★**, decorated for Cosimo's Spanish wife. Her **private chapel ★★★** is a masterpiece of mid–16th-century fresco painting by Bronzino. Under the coffered ceiling of the **Sala dei Gigli** is Ghirlandaio's fresco of "St. Zenobius Enthroned," with figures from Republican and Imperial Rome, and Donatello's original **"Judith and Holofernes"** ★ bronze (1455), one of his last works. In the palace basement are the **Scavi del Teatro Romano ★**, remnants of Roman Florentia's theater, upon which the medieval palace was built, with remains of the walls and an intact paved street.

Palazzo Vecchio.

Vasari's Corridor

The enclosed passageway that runs along the top of Ponte Vecchio is part of the **Corridoio Vasariano (Vasari Corridor)** ★, a private elevated link between the Palazzo Vecchio and Palazzo Pitti, and now hung with the world's best collection of artists' self-portraits. Duke Cosimo I found the idea of mixing with the hoi polloi on the way to work rather distressing—and there was a credible threat of assassination—and so commissioned Vasari to design his VIP route in 1565. It was previously open for guided visits only, and regularly closed for restoration. But a major policy change is set to bring back admission from inside the Uffizi. Ticketing plans are unclear at time of writing, although it is now scheduled to remain closed until (probably) mid-2019. Inquire at the tourist office for the latest news.

Visitors can also climb the **Torre di Arnolfo** ★★, the palace's crenellated tower. If you can bear small spaces and 218 steps, the views from the top of this medieval skyscraper are sublime. The 95m (312-ft.) Torre is closed during bad weather; the minimum age to climb it is 6, and children ages 17 and under must be accompanied by an adult.

Piazza della Signoria. www.museicivicifiorentini.comune.fi.it. © **055/276-8325**. Palazzo 10€; Torre 6.50€; Palazzo plus Torre 14€; Palazzo plus Scavi 14€; admission to all 18€. Palazzo/Scavi: Fri–Wed 9am–7pm (Apr–Sept until 11pm), Thurs 9am–2pm. Torre: Fri–Wed 10am–5pm (Apr–Sept 9am–9pm); Thurs 10am–2pm (Apr–Sept 9am–2pm). Bus: C1 or C2.

Ponte Vecchio ★ ARCHITECTURE   The oldest and most famous bridge across the Arno, the Ponte Vecchio was built in 1345 by Taddeo Gaddi to replace an earlier version. Overhanging shops have lined the bridge since at least the 12th century. In the 16th century, it was home to butchers, until Duke Ferdinand I moved into the Palazzo Pitti across the river. He couldn't stand the stench, so he evicted the meat cutters and moved in gold- and silversmiths, and jewelers, who occupy it to this day.

The Ponte Vecchio's fame saved it in 1944 from the Nazis, who had orders to blow up all the bridges before retreating out of Florence as Allied forces advanced. They couldn't bring themselves to reduce this span to rubble, so they blew up the ancient buildings on either end to block it off. Not so discriminating was the **Great Arno Flood** of 1966, which severely damaged the shops. A private night watchman saw waters rising alarmingly and called many of the goldsmiths at home. They rushed to remove their valuable stock before it was washed away.

Via Por Santa Maria/Via Guicciardini. Bus: C3 or D.

Santa Trínita ★★ CHURCH   Beyond Bernardo Buontalenti's late–16th-century **facade** lies a dark church, rebuilt in the 14th century but founded by the Vallombrosans sometime before 1177. The third chapel on the right has remains of detached frescoes by Spinello Aretino, which were found under Lorenzo Monaco's 1424 "Scenes from the Life of the Virgin" frescoes covering the next chapel along. In the right transept, Ghirlandaio frescoed the **Cappella Sassetti ★** in 1483 with a cycle on the "Life of St. Francis." He set the scenes against Florentine backdrops and peopled them with portraits of contemporary notables. His "Francis Receiving the Order from Pope Honorius" (in the lunette) takes place under an arcade on the north side of Piazza della Signoria. You'll recognize the Loggia dei Lanzi in the middle, and on the left, the Palazzo Vecchio (the Uffizi now between them hadn't been built yet).

Piazza Santa Trinita.

Tip: The south end of the piazza leads to the **Ponte Santa Trínita ★★**, Florence's most graceful bridge. In 1567, Ammannati built a span here that was set with four 16th-century statues of the seasons, in honor of the marriage of Cosimo II. After the Nazis blew up the bridge in 1944, it was rebuilt, and all was set into place—save the head on the statue of Spring, which remained lost until a team dredging the river in 1961 found it by accident. If you want to photograph the Ponte Vecchio at its best, head here at dusk or after dark.

Piazza Santa Trínita. ℘ **055/216-912.** Free. Mon–Sat 8:30am–noon and 4–6pm; Sun 8:30–10:45am and 4–6pm. Bus: C3, D, 6, or 11.

Catch an Exhibition at the Strozzi

The Renaissance **Palazzo Strozzi ★★**, Piazza Strozzi (www.palazzostrozzi.org; ℘ **055/264-5155**), and basement **Strozzina** are Florence's major spaces for temporary and contemporary art shows and have been experiencing a 21st-century renaissance of their own. Hits of recent years include 2012's "Americans in Florence: Sargent and the New World Impressionists" and Bill Viola's "Electronic Renaissance" in 2017. There's always plenty going on including talks, late-night events, late-night openings (usually Thurs), and discovery packs aimed at 3- to 9-year-olds. Check the website for the latest exhibition news.

Around San Lorenzo & the Mercato Centrale

Until a controversial—and *perhaps* temporary—move in 2014, the church of San Lorenzo was practically lost behind the leather stalls and souvenir carts of Florence's vast **San Lorenzo street market** (see "Shopping," p. 203). In fact, a bustle of commerce characterizes this whole neighborhood, centered on both the tourist market and nearby **Mercato Centrale,** whose upper floor is a showcase for Italian street food (see p. 170).

Cappelle Medicee (Medici Chapels) ★ MUSEUM   When Michelangelo built the New Sacristy between 1520 and 1533 (finished by Vasari in 1556), it was to be a tasteful monument to Lorenzo the Magnificent and his generation of relatively pleasant Medici. When work got underway on the adjacent **Cappella dei Principi (Chapel of the Princes)** in 1604, it was to become one of Italy's most god-awful and arrogant memorials, dedicated to the grand dukes, whose number includes some of Florence's most decrepit tyrants. Fittingly, the Cappella dei Principi is an exercise in bad taste, a mountain of cut marble and semiprecious stones—jasper, alabaster, mother-of-pearl, agate, and the like—slathered onto the walls and ceiling with no regard for composition and still less for chromatic unity. The pouring of ducal funds into this monstrosity lasted until the rarely conscious Gian Gastone de' Medici drank himself to death in 1737, without an heir. Teams kept doggedly at the thing, and they were still finishing the floor in 1962. Judge for yourself.

Michelangelo's **Sagrestia Nuova (New Sacristy)** ★★, built to jibe with Brunelleschi's Old Sacristy in San Lorenzo proper (see below), is much calmer. (An architectural tidbit: The windows in the dome taper as they get near the top to fool you into thinking the dome is higher.) Michelangelo was supposed to produce three tombs here (perhaps four) but ironically got only the two less important ones done. So, Lorenzo de' Medici ("the Magnificent")—wise ruler of his city, poet of note, grand patron of the arts, and moneybags behind much of the Renaissance—ended up with a mere inscription of his name next to his brother Giuliano's on a plain marble slab against the entrance wall. They did get one genuine Michelangelo sculpture to decorate their slab, an unfinished **"Madonna and Child"** ★.

On the left wall of the sacristy is Michelangelo's **"Tomb of Lorenzo"** ★, duke of Urbino (and Lorenzo the Magnificent's grandson), whose seated statue symbolizes the contemplative life. Below him on the curves of the tomb stretch "Dawn" (female) and "Dusk" (male), a pair of Michelangelo's most famous sculptures. This pair mirrors "Day" (male) and "Night" (female) across the way. Observing "Dawn" and "Night," one might wonder if Michelangelo perhaps hadn't seen many naked women.

Piazza Madonna degli Aldobrandini (behind San Lorenzo, where Via Faenza and Via del Giglio meet). ✆ **055/238-8602.** 8€. Daily 8:15am–5pm. Closed 1st, 3rd, and 5th Mon, and 2nd and 4th Sun of each month. Bus: C1, C2, or 22.

Palazzo Medici-Riccardi ★ PALACE   Built by Michelozzo in 1444 for the Medici "godfather" Cosimo il Vecchio, this is the prototypical Florentine *palazzo,* on which the more overbearing Strozzi and Pitti palaces were modeled. It remained the Medici's private home until Cosimo I officially declared his power as duke by moving to the city's civic nerve center, the Palazzo Vecchio. Its **Cappella dei Magi** is the oldest chapel to survive from a private Florentine palace; walls are covered with colorful Benozzo Gozzoli **frescoes ★★** (1459–63), classics of the International Gothic style. Rich as tapestries, they depict an extended "Journey of the Magi" to see the Christ child, who's being adored by Mary in the altarpiece. The third wise man is a flattering portrait of a young Lorenzo the Magnificent. Further highlights of the upper floor include the **Sala Luca Giordano ★**, with baroque decor by the Neapolitan painter, and a Filippo Lippi "Madonna."

Via Cavour 3. www.palazzo-medici.it. ℘ **055/276-0340.** 7€ adults (10€ during temporary exhibitions), 4€ ages 6 to 12. Thurs–Tues 8:30am–7pm. Bus: C1.

San Lorenzo ★ CHURCH   A rough brick anti-facade fronts what is most likely the oldest church in Florence, founded in A.D. 393. It was later the Medici family's parish church, and Cosimo il Vecchio, whose wise behind-the-scenes rule made him popular with the Florentines, is buried in front of the high altar. The plaque marking the spot is inscribed PATER PATRIAE, "Father of the Homeland." Off the left transept, the **Sagrestia Vecchia (Old Sacristy) ★** is one of Brunelleschi's purest pieces of early Renaissance architecture. The focal sarcophagus contains Cosimo il Vecchio's parents, Giovanni di Bicci de' Medici and his wife, Piccarda Bueri. A side chapel is decorated with a star map showing the night sky above the city in the 1440s—a scene that also features, precisely, in Brunelleschi's Pazzi Chapel in Santa Croce (see p. 196). On the wall of the left aisle is Bronzino's huge fresco of the **"Martyrdom of San Lorenzo" ★**, showing the poor saint being roasted on a grill in Rome.

Piazza San Lorenzo. www.operamedicealaurenziana.org. ℘ **055/214-042.** Church 6€. Mon–Sat 10am–5pm; Mar–Oct also Sun 1:30–5pm. Bus: C1.

Near Piazza Santa Maria Novella

The two squat obelisks in **Piazza Santa Maria Novella ★**, resting on Giambologna tortoises, once served as the turning posts for chariot races held here from the 16th to the mid–19th century. Once a down-at-the-heels part of the center, the area now is home to some of Florence's priciest lodgings.

Museo Marino Marini & Cappella Rucellai ★ MUSEUM   One of Florence's most unusual museums showcases the work of sculptor Marino Marini (1901–80). A native of nearby Pistoia, Marini worked mostly in bronze, with "horse and rider" a recurring theme in his semi-abstract work. The open spaces, minimal crowds, monumental sculptures, and fun themes in Marini's work make this museum—revamped in 2018—a good bet if kids in tow are becoming weary of the Renaissance. They won't escape it entirely, however—tagged onto the side of the museum is the **Cappella Rucellai,** a Renaissance chapel housing the **Tempietto ★★**, a polychrome marble tomb completed by L. B. Alberti for Giovanni de' Rucellai in 1467. Decorated with symbols of both the Rucellai and Medici families, and frescoed on the inside, the tomb was supposedly based on drawings of the Holy Sepulcher in Jerusalem.

Piazza San Pancrazio. www.museomarinomarini.it. ℂ **055/219-432.** 6€. Wed–Fri 10am–1pm; Sat–Mon 10am–7pm. Bus: C3, 6, or 11.

Museo Novecento ★ MUSEUM   Inaugurated in 2014, this museum covers 20th-century Italian art in a multitude of media. Crowds are often sparse—let's face it, you're in Florence for the 1400s, not the 1900s. But that's no reflection on the quality of the collection, which spans 100 years of visual arts. Exhibits include works by major names such as De Chirico and Futurist Gino Severini, and closer examinations of both Florence's role in fashion and Italy's relationship with European avant-garde art. Our favorite spot, though, is the top-floor **screening room** ★★ where a 20-minute movie-clip montage shows Florence as represented by a century of filmmakers, from Arnaldo Ginna's 1916 "Vita Futurista" to more recent films such as "Room with a View" and "Tea with Mussolini."

Piazza Santa Maria Novella 10. www.museonovecento.it/en. ℂ **055/286-132.** 8.50€. Apr–Sept Sat–Wed 11am–8pm, Thurs 11am–2pm, Fri 11am–11pm; Oct–Mar daily 11am–7pm (closes 2pm Thurs). Bus: 6 or 11.

Santa Maria Novella ★★ CHURCH   Of all Florence's major churches, this home of the Dominicans is the only one with an original **facade** ★★ matching the era of the church's greatest importance. The lower Romanesque half was started in the 1300s by architect Fra' Jacopo Talenti. Renaissance architect and theorist Leon Battista Alberti finished the facade, adding a classically inspired top that not only went seamlessly with the lower half but also created a Cartesian plane of perfect geometry. Inside, **Masaccio's "Trinità"** ★★★ (ca. 1425) is the first painting ever to use linear mathematical perspective. Florentine citizens and artists flooded in to see the fresco when it was unveiled, many remarking in awe that it seemed to punch a hole back into space, creating a chapel out of flat wall. Frescoed chapels by Filippino Lippi and others fill the **transept.**

The **Sanctuary** ★ behind the main altar was frescoed after 1485 by Ghirlandaio with the help of his assistants and apprentices, probably including a young Michelangelo. The left wall is covered with a cycle on the "Life of the Virgin" and the right with a "Life of St. John the Baptist." The works are also snapshots of the era's fashions and personages, full of portraits of the Tornabuoni family who commissioned them.

For years the church's frescoed cloisters were treated as a separate site; they are now reunited: The church and cloisters are now accessible on one admission ticket. (Although, confusingly, there are two separate entrances, through the church's garden and via the tourist office at the rear, on Piazza della Stazione.) The **Chiostro Verde (Green Cloister)** ★★ was partly frescoed between 1431 and 1446 by Paolo Uccello, a Florentine painter who became increasingly obsessed with the mathematics behind perspective. His Old Testament scenes include a "Universal Deluge," which ironically was badly damaged by the Great Arno Flood of 1966. Off the cloister, the **Spanish Chapel** ★ is a complex piece of Dominican propaganda, frescoed in the 1360s by Andrea di Bonaiuto. The **Chiostro dei Morti (Cloister of the Dead)** ★ is among the oldest parts of the convent and was another area badly damaged in 1966. Its low-slung vaults were decorated by Andrea Orcagna and others. Since 2017 visitors have also been permitted access to the **Chiostro Grande** ★ (Florence's largest cloister) and the papal apartments, frescoed by Florentine Mannerist Pontormo.

Piazza Santa Maria Novella/Piazza della Stazione 4. www.smn.it. ✆ **055/219-257.** 7.50€. Mon–Thurs 9am–5:30pm (Apr–Sept until 7pm); Fri 11am–5:30pm (Apr–Sept until 7pm); Sat 9am–5:30pm (July–Aug until 6:30pm); Sun 1–5:30pm (July–Aug noon–6:30pm; Sept noon–5:30pm). Bus: C2, 6, 11, or 22.

Near San Marco & Santissima Annunziata

Cenacolo di Sant'Apollonia ★ ART MUSEUM Painter Andrea del Castagno (1421–57) learned his trade painting portraits of condemned men in the city's prisons, and it's easy to see this influence in faces of the Disciples in his version of **"The Last Supper,"** the first of many painted in Florence during the Renaissance. This giant fresco, completed around 1447, covers an entire wall at one end of this former convent refectory. Judas is banished to the other side of a communal table. Above Castagno's "Last Supper," his "Crucifixion," "Deposition," and "Entombment" complete the sequence.

Via XXVII Aprile 1. ✆ **055/238-8608.** Free. Daily 8:15am–1:50pm. Closed 1st, 3rd, and 5th Sat–Sun of each month. Bus: 1, 6, 11, 14, 17, or 23.

Chiostro dello Scalzo ★ ART MUSEUM/ARCHITECTURE You'll need luck or great timing to catch this place open, but it is well worth a short detour from San Marco. Between 1509 and 1526 Mannerist painter Andrea del Sarto frescoed a cloister belonging to a religious fraternity dedicated to St. John the Baptist, who is the theme of an unusual monochrome *(grisaille)* fresco cycle. This place is usually blissfully empty, too.

Via Cavour 69. ✆ **055/238-8604.** Free. Mon and Thurs 8:15am–1:50pm; also open (same hours) 1st, 3rd, and 5th Sat, and 2nd and 4th Sun of each month. Bus: 1 or 17.

Galleria dell'Accademia ★★ ART MUSEUM **"David"** ★★★—"Il Gigante"—is much larger than most people imagine, looming 4.8m (16 ft.) on top of a 1.8m (6-ft.) pedestal. He hasn't faded with time, either; the marble still gleams as if it were unveiling day in 1504. Viewing the statue is a pleasure in the bright and spacious room custom-designed for him after his move to the Accademia in 1873, following 300 years of pigeons perching on his head in Piazza della Signoria. Replicas now take the abuse there, and at Piazzale Michelangiolo. The spot high on the northern flank of the Duomo, for which he was originally commissioned, stands empty.

But the Accademia is not only about "David"; you will be delighted to discover he is surrounded by an entire museum stuffed with notable Renais-sance works. Michelangelo's unfinished **"Prisoners"** ★★ statues are a contrast to "David," with their rough forms struggling to emerge from the raw stone. Michelangelo famously said that he tried to free the sculpture within from the block, and you can see this clearly here. Rooms showcase paintings by Perugino, Filippino Lippi, Giotto, Giovanna da Milano, Andrea Orcagna, and others.

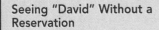

Seeing "David" Without a Reservation

The wait to get in to see "David" can be an hour or more if you didn't reserve ahead or buy a Firenze Card (p. 149). Try getting there before the museum opens in the morning or an hour or two before closing time.

Via Ricasoli 60. ©**055/238-8609.** (Prebook tickets at www.firenzemusei.it or ©055/294-883.) 12.50€. Tues–Sun 8:15am–6:50pm. Bus: C1, 1, 6, 14, 19, 23, 31, or 32.

Museo Archeologico (Archaeological Museum) ★ MUSEUM   If you can force yourselves away from the Renaissance, rewind a millennium or two at one of the most important archaeological collections in central Italy, which has a particular emphasis on the **Etruscan** period. You will need a little patience, however: The collection is not easy to navigate, and exhibits have a habit of moving around, but you will easily find the **"Arezzo Chimera"** ★★ , a bronze figure of a mythical lion–goat–serpent dating to the 4th century B.C. It is perhaps the most important bronze sculpture to survive from the Etruscan era, and at time of writing, it was displayed alongside the "Arringatore," a life-size bronze of an orator dating to the 1st century, just as Etruscan culture was being subsumed by Ancient Rome. On the top floor is the **"Idolino"** ★, an exquisite and slightly mysterious, lithe bronze. The collection is also strong on Etruscan-era *bucchero* pottery and funerary urns, and Egyptian relics that include several sarcophagi displayed in eerie galleries. With other travelers so focused on medieval and Renaissance sights, you may have the place almost to yourself.

Piazza Santissma Annunziata 9b. © **055/23-575.** 4€. Tues–Fri 8:30am–7pm; Sat–Mon 8:30am–2pm. Closed 2nd, 4th, and 5th Sun of each month. Bus: 6, 19, 31, or 32.

San Marco ★★★ ART MUSEUM   We have never understood why this place is not constantly mobbed. Showcasing the work of Fra' Angelico, Dominican monk and Florentine painter in a style known as "International Gothic," this is the world's most important collection of his altarpieces and painted panels, residing in the former 13th-century convent the artist-monk once called home. Seeing it all in one place allows you to appreciate how his decorative impulses and the sinuous lines of his figures place his work right on the cusp of the Renaissance. The most moving and unusual is his **"Annunciation"** ★★★, but a close second are the intimate frescoes of the life of Jesus—painted not on one giant wall, but scene by scene on the individual walls of small monks' cells that honeycomb the upper floor. The idea was that these scenes, painted by both Fra' Angelico and his assistants, would aid in the monks' prayer and contemplation. The final cell on the left corridor belonged to the firebrand preacher Savonarola, who briefly incited the populace of the most art-filled city in the world to burn their "decadent" paintings, illuminated manuscripts, and anything else he felt was a worldly betrayal of Jesus's ideals. (Ultimately, he ran afoul of the pope.) You'll see his notebooks, rosary, and what's left of the clothes he wore in his cell, as well as an anonymous panel painted to show the day in 1498 when he was burned at the stake in Piazza della Signoria. There is much more Fra' Angelico secreted around the cloisters, including a **"Crucifixion"** ★ in the Chapter House. The former Hospice is now a gallery dedicated to Fra' Angelico and his contemporaries; look out especially for his **"Tabernacolo dei Linaioli"** ★★ and a seemingly weightless **"Deposition"** ★★.

Piazza San Marco 3. ✆ **055/238-8608.** 4€; free if you show an Uffizi ticket. Mon–Fri 8:15am–1:50pm; Sat–Sun 8:15am–4:50pm. Closed 1st, 3rd, and 5th Sun and 2nd and 4th Mon of each month. Bus: C1, 1, 6, 7, 10, 11, 14, 17, 19, 20, 23, 25, 31, or 32.

Santissima Annunziata ★★ CHURCH This church's story begins humbly, in 1233, when seven Florentine nobles had a spiritual crisis, gave away all their possessions, and retired to the forest to contemplate divinity. In 1250, they returned to what were then fields outside the city walls and founded a small oratory, proclaiming themselves Servants of Mary (the "Servite Order"). Over the years, however, thanks to a miraculous painting (more on that later), the oratory grew into a grand basilica, enlarged by Michelozzo (1444–81) and later redecorated in unrestrained baroque style.

Visitors enter through the **Chiostro dei Voti (Votive Cloister),** which is today the church's main art draw, decorated with some of the city's finest **Mannerist frescoes** ★★ (1465–1515). A five-year restoration completed in 2017 has reinstated their original vibrancy. Rosso Fiorentino provided an "Assumption" (1513) and Pontormo a "Visitation" (1515) just to the right of the door. Their master, Andrea del Sarto, contributed a "Birth of the Virgin" (1513), in the far-right corner, one of his finest works. To the right of the door into the church is a damaged but still fascinating "Procession of the Magi" (1514) by del Sarto, who included a self-portrait at the far right, looking out at us from under his blue hat.

The church's interior is a flamboyant affair, smothered in multicolored marble and topped with a gilded coffered ceiling. In a side chapel to the left of the entrance, look for the ornate tabernacle housing a small 14th-century painting of the "Annunciation." Why such a grandiose setting? Well, according to legend, the friar who was painting the picture became vexed that he couldn't paint the Madonna's face as beautiful as she should be and went to take a nap. When he awoke, he found an angel had completed the face for him. The miraculous painting became an object of cult worship, and this once-humble church was changed forever.

On **Piazza Santissima Annunziata** ★★ outside, flanked by elegant Brunelleschi porticos, is an equestrian statue of Grand Duke Ferdinand I by Giambologna. It was his last work, cast in 1608 after his death by his student Pietro Tacca, who also did the two fountains of fantastical mermonkey-monsters. *Tip:* You can stay right on this spectacular piazza, at one of our favorite Florence hotels, the **Loggiato dei Serviti** ★★ (p. 161).

Piazza Santissima Annunziata. ✆ **055/266-181.** Free. Cloister: daily 7:30am–12:30pm and 4–6:30pm. Church: daily 4–5:15pm. Bus: 6, 19, 31, or 32.

Spedale degli Innocenti ★★ MUSEUM/ARCHITECTURE Originally funded by the silk guild, the "Nocenti" opened in 1419, and ever since has been one of the world's most famous childcare institutions. (The Institute still works with UNICEF and others.) Their landmark building was designed by Brunelleschi himself, with elegant Renaissance loggias on the façade and surrounding its interior "Women's" and "Men's" **Courtyards.** Inside, there's a three-floor museum, with multimedia exhibits tracing the history of the place and the fascinating stories of children who have benefited from its care. The Institute also has a fine **art collection,** including Renaissance works by Botticelli and Ghirlandaio displayed in a top-floor gallery alongside the original painted ceramic roundels by Della Robbia which elegantly completed Brunelleschi's sublime façade.

As you leave, notice the little window on the far north wall of the main loggia. Grated since 1875, this was where babies for centuries were delivered anonymously to the care of the orphanage.

Piazza Santissima Annunziata. www.istitutodeglinnocenti.it. ✆ **055/203-7308.** 7€. Daily 10am–7pm. Bus: 6, 19, 31, 32.

Around Piazza Santa Croce

Piazza Santa Croce is pretty much like any grand Florentine square—an open space ringed with souvenir and leather shops and thronged with tourists. Once a year (during late June) it's covered with dirt for a violent, Renaissance-style soccer tournament known as **Calcio Storico Fiorentino.**

Santa Croce ★★ CHURCH The center of Florence's Franciscan universe was begun in 1294 by Gothic master Arnolfo di Cambio to rival the church of Santa Maria Novella being raised by the Dominicans across the city. The church wasn't consecrated until 1442, and even then remained faceless until a neo-Gothic **facade** was added in 1857. This art-stuffed complex demands 2 hours of your time to see properly.

The Gothic **interior** is vast and populated with tombs of famous Florentines. Starting from the main door, immediately on the right is the recently restored tomb of the most venerated Renaissance master, **Michelangelo Buonarroti,** who died in Rome in 1564 at the ripe age of 89. The pope wanted him buried in the Eternal City, but Florentines managed to sneak his body back to Florence. Two berths down from Michelangelo's monument is a pompous 19th-century cenotaph to **Dante Alighieri,** one of history's great poets, whose "Divine Comedy" even laid the basis for the modern Italian language. (Exiled from Florence, Dante is buried in Ravenna.) Elsewhere are monuments to philosopher **Niccolò Machiavelli,** composer **Gioacchino Rossini,** sculptor **Lorenzo Ghiberti,** and scientist **Galileo Galilei.**

The right transept is richly decorated with **frescoes**. The **Cappella Castellani** was frescoed with stories of saints' lives by Agnolo Gaddi. Agnolo's father, Taddeo Gaddi—one of Giotto's closest followers—painted the **Cappella Baroncelli ★** (1328–38) at the transept's end. His frescoes depict scenes from the "Life of the Virgin," and include an "Annunciation to the Shepherds," the first night scene in Italian fresco. Giotto himself frescoed two chapels to the right of the high altar; whitewashed in the 17th century, they were uncovered in the 1800s and inexpertly restored. The **Cappella Peruzzi ★** is a late work with many references to antiquity, reflecting Giotto's trip to Rome's ruins. The more famous **Cappella Bardi ★★** appeared in the movie *A Room with a View;* key panels, featuring episodes in the life of St. Francis, include the "Trial by Fire Before the Sultan of Egypt" on the right wall; and one of Giotto's best-known works, the "Death of St. Francis," in which monks weep and wail with convincing pathos.

In the cloister is the **Cappella Pazzi ★**, one of Filippo Brunelleschi's architectural masterpieces (faithfully finished after his death in 1446). Giuliano da Maiano probably designed the porch that fronts the chapel, set with glazed terracottas by Luca della Robbia. The chapel is one of Brunelleschi's signature pieces, decorated with his trademark *pietra serena* gray stone. It is a defining example of and model for early Renaissance architecture. Curiously, the ceiling of the smaller dome depicts the same night sky as the Old Sacristy in San Lorenzo (p. 191). In the **Sacristy** is a Cimabue **"Crucifix" ★** that was almost destroyed by the Arno Flood of 1966. It became an international symbol of the ruination wreaked by a river that November day.

Piazza Santa Croce. www.santacroceopera.it. ✆ **055/246-6105.** 8€ adults, 6€ ages 11–17 (children 17 and under free with parent or guardian). Mon–Sat 9:30am–5pm; Sun 2–5pm. Bus: C1, C2, or C3.

The Oltrarno, San Niccolò & San Frediano

Giardino Bardini (Bardini Garden) ★ PARK/GARDEN   Hemmed in to the north by the city's medieval wall, the handsome Bardini Garden is less famous—and therefore less hectic—than its neighbor down the hill, the Boboli (see below). From a loftier perch over the Oltrarno, it beats the Boboli hands down for views and new angles on the city. The side view of Santa Croce—with the copper dome of the synagogue in the background—shows how the church's 19th-century facade was bolted onto a building dating to the 1200s.

Costa San Giorgio 2. www.villabardini.it. ✆ **055/2006-6233.** Combined ticket with Boboli Garden Mar–Oct 10€, Nov–Feb 6€. Same hours as Boboli; see below. Bus: C3 or D.

Giardino di Boboli (Boboli Garden) ★★ PARK/GARDEN   The statue-filled park behind the Pitti Palace is one of the earliest and finest Renaissance gardens, laid out mostly between 1549 and 1656 with box hedges in geometric patterns, groves of ilex (holm oak), dozens of statues, and rows of cypress. Just above the entrance through the courtyard of the Palazzo Pitti is an oblong **amphitheater** modeled on Roman circuses, with a **granite basin** from Rome's Baths of Caracalla and an **Egyptian obelisk** of Ramses II. In

1589 this was the setting for the wedding reception of Ferdinand de' Medici and Christine of Lorraine. (Brunelleschi's dome and Fiesole on a hill beyond must have made a sublime backdrop for the photos.) For the occasion, the family commissioned entertainment from Jacopo Peri and Ottavio Rinuccini, who decided to set a classical story entirely to music. They called it "Dafne," and it was the world's first opera. (Their follow-up hit "Erudice" was performed here in 1600; this is the first opera whose score has survived.) At the south end of the park, the **Isolotto** ★ is a dreamy island in a pond full of huge goldfish, with Giambologna's "L'Oceano" sculptural composition at its center. At the north end, down around the end of the Pitti Palace, are fake caverns filled with statuary, attempting to invoke a classical sacred grotto. The most famous, the **Grotta Grande,** was designed by Giorgio Vasari, Bartolomeo Ammannati, and Bernardo Buontalenti between 1557 and 1593; dripping with phony stalactites, it's set with replicas of Michelangelo's unfinished "Prisoners" statues. You can often get inside on the hour (but not every hour) for 15 minutes.

Entrance via Palazzo Pitti. ℭ **055/238-8791.** Mar–Oct 10€, Nov–Feb 6€; includes Giardino Bardini (see above). Open daily, June–Aug 8:15am–7:30pm; Apr–May and Sept–Oct 8:15am–6:30pm; Mar 8:15am–5:30pm; Nov–Feb 8:15am–4:30pm. Closed 1st and last Mon of month. Bus: C3, D, 11, 36, or 37.

Museo Zoologia "La Specola" ★ MUSEUM   Wax anatomical models are one reason this museum may be the only one in Florence where kids eagerly drag parents from room to room. Creepy collections of threadbare stuffed-animal specimens transition into rooms filled with lifelike human bodies suffering dismemberment, flaying, and evisceration. These wax models served as anatomical illustrations for medical students studying at this scientific institute from the 1770s. (Alas, since 2017, you must be accompanied to see many of them.) Grisly plague dioramas in the final room, created from wax in the early 1700s to satisfy the lurid tastes of Duke Cosimo III, can still be viewed unaccompanied.

Via Romana 17. www.msn.unifi.it. ℭ **055-275-6444.** 6€ adults, 3€ children 6–14 and seniors 65 and over; additional 3€ per person to see most of the waxworks. Tues–Sun 10:30am–5:30pm (Oct–May 9:30am–4:30pm). Guided visits to waxworks Tues–Fri 11:30am, 3pm; Sat–Sun 11:30am, 12:30pm, 3pm. Bus: 11, 36, or 37

Palazzo Pitti (Pitti Palace) ★★ MUSEUM/PALACE   Although built by and named after a rival of the Medici—the merchant Luca Pitti—in the 1450s, this gigantic *palazzo* soon came into Medici hands. It was the Medici family's principal home from the 1540s and continued to house Florence's rulers until 1919. The Pitti contains five museums, including one of the world's best collections of canvases by Raphael. Out back are elegant Renaissance gardens, the **Boboli** (see p. 197).

In the art-crammed rooms of the Pitti's **Galleria Palatina** ★★, paintings are displayed like cars in a parking garage, stacked on walls above each other in the "Enlightenment" method of exhibition. Rooms are alternately dimly lit or garishly bright; this is how many of the world's great art treasures were seen and enjoyed by their original commissioners. You will find important historical treasures amid the Palatina's vast and haphazard collection; some of the best efforts of Titian, Raphael, and Rubens line the walls. Botticelli and Filippo Lippi's **"Madonna and Child"** ★ (1452) provide the key works in the **Sala di Prometeo (Prometheus Room),** which also has Signorelli, Beccafumi, and Franciabigio paintings on show. Two giant versions of the "Assumption of the Virgin," both by Mannerist painter Andrea del Sarto, dominate the **Sala dell'Iliade (Iliad Room).** As in the Uffizi, a Biblical "Judith" is painted by Artemisia Gentileschi. Rosso Fiorentino and Bolognese baroque painter Annibale Caracci are also here. The **Sala di Saturno (Saturn Room)** ★ is stuffed with Raphaels; in the **Sala di Giove (Jupiter Room)** you'll find his sublime, naturalistic portrait of **"La Velata"** ★★, as well as **"The Ages of Man"** ★. The current attribution of this painting is awarded to Venetian Giorgione, though that is often disputed.

At the **Appartamenti Reali (Royal Apartments)** you get a feeling for the conspicuous consumption of Medici Grand Dukes, and their Austrian and Belgian Lorraine successors—and see some notable paintings in their original, ostentatious setting. Italy's first king lived here for several years during Italy's 19th-century unification process—when Florence was Italy's second capital, after Turin—until Rome was finally conquered and the court moved there. Much of the stucco, fabrics, furnishings, and general decoration is in thunderously poor taste, but you should look out for Caravaggio's subtle canvas, **"A Knight of Malta"** ★.

The Pitti's "modern" gallery, the **Galleria d'Arte Moderna** ★, has a good collection, this time of 19th-century Italian paintings with a focus on Romanticism, Neoclassical works, and the **Macchiaioli,** a school of Italian painters who worked in an "impressionistic style" (and before the French Impressionists). If you have only limited time, make directly for the major works of the latter, in Sala 18 through 20, which displays the Maremma landscapes of **Giovanni Fattori** ★ (1825–1908).

The Pitti's pair of lesser museums—the **Galleria del Costume** (Costume Gallery) and **Museo degli Argenti** (Museum of Silverware)—combine to show that wealth and taste do not always go hand in hand. One thing you will notice in the Costume Gallery is how much smaller locals were just a few centuries ago.

Piazza Pitti. Reserve tickets at www.firenzemusei.it or ℂ **055/294-883.** Mar–Oct 16€, Nov–Feb 10€; half-price admission before 9am. Tues–Sun 8:15am–6:50pm. Bus: C3, D, 11, 36, or 37.

Piazzale Michelangelo ★ SQUARE   This newly pedestrianized panoramic piazza is on the itinerary of every tour bus. The balustraded terrace was laid out in 1869 to give a sweeping **vista** ★★ of the entire city, spread out in the valley below and backed by the green hills of Fiesole beyond. A bronze replica of "David" here points directly at his original home, outside the Palazzo Vecchio.

Viale Michelangelo. Bus: 12 or 13.

San Miniato al Monte ★★ CHURCH   High atop a hill, its gleaming white-and-green marble facade visible from the city below, San Miniato is one of the few ancient churches of Florence to survive the centuries virtually intact. It celebrated its 1,000th birthday in 2018. The current building began to take shape in 1013, under the auspices of the powerful Arte di Calimala guild, whose symbol, a bronze eagle clutching a bale of wool, perches on the **facade** ★★. Above the central window is a 13th-century mosaic of "Christ Between the Madonna and St. Miniato" (a theme repeated in the apse). The **interior** has a few Renaissance additions, but they blend in well with an overall medieval aspect—an airy, stony space with a raised choir at one end, painted wooden trusses on the ceiling, and tombs interspersed with inlaid marble symbols of the zodiac paving the floor. Below the choir is an 11th-century **crypt** with remains of frescoes by Taddeo Gaddi. Off to the right of the raised choir is the **sacristy,** which Spinello Aretino covered in 1387 with elaborate frescoes depicting the **"Life of St. Benedict"** ★. Off the left aisle of the nave is the 15th-century **Cappella del Cardinale del Portogallo** ★★, a collaborative effort by Renaissance artists to honor a Portuguese humanist cardinal, Jacopo di Lusitania. It's worth timing your visit to come here when the Benedictine monks are celebrating mass and Vespers in Gregorian chant (usually 6:30pm summer, 5:30pm winter).

Around the back of the church is San Miniato's **monumental cemetery** ★, one enormous "city of the dead," whose streets are lined with tombs and mausoleums built in elaborate pastiches of every generation of Florentine architecture. It's a peaceful spot, soundtracked only by birdsong and the occasional tolling of church bells.

Via Monte alle Croci/Viale Galileo Galilei (behind Piazzale Michelangiolo). ✆ **055/234-2731.** Free. Mon–Sat 9:30am–1pm and 3pm till dusk; Sun 1pm till dusk. Bus: 12 or 13.

Santa Felicita ★ CHURCH   Greek sailors who lived in this neighborhood in the 2nd century brought Christianity to Florence, and this little church was probably the second to be established in the city, its first version rising in the late 4th century. The current nave and transept were built in the 1730s. The star works predate this and are in the first chapel on the right: the Brunelleschi-designed **Cappella Barbadori–Capponi,** with paintings by Mannerist master Pontormo (1525–27). His **"Deposition"** ★★ and frescoed "Annunciation" are rife with his garish color palette of oranges, pinks, golds, lime greens, and sky blues, and exhibit his trademark surreal sense of figure.

Piazza Santa Felicita (on left off Via Guicciardini across Ponte Vecchio). ✆ **055/213-018.** Free (1€ to illuminate chapel lights). Mon–Sat 9:30am–12:30pm and 3:30–5:30pm. Bus: C3 or D.

Santa Maria del Carmine ★★★ CHURCH   Following a 1771 fire that destroyed everything but the transept chapels and sacristy, this Carmelite church was almost entirely reconstructed in high baroque style. To see the **Cappella Brancacci** ★★★ in the right transept, you have to enter through the cloisters and pay admission. The frescoes here were commissioned by an enemy of the Medici, Felice Brancacci, who in 1424 hired Masolino and his student Masaccio to decorate it with a cycle on the "Life of St. Peter." Masolino probably worked out the cycle's scheme and painted a few scenes along with his pupil before taking off for 3 years to serve as court painter in Budapest, while Masaccio kept painting, quietly creating the early Renaissance's greatest frescoes. Masaccio eventually left for Rome in 1428, where he died at age 27; the cycle was completed between 1480 and 1485 by Filippino Lippi.

Masolino painted "St. Peter Preaching," the upper panel to the left of the altar, and the two top scenes on the right wall, which shows his fastidious, decorative style in a long panel of "St. Peter Healing the Cripple" and "Raising Tabitha," and his "Adam and Eve." Contrast this first man and woman, about to take the bait offered by the snake, with the **"Expulsion from the Garden"** ★★★, opposite it, painted by Masaccio. Masolino's figures are highly posed, expressionless models, while Masaccio's Adam and Eve burst with intense emotion. The top scene on the left wall, the **"Tribute Money"** ★★, is also by Masaccio, and showcases his use of linear perspective. The scenes to the right of the altar are Masaccio's as well: **"Baptism of the Neophytes"** ★★ is among his masterpieces.

Piazza del Carmine. www.museicivicifiorentini.comune.fi.it. ℂ **055/276-8224.** Church free; Cappella Brancacci 6€ (7€ Sat–Mon). Mon and Wed–Sat 10am–5pm; Sun 1–5pm. Bus: D.

Santo Spirito ★ CHURCH   One of Filippo Brunelleschi's masterpieces of architecture, this 15th-century church doesn't look like much from the outside (no proper facade was ever built). But the **interior** ★ is a marvelous High Renaissance space—an expansive landscape of proportion and mathematics in classic Brunelleschi style, with coffered ceiling, lean columns with Corinthian capitals, and the stacked perspective of arched arcading. Good late-Renaissance and baroque paintings are scattered throughout, but the best stuff lies in the transepts, especially the **Cappella Nerli** ★, with a panel by Filippino Lippi (right transept). The church's extravagant **baroque altar** has a ciborium inlaid in *pietre dure* around 1607—and frankly, looks a bit silly against the restrained elegance of Brunelleschi's architecture.

A separate entrance (with a 3€ admission fee) gets you into the **Sacristy**—which displays a wooden "Crucifix" that has, controversially, been attributed to Michelangelo—as well as Santo Spirito's 17th-century cloister and refectory.

Tip: Tree-shaded Piazza Santo Spirito ★ is one focal point of the Oltrarno, lined with cafes that see action late into the evening. Sometimes a few farmers sell their produce on the piazza.

Piazza Santo Spirito. www.basilicasantospirito.it. ℂ **055/210-030.** Church free; cloister/sacristy 3€. Church: Mon–Tues and Thurs–Sat 10am–12:30pm and 4–5:30pm; Sun 4–5:30pm. Cloister/sacristy: Mon–Tues and Thurs–Sat 10am–5:30pm; Sun 2–4:30pm. Bus: C3, D, 11, 36, or 37.

Organized Tours

To really get under Florence's surface, book an insightful culture tour with **Context Travel ★★** (www.contexttravel.com; ✆ **800/691-6036** in the U.S. or 06/9672-7371 in Italy). Led by academics and other experts in their field on a variety of themes, from the gastronomic to the archaeological and artistic, these tours are limited to six people and generally cost around 85€ per person. The quality of Context's walks is unmatched, and well worth the above-average cost. Recommended tours include "Galileo and Science in the Renaissance" and "Secret Gardens of Florence: Boboli and Giardino Torrigiani."

Offerings from **CAF Tours** (www.caftours.com; ✆ **055/283-200**) include several themed walks and cooking classes costing from 19€ to over 100€. **I Just Drive** (www.ijustdrive.us; ✆ **055/093-5928**) offers fully equipped cars (Wi-Fi, complimentary bottle of Prosecco) plus an English-speaking driver for various themed visits; for example, you can book a private ride in a luxury Bentley or Mercedes up to San Miniato al Monte at dusk (1½ hr.; 129€). They also operate full-day and half-day private and group food and wine tours into the Chianti hills. **Viator.com** also has a range of locally organized tours and activities, reviewed by travelers.

Especially for Kids

You have to put in a bit of work to reach some of Florence's best views—and the climbs, up claustrophobic, medieval staircases, are a favorite with many kids. The cupola of **Santa Maria del Fiore** (p. 178), the **Palazzo Vecchio**'s (p. 186) Torre di Arnolfo, and the **Campanile di Giotto** (p. 178) are perfect for any youngster with a head for heights.

The best activities with an educational component are run by **Mus.e ★★** (www.musefirenze.it; ✆ **055/276-8224**), a program that offers child's-eye tours in English around the Palazzo Vecchio, led by guides in period costumes. Lively, affordable activities focus on life at the ducal court—pitched at children ages 4–7 ("The Turtle and the Snail") or 10-plus ("At Court with Donna Isabella" and "Secret Passages")—or take kids into the workshop to learn fresco painting (ages 8-plus). Programs cost 4€ per person; book online or at the desk next to the Palazzo Vecchio ticket booth.

If youngsters just need a crowd-free timeout space, head for the **Biblioteca delle Oblate,** Via dell'Oriuolo 26 (www.biblioteche.comune.fi.it; ✆ **055-261-6512**), where you'll find a library with books for little ones (including in English), as well as space to spread out, color, or draw. It's free and open 9am to 6:45pm, except for Monday morning and all day Sunday (closed 1 week mid-Aug). *Tip:* The Oblate's **cafe** (p. 207) is an excellent place to kick back and has a great view of Brunelleschi's dome which few visitors see.

There's only one game in town when it comes to spectator sports: *calcio.* To Italians, soccer/football is akin to a second religion, and an afternoon at the stadium can offer you more insight into local culture than a lifetime in the Uffizi. Florence's team, **Fiorentina ★** (nicknamed *i viola,* "the purples") is often among the best in Italy's top league, *Serie A.* You can usually catch them alternate Sundays from September through May at the **Stadio Comunale Artemio Franchi,** Via Manfredo Fanti 4 (www.violachannel.tv). Book tickets online or head for an official ticket office on arrival (you must take photo I.D.): There is a sales desk on the Mercato Centrale's upper floor (p. 170) and at Via dei Sette Santi 28R, open from 10am on match days. With kids, get seats in a Tribuna (stand) rather than a Curva, where the fanatical fans sit. To reach the stadium, take match-day-only bus no. 52 or 17 from Santa Maria Novella (15 min.). You can get kitted out in home colors at **Alè Viola,** Via del Corso 58R (✆ **055/295-306**), or from stalls around the ground on match day.

You can skip the subtitles at an original 1920s movie theater right in the center, where films show in their original language (usually English): **Odeon Firenze** ★, Piazza Strozzi (www.odeonfirenze.com; ✆ **055/214-068**).

Cycling is a pleasure in the riverside Parco delle Cascine. And remember: You are in the **gelato** capital of the world. At least one multiscoop gelato per day is the minimum recommended dose; see p. 173. Better still, be in town during the **Gelato Festival** (www.gelatofestival.it).

SHOPPING IN FLORENCE

After Milan, Florence is **Italy's top shopping city**—beating even the capital, Rome. Here's what to buy: leather, fashion, shoes, marbleized paper, hand-embroidered linens, artisan and craft items including ceramics, Tuscan wines, handmade jewelry, *pietre dure* (known also as "Florentine mosaic," inlaid semiprecious stones), and antiques. *Note:* It is illegal to knowingly buy fake goods anywhere in the city (and yes, a "Louis Vuitton" bag at 10€ counts as *knowingly*). You may be served a hefty on-the-spot fine if caught.

Standard Florentine **shopping hours** are Monday through Saturday from 9:30am to noon or 1pm and 3 or 3:30 to 7:30pm, although increasingly shops stay open on Sunday and through the midafternoon *riposo* or "nap." Large stores and those around tourist sites have almost all gone that way already. Some small or family-run places close Monday mornings instead of Sundays.

The Top Shopping Streets & Areas

AROUND SANTA TRÍNITA   The cream of the crop of Florentine shopping lines both sides of elegant **Via de' Tornabuoni,** with extensions along **Via della Vigna Nuova, Via Strozzi, Via della Spada,** and surrounding streets. Here you'll find big Florentine fashion names like **Gucci** ★ (at no. 73R; www.gucci.com; ✆ **055/264-011**), **Pucci** ★ (at no. 22R; www.emilio pucci.com; ✆ **055/265-8082**), and **Ferragamo** ★ (at no. 4R; www.ferragamo. com; ✆ **055/292-123**) ensconced in old palaces or minimalist boutiques; couture meets streetwear at concept sneaker store **SOTF** ★ (at no. 17R; www. sotf.com; ✆ **055/588-302**). Stricter traffic control has made shopping Via de' Tornabuoni a more sedate experience, though somewhat at the expense of surrounding streets.

AROUND VIA ROMA & VIA DEI CALZAIUOLI These are some of Florence's busiest streets, packed with storefronts showcasing mainstream fashions. Here, too, you find the city's major department stores, **Coin,** Via dei Calzaiuoli 56R (www.coin.it; ✆ **055/280-531**), and **La Rinascente,** Piazza della Repubblica (www.rinascente.it; ✆ **055/219-113**) alongside such quality clothing chains as Geox and Zara. **La Feltrinelli RED,** Piazza della Repubblica 26 (www.lafeltrinelli.it; ✆ **199/151-173**), is the center's best bookstore and carries some English titles. A three-floor branch of upscale food-market minichain **Eataly,** Via de' Martelli 22 (www.eataly.net; ✆ **055/015-3601**), is just north of the Baptistery. Online couture sales sensation **Luisa Via Roma ★** (www.luisaviaroma.com) also has its physical store here, at Via Roma 21R.

AROUND SANTA CROCE The eastern part of the center has seen a flourishing of one-off stores, with an emphasis on young, independent fashions. **Borgo degli Albizi** and its tributary streets are worth roaming—**Sabatini ★** (at no. 75R; www.sabatiniscarpe.it; ✆ **055/234-0240**) is a longstanding go-to for affordable casual footwear.

Florence's Best Markets

Mercato Centrale ★★ The center's main food market stocks the usual fresh produce, but you can also browse for (and taste) cheeses, salamis and cured hams, Tuscan wines, takeout food, and more. It is picnic-packing heaven and runs Monday to Saturday 7am until 2pm (until 5pm Sat for most of the year). Upstairs is street-food nirvana, all day, every day: See p. 170. Btw. Piazza del Mercato Centrale and Via dell'Ariento. No phone. Bus: C1.

Mercato di San Lorenzo ★ The city's tourist street market is a fun place to pick up T-shirts, marbleized paper, a leather-bound notebook, or some other city souvenir. Leather wallets, purses, bags, and jackets are another popular purchase—be sure to assess the workmanship, and haggle shamelessly. The market runs daily. Watch out for pickpockets. Via dell'Ariento and Via Rosina. No phone. Bus: C1.

Mercato di Sant'Ambrogio ★ A proper slice of Florentine life, six mornings a week (closed on Sun). The piazza outside has fruit, vegetables, costume jewelry, preserves, and end-of-line clothing. Go inside the market building for meat, olive oil, or a tasty budget lunch at **Da Rocco ★**. Piazza Ghiberti. No phone. Bus: C2 or C3.

Crafts & Artisanal Goods

Florence has a longstanding reputation for its craftsmanship. Although storefront display windows along heavily touristed streets are often stuffed with cheap imports and mass-produced goods, if you search around you can still find genuine handmade, top-quality items.

To get a better understanding of Florence's artisans, including a visit to a workshop, join the guided "Made in Florence" walk run by **Context Travel** (p. 202), which explores the Oltrarno, Florence's traditional craft area. The tour costs 80€ and lasts 3 hours.

Shopping for leather goods in the San Lorenzo market.

Madova ★★   For a century, this has been the best city retailer for handmade leather gloves lined with silk, cashmere, or lambs' wool. Expect to pay between 40€ and 70€ for a pair. You may not expect it this close to the Ponte Vecchio, but Madova is the real deal. Closed Sunday. Via Guicciardini 1R. www.madova.com. ✆ **055/239-6526.** Bus: C3 or D.

Marioluca Giusti ★★   The boutique of this renowned Florentine designer sells only his trademark synthetic glassware. The range includes colorful reinventions of cocktail and wine glasses, jugs, and tumblers—every piece tough and chic. Via della Spada 20R. www.mariolucagiusti.it. ✆ **055/214-583.** Bus: 6 or 11. Also at Via della Vigna Nuova 88R.

Masks of Agostino Dessi ★   This little shop is stuffed floor to ceiling with Venetian Carnevale and *commedia dell'arte* masks, handmade from papier-mâché, leather, or ceramics, and then finished expertly. From 20€ to hundreds. Via Faenza 72R. ✆ **055/287-370.** Bus: C1 or 4.

Officina Profumo-Farmaceutica di Santa Maria Novella ★★★   A shrine to scents and skincare, and Florence's most historic herbal pharmacy with roots in the 17th century, when it was founded by Dominicans in the adjacent convent of Santa Maria Novella. It's not inexpensive, but perfumes, cosmetics, moisturizers, and other products are made from natural ingredients and packaged exquisitely. Via della Scala 16. www.smnovella.it. ✆ **055/216-276.** Bus: C2.

Parione ★★   This traditional Florentine stationer close to the Duomo stocks notebooks, marbleized paper, fine pens, and souvenirs like handmade wooden music boxes and playing cards with 17th-century Florentine designs. Via dello Studio 11R. www.parione.it. ✆ **055/215-030.** Bus: C1 or C2.

Richard Ginori ★★ The city-center home for a reborn icon of painted porcelain. Nothing is cheap, but Ginori is a piece of Florence history. Via dei Rondinelli 17R. ℂ **055/265-4573.**

Scuola del Cuoio ★★ Florence's leading leather school is also open house for visitors. You can watch trainee artisans at work (Mon–Fri), then visit the small shop for the best soft leather. Portable items like wallets and bags are a good buy. Closed Sundays in off-season. Via San Giuseppe 5R (or enter through Santa Croce, via right transept). www.scuoladelcuoio.com. ℂ **055/244-534.** Bus: C3.

ENTERTAINMENT & NIGHTLIFE

Florence has excellent, mostly free, listings publications. At the tourist offices, pick up the free monthly **"Informacittà"** (www.informacitta.net), which is strong on theater, concerts, and other arts events, as well as one-off markets. Younger and hipper **"Zero"** (www.zero.eu/firenze) is hot on the latest eating, drinking, and edgy nightlife. It is available free from trendy cafe-bars and shops and updated online. **"Firenze Spettacolo,"** a 2€ Italian-language monthly sold at newsstands, has the most detailed and up-to-date listings of nightlife, arts, and entertainment. English-language magazine "The Florentine" runs a weekly events and listings section, at **www.theflr.net/weekly**.

If you just want to wander and see what grabs you, you will find plenty of tourist-oriented action in bars around the city's main squares. For something a little livelier—with a more local focus—visit **Borgo San Frediano, Piazza Santo Spirito,** or the northern end of **Via de' Macci,** close to where it meets Via Pietrapiana. **Via de' Benci** is usually buzzing around *aperitivo* time, and is popular with an expat crowd. **Via de' Renai** and the bars of San Niccolò around the **Porta San Miniato** are often lively too, with a mixed crowd of tourists and locals.

Performing Arts & Live Music

Florence does not have the musical cachet or grand opera houses of Milan, Venice, Naples, or Rome, but there are two symphony orchestras and a fine music school in Fiesole (p. 210), as well as great expectations for its new opera house (see p. 207). The city's theaters are respectable, and most major touring companies stop in town. Get tickets to all cultural and musical events online; they will e-mail collection instructions, or buy in person at **Box Office,** Via Vecchie Carceri 1 (www.boxofficetoscana.it; ℂ **055/210-804**).

Many classical chamber music performances are sponsored by the **Amici della Musica** (www.amicimusica.fi.it; ℂ **055/607-440**), so check their website to see what is scheduled while you are in town. Their venue is often historic **Teatro della Pergola,** where Verdi's opera "Macbeth" premiered in 1847.

Libreria-Café La Cité ★★ A relaxed cafe/bookshop by day, after dark this place becomes a bar and small-scale live-music venue. The lineup is eclectic, often offbeat or world music, one night forrò or swing, the next

Italian folk or chanteuse. Borgo San Frediano 20. www.lacitelibreria.info. ℰ **055/210-387.** Bus: C3, D, 6, 11, 36, or 37.

Opera di Firenze ★★   This vast new concert hall and arts complex seats up to 1,800 in daring modernist surroundings on the edge of the Cascine Park. Its program incorporates opera, ballet, and orchestral music. In May and June, the venue hosts the **Maggio Musicale Fiorentino,** one of Italy's most prestigious music festivals. Piazzale Vittorio Gui. www.operadifirenze.it. ℰ **055/277-9350.** Tickets 10€–100€. Tram: T1.

St. Mark's ★   Operatic duets and budget full-scale operas in costume are the lure. The program sticks to crowd pleasers like "Carmen," "La Traviata," and "La Bohème," and runs most nights of the week all year. Via Maggio 18. www.concertoclassico.info. ℰ **340/811-9192.** Tickets 15€–35€. Bus: D, 11, 36, or 37.

Teatro Verdi ★   Touring shows, "serious" popular music, one-off revues, classical and dance, and the Orchestra della Toscana occupy the stage at Florence's leading theater. Via Ghibellina 97. www.teatroverdionline.it. ℰ **055/212-320.** Closed 2nd half of July and all Aug. Bus: C1, C2, or C3.

Volume ★   By day, it's a laid-back cafe and arts space selling coffee, books, and crepes. By night, it's a cocktail bar with regular acoustic sets. Piazza Santo Spirito 5R. www.volumefirenze.com. ℰ **055/238-1460.** Bus: D, 11, 36, or 37.

Cafes

Florence no longer has a glitterati or intellectuals' cafe scene, and when it did—from the late-19th-century Risorgimento era through 1950s *Dolce Vita*—it was basically copying the idea from Paris. Although they're often overpriced tourist spots today—especially around **Piazza della Repubblica**—Florence's high-toned cafes are fine if you want pastries served while you sit and people-watch.

Caffetteria delle Oblate ★   A relaxing terrace popular with local families and students, and well away from the tourist crush (and prices) on the streets outside. As a bonus, it has a unique view of Brunelleschi's dome. Also serves light lunch and *aperitivo.* Closed Monday morning. Top floor of Biblioteca delle Oblate, Via del Oriuolo 26. www. caffetteriadelleoblate.it. ℰ **055/263-9685.** Bus: C1 or C2.

Ditta Artigianale Oltrarno ★★   This on-trend spot mixes modernist Scandinavian design with a bit of everything, at any time of day. Highlights are evening gin cocktails (10€) and a fantastic "flat white" coffee made with their own small-batch grind. There's also daily brunch, wines by the glass, and artisan beers. Via dello Sprone 5R. www.dittaartigianale.it. No phone. Bus: C3 or D.

La Menagere ★   In the former premises of a vast 19th-century homewares store, this trendy all-day café is a favorite stop for breakfast, brunch, lunch, a caffeine pick-me-up, aperitif, or even to buy a bunch of fresh flowers. Via de' Ginori 8R. www.lamenagere.it. ℰ **055-/750-600.** Bus: C1.

La Terrazza ★ The prices, like the perch, are a little elevated (3€–5€ for a coffee). But you get to enjoy your drink on a hidden terrace in the sky, with just rooftops, towers, and Brunelleschi's dome for company. Top floor of La Rinascente, Piazza della Repubblica. www.larinascente.it. ⟨⟩**055/219-113.** Bus: C3 or D.

Procacci ★ This historic cafe and wine bar, with royal patronage, has an elegant mahogany and gilded interior. Truffled *panini* (mini-sandwiches) are the classic snack; pair with Antinori wines by the glass. Via Tornabuoni 64R. www.procacci1885.it. ⟨⟩**055/211-656.** Bus: C2, 6 or 11.

Rivoire ★ If you want to pick one overpriced pavement cafe, make it this one. The steep prices (6€ a cappuccino, 10€ for a small bowl of ice-cream) help pay the rent of one of the prettiest slices of real estate on the planet. Piazza della Signoria (at Via Vaccherreccia). www.rivoire.it. ⟨⟩**055/214-412.** Bus: C2.

Wine Bars, Cocktail Bars & Craft Beer Bars

To party into the small hours, you will likely find Italian **nightclubs** to be rather cliquey. People usually go in groups to hang out and dance only with one another. There's plenty of flesh showing, but no meat market. Out in the northwestern 'burbs, **Tenax,** Via Pratese 46 (www.tenax.org; ⟨⟩ **335/523-5922**), attracts big-name DJs on Friday and Saturday nights.

Beer House Club ★ Artisan beers from Tuscany, Italy, and farther afield. Their own line, brewed in nearby Prato, includes IPA, Imperial Stout, and Saison styles. They also show major sports. Corso Tintori 34R. ⟨⟩**055/247-6763.** Bus: C1, C3, or 23.

Bitter Bar ★★ Impeccable mixology adds a bit of theater at this bar, with a menu of Prohibition and creative modern cocktails. The decor lies somewhere between a 1920s speakeasy and a gentleman's club, with low-watt lighting, velvet, and Italian and U.S. jazz. Via di Mezzo 28R. www.bitterbarfirenze. it. ⟨⟩**340/5499258.** Bus: C2 or C3.

Cantinetta dei Verrazzano ★★ One of the coziest little wine and food bars in the center is decked out with antique wooden wine cabinets, in genuine *enoteca* style. Wines come from the first-rate Verrazzano estate, in Chianti. Closes at 9pm (4:30pm on Sun). Via dei Tavolini 18R. www.verrazzano.com. ⟨⟩**055/268-590.** Bus: C2.

Fermento ★ In a handy location by the Medici Chapels, this bar serves Italian and Belgian craft beers in every style from IPA to stout, along with carb-rich food to soak it up. Via Canto dei Nelli 38R. http://fermentofirenze.com. ⟨⟩**055/267-5817.** Bus: C1.

Fuori Porta ★ At this friendly San Niccolò wine bar with a terrace at the foot of the climb to Piazzale Michelangiolo, cold cuts accompany the wine, as the kitchen knocks out excellent pasta and larger dishes. You can order wines by the glass from 3.50€ and a few Tuscan craft beers by the bottle. It is often open all day in high season (Apr–Oct), with an afternoon closure the rest of the year. Via Monte alle Croci 10R. www.fuoriporta.it. ⟨⟩**055/234-2483.** Bus: D or 23.

Lo Sverso ★ New-breed craft cocktails and classics with a twist (like the rosemary Collins, with herb-infused gin), all at sub-10€ prices. It has a few outdoor seats under the loggia facing the market. Free snacks from 6pm to 9pm. Via Panicale 7R. www.facebook.com/losverso.firenze. No phone. Bus: C1.

Mayday ★ A Florence original, this laidback cocktail bar offers eccentric signature drinks commemorating events in local 20th-century history. Decked out like a mismatched junk store, there's a randomness that's genuinely effective. Via Dante Alighieri 16R. www.maydayclub.it. ⓒ **055/238-1290.** Bus: C2.

Mostodolce ★ Burgers, pizza, Wi-Fi, and sports on the screen: so far, so good. Mostodolce also has its own artisan beer on tap, brewed just outside Florence at Prato (some are very strong). Happy hour is 3:30 to 7:30pm, when house beers are 4€ for a half-liter. Via Nazionale 114R. www.mostodolce.it/firenze. ⓒ **055/230-2928.** Bus: C1.

O' Cafe ★★ An elegant, minimalist *aperitivo* spot. Pay 10€ to 15€ for a cocktail or glass of bubbly and help yourself to a buffet between 6:30 and 9:30pm every night. Live jazz plays 3 nights a week from 9:15pm. Via dei Bardi 58R. www.goldenviewopenbar.com. ⓒ **055/214-502.** Bus: C3 or D.

Sant'Ambrogio ★ This wine and cocktail bar is in a lively part of the center, northeast of Santa Croce. It is popular with locals without being too achingly hip. In summer, the action spills out onto the little piazza and church steps outside. Piazza Sant'Ambrogio 7R. No phone. Bus: C2 or C3.

Santino ★★ This tiny wine bar stocks niche labels from across Italy and serves exquisite "Florentine tapas" and cold-cut plates (5€–11€) to munch while you sip. Via Santo Spirito 60R. ⓒ **055/230-2820.** Bus: D, 11, 36, or 37.

La Terrazza Lounge at the Continentale ★★ The list has few surprises—a well-made Negroni, Moscow Mule, Bellini, and the like—and prices are a little steep at around 15€ to 18€ a cocktail. But the setting, on a rooftop right by the Ponte Vecchio, makes them practically a steal. The atmosphere is fashionable but casual (wear what you like), and staff is supremely welcoming. Arrive at sundown to watch the city start to twinkle. Closed in bad weather. Inside the Continentale Hotel, Vicolo dell'Oro 6R. ⓒ **055/27-262.** Bus: C3 or D.

DAY TRIPS FROM FLORENCE

By Donald Strachan

E ven for other Italians, Tuscany is the epitome of everything that's good about their country: Beguiling landscapes carpeted with cypresses and vineyards, delicious
food and wine, and some of the greatest art and architecture
of the Renaissance—the Leaning Tower of Pisa, Ambrogio
Lorenzetti's "Allegories" in Siena's Palazzo Pubblico, and the
perfectly preserved Gothic hill town of Sam Gimignano. As
Tuscany's transportation hub, Florence is perfectly situated
within easy day-trip reach of several of these sights—you
don't even have to switch hotels to see the highlights of central Italy.

FIESOLE ★

11km (6 miles) NE of Florence

An oasis of cultivated greenery separates the hilltop village of Fiesole from Florence. Fiesole preserves the character of a Tuscan
small town, which makes it a perfect escape from summertime
crowds. Sitting at a cafe on Piazza Mino, sipping an iced cappuccino, you'll feel that the lines at the Uffizi and throng around the
Duomo seem very distant indeed.

Fiesole predates Florence by centuries—Etruscans from Arezzo
probably founded a town here in the 6th century B.C., on the site of
an earlier Bronze Age settlement. *Faesulae* became the most important Etruscan center in the region, and although it became a Roman
town in 90 B.C., it always retained a bit of otherness. After the barbarian invasions, in the 9th century it became part of Florence's
administrative district yet continued to struggle for self-govern-
ment. Medieval Florence settled things in 1125 by attacking and
razing the entire settlement.

Essentials

ARRIVING   Bus no. 7 from Florence departs from Via La Pira, to
the right of San Marco. The trip to Fiesole takes 25 minutes, arriving in Fiesole's main square, Piazza Mino. Fare is 1.20€.

VISITOR INFORMATION   The tourist office is at Via Portigiani 3 (www. fiesoleforyou.it; ☎ 055/596-1311). It's open daily (Apr–Sept 9am–7pm, Mar and Oct 10am–6pm). At the tourist office, you can buy a single admission ticket to all of Fiesole's sights for 12€ adults, 8€ ages 7–18; family ticket 24€, or 2€ per person less without the Museum Bandini (which is missable). For more information, visit **www.museidifiesole.it** or call ☎ **055/596-1293.**

Exploring Fiesole

Off Piazza Mino, the ancient high-point of the Etruscan and Roman town is now occupied by the tiny 14th-century church and monastery of **San Francesco** ★ (Via San Francesco 13; ☎ **055/59-175;** admission free; Tues–Sun 9:30am–noon and 2:30–5pm [6pm in summer]). At the end of a small nave hung with devotional works—Piero di Cosimo and Cenni di Francesco are both represented—is a fine "Crucifixion and Saints" altarpiece by Neri di Bicci. Off the cloisters, a quirky little ethnographic museum is stuffed with objects picked up by Franciscan missionaries, including an Egyptian mummy and Chinese jade and ceramics. Entrance to the church's painted, vaulted crypt is through the museum. To reach San Francesco, you will climb a sharp hill—pause close to the top, where a little balcony provides perhaps the best **view** of Florence, and the wine hills of the Chianti beyond.

Terraced into a hill with views over the olive groves and forests north of Florence, Fiesole's romantically overgrown archaeological area (Via Portigiani 1; ☎ **055/596-1293**) is scattered with sections of columns, broken friezes, and other remnants of the ancient world. Beyond the **Roman Theater** ★ (which seated 1,500 in its day), three rebuilt arches mark the remains of 1st-century-A.D. **baths.** Near the arches, a cement balcony over the far edge of the archaeological park gives a good view of the best remaining stretch of Fiesole's 4th-century-B.C. **Etruscan walls.** At the other end of the park from the baths, the floor and steps of a 1st-century-B.C. **Roman Temple** were built on top of a 4th-century-B.C. Etruscan one dedicated to Minerva. To the left are oblong **Lombard tombs** from the 7th century A.D., when this part of Fiesole was a necropolis.

SIENA ★★★

70km (43 miles) S of Florence

With its uniquely preserved medieval core, Siena is for many admirers the most beautiful town in Italy. Viewed from the summit of the Palazzo Pubblico's tower, its sea of roof tiles and red brick blends into a labyrinth of steep, twisting stone alleys. This cityscape hides dozens of Gothic palaces and pastry shops galore, longstanding neighborhood rivalries, and painted altarpieces of unsurpassed elegance.

Founded as a Roman colony by Emperor Augustus (see p. 25), the city enjoyed its heyday in the 13th and 14th centuries. In 1270, Sienese merchants established the Council of Nine, an oligarchy that ruled over Siena's great republican era, when civic projects and artistic prowess reached their heights. Artists like Duccio di Buoninsegna, Simone Martini, and the Lorenzetti brothers invented a distinctive Sienese art, a highly developed Gothic style that was an artistic foil to the emerging Florentine Renaissance. Then in 1348, a plague known as the "Black Death" hit the city, killing perhaps three-quarters of its 100,000 population, destroying the social fabric and devastating the economy. Siena never recovered, and much of it has barely changed since.

Essentials

ARRIVING The **bus** is more convenient than the train, because Siena's rail station is way outside of town. **Tiemme** (www.tiemmespa.it) runs express (*rapida;* 75 min.) and slower buses (*ordinaria;* 95 min.) from Florence's main bus station to Siena's Piazza Gramsci. It costs 8€ each way, and there is no need to reserve ahead.

Bell tower of the Palazzo Pubblico.

Buses run at least hourly in the morning. Try not to make the trip on a Sunday, when the bus service is much reduced. The last bus back usually departs at 8:45pm (7:10pm on weekends; but check ahead as schedules have been known to change).

If you have a **car,** there's a fast road direct from Florence (it has no route number; follow the green or blue signs toward Siena), about a 90-minute drive; the more scenic route, down the **Chiantigiana wine road,** the **SS222,** takes 2 hours or so. But the bus makes more sense for a day trip.

VISITOR INFORMATION The **tourist office** is inside Santa Maria della Scala, at Piazza del Duomo 2 (www.enjoysiena.it; ✆ **0577/280-551**). It is open daily from 9am to 5:30pm. Winter hours are generally a little shorter.

PARKING Siena's most convenient **parking lots** (www.sienaparcheggi.com; ✆ **0577/228-711**) charge around 2€ per hour. All lots are well marked, with locations just outside the city gates. An especially handy lot is Santa Caterina, from which escalators whisk you up to town.

Exploring Siena

Be prepared for one *seriously* busy day (and even then you can't see it all). Several stepped alleys lead down into **Piazza del Campo ("Il Campo")** ★★, arguably the most beautiful piazza in Italy. Crafted like a sloping scallop shell, the Campo was first laid out in the 1100s on the former site of the Roman forum. The herringbone brick pavement is divided by white marble lines into nine sections representing the city's medieval ruling body, the Council of Nine.

Overlooking the Campo, the crenellated town hall, **Palazzo Pubblico ★★** (built 1297–1310), is the city's (maybe all Tuscany's) finest Gothic palace, and the **Museo Civico** (_©_ **0577/292-615**) inside is home to Siena's best artworks. Frescoed on the wall of the Sala del Mappamondo, Simone Martini's 1315 **"Maestà" ★★** honors the Virgin Mary (she is Siena's saintly protector). Next door, in the Sala della Pace, Ambrogio Lorenzetti covered the walls in his **"Allegories of Good and Bad Government" ★★★** (1338), full of detail of medieval Sienese life; it was painted to provide encouragement to the city's governing body, which met inside the room. The museum is open daily from 10am to 6pm (mid-Mar–Oct until 7pm). Admission costs 9€, 8€ for students and seniors, free for ages 10 and under.

Having seen Siena's civic heart, visit its religious monuments on **Piazza del Duomo** (www.operaduomo.siena.it; _©_ **0577/286-300**) on a single ticket, the **Opa Si Pass** (15€ in high season; sold at the Museo dell'Opera, see below). Siena's **Duomo ★★** is stuffed with art treasures, including Bernini's **Cappella Chigi ★** (1659) and the **Libreria Piccolomini ★★**, frescoed in 1507 with scenes from the life of Sienese Pope Pius II, by Pinturicchio. If you are visiting between mid-August and October, you will find the cathedral's **floor ★★★** uncovered; its 59 etched and inlaid marble panels were created between 1372 and 1547 by Siena's top artists, including Domenico di Bartolo, Matteo di Giovanni, Pinturicchio, and especially Domenico Beccafumi. (Admission is 2€ more when the floors are uncovered.) The **Battistero (Baptistery) ★★** has a baptismal font (1417–30) with gilded brass panels cast by the foremost Siencse and Florentine sculptors of the early Renaissance, including Jacopo della Quercia, Lorenzo Ghiberti, and Donatello. Inside the **Museo dell'Opera del Duomo ★** is Siena's most precious work of art, Duccio di Buoninsegna's 1311 **"Maestà" ★★★**. It shows the Virgin and Child in majesty, adored by a litany of saints including St. Paul (holding the sword) and St. John the Baptist (pointing at Jesus and wearing animal skins). From the museum, climb to the top of the **Facciatone ★★** for the best view in Siena, over the rooftops and down into the Campo. Opening hours for most of the Duomo sights are

Mosaic floors inside Siena Cathedral.

10:30am to 5:30pm, although it stretches to 6 or 7pm in summer. The cathedral is closed to visitors on Sunday mornings.

You also just about have time for **Santa Maria della Scala** ★★ (www.santamariadellascala.com; ℂ **0577/534-571**), opposite the cathedral. It's always much less busy than other sites in the city—and we have no idea why. An "old hospital" might not sound too enticing, but this huge building has treasures hidden away in its eerie corridors. The **Pellegrinaio** ★★ was frescoed in the 1440s with sometimes grisly scenes of life in this medieval hospital; the Old Sacristy has an even more gruesome **"Massacre of the Innocents"** ★★, painted in 1482 by Matteo di Giovanni. Also here is the spooky oratory where St. Catherine of Siena used to pray during the night; the city's **National Archaeological Museum** occupies the labyrinthine lower floor; in **Bambimus,** art is displayed at child's-eye height. Admission costs 9€, or 7€ for students 12–19 and seniors 65 and over. It's open 10am to 7pm (Fri till 10pm), closing at 5pm November through March (also closed Tues Nov–Mar).

Tip: Discount combo tickets for Santa Maria Della Scala and the Museo Civico cost 13€; the Acropoli Pass adds Santa Maria della Scala to the Opa Si Pass for an additional 5€ (see above).

Where to Eat

Sienese cooking is rustic and simple, making liberal use of meat from the local *Cinta Senese* breed of pig. **L'Osteria** ★★, Via de' Rossi 81 (ℂ **0577/287-592**), does a mean line in local grilled meats, including veal and *Cinta.* Main courses range from 8€ to 17€. At the **Osteria del Gusto** ★, Via dei Fusari 13 (www.osteriadelgusto.it; ℂ **0577/271-076**), pasta dishes are a great value and served in filling portions. Think *pici* (fat, hand-rolled spaghetti) served with a *ragù* of *Cinta* and porcini mushrooms for around the 10€ mark. A buffet "light lunch" is served from 12:15 to 2:30pm Monday to Saturday at the gourmet food shop **Morbidi** ★, Via Banchi di Sopra 75 (www.morbidi.com; ℂ **0577/280-268**). Expect the likes of porcini risotto, roast pork, and sliced artichokes, all freshly prepared. It costs 12€, including water, an excellent value.

If you prefer a sandwich to a sit-down meal, walk around the back of the Palazzo Pubblico to **Gino Cacino di Angelo** ★, Piazza del Mercato 31 (ℂ **0577/223-076**). Sublime offerings include aged pecorino cheese, Tuscan salami, anchovies, and pretty much anything else that can go on bread or a tasting platter, all carefully sourced. It is open daily until 8pm, but often closes for a couple of weeks in August. The best gelato in the city is churned at **Kopakabana** ★, Via de' Rossi 52–54 (www.gelateriakopakabana.it; ℂ **0577/284-124**); it's open daily 11am to midnight mid-February through November.

PISA ★★

76km (47 miles) W of Florence

On a grassy lawn against the northwest corner of the city walls, medieval Pisans created one of the most dramatic (and now most photographed) squares

Pisa's Campo dei Miracoli, with the Leaning Tower.

in the world. Dubbed the **Campo dei Miracoli** (or "Field of Miracles"), Piazza del Duomo contains an array of elegant buildings that heralded the Pisan-Romanesque style—including the *Torre Pendente,* better known as the **Leaning Tower of Pisa.**

Founded as a seaside settlement around 1,000 B.C., Pisa expanded into a naval trading port under the Romans in the 2nd century B.C. By the 11th century, it had grown into one of Europe's most powerful maritime republics. Extensive trading in the Middle East helped Pisa import Arab ideas—both decorative and scientific—to Italy. In 1284, Pisa's battle fleet was destroyed by Genoa at Meloria, off Livorno, a staggering defeat that allowed the Genoese to take control of the Tyrrhenian Sea and forced Pisa's long gradual slide into twilight. Florence took control in 1406, and despite a few minor rebellions, remained in charge until Italian unification in the 1860s.

Essentials

ARRIVING From Florence's Santa Maria Novella station, around 50 daily **trains** make the trip (45–80 min.; 8.40€) to Pisa Centrale station. The last fast connection back to Florence departs around 9:30pm, but check **www.trenitalia. com** for timetable updates. There's also a fast, direct, and (for now) free **road**—the so-called *FI–PI–LI*—from Florence to Pisa along the Arno valley. Journey time is usually around 1¼ hours, subject to traffic.

VISITOR INFORMATION The most convenient tourist office for the sights is at Piazza del Duomo 7 (www.pisa.turismo.it; ✆ **050/550-100**). It is open daily 9:30am to 5:30pm (till 5pm in winter).

GETTING AROUND It's a long walk from the main station to the major sights. A **CPT** (www.pisa.cttnord.it) city bus no. 4, or the LAM Rossa bus, run from the train station to near the Tower (10 min.; 1.40€). Buy tickets from the station newsstand.

PARKING Much of central Pisa is a controlled traffic zone. However, the Pietrasantina lot, in the northwest corner of the city (exit the autostrada at Pisa Nord) offers free parking within walking distance of the Campo; there's also a shuttle bus from here to the Campo (1€ on the bus or at the cafe in the lot).

Exploring Pisa

At the **Campo dei Miracoli ★★★**, your main destination in Pisa, most of the monuments are linked on a combo ticket (admission to the Leaning Tower is separate). The cathedral is free, although you still need a ticket to reserve an admission time. Any other single admission is 5€; any two sites costs 7€; to access everything except the Leaning Tower costs 8€. (Accompanied children 10 and under enter everything except the Tower for free.) The **Leaning Tower** costs 18€ (no reductions), with admission via timed half-hour slots. To book a slot, visit **www.opapisa.it**. *You should reserve up to 20 days ahead of arrival in peak season, or if you are on a tight schedule.* Anyone under 18 must be accompanied by an adult; children 8 and under are not allowed in the tower. Main ticket offices are behind the Tower and Duomo, on the north edge of the piazza, and inside the Museo delle Sinopie: If you have no Tower reservation, head to one of them immediately to book for later in the day.

First, spend a moment looking at the layout of **Piazza del Duomo**. A hidden part of the square's appeal is its spatial geometry: If you take an aerial photo of the square and draw connect-the-dot lines between the centers, doors, and other focal points, you'll come up with an array of perfect triangles and tangential lines of mathematical grace.

Buschetto, the architect who laid the **Cathedral**'s first stone in 1063, kicked off a new era in art by building what was to become the model for the Pisan-Romanesque style. All the key elements are here on the **facade ★**, designed and built by Buschetto's successor, Rainaldo: alternating light and dark banding, rounded blind arches with Moorish-inspired lozenges at the top and colored marble inlay designs, and Lombard-style open galleries of mismatched columns, stacked to make the facade much higher than the church roof. The **main door** was cast by students of Giambologna after a 1595 fire destroyed the original (the last surviving original door, which you can see in the **Museo dell'Opera,** was cast by Bonnano Pisano in 1180). On the back of the right transept, across from the bell tower, is a 2008 cast of the bronze **Door of San Ranieri ★★★**. Inside the Cathedral, on the north side of the nave, is Giovanni Pisano's masterpiece **pulpit ★★** (1302–11)—it's the last and perhaps greatest of the Pisano pulpits. Head over to the **Battistero (Baptistery) ★** to see its prototype: a carved stone **pulpit ★★** by Nicola Pisano (1255–60), Giovanni's father. This father-and-son team created a number of masterful pulpits over the years, following this model. Heavily influenced by classical works, Nicola's high-relief panels (a synopsis of Christ's life) include pagan gods converted to Christianity as Madonnas and saints.

Now on to the main attraction. Why does the **Leaning Tower ★★★** lean? The main problem—and the bane of local engineers for 8 centuries—is that you can't stack that much heavy marble on shifting subsoil and keep it all upright. Building began in 1173 under Guglielmo and Bonnano Pisano, who also cast the Duomo's doors (see above). They reached the third level in 1185 when they noticed a lean, at that point only about 3.8cm (1½ in.). Work stopped until 1275, under Giovanni di Simone. He tried to correct the tilt by curving the structure back toward the perpendicular, giving the tower its slight banana shape. In 1284, work stopped yet again. In 1360, Tommaso di Andrea da Pontedera capped it off at about 51m (167 ft.) with a vaguely Gothic belfry.

The walls of the **Camposanto ★**, or cemetery, were once covered with important 14th- and 15th-century frescoes by Taddeo Gaddi, Spinello Aretino, and Benozzo Gozzoli, among others. On July 27, 1944, however, American warplanes launched an attack against the city (which was still in German hands) and the Camposanto was accidentally bombed. The most fascinating panel to survive the bombing is the 1341 **"Triumph of Death" ★**, attributed to Florentine Buonamico Buffalmacco.

Where to Eat

If you want a genuine taste of Pisa, get away from the crowds around the Tower. Head south on Via Santa Maria as far as Piazza Cavalotti, then along Via dei Mille into Piazza dei Cavalieri. Continue through this vast, polygonal square to the center of the "real" city—it is less than 10 minutes' walk away. At **Osteria dei Cavalieri ★**, Via San Frediano 16 (www.osteriacavalieri.pisa.it; © **050/580-858**), you'll find plenty of grilled meats, daily fresh fish, and traditional Pisan dishes like rabbit stewed with oregano. Main courses range from 10€ to 18€. Osteria dei Cavalieri is closed Sundays and most of August; there's no lunch on Saturdays. Just across the River Arno, you'll find a great-value lunch at **La Taverna di Pulcinella ★**, Via Garofani 10 (© **050/520-2704**). Pizzas are 10.50€ to 22€, or you can opt for a 10€ two-course menu, which may be the likes of spelt with garbanzo beans and porcini mushrooms followed by a rustic pork steak with garlic and rosemary. It's closed Sunday and Monday.

For pizza or *cecina* (warm garbanzo-bean-flour flatbread) and a cold beer, stop at **Il Montino ★**, Vicolo del Monte 1 (www.pizzeriailmontino.com; © **050/598-695**), a slice spot often busy with students.

SAN GIMIGNANO ★★

52km (32 miles) SW of Florence

An otherworldly scene hits you when you pass through the Porta San Giovanni gate, inside the walls of **San Gimignano:** a thoroughly medieval center peppered with the tall towers that made *San Gimignano delle Belle Torri* ("of the beautiful towers") the poster child for Italian hill towns everywhere. At one time there were around 70 of the things spiking the sky above this little village. Only a dozen or so remain. The towers started rising in the bad old days of the 1200s, partly to defend against outside invaders but mostly as command centers for San Gimignano's warring families. As several successive waves of plague swept through (1348, 1464, 1631), the economy—based on textiles and hosting pilgrims on the Via Francigena route to Rome—crumbled. San Gimignano slowly became a provincial backwater. As a result, when tourism began picking up in the 19th century, visitors found a delightfully preserved medieval village of decaying stone towers.

Essentials

ARRIVING   Your best bet is the **bus.** From Florence's main bus station, **Tiemme** (www.tiemmespa.it) runs buses for most of the day, a 50-minute journey to Poggibonsi, where many services are timed to connect on to San Gimignano (a further 20–25 min.). Buy through-tickets for the whole journey in Florence (7€). The last bus back usually departs around 8:30pm, but check when you leave Florence or in San Gimignano's tourist information office. *Tip:* Avoid making this day trip on a Sunday, when bus service is much reduced.

Arriving by **car,** take the Poggibonsi Nord exit off the Florence–Siena highway or the SS2. San Gimignano is 12km (7½ miles) from Poggibonsi, through very pretty country.

VISITOR INFORMATION   The friendly tourist office at Piazza Duomo 1 (www.sangimignano.com; *℄* **0577/940-008**) is open daily 10am to 1pm and 3 to 7pm (Nov–Feb 10am–1pm and 2–6pm).

PARKING   The most convenient parking is at Parcheggio Montemaggio, outside the Porta San Giovanni (2€ an hour, 20€ a day). You can easily walk into town from here, but shuttle buses also take you up to Piazza della Cisterna (1€). P1, the farthest lot from town, is the cheapest (1.50€ per hour; 6€ for full day). Drive right up to the town gate, drop any passengers, then return to park—it is a stiff uphill walk of 7 to 10 minutes back.

Exploring San Gimignano

Anchoring the town at the top of Via San Giovanni are its two interlocking triangular *piazze:* **Piazza della Cisterna ★★**, centered on a 1237 well, and **Piazza del Duomo,** flanked by the city's main church and civic palace. It is easy to find them: From any direction, just keep walking uphill.

The town's key art site is the **Collegiata ★★**, Piazza del Duomo (www.duomosangimignano.it; *℄* **0577/286-300**). The right wall of this collegiate church was frescoed from 1333 to 1341—most likely by Lippo Memmi—with three levels of **New Testament scenes** (22 in all) on the life and Passion of Christ. In 1367, Bartolo di Fredi frescoed the left wall with 26 scenes from the **Old Testament;** Taddeo di Bartolo added a **"Last Judgment"** peppered with gruesome details (just above and left of the main door) in 1410.

In 1468, Giuliano da Maiano built the **Cappella di Santa Fina ★★** off the right aisle; his brother Benedetto carved the relief panels for the altar, and Florentine painter Domenico Ghirlandaio decorated the tiny chapel's walls with some of his finest, airiest works, including two scenes depicting the life of Santa Fina, a local girl who, although never officially canonized, is one of

Piazza della Cisterna, San Gimignano.

San Gimignano's patron saints. Admission to the Collegiata costs 4€, 2€ ages 6 to 17. From April through October it's open Monday to Friday 10am–7:30pm, Saturday 10am–5:30pm, and Sunday 12:30–7:30pm; November to March hours are Monday to Saturday 10am–5pm, Sunday 12:30–5pm. It is closed the second half of November and the second half of January.

The town's small **Museo Civico (Civic Art Museum)** ★, Piazza del Duomo 2 (www.sangimignanomusei.it; ✆ **0577/286-300**), inside the Palazzo del Popolo, houses a **"Maestà"** ★★ (1317) by Sienese painter Lippo Memmi, and some rather racy medieval "wedding night" frescoes by Lippo's father, Memmo di Filippuccio. Admission costs 9€. The same ticket gets you up the tallest tower still standing, the **Torre Grossa** ★. From 54m (175 ft.) up, you can gaze for miles across hills and grapevines. The museum and tower are open daily: 10am to 7:30pm April through September, 11am to 5:30pm October through March.

At **Sant Agostino,** Piazza Sant'Agostino (✆ **0577/907-012**), Florentine painter Benozzo Gozzoli spent 2 years frescoing the walls behind the main altar floor to ceiling with scenes rich in architectural detail from the **"Life of St. Augustine"** ★★. The church is generally open daily 10am–noon and 3–7pm (Nov–Mar it closes at 6pm; Jan–Mar it's also closed Mon mornings). Admission is free.

Where to Eat

The handiest restaurant for a day trip, **Chiribiri ★**, Piazzetta della Madonna 1 (www.ristorantechiribiri.it; © **0577/941-948**) is open all day—you can dine early before heading for the bus or car parks. It is a small place, with a simple, well-executed menu of Italian and Tuscan classics such as lasagna, *osso buco,* and wild boar stew. Main courses are priced fairly at 8€ to 12€. No credit cards. The town's essential foodie stop, however, isn't a restaurant, but the **Gelateria Dondoli ★★**, Piazza della Cisterna 4 (www.gelateriadondoli. com; © **0577/942-244**), for creative combinations like raspberry and rosemary (it works) and their signature *crema di Santa Fina,* made with saffron and pine nuts.

VENICE

By Stephen Keeling

N o other place in the world quite looks like Venice. This vast, floating city of grand *palazzi*, elegant bridges, gondolas, and canals is a magnificent spectacle, truly magical when approached by sea for the first time, when its golden domes and soaring bell towers seem to rise straight from the sea. While it can sometimes appear that Venice is little more than an open-air museum where tourists outnumber locals—by a large margin—it is still surprisingly easy to lose the crowds. Indeed, the best way to enjoy Venice is to simply get lost in its labyrinth of narrow streets, stumbling upon a quiet *campo* (square), market stall, or cafe far off the beaten track, where even the humblest medieval church might contain masterful work by Tiepolo, Titian, or Tintoretto.

The origins of Venice are as muddy as parts of the lagoon it now occupies, but most histories begin with the arrival of refugees from Attila the Hun's invasion of Italy in 453 A.D. The mudflats were gradually built over and linked together, channels and streams eventually becoming canals. By the 11th century, Venice had emerged as a major independent trading city, and by the 13th century a seaborne empire (which included Crete, Corfu, and Cyprus) was held together by a huge navy and commercial fleet. Though embroiled with wars against rival Italian city Genoa and the Turks for much of the ensuing centuries, these were golden years for Venice, when booming trade with the Far East funded much of its grand architecture and art. Although it remained an outwardly rich city, by the 1700s the good times were over, and in 1797 Napoleon dissolved the Venetian Republic. You'll gain a sense of some of this history touring **Piazza San Marco** and **St. Mark's Basilica,** or by visiting the **Accademia,** one of Italy's great art galleries, but only when you wander the back *calli* (streets), will you encounter the true, living, breathing side of Venice, still redolent of those glory days.

Piazza San Marco (St. Mark's Square).

STRATEGIES FOR SEEING VENICE

Wandering aimlessly around back streets and canals is a marvelous way to experience Venice, but you'll still want to hit all the must-see sights—preferably without over-spending or getting stuck in San Marco tourist gridlock. These strategies and time-tested tips will help you make the most of your time here.

- **Avoid the lines:** It pays to book ahead (online) for the Palazzo Ducale and the Accademia, which guarantees you an entry time. Venice offers several discount cards (see p. 273) that also let you skip ticketing lines (the **Museum Pass** is recommended).

- **Plan your sightseeing around lunch:** Some sights do close for lunch in Venice (12:30–3pm), but most (including the churches) stay open, meaning a lot fewer people at each location.

- **Walk:** Aside from on boats, the only way to explore Venice is on foot. Though the layout of the city is confusing, getting lost in its streets is part of the fun. Indeed, explore the far reaches of the city and you'll be guaranteed to lose the crowds, even in summer—most folks rarely stray beyond the main routes. See p. 228 for tips on getting around Venice.

- **Be prepared for Sunday closures:** While most sights in Venice are open every day (some museums close on Tuesday), much of the city's art is in churches, and many of those are closed to tourists on Sundays, either for the morning or all day. There's one way to get around this: Attend a Sunday service as a worshipper. You may not be able to study the art at length, but it's the best way to put this great religious art in context.

o **Avoid the crowds:** Late February and March, just after Carnevale, is a great time to visit; it can be cool and misty, but you'll have the streets and canals (largely) to yourself. Otherwise, get up at sunrise in summer at least once, just to wander the city before the crowds emerge—it's a magical experience.

o **Save money on meals:** Eating in Venice can be expensive, but there are plenty of budget options (see p. 246). You'll save loads by frequenting neighborhood bars known as *bacari* (normally 5–7pm), where you can stand or sit with small plates of *"cicchetti"* (tapaslike finger foods), washed down with a small glass of wine. Anywhere near Piazza San Marco is likely to be expensive; it's best to avoid places with *"menù turistico"* options altogether.

ESSENTIALS

Arriving

BY PLANE   From North America, the cheapest flights to Venice tend to route through Rome or Milan via **Alitalia,** though **Swissair** (via Zurich), **Lufthansa** (via Frankfurt), **KLM** (via Amsterdam), and **Air France** (via Paris) usually offer cheap fares in low season (code-sharing with US carriers). If travelling in the peak spring and summer seasons however, it's worth considering far more convenient seasonal non-stop flights, which are often priced competitively (assuming you buy far enough in advance). **Delta Airlines** (www.delta.com) flies from Atlanta (late June–Aug only) and New York-JFK (Apr–Sept only), **United Airlines** (www.united.com) from Newark (June–late Sept), and **American Airlines** (www.aa.com) from Chicago and Philadelphia (May–Oct). For those already in Europe, numerous budget airlines serve Venice, offering rock-bottom prices. No-frills **easyJet** (www.easyjet.com) flies from Amsterdam, Berlin, London-Gatwick, Manchester, Paris, and Zurich, while **Ryanair** (www.ryanair.com) flies from Bristol and Barcelona, with many more of its flights routed through nearby **Treviso** (a 1-hr. bus ride to Venice).

Flights land at the **Aeroporto di Venezia Marco Polo,** 7km (4¼ miles) north of the city on the mainland (www.veniceairport.it; ✆ **041/2609260**). There are several alternatives for getting into town. The **cheapest** is by **bus,** though this is not recommended if you have heavy luggage; you'll have to walk to or from the final stop at Piazzale Roma (the closest point to Venice's attractions accessible by car or bus), to the nearby *vaporetto* stop for the final connection to your hotel. (See "The Vaporetto Lowdown," p. 225.) It's rare to find porters who'll help with luggage, so pack light. The **ATVO airport shuttle bus** (www.atvo.it; ✆ **0421/594672**) connects with Piazzale Roma not far from Venice's Santa Lucia train station (and the closest point to Venice's attractions accessible by car or bus). Buses leave for/from the airport about every 20 minutes, cost 8€ (15€ return), and make the trip in about 20 minutes. Buy tickets at the automatic ticket machines in the arrivals baggage hall, or the Public Transport ticket office (daily 8am–midnight). The local **ACTV bus**

no. 5 (📞 041/2424) also costs 8€, also takes 20 minutes, and runs between two and four times an hour depending on the time of day; the best option here is to buy the combined ACTV and "Nave" ticket for 14€ (valid for 90 minutes), which includes your first *vaporetto* ride at a slight discount (the "vaporetto" is the seagoing streetcar of Venice, which goes to all parts of the city). Buy tickets at machines just outside the terminal. With either bus, you'll have to walk to or from the final stop at Piazzale Roma to the nearby **vaporetto** (water bus) stop for the final connection to your hotel. It's rare to see porters around who'll help with luggage, so pack light.

It's also possible to take a **land taxi** (www.radiotaxivenezia.com; 📞 **041/5964**) from the airport to Piazzale Roma (where you get the *vaporetto*) for about 40€, but while this is more convenient and a bit faster (15min) than the bus, it still doesn't take you to your hotel (unless it's right by Piazzale Roma)—you are better off spending the extra euros on water transport.

The most evocative and traditional way to arrive in Venice is by sea. For 15€, 14€ if you buy online, the **Cooperative San Marco/Alilaguna** (www.alilaguna.it; 📞 **041/2401701**) operates a large *motoscafo* (shuttle boat) service from the airport with two primary routes. The *Linea Blu* (blue line) runs almost every 30 minutes from 6:15am to 12:30am, stopping at Murano (8€) and the Lido before arriving, after about 1 hour and 30 minutes, in Piazza San Marco (this service continues on to the cruise ship terminal). The *Linea Arancio* (orange line) runs almost every 30 minutes from 7:45am to midnight, taking 1 hour and 15 minutes to arrive at San Marco, but gets there through the Grand Canal, which is much more spectacular and offers the possibility to get off at one of the stops along the way. This might be convenient to your hotel and could save you from having to take another means of transportation. If you arrive at Piazza San Marco and your hotel isn't in the area, you'll have to make a connection at the *vaporetto* launches. (If you're booking a hotel in advance, ask for specific advice how to get there.)

A good alternative is the **Venice Shuttle** (www.venicelink.com; daily 8am–10:30pm; minimum 2 people for reservations), a shared water taxi (they carry 6–8 people) that will whisk you directly from the airport to many hotels and most of the major locations in the city for 25€ to 32€ (add 6€ after 8pm). You must reserve online in advance.

A **private water taxi** (20–30 min. to/from the airport) is the most convenient option but costly—a trip to the city costs 107–120€ (discounts at www.venicelink.com) for up to four passengers with one bag each (10€ more for each extra person up to a maximum of 10, 5€ for each extra suitcase, and another 20€ for trips 10pm–7am). It's worth considering if you're pressed for time, have an early flight (taxis run 24 hrs.), are carrying a lot of luggage (a Venice no-no), or can split the cost with a friend or two. It may be able to drop you off at the front (or side) door of your hotel or as close as it can maneuver given your hotel's location (check with the hotel before arriving). Your taxi captain should be able to tell you before boarding just how close he can get

The Vaporetto Lowdown

Whether you're arriving by train, bus, or car, your first challenge upon arriving in Venice will be to take a vaporetto (water bus) on to your final destination in the city. Here's how to do it right.

Finding the right boat is a little easier if you're arriving by bus or car, because you'll be in Piazzale Roma, the vaporetto terminus, and all the boats will be going the right direction. (See "Getting Around Venice," p. 228, for information on tickets). Exiting the train station, however, you'll find the Grand Canal immediately in front of you, with the docks for a number of *vaporetti* lines to your left and right. Head to the booths to your left, near the bridge, to buy tickets, then head for the docks farther to your right.

The most useful routes are the two lines plying the Grand Canal: the **no. 2 express** (from bay "D"), which stops only at the San Marcuola, Rialto Bridge, San Tomà, San Samuele, and Accademia before hitting San Marco (30 min. total);

and the slower **no. 1** (from bay "E"), which makes 13 stops before arriving at San Marco (a 36-min. trip). Both leave every 10 minutes or so, but before 9am and after 8pm, the no. 2 sometimes stops short at Rialto, meaning you'll have to disembark and hop on the next no. 1 or 2 that comes along to continue to San Marco.

Word to the wise: The *vaporetti* go in two directions from the train station. Those heading left go down the Grand Canal toward San Marco—which is the (relatively) fast and scenic way. The no. 2 route heading right also eventually gets you to San Marco (at the San Zaccaria stop) but takes more than twice as long because it goes the long way around Dorsoduro (this line serves mainly commuters). As for the no. 1 line going to the right from the train station, it will go only one more stop before it hits its terminus at Piazzale Roma. **Make sure the *vaporetto* you get on is heading to the left.**

you. Try **Corsorzio Motoscafi Venezia** (www.motoscafivenezia.it; ✆ **041/5222303**) or **Venezia Taxi** (www.veneziataxi.it; ✆ **041/723112**).

BY TRAIN Trains from Rome (3¾ hr.), Milan (2½ hr.), Florence (2 hr.), and all over Europe arrive at the **Stazione Venezia Santa Lucia.** To get there, all must pass through (although not necessarily stop at) a station marked Venezia-Mestre. Don't be confused: Mestre is a charmless industrial city that's the last major stop on the mainland (some trains also stop at the next station, Venezia Porto Marghera, before continuing to Venice proper). Occasionally trains end in Mestre, in which case you'll have to catch one of the frequent 10-minute shuttles connecting with Venice; it's inconvenient, so when you book your ticket, confirm that the final destination is Venezia Santa Lucia.

BY BUS Although rail travel is more convenient and commonplace, Venice is serviced by long-distance buses from all over mainland Italy and some international cities. The final destination is Piazzale Roma, where you'll need to pick up *vaporetto* no. 1 or no. 2 (see "The Vaporetto Lowdown," p. 225) to connect you with stops in the heart of Venice and along the Grand Canal.

BY CAR The only wheels you'll see in Venice are those attached to luggage. **No cars are allowed,** or more to the point, no cars could drive through the narrow streets and over the footbridges—even the police, fire department, and ambulance services use boats. You can drive across the Ponte della Libertà from Mestre to Venice, but you can go no farther than Piazzale Roma at the Venice end, where many garages eagerly await your euros (and in high season are often full). The **Autorimessa Comunale garage** (www.avmspa.it; ℂ **041/ 2727301**) charges 26€ for a 24-hour period, while **Garage San Marco** (www. garagesanmarco.it; ℂ **041/5232213**) costs 32€ for 24 hours. From Piazzale Roma, you can catch *Vaporetti* lines 1 and 2 (see "The Vaporetto Lowdown," p. 225), which go down the Grand Canal to the train station and, eventually, Piazza San Marco.

Visitor Information

TOURIST OFFICES The most central office lies in the arcade at the western end of Piazza San Marco (Calle Larga de l'Ascensione 71F), near Museo Correr (daily 9am–7pm; ℂ **041/2424**). There are also offices at Piazzale Roma (inside the Autorimessa Comunale garage; daily 7am–8pm), the train station (opposite platform 2; daily 7am–9pm), and in the arrivals hall at Marco Polo Airport (daily 8:30am–7pm). See also **www.veneziaunica.it**.

The info-packed monthly *Un Ospite di Venezia* (www.unospitedivenezia.it) is a useful source of information (published in Italian and English); most hotels have free copies. Also useful is *VeNews* (www.venezianews.it), a monthly sold at newsstands all over the city (also in English and Italian).

City Layout

Even armed with the best map or a hefty smartphone data plan, expect to get a little bit lost in Venice, at least some of the time (GPS directions are notoriously unreliable here). Just view it as an opportunity to stumble across Venice's most intriguing corners. Keep in mind as you wander seemingly hopelessly among the *calli* (streets) and *campi* (squares) that the city wasn't built to make sense to those on foot but rather to those plying its canals.

Venice lies 4km (2½ miles) from terra firma, connected to the mainland burg of Mestre by the Ponte della Libertà, which leads to Piazzale Roma. Snaking through the city is the **Grand Canal,** the wide main artery of aquatic Venice. Central Venice refers to the built-up block of islands in the lagoon's

---

A Note on Addresses

Within each *sestiere* is a most original system of numbering the *palazzi*, using one continuous string of 6,000 or so numbers. The format for addresses in this chapter is, where possible, the number with the actual street or *campo* on which you'll find that address. But official mailing addresses (and what you'll see written down in most places), are simply the *sestiere* name followed by the building number, which isn't especially helpful—for example, San Marco 1471 may not necessarily be found close to San Marco 1473. Many buildings aren't numbered at all.

Canals on Burano Islands.

center, the six main *sestieri* (districts) that make up the bulk of the tourist city. Greater Venice includes all the inhabited islands of the lagoon—central Venice plus Murano, Burano, Torcello, and the Lido.

The Neighborhoods in Brief

San Marco   The most visited, and most central, *sestiere* is anchored by the magnificent Piazza San Marco and St. Mark's Basilica to the south and the Rialto Bridge to the north. This has been the commercial, religious, and political heart of the city for more than a millennium. Unfortunately, ever-rising rents have persuaded most locals to look for housing in other neighborhoods, but the area is laced with first-class hotels—see p. 236 for suggestions on where to stay in the heart of Venice without going broke.

Castello   Just east of Piazza San Marco, Castello's tony waterside esplanade Riva degli Schiavoni follows the Bacino di San Marco (St. Mark's Basin), skirting Venice's most congested area to the north and east. Riva degli Schiavoni is often thronged, but if you head farther east in the direction of the Arsenale or inland away from the *bacino,* the crowds thin out. Here you'll find such major sights as Campo SS. Giovanni e Paolo and the Scuola di San Giorgio.

Dorsoduro   Residential Dorsoduro, the largest of the *sestieri,* lies across the Accademia Bridge from San Marco. Home to the Accademia and Peggy Guggenheim museums, it was known as an artists' haven until rising rents forced many residents to relocate. Come here for good neighborhood restaurants, a charming gondola boatyard, lively Campo Santa Margherita, and the sunny canalside quay of le Zattere.

San Polo   This mixed bag of residential corners and tourist sights stretches northwest of the Rialto Bridge to the church of Santa Maria dei Frari. At the foot of the bridge you'll find the bustling Rialto Market. Some of the city's best restaurants flourish here, alongside some of its worst tourist traps. Spacious Campo San Polo is the main piazza.

Santa Croce   North and northwest of the San Polo district and across the Grand Canal from the train station, Santa Croce stretches all the way to Piazzale Roma. Less lively than San Polo but just as authentic, it feels light-years away from San Marco; its little-visited eastern section is a great place for curious visitors to explore. Quiet, lovely Campo San Giacomo dell'Orio is its heart.

Cannaregio On the same side of the Grand Canal as San Marco and Castello, Cannaregio stretches north and east from the train station to include the old Jewish Ghetto. One-quarter of Venice's ever-shrinking population of 60,000 lives here. Many one-star hotels are clustered about the train station—not a dangerous neighborhood but not known for its charm, either. Strada Nova is Cannaregio's main thoroughfare, leading to the Rialto bridge.

La Giudecca Across the Giudecca Canal from Piazza San Marco and Dorsoduro, tranquil La Giudecca is a residential island where you'll find a youth hostel and a few hotels (including the deluxe Cipriani, see p. 245).

Lido di Venezia This slim, 11km-long (6¾-mile) island, the only spot in the Venetian lagoon where cars circulate, is the city's beach, fronting the open sea. It's also base for the annual Venice Film Festival.

Getting Around Venice

Aside from traveling by boat, the only way to explore Venice is by walking—and by getting lost repeatedly. You'll navigate many twisting streets whose names change constantly and don't appear on any map, and streets that may very well end in a blind alley or spill abruptly into a canal. You'll also cross dozens of footbridges. Treat getting bewilderingly lost in Venice as part of the fun, and budget more time than you'd think necessary to get wherever you're going.

STREET MAPS & SIGNAGE   The map sold by the tourist office (5€) and free maps provided by most hotels don't always show—much less name or index—all the *calli* (streets) and pathways of Venice. For that, pick up a more detailed map (ask for a *pianta della città* at news kiosks—especially those at the train station and around San Marco or most bookstores). The best (and most expensive) is the highly detailed **Touring Club Italiano map,** available in a variety of forms (folding or spiral-bound) and scales. Almost as good, and easier to carry, is the simple and cheap 1:6,500 folding map put out by Storti Edizioni. If using your phone, note that GPS directions are often unreliable in Venice, though Google Maps has definitely improved in recent years (and has added its "streetview" option to the city).

Still, Venice's confusing layout confounds even the best maps and navigators. You're often better off just stopping and asking a local to point you in the right direction (always know the name of the *campo*/square or major sight closest to the address you're looking for and ask for that).

As you wander, look for the ubiquitous yellow signs (well, *usually* yellow) whose destinations and arrows direct you toward five major landmarks: **Ferrovia** (the train station), **Piazzale Roma** (the parking garage), **Rialto** (one of the four bridges over the Grand Canal), **San Marco** (the city's main square), and the **Accademia** (the southernmost Grand Canal bridge).

BY VAPORETTO   The various *sestieri* are linked by a comprehensive *vaporetto* (water bus/ferry) system of about a dozen lines operated by the **Azienda del Consorzio Trasporti Veneziano (ACTV;** actv.avmspa.it;

The Grand Canal with Basilica di Santa Maria della Salute in the background.

© **041/5287886**). Transit maps are available at the tourist office and most ACTV ticket offices. It's easier to get around the center on foot, as the *vaporetti* principally serve the Grand Canal, the outskirts, and the outer islands. The crisscross network of small canals is the province of delivery vessels, gondolas, and private boats.

A *vaporetto* ticket (good for 75 minutes after validation) is a steep 7.50€, while the 24-hour **ACTV travel card** is 20€—it only takes three rides to begin saving money with the card. (For even more savings, there are also ACTV travel cards for 48 hr. [30€] and 72 hr. [40€]). Most lines run every 10 to 15 minutes from 7am to midnight, and then hourly until morning. Most *vaporetto* docks have timetables posted. You can buy tickets at Venezia Unica offices, authorized retailers displaying the ACTV/Venezia Unica sticker, and usually at the dock itself, though not all have machines or kiosks that sell tickets. If you haven't bought a pass or tickets beforehand, you can pay the conductor onboard (find immediately him upon boarding—he won't come looking for you) or risk a stiff fine of at least 60€ plus ticket price and admin fees, no excuses accepted. You **must validate** (stamp) all tickets in the yellow machines at the docks before getting aboard. ***Tip:*** If you're staying in Venice for a week and intend to use the *vaporetto* service a lot, it makes sense to get a **Venezia Unica city pass** (see "Venice Discounts," p. 273), which lets you buy *vaporetto* tickets for 1.50€.

BY TRAGHETTO   Just four bridges span the Grand Canal, and to fill in the gaps, *traghetti* skiffs (oversize gondolas rowed by two standing *gondolieri*) cross the Grand Canal at several intermediate points (during daylight hours only). You'll find a station at the end of any street named Calle del Traghetto

CRUISING THE canals

A leisurely cruise along the **Grand Canal ★★★** (p. 265) from Piazza San Marco to the train station (Ferrovia)—or the reverse—is one of Venice's must-dos. It's the world's most unusual Main Street, a watery boulevard whose *palazzi* have been converted into condos. Lower water-lapped floors are now deserted, but the higher floors are still coveted by the city's titled families, who have inhabited these glorious residences for centuries; others have become the summertime dream homes of privileged expats, drawn here as irresistibly as the romantic Venetians-by-adoption who preceded them: Richard Wagner, Robert Browning, Lord Byron among them.

As much a symbol of Venice as the winged lion, the **gondola ★★★** is one of Europe's great traditions, incredibly and inexplicably expensive but truly as romantic as it looks (detractors who write it off as too touristy have most likely never tried it). The official fixed rate is 80€ for a 40-minute gondola tour for up to six passengers. The rate bumps up to 100€ from 7pm to 8am (for 40 min.), and it's 40€ for every additional 20 minutes (50€ at night). That's not a typo: 150€ for a 1-hour evening cruise. **Note:** Although the price is fixed by the city, a good negotiator at the right time of day (when business is slow) can sometimes grab a small discount for a shorter ride. And at these ridiculously inflated prices, there is no need to tip the gondolier. You might also find **discounts online.**

Aim for late afternoon before sundown, when the light does its magic on the canal reflections (and bring a bottle of prosecco and glasses). If the gondola price is too high, find someone—other hotel guests, say—to share it. Though the price is "fixed," before setting off establish with the gondolier the cost, time, and route (back canals are preferable to the trafficked and often choppy Grand Canal). They're regulated by the **Ente Gondola** (www.gondolavenezia.it; © 041/5285075), so call if you have any questions or complaints.

And what of the serenading gondolier immortalized in film? Frankly, you're better off without. But if warbling is de rigueur for you, here's the scoop. An ensemble of accordion player and tenor is so expensive that it's shared among several gondolas traveling together. A number of travel agents around town book the evening serenades for around 50€ per person.

Venice has 12 gondola stations, including Piazzale Roma, the train station, the Rialto Bridge, and Piazza San Marco. There are also a number of smaller stations, with *gondolieri* in striped shirts standing alongside their sleek 11m (36-ft.) black wonders looking for passengers. All speak enough English to communicate the necessary details. Remember, if you just want a quick taste of being in a gondola, you can take a cheap *traghetto* across the Grand Canal.

on your map (though not all of them have active ferries today; ask a local before walking to the canal), indicated by a yellow sign with the black gondola symbol. These days only a handful operate regularly, primarily at San Tomà, Santa Maria del Giglio and Santa Sofia (check with a local if in doubt). The fare is 2€ for non-residents (locals pay 0.50€), which you hand to the gondolier when boarding. Most Venetians cross standing up. For the experience, try the Santa Sofia crossing (daily: 7:30am–6:30pm Oct–Mar, 7:30am–7pm Apr–Sep) that connects the Ca' d'Oro and the Pescheria fish market, opposite each other on the Grand Canal just north of the Rialto Bridge—the gondoliers expertly dodge water traffic at this point of the canal, where it's the busiest and most heart-stopping.

BY WATER TAXI *Taxi acquei* (water taxis) charge high prices and aren't for visitors watching their euros. Trips in town are likely to cost at least 40€ to 70€, depending on distance, time of day, and whether you've booked in advance or just hired on the spot. Each trip includes allowance for up to four to five pieces of luggage—beyond that there's a surcharge of 3€ to 5€ per piece (rates differ slightly according to company and how you reserve a trip). Plus there's a 20€ supplement for service from 10pm to 7am, and a 5€ charge for taxis on-call. Those rates cover up to four people; if any more squeeze in, it's another 5€ to 10€ per extra passenger (maximum 10 people). Taking a taxi from the train station to Piazza San Marco or any of the hotels in the area will put you back about 80€ (the Lido is 90€), while fixed fees to the airport range 107–120€ (for up to four people). Taxis to Burano or Torcello will be at least 120€. Note that only taxi boats with a yellow strip are the official operators sanctioned by the city. You can book trips with Consorzio Moscafi Venezia online at **www.motoscafivenezia.it** or call © **041/5222303.** Six water-taxi stations serve key points in the city: the Ferrovia, Piazzale Roma, the Rialto Bridge, Piazza San Marco, the Lido, and Marco Polo Airport.

BY GONDOLA If you've come all this way and don't indulge in a gondola ride, you might be kicking yourself long after you have returned home. Yes, it's touristy, and, yes, it's expensive (see "Cruising the Canals" on p. 230), but only those with a heart of stone will be unmoved by the quintessential Venetian experience. Don't initiate your trip, however, until you have agreed on a price and synchronized watches. Oh, and don't ask them to sing.

A gondola near the Rialto Bridge.

COME HELL OR high water

During the tidal *acqua alta* (high water) floods, Venice's lagoon rises until it engulfs the city, leaving up to 1.5 to 1.8m (5–6 ft.) of water in the lowest-lying streets. Piazza San Marco, as the lowest point in the city, goes first. As many as 50 floods a year have been recorded since they first started keeping track in the late 1700s.

Significant *acqua alta* can begin as early as late September or October, but usually takes place November to March (there is no way to predict them in advance). Remember, though, the waters usually recede after just a few hours— there is no need to get wet and the city doesn't shut down. Walkways are set up along the main routes, but if you intend to wander around, do as the locals do and buy rubber wading boots, available from most stores from 20€ (souvenir shops and stands in Piazza San Marco also sell disposable knee-high plastic waterproof slippers for about 10€, good for a couple of days). A complex system of hydraulic gates—the Modulo Sperimentale Elettromeccanico or just "MOSE"—is being built out in the lagoon to cut off the highest of these tides (controversial because of its environmental impact and the seemingly endless delays that have plagued construction); it is expected to be operational sometime in 2022.

[FastFACTS] VENICE

Consulates See chapter 10.

Doctors & Hospitals The **Ospedale Civile Santi Giovanni e Paolo** (✆ 041/5294111), on Campo Santi Giovanni e Paolo, has English-speaking staff and provides emergency service (go to the emergency room, *pronto soccorso*) 24 hours a day (*vaporetto:* Ospedale).

Emergencies The best number to call in Italy (and the rest of Europe) with a **general emergency** is ✆ **112;** this connects you to the military-trained (and English-speaking) **Carabinieri** who will transfer your call as needed. For the **police,** dial ✆ **113;** for a medical emergency and to call an **ambulance,** the number is ✆ **118;** for the **fire department,** call ✆ **115.** All are free calls.

Internet Access Venice offers citywide Wi-Fi through the **VeniceConnected** (www.veneziaunica. it) network of 200 hotspots. Buy packages online (5€/24 hr., 15€/3 days, or 20€/7 days); access codes are then sent via e-mail.

Mail The most convenient post offices are: **Venezia Centro** at Calle de la Acque, San Marco (✆ 041/2404149; Mon–Fri 8:25pm– 7:10pm and Sat 8:25am– 12:35pm); **Venezia 4** at Calle de l'Ascension 1241 (✆ 041/2446711), off the west side of Piazza San Marco (Tues–Fri 8:25am– 1:35pm, Sat 8:25am– 12:35pm); and **Venezia 3** at Campo San Polo 2012 (✆ 041/5200315; same hours).

Pharmacies Venice's pharmacies take turns staying open all night. To find out which one is on call in your area, ask at your hotel or check the rotational duty signs posted outside all pharmacies.

Safety Be aware of petty crime like pickpocketing on the crowded *vaporetti*, particularly the tourist routes, where passengers are more intent on the passing scenery than on watching their bags. Venice's often deserted back streets are virtually crime-free, though occasional crime tales of theft have circulated. Generally speaking, Venice is one of Italy's safest cities.

WHERE TO STAY IN VENICE

Few cities boast as long a high season as that of Venice, beginning with the Easter period. May, June, and September are the best months weather-wise and, therefore the most crowded. July and August are hot (few of the one- and two-star hotels offer air-conditioning, and when they do, it usually costs extra). Like everything else, hotels are more expensive here than in any other Italian city, with no apparent upgrade in amenities. The least special of those below are clean and functional; at best, they're charming and thoroughly enjoyable, with the serenade of a passing gondolier thrown in for good measure. Some may even provide you with your best stay in all of Europe.

It's highly advisable to reserve your lodging as far in advance as possible, even in the off-season.

Hotels by Price

EXPENSIVE

Al Ponte Antico ★★★, p. 244
Antiche Figure ★★★, p. 243
Baglioni Hotel Luna ★★★, p. 236
Corte Di Gabriela ★★★, p. 236
Londra Palace ★★, p. 238
Metropole ★★★, p. 238
Moresco ★★★, p. 240

Casa Verardo ★★★, p. 239
Galleria ★★, p. 241
Giorgione ★★, p. 245
Locanda Fiorita ★★, p. 237
Locanda Orseolo ★★★, p. 237
Pensione Accademia ★★, p. 241
Pensione Guerrato ★★★, p. 242
Violino d'Oro ★★★, p. 238

MODERATE

Ai Due Fanali ★★, p. 243
Al Piave ★★, p. 238
American Dinesen ★★, p. 240
Antica Locanda al Gambero ★, p. 237
Arcadia ★★★, p. 244
Ca' Barba B&B ★★, p. 242

INEXPENSIVE

Ai Tagliapietra ★★★, p. 239
B&B San Marco ★★★, p. 240
Bernardi ★★, p. 245
Falier ★, p. 243
San Geremia ★, p. 245

Self-Catering Apartments

Anyone looking to get into the local swing of things in Venice should stay in a **short-term rental apartment.** For the same price or less than a hotel room, you could have your own one-bedroom apartment with a washing machine, A/C, and a fridge to keep your wine in. Properties of all sizes and styles, in every price range, are available for stays of 3 nights to several weeks.

In terms of **location,** San Marco is the most convenient part of the city, though anywhere near the Grand Canal will allow you easy access to the best of Venice. Apartments in the further reaches of Santa Croce, Cannaregio, Giudecca and Castello may be slightly cheaper and allow a glimpse of residential life in the city, but getting to and from the main sights will take a lot of time.

For those renting apartments, rather than staying in hotels, secure **luggage storage facilities** are available through BAGBNB (which acts as an agent for businesses prepared to look after your bags throughout the city), from 5€ per day (bagbnb.com).

Venice Hotels

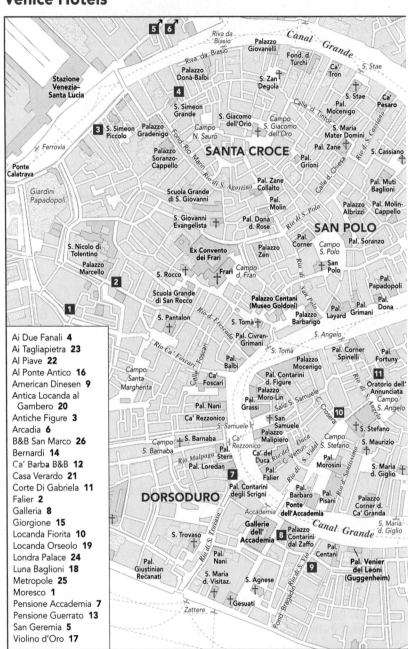

Ai Due Fanali **4**
Ai Tagliapietra **23**
Al Piave **22**
Al Ponte Antico **16**
American Dinesen **9**
Antica Locanda al
  Gambero **20**
Antiche Figure **3**
Arcadia **6**
B&B San Marco **26**
Bernardi **14**
Ca' Barba B&B **12**
Casa Verardo **21**
Corte Di Gabriela **11**
Falier **2**
Galleria **8**
Giorgione **15**
Locanda Fiorita **10**
Locanda Orseolo **19**
Londra Palace **24**
Luna Baglioni **18**
Metropole **25**
Moresco **1**
Pensione Accademia **7**
Pensione Guerrato **13**
San Geremia **5**
Violino d'Oro **17**

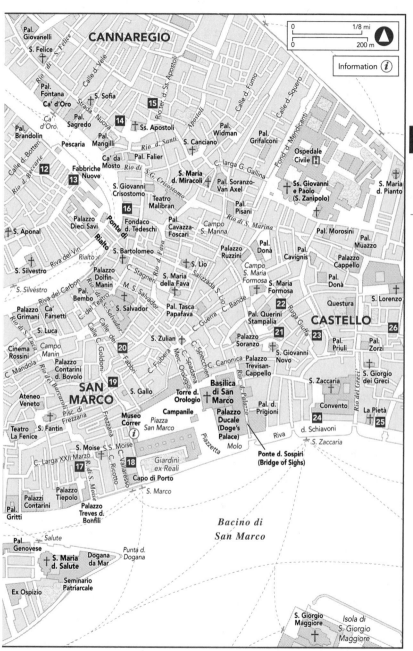

RECOMMENDED AGENCIES

Airbnb (www.airbnb.com), **VRBO.com,** and **Homeaway.com** are now major players in Venice, each with more than 300 properties listed. On Airbnb you can rent a room in someone's home from just 25€ per night. **Couchsurfing** (www.couchsurfing.com) is also popular and generally safe in Venice, though take the usual precautions (for those who don't know the company, it allows locals to offer free rooms to travelers). **Cities Reference** (www.cities reference.com; 𝒸 **06/48903612**) is the best traditional rental agency for Venice, with around 119 properties listed. The company's no-surprises property descriptions come with helpful information and lots of photos. **Cross Pollinate** (www.cross-pollinate.com; 𝒸 **06/99369799**) is a multi-destination agency with a decent roster of personally inspected apartments and B&Bs in Venice, created by the American owners of the Beehive hotel in Rome (p. 66). **Rental in Venice** (www.rentalinvenice.com; 𝒸 **041/718981**) has an alluring website—with video clips of the apartments—and the widest selection of midrange and luxury apartments in the prime San Marco zone (there are less expensive ones, too).

It's standard practice for local rental agencies to collect 30% of the total rental amount upfront to secure a booking. When you check in, the balance of your rental fee is normally payable in cash only, so make sure you have enough euros in hand. Upon booking, the agency should provide you with detailed check-in procedures. Most apartments provide a list of nearby shops and services; beyond that, you're on your own, which is what makes an apartment stay a great way to do as the Venetians do.

San Marco

EXPENSIVE

Baglioni Hotel Luna ★★★ Perfectly situated on the lagoon just around the corner from the bustle of Piazza San Marco, this is the oldest hotel in Venice, housed in a building from 1118 that was once a church before Napoleon destroyed its sacristy. Today, the boutique property, a member of Leading Hotels of the World, is a cocoon of privacy and comfort; the bright lobby with Murano chandeliers gives way to plush rooms decorated with antique furnishings, brocade, and original artwork from the 1700s. The breakfast room is especially noteworthy: With a room-length mural and intricately painted ceiling frescoes created in the 18th century by students of Tiepolo, it makes every cup of coffee feel like a regal break. Staff here is especially attentive and professional.

San Marco, 1243. www.baglionihotels.com. 𝒸 **041/5289840.** 91 units. 290€–800€. *Vaporetto:* San Marco. **Amenities:** Restaurant; lounge; babysitting; concierge; Wi-Fi (free).

Corte Di Gabriela ★★★ This gorgeous boutique hotel just a short walk from Piazza San Marco combines contemporary design and classical Venetian style—ceiling murals, marble pillars, and exposed brick blend with designer furniture and appliances (including free use of iPads, strong Wi-Fi, and satellite TV). The fully renovated property dates from 1870, once serving as the home and offices of Venetian lawyers. It's the attention to detail that makes a stay here so memorable, with breakfast one of the highlights. It's well worth lingering over: decent espresso, fresh pastries made by the owners the night before, and crepes and omelets made on request.

Calle degli Avvocati 3836. www.cortedigabriela.com. ℂ **041/5235077.** 10 units. 245€–410€ double. Rates include breakfast. *Vaporetto:* Sant' Angelo. **Amenities:** Bar; babysitting; concierge; room service (limited hours); Wi-Fi (free).

MODERATE

Antica Locanda al Gambero ★ The best attribute of this small, typically cute Venetian hotel is the location, just a 2-minute walk from Piazza San Marco. Rooms are dressed in a bright rococo style with modern extras like satellite TV and A/C, and most have lovely views of the local canal (but not all—check when you book to avoid disappointment). It has no elevator (remember that a "fourth floor" room in Italy is actually on the fifth floor, quite a climb) and the breakfast buffet is small, but it does have free Internet terminals in the lobby and a small rooftop patio that few guests seem to use.

Calle dei Fabbri 4687. www.locandaalgambero.com. ℂ **041/5224384.** 30 units. 138€–175€ double. Rates include breakfast. *Vaporetto:* Rialto (turn right along canal, cross bridge over Rio San Salvador, then left onto Calle Bembo/Calle dei Fabbri; hotel is 5 blocks ahead on left). **Amenities:** Restaurant; bar; concierge; Wi-Fi (free).

Locanda Fiorita ★★ Hard to imagine a more picturesque location for this little hotel, a charming, quiet *campiello* draped in vines and blossoms— no wonder it's a favorite of professional photographers. Standard rooms are small (bathrooms are tiny), but all are furnished in an elegant 18th-century style, with wooden floors, shuttered windows, and richly patterned fittings (A/C and satellite TV are included). The helpful staff more than make up for any deficiencies, and breakfast is a real pleasure, especially when taken outside on the *campiello*.

Campiello Novo 3457a. www.locandafiorita.com. ℂ **041/5234754.** 10 units. 110€– 175€ double. Rates include breakfast. *Vaporetto:* Sant'Angelo (walk to tall brick building and go around it, turn right into Ramo Narisi; at small bridge turn left, walk along Calle del Pestrin; Campiello Novo will be on your right. **Amenities:** Babysitting; concierge; room service; Wi-Fi (free).

Locanda Orseolo ★★★ This enticing inn comprises three elegant guesthouses operated by the friendly Peruch family, located right behind Piazza San Marco. This place really oozes character, with exposed wood beams and heavy drapes, and rooms lavishly decorated with Venetian-style furniture and tributes to the masks of the Carnevale—a cross between an artist's studio and Renaissance palace. Lounge with an aperitif on the terrace overlooking the Orseolo canal, and enjoy eggs and crepes made to order at breakfast, while watching the gondolas glide by.

Corte Zorzi 1083. www.locandaorseolo.com. ℂ **041/5204827.** 15 units. 150€–240€ double. Rates include breakfast. *Vaporetto:* San Marco. **Amenities:** Babysitting; concierge; Wi-Fi (free).

Violino d'Oro ★★   The relatively spacious rooms in this handsome 18th-century building have been adorned in a neoclassical Venetian style with exposed wooden beams, crystal chandeliers, and heaps of character. Most rooms also overlook the romantic San Moisè canal, and Piazza San Marco is just a 5-minute stroll. At this price (with incredible low-season deals), it's reassuring to know you get A/C, satellite TV, and an elevator. Breakfast is a vast spread of homemade cakes and muffins paired with one of the best cappuccinos in the city.

Calle Larga XXII Marzo 2091. www.violinodoro.com. ℂ **041/2770841.** 26 units. 112€–214€ double. Rates include breakfast. *Vaporetto:* San Marco–Vallaresso (walk up Calle di Ca' Vallaresso, turn left on Salizada San Moisè and cross the footbridge; the hotel is across the *campiello* on the left). **Amenities:** Bar; concierge; room service; Wi-Fi (free).

Castello
EXPENSIVE
Londra Palace ★★   This white-marble beauty, part of the Relais & Chateaux stable, occupies a prime location overlooking the waterfront promenade—get a room with a balcony to make the most of the spectacular views. All rooms are spacious, with lofty ceilings, 19th-century Biedermeier-style furniture, and satellite TV. This is another place with an intriguing history: The core of the hotel dates back to 1853 when it was the Hotel d'Angleterre, beefed up by a "neolombardesque-style" extension in the 1860s. Tchaikovsky was a guest here in December 1877; legend has it he composed the first three movements of his Symphony No. 4 in room no. 106.

Riva degli Schiavoni 4171. www.londrapalace.com. ℂ **041/5200533.** 53 units. 350€–450€ double. Rates include breakfast. *Vaporetto:* San Zaccaria. **Amenities:** Restaurant; bar; babysitting; concierge; room service; Wi-Fi (free).

Metropole ★★★   This five-star behemoth with a waterfront location is part luxury hotel, part eclectic art museum, with antiques, Asian artworks, and tapestries dotted throughout. But it's no dusty grand dame; on the contrary, the hotel is a chic boutique with rooms opulently furnished in white, red, and gold color schemes. For many guests, however, the main reason to stay here is the building's inspiring history. It began life in the Middle Ages as the Ospedale della Pietà, serving as a charitable institution for orphans and abandoned girls, and later a music school where Vivaldi taught violin in the early 1700s. After it was converted into a hotel in 1895, Sigmund Freud was an early guest, as was Thomas Mann, who allegedly wrote parts of *Death in Venice* here.

Riva degli Schiavoni 4149. www.hotelmetropole.com. ℂ **041/5205044.** 67 units. 210€–436€ double. Rates include breakfast. *Vaporetto:* San Zaccaria (walk along Riva degli Schiavoni to the right; the hotel is next to La Pietà church). **Amenities:** Restaurant; bar; babysitting; concierge; room service; Wi-Fi (free).

MODERATE
Al Piave ★★   Al Piave is a cozy, old-fashioned family-run hotel just 5 minutes from Piazza San Marco. Rooms are simply but attractively furnished with richly woven rugs, marble floors, and original wood beams exposed.

Some rooms come with a terrace, while the family suites are a good value for groups. Bathrooms are relatively big, and the A/C is a welcome bonus in the summer, but there are no elevators, so be prepared if you get a higher floor. Outside of peak months (July, Sept), Piave is an exceptionally good value, given its proximity to the *piazza*.

Ruga Giuffa 4838. www.hotelalpiave.com. ⓒ **041/5285174.** 20 units. 115€–260€ double. Rates include breakfast. Closed Jan 7 to Carnevale. *Vaporetto:* San Zaccaria (beyond Palazzo Danieli, find Calle delle Rasse and walk to end of street; turn left and then immediately right; cross tiny Ponte Storto, continue to Ruga Giuffa—hotel is on left). **Amenities:** Babysitting; concierge; Wi-Fi (free).

Casa Verardo ★★★   Tucked away across a small bridge in the warren of central Castello, this enchanting hotel occupies a 16th-century *palazzo*, though it's been a hotel since 1911. Rooms sport an old-fashioned Venetian style, with Florentine furniture, hand-painted beds, and colorful textiles (antiques and paintings are scattered throughout), but are updated with air-conditioning and satellite TV. Some rooms have a view over a canal, others over the shady courtyard and the city. Don't miss the top floor, where the panoramic terrace is a pleasant spot for an aperitif. They'll also take you to Murano for free, but you have to find your own way back.

Calle Drio La Chiesa 4765 (at foot of Ponte Storto). www.casaverardo.it.ⓒ **041/5286138.** 25 units. 150€–300€ double. Rates include breakfast. *Vaporetto:* San Zaccaria (walk straight on Calle delle Rasse to Campo SS. Filippo e Giacomo; cross *campo* to Calle della Sacrestia, then Calle Drio La Chiesa to Ponte Storto, look for hotel on left). **Amenities:** Bar; babysitting; concierge; room service; Wi-Fi (free).

INEXPENSIVE

Ai Tagliapietra ★★★   This cozy B&B is run by the amicable Lorenzo, who works hard to make guests' stay a memorable one. It's a real bargain in this part of town. Rooms are basic, but spotless, modern, and relatively spacious with private bathrooms. The small, shared kitchenette is for guests' use (with refrigerator and free tea). Lorenzo will usually meet you at San Zaccaria, give you a map, print your boarding passes, and generally organize your trip if you desire, making this an especially recommended option for first-time visitors.

Casa Verardo.

Salizada Zorzi 4943. www.aitagliapietra. com. ⓒ **347/3233166.** 3 units. 75€–100€ double. Rates include breakfast. *Vaporetto:* San Zaccaria (walk straight on Calle delle Rasse to Campo SS. Filippo e Giacomo; cross *campo* to Calle della Sacrestia; take first left; cross Salita Corte Rotta and continue to Salizada Zorzi). **Amenities:** Wi-Fi (free).

B&B San Marco ★★★ With just three rooms, this exquisite B&B in a peaceful, residential neighborhood fills up fast, so book ahead. It's a comfortable, charming yet convenient option, the kind of place that makes you feel like a local, but not too far from the main sights. Your hosts are the bubbly Marco and Alice Scurati, who live in the attic upstairs, happy to provide help and advice. Furnished with antique furniture, rooms overlook the Scuola di San Giorgio degli Schiavoni and offer wonderful views of the canal and streetscapes nearby. Two rooms share a bathroom; the third has private facilities. Breakfast is self-service in the shared kitchen; yogurts, pastries, espresso, cappuccino, juice, and tea.

Fondamenta San Giorgio dei Schiavoni 3385. www.realvenice.it. ℭ **041/5227589.** 3 units. 100€–160€ double. Rates include breakfast. Closed Aug and Jan 7 to Carnevale. *Vaporetto:* San Zaccaria (walk on Calle delle Rasse to Campo SS. Filippo e Giacomo; cross *campo* to Calle della Sacrestia, cross canal and turn left at Campo S Provolo along Fondamenta Osmarin; turn left where canal ends, walk to bridge that connects to Calle Lion; at end of street turn left along the canal onto Fondamenta San Giorgio dei Schiavoni). **Amenities:** Wi-Fi (free).

Dorsoduro
EXPENSIVE
Moresco ★★★ An incredibly attentive staff, a decadent breakfast that includes prosecco (to mix with orange juice, ahem), and lavish 19th-century Venetian decor make this a popular choice, away from the tourist hubbub. Rooms seamlessly blend Venetian style with modern design. Some have a terrace (with canal or garden views), while others have spa bathtubs; all have flatscreen TVs with satellite channels. If the weather cooperates, take breakfast in the courtyard garden. The hotel is a 5- to 10-minute walk from Piazzale Roma and the train station, but you'll have a number of bridges and stairs to negotiate along the way.

Fondamenta del Rio Novo 3499, Dorsoduro. www.hotelmorescovenice.com. ℭ **041/2440202.** 23 units. 221€–415€ double. Rates include breakfast. *Vaporetto:* Ferrovia/Piazzale Roma (from train station walk southwest along Fondamenta Santa Lucia, cross Ponte della Costituzione, turn left onto Fondamenta Santa Chiara; cross Ponte Santa Chiara and turn right onto Fondamenta Papadopoli; continue across Campiello Lavadori then along Fondamenta del Rio Novo). **Amenities:** Bar; concierge; free trips to Murano; room service; Wi-Fi (free).

MODERATE
American Dinesen ★★ Overlooking the San Vio Canal close to the Accademia, this 17th-century Venetian town house offers elegant rooms decorated in a classical Venetian style, with all the usual modern amenities including LCD TV. All the "superior canal"-view rooms have picture-perfect views of the San Vio, many with a balcony (check if this is important to you), and even partial views of the Grand Canal. Cheaper, modern "dependence rooms" are located in the annex next door and do not include breakfast.

San Vio 628 (on Fondamenta Bragadin). www.hotelamerican.it. ℭ **041/5204733.** 30 units. 250€–480€ double. Rates include breakfast. *Vaporetto:* Accademia (veer left around Accademia, take 1st left turn, then straight ahead to cross 1st small footbridge;

turn right along Fondamenta Bragadin; hotel is on left). **Amenities:** Bar; babysitting; concierge; room service; free Murano trips; Wi-Fi (free).

Galleria ★★   Just around the corner from the Accademia, right on the Grand Canal, this hotel occupies a 19th-century *palazzo* in one of the most inviting locations in the city. It's been a hotel since the 1800s, hosting poet Robert Browning in 1878, and maintains an 18th-century Venetian theme in the rooms, with wood furniture and rococo decor. Hosts Luciano and Stefano serve a simple breakfast in your room. The smallest rooms here really are tiny, and there is no A/C (rooms are supplied with fans when it gets hot), but the fridge of free water and sodas is a lifesaver in summer.

Dorsoduro 878a (at foot of Accademia Bridge). www.hotelgalleria.it. ℂ**041/5232489.** 9 units, 6 with bathroom. 140€–290€ double. Rates include breakfast. *Vaporetto:* Accademia (with Accademia Bridge behind you, hotel is just to your left). **Amenities:** Babysitting; concierge; room service; Wi-Fi (free in public areas).

Pensione Accademia ★★   This spellbinding hotel with a tranquil blossom-filled garden has a fascinating history. The Gothic-style Villa Maravege was built in the 17th century as a family residence, but served as the Russian Embassy between the wars, before becoming a hotel in 1950. If that's not enticing enough, the rooms are fitted with Venetian-style antique reproductions, wood furnishings, handsome tapestries, and A/C, with views over either the Rio San Trovaso or the garden. Breakfast is served in your room, in the dining hall, or on the patio.

Fondamenta Bollani 1058. www.pensioneaccademia.it. ℂ **041/5210188.** 27 units. 120€–330€ double. Rates include breakfast. *Vaporetto:* Accademia (turn right down Calle Gambara/Calle Corfu, which ends at a side canal; walk left to cross over bridge, turn right back toward Grand Canal and the hotel). **Amenities:** Bar; babysitting; concierge; room service; Wi-Fi (free).

A character-filled room at Hotel Galleria.

The dining room and patio at Pensione Accademia (see p. 241).

San Polo

MODERATE

Ca' Barba B&B ★★   What you'll remember most about Ca' Barba may well be the host, Alessandro, who usually meets guests at the Rialto *vaporetto* stop; inspires daily wanderings with tips, maps, and books; and provides fresh breads and pastries from the local bakery for breakfast. Of the four rooms, no. 201 is the largest and brightest, with a Jacuzzi tub (202 also has one). All rooms come with antique furniture, 19th-century paintings, wood-beamed ceilings, LCD TVs, A/C, and strong Wi-Fi.

Calle Campanile Castello 1825. www.cabarba.com. ℰ **041/5242816.** 4 units. 80€–150€ double. Rates include breakfast. *Vaporetto:* Rialto (walk back along Grand Canal, turn left at Calle Campanile Castello). **Amenities:** Concierge; Wi-Fi (free).

Pensione Guerrato ★★★   Dating, incredibly, from 1227, this is definitely one of the city's most historic places to stay. The building's long history—it was once the "Inn of the Monkey," run by nuns, with the original structure mostly destroyed by fire in 1513—is worth delving into (the owners have all the details). Rooms are simply but classically furnished, with wood floors, exposed beams, A/C, and private baths—many with original frescos that may date from the medieval inn. Note that some rooms are on the sixth floor—and there's no elevator.

Calle Drio La Scimia 240a (near the Rialto Market). www.hotelguerrato.com. ℰ **041/5227131.** 19 units. 100€–150€ double. Rates include breakfast. Closed Dec 22–26 and Jan 8–early Feb. *Vaporetto:* Rialto (from north side of Ponte Rialto, walk through the market to corner with UniCredit Banca; go 1 more short block and turn right; hotel is halfway along Calle Drio La Scimia). **Amenities:** Babysitting; concierge; Wi-Fi (free).

Santa Croce

EXPENSIVE

Antiche Figure ★★★   The most convenient luxury hotel in Venice lies directly across the Grand Canal from the train station, a captivating 15th-century *palazzo* adjacent to an ancient gondola workshop. History aside, this is a very plush choice, with rooms decorated in neoclassical Venetian style, with gold leaf, antique furniture, red carpets, silk tapestries, and aging Murano glass and chandeliers, but also LCD satellite TVs and decent Wi-Fi. With the soothing nighttime views across the water, it's certainly a romantic choice, and the staff is worth singling out—friendly and very helpful. There is an elevator, just in case you were wondering.

Fondamenta San Simeone Piccolo 687. www.hotelantichefigure.it. ℗ **041/2759486.** 22 units. 120€–340€ double. Rates include breakfast. *Vaporetto:* Ferrovia (from train station, cross Scalzi Bridge on your left and turn right). **Amenities:** Restaurant; bar; babysitting; concierge; room service; Wi-Fi (free).

MODERATE

Ai Due Fanali ★★   Originally a wooden oratory frequented by fishermen and farmers (later rebuilt), this beguiling hotel features small but artsy rooms, even for Venice: Headboards have been hand-painted by a local artist, exposed wood beams crisscross the ceiling, and vintage drapes and curtains add a cozy feel (work by Jacopo Palma the Younger, the 16th-c. Mannerist painter, adorns the public areas). The bathrooms are embellished with terracotta tiles and Carrera marble. The location is excellent for the train station, while the roof terrace on the third floor is the best place to soak up a panorama of the city (breakfast is served here). It's incredibly popular—book months ahead.

Campo San Simeon Profeta 946. www.aiduefanali.com. ℗ **041/718490.** 16 units. 120€–215€ double. Rates include breakfast. Closed most of Jan. *Vaporetto:* Ferrovia (cross Scalzi bridge over Grand Canal, continue straight, take 2nd left, keep walking to Campo San Simeon Profeta). **Amenities:** Bar; concierge; room service; Wi-Fi (free).

INEXPENSIVE

Falier ★   This tranquil budget hotel is set in a quiet neighborhood, next to the Frari Church and just a 10-minute walk from the train station. Rooms are fairly compact (and could be a little cramped for some), but par for this price point in Venice; all are air-conditioned and come with free Wi-Fi and satellite TV (although there rarely seem to be any English-language channels). The elegant garden is a great place for breakfast (you can also have it in the dining room), with warm croissants, cheese, and a selection of yogurts and cereals, teas and coffees, and fruit juices. The hotel provides free entrance to the Venice casino and a free tour of a Murano glass factory; the friendly, English-speaking staff will also set you up with all manner of other tour options.

Salizada San Pantalon 130. www.hotelfalier.com. ℗ **041/710882.** 19 units. 90€–120€ double. Rates include breakfast. *Vaporetto:* Ferrovia (from train station, cross Scalzi Bridge, turn right along Grand Canal, walk to first footbridge; turn left before crossing bridge and continue along smaller canal to Fondamenta Minotti; turn left here; the street becomes Salizada San Pantalon.) **Amenities:** Concierge; Wi-Fi (free).

Cannaregio

EXPENSIVE

Al Ponte Antico ★★★ To indulge your James Bond fantasy, look no further. Yes it's expensive, but this is one of the most exclusive hotels in Venice, steps from the Rialto Bridge, with a private wharf on the Grand Canal. Part of the attraction is its relatively small size; with just seven rooms, it feels far more intimate than most hotels in this price range, and service is always superior. Rococo wallpaper, rare tapestries, elegant beds, and Louis XV–style furnishings make this place seem like Versailles on the water. The building was originally a 16th-century *palazzo;* one of the many highlights is the charming balcony where breakfast is served and where Bellinis are offered in the evenings.

Calle dell'Aseo 5768. www.alponteantico.com. © **041/2411944.** 7 units. 240€–510€ double. Rates include breakfast. *Vaporetto:* Rialto (walk up Calle Large Mazzini, take 2nd left, cross Campo San Bartolomeo; walk north along Salizada S.G. Grisostomo to Calle dell'Aseo on left). **Amenities:** Bar; concierge; room service; Wi-Fi (free).

MODERATE

Arcadia ★★★ This sensational, modestly advertised boutique set in a 17th-century *palazzo* has an appealing blend of old and new: The theme is Byzantium east-meets-west, combining elements of Venetian and Asian style, but the rooms are full of cool, modern touches: rainfall showers, A/C, flatscreen TVs, bathrobes, and posh toiletries. The lobby is crowned with a Murano glass chandelier. It's a 5-minute walk from the train station.

Rio Terà San Leonardo 1333, Cannaregio. www.hotelarcadia.net. © **041/717355.** 17 units. 105€–285€ double. Rates include breakfast. *Vaporetto:* Guglie (take left into Rio Terà San Leonardo; Arcadia is 30m [98 ft.] on left). **Amenities:** Bar; concierge; room service; Wi-Fi (free).

Breakfast is prepared at Hotel Al Ponte Antico.

Giorgione ★★ Set in a grand 18th-century building, the Giorgione is an elegant gem of a hotel—staying here really is like taking a trip back to old Venice. The combination of old and new works well: Rooms are a little worn, but that adds to the historic ambience, with antique furniture and Venetian decor, fabrics, Murano glass chandeliers, and also satellite TV. In the summer, the generous breakfast is served in the pretty fountain courtyard.

Campo SS. Apostoli 4587. www.hotelgiorgione.com. ✆ **041/5225810.** 76 units. 95€–260€ double. Rates include breakfast. *Vaporetto:* Ca' d'Oro (walk up Calle Ca' d'Oro and turn right onto Strada Nuova, which ends in Campo SS Apostoli). **Amenities:** Bar; babysitting; concierge; room service; Wi-Fi (free).

INEXPENSIVE

Bernardi ★★ An excellent deal, this hotel offers small, basic but spotless rooms in a 16th-century *palazzo* (the superior rooms are bigger), owned and managed by the congenial Leonardo and his wife, Teresa. Most rooms come with one or two classical Venetian touches: Murano chandeliers, hand-painted furniture, exposed wood beams, or tapestries. The shared showers are kept very clean (11 rooms have private bathrooms), and fans are provided in the hot summer months for the cheaper rooms with no A/C. Breakfast is very basic, however, and note that the more spacious annex rooms (near the main building), have A/C but don't appear to get good Wi-Fi coverage.

Calle de l'Oca 4366. www.hotelbernardi.com. ✆ **041/5227257.** 18 units, 11 with private bathroom. 90€–135€ double, includes breakfast. *Vaporetto:* Ca' d'Oro (walk to Strada Nova, turn right to Campo SS. Apostoli; in the square, turn left and take the 1st left onto Calle de l'Oca). **Amenities:** Concierge; room service; Wi-Fi (free).

San Geremia ★ At this excellent budget option just 10 minutes from the train station, rooms are simple but adequate, and most have air-conditioning and views across the canal or *campo*. Note that there is no elevator (some rooms are up 3 flights of stairs), and no breakfast is provided (but you get 50% off breakfast next door). Rooms have no TVs, but Wi-Fi is strong. The dorm rooms are a good deal (21€–25€ per night; guests under 35 only). Cash only.

Campo San Geremia 283. www.hotelsangeremia.com. ✆ **041/715562.** 20 units, 14 with private bathroom. 100€–148€ double. Closed Christmas week. *Vaporetto:* Ferrovia (exit train station, turn left onto Lista di Spagna, and continue to Campo San Geremia). **Amenities:** Babysitting; concierge; room service; Wi-Fi (free).

Giudecca

A quick ferry straight across from the cacophony of Piazza San Marco brings you to the quiet charms of Giudecca Island and its spectacular views across the lagoon to Venice. This is where you'll find **Belmond Hotel Cipriani** (Giudecca 10; www.belmond.com/hotel-cipriani-venice; ✆ **041/240801**), the most famous hotel in Venice, if not all of northern Italy, with its enormous saltwater pool, decadent spa, and rambling gardens. It's extremely expensive, but keep an eye out for shoulder-season deals (the hotel is closed in winter). Or just come for a meal at the waterside **Cip's Club,** where dinner comes with a sparkling view of Piazza San Marco.

WHERE TO EAT IN VENICE

Eating cheaply in Venice is not easy, though it's by no means impossible. The city's reputation for mass-produced menus, bad service, and wildly overpriced food is, sadly, well-warranted, and if you've been traveling in other parts of the country, you may be a little disappointed here. Having said that, everything is relative—this is still Italy after all—and you'll find plenty of excellent dining options in Venice. As a basic rule, value for money tends to increase the farther you travel away from Piazza San Marco, and anything described as a *menù turistico,* while cheaper than a la carte, is rarely any good in Venice (exceptions noted below). Note also that compared with Rome and other points south, Venice is a city of early meals: You should be seated by 7:30 to 8:30pm. Most kitchens close at 10 or 10:30pm, even though the restaurant may stay open later.

While most restaurants in Italy include a cover charge *(coperto)* that usually runs 1.50€ to 3€, in Venice they tend to instead tack on 10% to 12% to the bill for "taxes and service." Some places in Venice will very annoyingly charge you the cover and still add on 12%. A menu should state clearly what extras the restaurant charges (sometimes you'll find it in fine print at the bottom) and if it doesn't, take your business elsewhere.

VENETIAN CUISINE   Venice has a distinguished culinary history, much of it based on its geographical position on the sea. For first courses, both pasta and risotto are commonly prepared with fish or seafood: Risotto *al nero di seppia* or *alle seppioline* (tinted black by the ink of cuttlefish, also called *risotto nero* or black risotto) or *spaghetti alle vongole* (with clams; clams without their shells are not a good sign) are two specialties. Both appear with *frutti di mare,* "fruit of the sea," which is mixed shellfish. *Bigoli,* a thick

bacari & CICCHETTI

One of the essential culinary experiences of Venice is trawling the countless neighborhood bars known as **bacari,** where you can stand or sit with *tramezzini* (small, triangular white-bread half-sandwiches filled with everything from thinly sliced meats and tuna salad to cheeses and vegetables), and **cicchetti** (tapaslike finger foods, such as calamari rings, speared fried olives, potato croquettes, or grilled polenta squares), traditionally washed down with an *ombra* or a small glass of wine, Veneto prosecco, or spritz (a fluorescent cocktail of prosecco and orange-flavored Aperol). All of the above will cost approximately 1.50€ to 6€ if you stand at the bar, as much as double when seated. Bar food is displayed on the countertop or in glass counters and usually sells out by late afternoon, so though it can make a great lunch, don't rely on it for a light dinner. A concentration of popular, well-stocked bars can be found along the **Mercerie** shopping strip that connects Piazza San Marco with the Rialto Bridge, the always lively **Campo San Luca** (look for Bar Torino, Bar Black Jack, or the character-filled Leon Bianco wine bar), and **Campo Santa Margherita.**

spaghetti that's perfect for catching lots of sauce, is a Venetian staple, as is creamy polenta, often served with *gamberetti* (small shrimp) or tiny shrimp called *schie,* or as an accompaniment to *fegato alla veneziana* (calf's liver cooked with onions and white wine). Some of the fish and seafood dishes Venice does particularly well include *branzino* (a kind of seabass), *rombo* (turbot or brill), *moeche* (soft-shelled crab) or *granseola* (crab), and *sarde in saor* (sardines in onions, vinegar, pine nuts, and raisins).

Try the dry white Tocai and pinot from the Friuli region to the northeast of Venice and the light, sparkling prosecco that Venetians consume almost like a soft drink. Popular local red wines include Bardolino, Valpolicella, and Soave, all of which come from the surrounding Veneto region. *Grappa,* the local firewater, is an acquired taste and is often offered in many variations.

Restaurants by Cuisine

CAFE
Caffè dei Frari ★★★, p. 287
Caffè Florian ★★, p. 287
Caffè Lavena ★★, p. 287
Gran Caffè Quadri ★, p. 288
Il Caffè (aka Caffe Rosso) ★★★, p. 288
Marchini Time ★★, p. 288
Pasticceria Nobile ★★, p. 288

DELI
Rosticceria San Bartolomeo ★★, p. 251

GELATO
Gelato Fantasy ★, p. 258
Il Doge ★★, p. 258
La Mela Verde ★★, p. 259
Nico ★, p. 260

ITALIAN
Al Bacco Felice ★, p. 256
Alle Testiere ★★★, p. 252
Al Vecio Canton ★, p. 253
Bacaromi ★★, p. 258
San Trovaso ★, p. 255

PIZZA
Al Vecio Canton ★, p. 253

SEAFOOD
Al Covo ★★, p. 251
Alle Corone ★★, p. 252
Ostaria Da Rioba ★★, p. 257

SICILIAN
A Beccafico ★, p. 250

VENETIAN
Ai Artisti ★★★, p. 253
Ai Cugnai ★★, p. 254
Al Covo ★★, p. 251
Alle Corone ★★, p. 252
Alle Testiere ★★★, p. 252
Bacareto Da Lele ★★★, p. 256
Bacaromi ★★, p. 258
Bistrot de Venise ★★★, p. 250
Da Fiore ★★, p. 250
Do Mori ★★★, p. 255
Do Spade ★, p. 255
Locanda Montin ★★, p. 254
L'Orto dei Mori ★★, p. 257
Osteria Alla Ciurma ★★★, p. 256
Osteria Al Squero ★★★, p. 254
Ostaria Da Rioba ★★, p. 257
Rosticceria San Bartolomeo ★★, p. 251
San Trovaso ★, p. 255
Taverna al Remer ★★, p. 257

WINE BAR
Bacareto Da Lele ★★★, p. 256
Do Mori ★★★, p. 255
Osteria Alla Ciurma ★★★, p. 256
Osteria Al Squero ★★★, p. 254

Venice Restaurants

A Beccafico **11**
Ai Artisti **4**
Ai Cugnai **10**
Al Covo **26**
Alle Corone **20**
Alle Testiere **21**
Al Bacco Felice **2**
Al Vecio Canton **24**
Bacareto De Lele **1**
Bacaromi **6**
Bistrot de Venise **22**
Da Fiore **12**
Do Mori **15**
Do Spade **13**
Gelateria Il Doge **3**
Gelateria La Mela
    Verde **25**
Gelateria Nico **7**
Gelato Fantasy **23**
Locanda Montin **5**
L'Orto dei Mori **17**
Ostaria Da Rioba **16**
Osteria Al Squero **8**
Osteria Alla Ciurma **14**
Rosticceria San
    Bartolomeo **19**
San Trovaso **9**
Taverna al Remer **18**

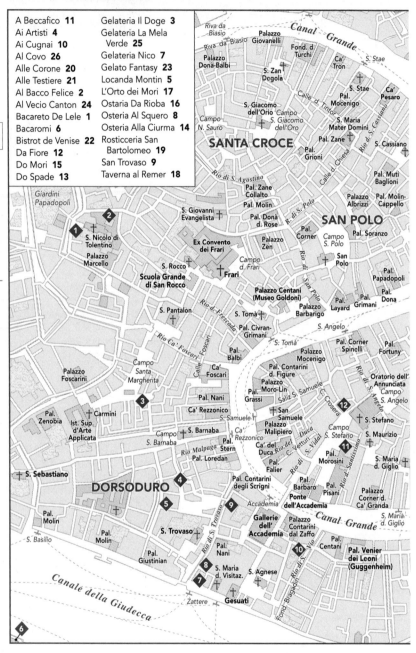

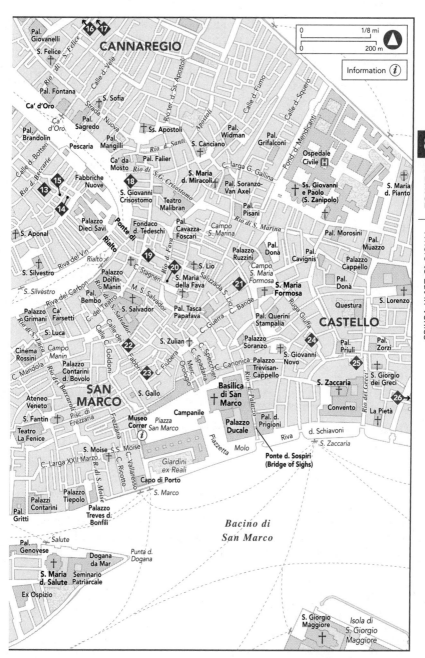

San Marco

EXPENSIVE

A Beccafico ★ SICILIAN   Take a trip to Sicily for a refreshing change from Venetian cuisine, with a menu rich in seafood pastas (such as a simple but delicious *spaghetti alle vongole*) and fresh tuna, sea bream, fabulous calamari, and swordfish—the waiters will advise on the fish of the day and specials such as eggplant ragout. For dessert, you'd be remiss to ignore the utterly addictive tiramisu, and the evening is usually rounded off with complimentary *limoncello*. The location is charming; sit outside to enjoy the people-watching in Campo Santo Stefano. On the downside, service can be hit or miss, and though the food is good, the high prices reflect the location rather than overall quality.

Campo Santo Stefano 2801. www.abeccaficovenezia.com. ✆ **041/5274879.** Reservations recommended. Main courses 17€–38€. Daily noon–3pm and 7–11pm. *Vaporetto:* Accademia (cross bridge to San Marco side and walk straight ahead to Campo Santo Stefano; the restaurant is on your right and toward the back end of the *campo*).

Bistrot de Venise ★★★ VENETIAN   Though it looks a bit like a wood-paneled French bistro, the menu here is primarily old-school Venetian, specializing in rare wines and historical recipes from the 14th to 18th centuries. It's gimmicky, but it works; think fried soft crabs with artichoke salad, scallops, cream of cauliflower and white chocolate, and suckling pig with spices *(civiro)*, quince and bitter orange compote. The "historical" tasting menu is a splurge, but we recommend it as the best introduction. Whatever you opt for, expect service to be topnotch.

4685 Calle dei Fabbri. www.bistrotdevenise.com. ✆ **041/5236651.** Main courses 28€–38€; classic 4-course Venetian tasting menu 74€; historical 5-course Venetian menu 110€. Daily: bar 10am–midnight, restaurant noon–3pm and 7pm–midnight. *Vaporetto:* Rialto (turn right along canal, cross small footbridge over Rio San Salvador, turn left onto Calle Bembo, which becomes Calle dei Fabbri; Bistrot is about 5 blocks ahead).

Da Fiore ★★ VENETIAN   At this classy but laid-back Venetian trattoria (not to be confused with the posher *osteria* with the same name), the menu features typical Venetian dishes like squid ink pasta, but the specials here are the most fun, with *moeche* (local soft-shell crab) a particular treat (the two main seasons are Mar–Apr and Oct–Nov). Desserts see all sorts of sugary *golosessi* on offer, from *buranelli* to *zaletti* (cornmeal cookies, typically eaten dipped in sweet wine or chocolate) and an exceptional *sgroppino al limone* (lemon sherbet). Make sure you visit the bar and *cicchetteria* next door, the **Bacaro di Fiore** (Wed–Mon 9am–10pm), which has been around since 1871, serving cheap wine and finger food like fried sardines and squid, fried vegetables, and crostini with creamed cod.

Calle delle Botteghe 3461, off Campo Santo Stefano. www.dafiore.it. ✆ **041/5235310.** Main courses 16€–30€. Wed–Mon noon–3pm and 7–10pm. Closed 2 weeks in Jan and 2 weeks in Aug. *Vaporetto:* Accademia (cross bridge to San Marco side and walk straight to Campo Santo Stefano; as you are about to exit the *campo* at northern end, take a left onto Calle delle Botteghe; also close to Sant'Angelo *vaporetto* stop).

MODERATE

Rosticceria San Bartolomeo ★★ DELI/VENETIAN   Also known as Rosticceria Gislon, this no-frills spot is incredibly popular with locals, with a handful of small tables and bar stools and bigger tables in the upstairs dining room. Don't be fooled by appearances—the food here is excellent, with a range of grilled fish and seafood pastas on offer, and a tasty "mozzarella in carrozza" (fried cheese sandwich; 2€). There is a discount if you order to take out. Otherwise just sit at the counter and soak up the animated scene, as the cooks chop, customers chat, and people come and go. Order the roast chicken, salt cod, or polenta—typical Venetian fare without all those extra charges.

Calle della Bissa 5424. ℂ **041/5223569.** Main courses 8€–25€. Daily 9:30am–9:30pm (Mon until 3:30pm). *Vaporetto:* Rialto (with bridge at your back on San Marco side of canal, walk straight to Campo San Bartolomeo; take underpass slightly to your left marked SOTTOPORTEGO DELLA BISSA; the *rosticceria* is at the 1st corner on your right; look for GISLON above the entrance).

Castello

EXPENSIVE

Al Covo ★★ SEAFOOD/VENETIAN   For years, this high-quality Venetian restaurant from Diane and Cesare Benelli has been deservedly popular with American food writers (and TV chefs such as Anthony Bourdain), so expect to be eating with plenty of fellow tourists. It features two cozy dining rooms adorned with art (plus some outdoor seating in summer), but it's the food that takes center stage here: fresh fish from the lagoon or the Adriatic, fruits and vegetables from local farms, and meat sourced from esteemed Franco Cazzamali Butchers. The pasta, desserts, and sauces are all homemade. Begin with Venetian *saor,* sweet and sour fish and shellfish, or fried zucchini flowers, followed by salt cod in cocotte, taggiasca olives, salina capers and rosemary, or Piemontese beef tagliata with potato fries, chicory sprouts, and homemade ketchup. Diane's desserts might include rustic pear and prune cake with grappa-cinnamon sauce or green apple sorbet with Calvados.

Al Covo chef Cesare Benelli preparing Carmelli Veneziani, a dessert of caramelized fruits and nuts.

Campiello della Pescheria 3968. www.ristorantealcovo.com. ℂ **041/5223812.** Reservations required. Main courses 26€–38€. Fri–Tues 12:45–3:30pm (kitchen closes 2pm) and 7:30pm–midnight (kitchen closes 10pm); closed usually in Jan and 10 days in Aug. *Vaporetto:* Piazza San Marco (walk along Riva degli Schiavoni toward Arsenale, take 3rd narrow street left [Calle della Pescaria] after Hotel Metropole).

Alle Corone ★★★ SEAFOOD/VENETIAN   This is one of Venice's finest restaurants, an elegant 19th-century dining room inside the Hotel Ai Reali and overlooking the canal. Start with a selection of classic Venetian *cicchetti* (25€) before moving on to grilled scallops with black truffle (19.50€) or main courses such as fillets of sea bass with fennel, small squid and olives, or roast veal with celery mashed turnip and fresh broad beans. To finish, the homemade tiramisu is spectacular. Reservations recommended.

Campo della Fava 5527 (Hotel Ai Reali). www.ristorantealleccorone.com. ℂ **041/ 2410253.** Main courses 29€–30€; 6-course tasting menu 79€; Daily noon–2:30pm and 7–10:30pm. *Vaporetto:* Rialto (walk east along Calle Larga Mazzini, turn left at Merceria then right on Calle Stella until you reach the hotel).

Alle Testiere ★★★ ITALIAN/VENETIAN   This tiny restaurant (with only nine tables) is the connoisseur's choice for fresh fish and seafood, with a menu that changes frequently and a shrewd selection of wines. Dinner is served at two seatings, where you choose from appetizers such as scallops with orange and leeks, or razor clams that seem to have been literally plucked straight from the sea. The fresh seabass fillet with capers and Ligurian black olives is always an exceptional main choice, and seasonal pastas—like pumpkin and ricotta ravioli with prawns, or spaghetti with clams—are all superb. Finish off with homemade peach pie or chestnut pudding. In peak season, plan

Dining room of Alle Corone.

Opening wine at Alle Testiere.

to make reservations at least a month in advance, and note that you'll have a less rushed experience in the second seating.

Calle del Mondo Novo 5801. www.osterialletestiere.it. ℗ **041/5227220.** Main courses 26–28€; many types of fish sold by weight. Tues–Sat noon–3pm and two dinner seatings (7pm and 9:30pm). *Vaporetto:* Rialto or San Marco (look for Salizada San Lio west of Campo Santa Maria Formosa; from there ask for Calle del Mondo Novo).

MODERATE

Al Vecio Canton ★ ITALIAN/PIZZA   Venice is not known for pizza, partly because fire codes restrict the use of traditional wood-burning ovens, but the big, fluffy-crusted pies here—made using natural mineral water—are the best in the city. They also do a mean T-bone steak, cooked tableside on a granite slab, accompanied by truffle or red pepper sauce. Pastas are pretty good, too—stick with seafood versions like cuttlefish, the seasonal *moeche* (soft-shell crabs), and *schie,* small shrimp from the lagoon. Wash it all down with the drinkable house wine, or for a change, tasty craft beers from Treviso-based 32 Via dei Birrai.

Castello 4738a (at the corner of Calle Ruga Giuffa). www.alveciocanton.it. ℗ **041/5287143.** Pizza 7€–15€. Main courses 14€–22€. Wed–Mon noon–3pm and 6:30–10:30pm. *Vaporetto:* San Zaccaria (head down road on left side of Hotel Savoia e Jolanda to Campo San Provolo; take Salizada San Provolo on north side of *campo,* cross 1st footbridge on your left; the pizzeria is on the 1st corner on the left).

Dorsoduro
EXPENSIVE

Ai Artisti ★★★ VENETIAN   This unpretentious family-owned osteria enoteca is one of the best dining experiences in Venice, with a menu that changes daily according to what's available at the market (no fish is served Mon, when the fish market is closed). Grab a table by the canal and feast on octopus salad, swordfish steak, and an amazing buttery beef cheek with celery cream, or opt for one of the truly wonderful pastas (such as tortellini stuffed with spidercrab). The tiramisu and chocolate torte are standouts for dessert. Something that's likely to stay with you in addition to the food is the impeccable service, with waitstaff happy to guide you through the menu and offer brilliant suggestions for wine pairing. Reservations recommended—it's a tiny place, with seating for just 20.

Fondamenta della Toletta 1169A. www.enotecaartisti.com. ℂ **041/5238944.** Main courses 25€–28€. Mon–Sat 12:45–2:30pm and two dinner seatings (7–9pm and 9–11pm). *Vaporetto:* Accademia (walk around Accademia and turn right onto Calle Gambara; when it ends at Rio di San Trovaso, turn left onto Fondamenta Priuli; take 1st bridge onto road that soon leads into Fondamenta della Toletta).

Locanda Montin ★★ VENETIAN   Montin was the famous ex-hangout of Peggy Guggenheim in the 1950s, frequented by Jimmy Carter, Robert De Niro, and Brad Pitt, among many other celebrities, but is the food still any good? Well, yes. Grab a table in the wonderfully serene back garden (covered by an arching trellis), itself a good reason to visit, and sample Venetian classics such as sardines in *soar* (a local marinade of vinegar, wine, onion, and raisins) and an exquisite *seppie in nero* (cuttlefish cooked in its ink). For a main course, it's hard to beat the crispy seabass *(branzino)* or legendary monkfish, while the lemon sorbet with vodka is a perfect, tangy conclusion to any meal.

Fondamenta di Borgo 1147. www.locandamontin.com. ℂ **041/5227151.** Main courses 18€–28€. Daily 12:15–2:30pm and 7:15–10pm (closed on Wed Nov–Apr). *Vaporetto:* Ca'Rezzonico (walk straight along Calle Lunga San Barnaba, then turn left along Fondamenta di Borgo).

MODERATE

Ai Cugnai ★★ VENETIAN   The name of this small trattoria means "at the in-laws," and in that spirit the kitchen knocks out solid, home-cooked Venetian food, beautifully prepared and very popular with locals and hungry gondoliers. The classics are done especially well: The *spaghetti vongole* here is crammed with sea-fresh mussels and clams, the *caprese* and baby octopus salad are perfectly balanced appetizers, and the house red is top value. Our favorite, though, is the sublime spaghetti with scallops, a slippery, salty delight. Just two small tables outside, so get here early if you want to eat alfresco.

Calle Nuova Sant'Agnese 857. ℂ **041/5289238.** Main courses 15€–28€. Mon and Wed–Sun noon–3pm and 6–10pm. *Vaporetto:* Accademia (head east of bridge and Accademia in direction of Guggenheim Collection; restaurant will be on your right, off the straight street connecting the two museums).

Osteria Al Squero ★★★ WINE BAR/VENETIAN   Perhaps the most beguiling view in Venice is from this enticing *osteria,* right opposite the Squero di San Trovaso (p. 276). Sip coffee and nibble *cicchetti* while observing the activity at the medieval gondola boatyard and workshop, on the other side of the Rio di San Trovaso. It's essentially a place for a light lunch or *aperitivi* rather than a full meal. Snack on such delights as Carnia smoked sausage, baccalà crostini (cod), anchovies, blue cheese, tuna, and sardines in *saor* for a total of around 16€ to 18€ per person. Spritz from 2.50€.

Fondamenta Nani 943–944. © **335/6007513.** *Cicchetti* 1.20–2.80€ per piece. Tues–Sun 7am–8pm. *Vaporetto:* Zattere (walk west along waterside to Rio di San Trovaso, turn right up Fondamenta Nani).

San Trovaso ★ ITALIAN/VENETIAN   Perfect for a lunch or dinner of tasty Italian comfort food, this no-frills tavern's three-course *menu turistico* (21€) features classics such as spaghetti with pesto, *spaghetti vongole,* and an utterly addictive *gnocchi ai 4 formaggi* (gnocchi with four cheeses). The seafood menu is huge, with *salmone alla griglia* (grilled salmon) and a delightful *scaloppini* (finely sliced scallops) with lemon sauce in addition to the usual Venetian lineup of scampi, monkfish, and seabass. Tends to be touristy, of course, but a good value all the same.

Dorsoduro 1016 (on Fondamenta Priuli). © **041/5230835.** Reservations recommended. Main courses 12€–22€. Tues–Sun noon–2:45pm and 7pm–9:45pm. *Vaporetto:* Accademia (walk right around Accademia, then right onto Calle Gambara to where it ends at Rio di San Trovaso; turn left onto Fondamenta Priuli).

San Polo
MODERATE
Do Spade ★ VENETIAN   It's tough to find something so authentic this close to the Rialto Bridge these days, but Do Spade has been around since 1415. Most locals come here for the *cicchetti* (you can sit on benches outside if it's too crowded indoors), small plates such as fried calamari, meatballs, mozzarella, salted cod (1.50€–3.50€), and decent Italian wines (3€ a glass). The more formal menu is also worth a try, with seafood highlights including a delicately prepared monkfish, scallops served with fresh zucchini, and a rich seafood lasagna. The seasonal pumpkin ravioli is one of the best dishes in the city.

Sottoportego do Spade 860. www.cantinadospade.com. © **041/5210574.** Main courses 12€–25€; tasting menu 18€. Daily 10am–3pm and 6–10pm. *Vaporetto:* Rialto Mercato (with your back to Grand Canal, walk up Ruga Vecchia San Giovanni, turn right on Ruga dei Spezieri; at the end turn left on Calle de le Beccarie O Panataria, and then take 2nd right onto covered Sottoportego do Spade).

INEXPENSIVE
Do Mori ★★★ WINE BAR/VENETIAN   Serving good wine and *cicchetti* since 1462 (check out the antique copper pots hanging from the ceiling), Do Mori is above all a fun place to have a genuine Venetian experience, a small, dimly lit *bàcari* that can barely accommodate 10 people standing up. Sample the baby octopus and ham on mango, lard-smothered *crostini,* and pickled onions speared with salty anchovies, or opt for the *tramezzini* (tiny sandwiches). Local TV (and BBC) star Francesco Da Mosto is a regular, but note that this institution is very much on the well-trodden tourist trail—plenty of *cicchetti* tours stop by in the early evening. Sip local wine for 3€ to 4€ a glass.

Calle Do Mori 429 (also Calle Galeazza 401). ✆ **041/5225401.** *Tramezzini* and *cicchetti* 1.80€–3.50€ per piece. Mon–Sat 8am–8pm (June–Aug closed daily 2–4:30pm). *Vaporetto:* Rialto Mercato (with your back to Grand Canal, walk straight up Ruga Vecchia San Giovanni and turn right on Calle Galeazza).

Osteria Alla Ciurma ★★★ WINE BAR/VENETIAN With a dining room decked out like a traditional Venetian boat, this *cicchetteria* offers some of the freshest seafood snacks in the city—sourcing fresh fish from the daily market just around the corner—washed down with quality wines, spritz, and prosecco. Mouth-watering *cicchetti* include cod fillets, fried zucchini flowers, fried artichokes, and shrimp wrapped in bacon. More substantial sandwiches and lunch specials (noon–3pm) are also available.

Calle Galeazza 406. ✆ **340/6863561.** *Cicchetti* 1.80€–6€ per piece. Mon–Sat 9am–3pm and 5:30–9pm; Sun 10:30am–3pm (May–Sept only). *Vaporetto:* Rialto Mercato (with your back to Grand Canal, walk straight up Ruga Vecchia San Giovanni and turn right on Calle Galeazza).

Santa Croce
MODERATE
Al Bacco Felice ★ ITALIAN This quaint, friendly restaurant is convenient for the train station and popular with locals, with a real buzz most nights. Stick with the basics and you won't be disappointed—the pizzas, pastas, and fish dishes are always outstanding, with classic standbys *spaghetti alle vongole,* pasta with spicy *arrabbiata,* and *carpaccio* of swordfish especially well done. The meal usually ends with complimentary plates of Venetian cookies, a nice touch.

Santa Croce 197E (on Corte dei Amai). ✆ **041/5287794.** Main courses 15€–28€. Mon–Fri noon–3:30pm and 6:30–midnight, Sat and Sun noon–midnight. *Vaporetto:* Piazzale Roma (keeping Grand Canal on your left, head toward train station; cross small canal at end of park, immediately turn right onto Fondamenta Tolentini; at Campo Tolentini, turn left onto Corte dei Amai).

INEXPENSIVE
Bacareto Da Lele ★★★ WINE BAR/VENETIAN This tiny hole-in-the-wall *bacaro* is worth seeking out for its fresh snacks, sandwiches, and *cicchetti.* Tiny glasses or *ombras* of wine and prosecco are just 0.60€ to 1.50€. There are no seats, so do as the locals do and grab a space on the nearby church steps, outside by the canal, while you sip and nibble. Opt for a tiny *porchetta* and mustard or the bacon and artichoke panini (around 2.50€), antipasti plates (cheese and salami), or a simple, freshly baked crostini for 1€ to 2€. Expect long lines here in peak season; the secret is definitely out.

Campo dei Tolentini 183. No phone. *Cicchetti* 1.50€–3.50€ per piece. Mon–Fri 6am–8pm; Sat 6am–2pm. *Vaporetto:* Piazzale Roma (walk left along Grand Canal past Ponte della Costituzione, into Giardino Papadopoli; turn right on Fondamenta Papadopoli, then left. Cross park at 1st bridge; the next canal is Rio del Tolentini, across bridge from the campo; Da Lele is on southwest corner).

Cannaregio

EXPENSIVE

L'Orto dei Mori ★★ VENETIAN   Traditional Venetian cuisine is cooked up here by a young Sicilian chef, so expect some subtle differences to the usual flavors and dishes. Everything on the relatively small menu is exceptional—the codfish and clams stewed with artichokes especially so—and the setting next to a small canal is enhanced by candlelight at night. This place can get very busy—the waiters are normally friendly, but expect brusque treatment if you turn up late or early for a reservation. Don't be confused: The restaurant prefers to serve dinner, broadly, within two seatings, one early (7–9pm) and one late, so that's why waiters will be reluctant to serve diners who arrive early for the second sitting—even if there's a table available, you'll be given water and just told to wait.

Campo dei Mori 3386. www.osteriaortodeimori.com. ✆ **041/5243677.** Main courses 21€–28€. Wed–Mon 12:30–3:30pm and 7pm–midnight, usually in two seatings (July–Aug closed for lunch Mon–Fri). *Vaporetto:* Madonna dell'Orto (walk through campo to canal, turn right; take 1st bridge on left, walk down street and turn left at canal onto Fondamenta dei Mori; go straight until you hit Campo dei Mori).

Ostaria Da Rioba ★★ SEAFOOD/VENETIAN   Fresh, creative, and absolutely scrumptious Venetian food is served right alongside a serene canal in a lively—but not touristy—area. Plenty of locals eat here, enticed by the beautifully executed seafood: monkfish, seabass, scampi, turbot, mackerel, tuna, and lots of cod. Top choices include a lightly grilled scampi (massive prawns sliced down the middle) and "spaghetti noir," the kitchen's interpretation of that Venetian classic, spaghetti with cuttlefish ink. But for a real treat, order the grilled duck, a rich, sumptuous dish served with seasonal vegetables. Note that there are only 35 seats along the canal, so to watch that gorgeous summer sunset, reservations are a must.

Fondamenta della Misericordia 2553. www.darioba.com. ✆ **041/5244379.** Reservations highly recommended. Main courses 24€–28€. Tues–Sun 11am–3pm and 6–10pm. *Vaporetto:* San Marcuola (walk behind church, go straight 5 blocks to 1st bridge; cross and turn right on Misericordia).

INEXPENSIVE

Taverna al Remer ★★ VENETIAN   Eating on a budget in Venice doesn't always mean panini and pizza. This romantic *taverna* overlooks the Grand Canal from a small, charming piazza, and while the a la carte options can be pricey, the secret is to time your visit for the buffets. The 21€ weekday lunch is a fabulous deal: a choice of two fresh pastas plus a buffet of antipasto that includes vegetables, salads, cold cuts, a choice of two or three quality hot dishes (such as Venice-style liver with polenta, or pan-fried squid), a choice of two or three desserts, and coffee, water, and a quarter liter of wine (per person). The evening *aperitivo* is an even better deal, from just 5€ for as much smoked meat, sausage, salads, seafood risotto, and pasta as you can eat, plus one Aperol spritz, Bellini, vino, or Prosecco. Normal service resumes after the buffet is cleared, with live music (Latin, soul, jazz) most nights at 8:30pm, but as long as you order a few drinks it's fine to stick around and take in the scene.

Cannaregio 5701 (off Salizada S. Giovanni Grisostomo). www.alremer.it. © 041/5228789. Lunch buffet 21€ weekdays only; aperitivo (5:30–7:30pm) from 5€. Mon, Tues, and Thurs–Sun noon–2:30pm and 5:30pm–midnight. *Vaporetto:* Ca' d'Oro or Rialto (heading south on Salizada S. Giovanni Grisostomo, look for narrow passage on right, just beyond Ponte S. Giovanni footbridge).

La Giudecca

EXPENSIVE

Bacaromi ★★ ITALIAN/VENETIAN   This hotel restaurant is well worth visiting Giudecca for, even if you're not spending the night. It's a faux rustic Venetian canteen where you can sample *cicchetti* and a glass of local wine in the company of welcoming and incredibly helpful English-speaking staff led by the indomitable Giuseppe Russo. Combine that with views across the canal and this is a pricy but pleasurable experience, especially for those new to Venice. Menus change regularly, but seafood dominates. If available, order the crab and squid ink risotto, John Dory baked with olives, or just a simple pasta with prawns, but don't be afraid to create a meal from several *cicchetti*—these also change regularly, but the *baccala* (cod) mousse is a taste sensation.

Fondamenta San Biagio 810 (in the Hilton Molino Stucky). www3.hilton.com. © 041/2723311. Main courses 25€–30€. Daily 6–10:30pm (Apr–Sep also daily noon–3pm). *Vaporetto:* Palanca, then walk 5 min. along canal (to the right) to the hotel.

Gelato

Is the gelato any good in Venice? Italians might demur, but by international standards, the answer is most definitely yes. As always, remember that gelato parlors aimed exclusively at tourists are notorious for poor quality and extortionate prices, especially in Venice. Try to avoid places near Piazza San Marco altogether. Below are some of our favorite spots in the city. Each generally opens midmorning and closes late. Winter hours are more erratic.

Gelato Fantasy ★ GELATO   Since 1998, this tiny gelato shop has been doling out tasty scoops dangerously close to Piazza San Marco, but the quality remains high and portions generous. Fresh, strong flavors, with standouts including the pistachio, tiramisu, and strawberry cheesecake.

Calle dei Fabbri 929, San Marco. www.gelatofantasy.com. ©041/5225993. Cones and cups from 3.50€. Daily 10am–11:30pm. *Vaporetto:* Rialto or San Marco.

Il Doge ★★ GELATO   A definite contender for best gelato in Venice, with a great location at the southern end of the Campo Santa Margherita since 1986. These guys use only natural, homemade flavors and ingredients, from an exceptional spicy chocolate to their specialty, "Crema de Doge," a rich concoction of eggs, cream, and real oranges. Try a refreshing *granita* in summer.

Campo Santa Margherita, Dorsoduro. www.gelateriaildoge.com. © 041/5234607. Cones and cups 1.50€–5.50€. Open daily 11am–10pm. *Vaporetto:* Ca'Rezzonico.

EATING alfresco IN VENICE

You don't have to eat in a fancy restaurant to enjoy good food in Venice. Prepare a picnic, and while you eat alfresco, you can observe the life in the city's *campi* or the aquatic parade on its main thoroughfare, the Grand Canal.

Mercato Rialto Venice's principal open-air market has two parts, beginning with the produce section, whose many stalls unfold north on the San Polo side of the Rialto Bridge. Vendors are here Monday to Saturday 7am to 1pm, with some staying on in the afternoon. Behind these stalls are a few permanent food stores that sell cheese, cold cuts, and bread. At the market's farthest point, you'll find the covered **fish market,** still redolent of the days when it was one of the Mediterranean's great fish bazaars. The fish merchants take Monday off and work mornings only.

Campo Santa Margherita On this spacious *campo* in Dorsoduro, Tuesday through Saturday from 8:30am to 1pm, a number of open-air stalls set up shop, selling fresh fruit and vegetables. A conventional supermarket, **Punto Simply** (Mon–Sat 8:30am–8pm, Sun 9am–2pm), is just off the *campo* in the direction of the quasi-adjacent *campo* San Barnaba, at no. 3019.

San Barnaba This is where you'll find Venice's heavily photographed **floating market** (mostly fruit and vegetables), operating from a boat moored just off San Barnaba at the Ponte dei Pugni in Dorsoduro. This market is open daily from 8am to 1pm and 3:30 to 7:30pm, except Wednesday afternoon and Sunday.

The Best Picnic Spots Given its aquatic roots, you won't find much in the way of green space in Venice (if you are really desperate for green, you can walk 30 min. past San Marco along the water, or take a *vaporetto* to the Giardini Pubblici, Venice's only green park, but don't expect anything great). A much more enjoyable alternative is to find one of the larger *campi* that have park benches, such as Campo San Giacomo dell'Orio (in the quiet *sestiere* of Santa Croce). The two most central are **Campo Santa Margherita** (*sestiere* of Dorsoduro) and **Campo San Polo** (*sestiere* of San Polo).

The **Punta della Dogana (Customs House),** near La Salute Church, is a prime viewing site at the mouth of the Grand Canal. Pull up on a piece of the embankment here and watch the flutter of water activity against a backdrop deserving of the Accademia Museum. In this same area, another superb spot is the small **Campo San Vio,** near the Guggenheim, which is directly on the Grand Canal (not many *campi* are) and even boasts two benches and the chance to sit on an untrafficked small bridge.

A bit farther afield, you can take the *vaporetto* out to Burano and then no. 9 for the 5-minute ride to the near-deserted island of **Torcello.** If you bring a basketful of bread, cheese, and wine you can do your best to reenact the romantic scene between Katharine Hepburn and Rossano Brazzi from the 1955 film *Summertime.*

La Mela Verde ★★ GELATO   The popular rival to Il Doge for best scoop in the city, with sharp flavors and all the classics done sensationally well: pistachio, chocolate, *nocciola* (hazelnut), and a mind-blowing lemon and basil. The overall champions: *mela verde* (green apple), like creamy, frozen fruit served in a cup, and the addictive tiramisu.

Fondamenta de L'Osmarin, Castello. www.gelaterialamelaverde.it. ℂ **349/1957924.**
Cones or cups from 1.75€. Daily 11am–11pm. Usually closed mid-Nov to mid-Feb.
Vaporetto: Zaccaria.

Nico ★ GELATO   Founded in 1935, this is one of the city's more historic
gelato counters, with a handful of chairs on the waterfront (these are only for
"table service," at extra charge). Quality is good (the mint, amaretto, and the
signature *gianduiotto*, a chocolate and nut blend, are crazy good), but lines are
always long in the afternoons and evenings, and service can be a little surly.

Fondamenta Zattere al Ponte Longo 922, Dorsoduro. www.gelaterianico.com.
ℂ **041/5225293.** Cone from 2–3.50€. Mon–Wed & Fri–Sat 6:45am–8:30pm, Sun
7:30am–8:30pm. *Vaporetto:* Zattere.

EXPLORING VENICE

Venice is notorious for changing and extending the opening hours of its museums and, to a lesser degree, its churches. Before you begin your exploration of
Venice's sights, ask at the tourist office for the season's list of museum and
church hours. During the peak months, you can enjoy extended museum
hours—some places stay open until 7 or even 10pm. Unfortunately, these hours
are not released until approximately Easter of every year. Even then, little is
done to publicize the information, so you'll have to do your own research.

Index of Attractions & Sights

San Marco

Basilica di San Marco (St. Mark's Cathedral) ★★★ CATHE-DRAL   One of the grandest, and certainly the most exotic of all cathedrals in Europe, **Basilica di San Marco** is a treasure heap of Venetian art and all sorts of booty garnered from the eastern Mediterranean. Legend has it that **St. Mark,** on his way to Rome in the 1st century A.D., was told by an angel his body would rest near the lagoon that would one today become Venice. Hundreds of years later, the city fathers were looking to replace their original patron St. Theodore with a saint of high stature, someone more in keeping with their lofty aspirations. In 828 the prophecy was fulfilled when Venetian merchants stole the body of St. Mark from Alexandria in Egypt (the story goes that the body was packed in pickled pork to avoid the attention of the Muslim guards). Today the high altar's green marble canopy on alabaster columns is believed to cover the remains of St Mark and continues to be the focus of the basilica, at least for the faithful.

Modeled on Constantinople's Church of the Twelve Apostles, the original shrine of St. Mark was consecrated in 832, but in 976 the church burned down. The present incarnation was completed in 1094, then extended and embellished over the years it served as the personal church of the doge. Today San Marco looks more Byzantine cathedral than Roman Catholic church, with a cavernous interior gilded with Byzantine mosaics added over 7 centuries, covering every inch of both ceiling and pavement.

For a closer look at many of the most remarkable ceiling mosaics and a better view of the Oriental-carpet-like patterns of the pavement mosaics, pay the admission to go upstairs to the **Museo di San Marco** (the entrance is in the atrium at the principal entrance); this was originally the women's gallery, or *matroneum,* and includes access to the outdoor **Loggia dei Cavalli.** Here you can admire a panoramic view of the piazza

The facade and dome of the Basilica di San Marco.

Venice Attractions

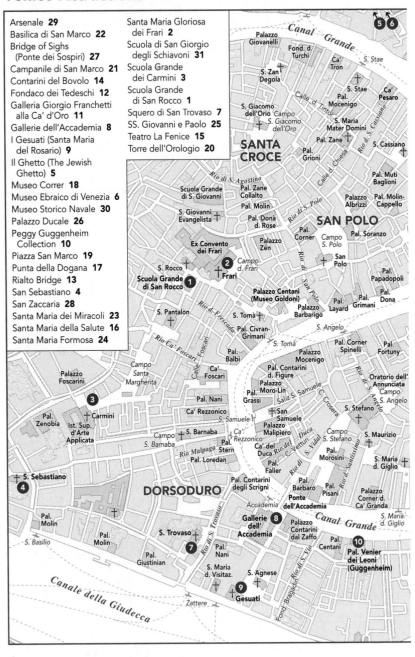

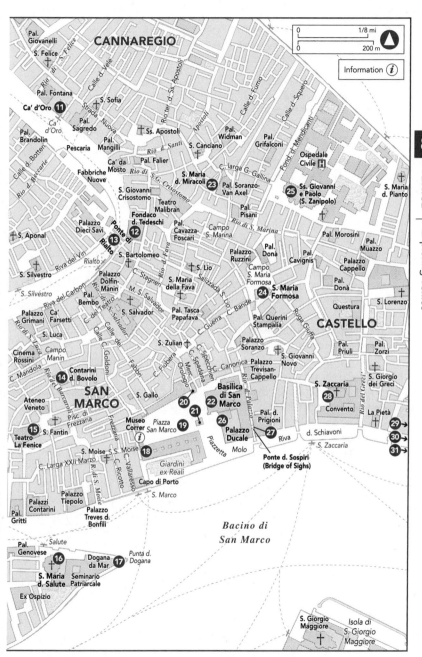

Lines can be long at the basilica (average 45 min), but you can avoid waiting by **reserving access in advance** online (www.venetoinside.com; 3€), up to 10 minutes before your chosen entry time. This service is only available April through October; at other times try to arrive 30 minutes before opening time to avoid the worst of the crush (and skip holidays altogether). You can also use the same website to skip the line at the Campanile di San Marco (p. 264). The guards at St. Mark's entrance are serious about forbidding entry to anyone in **inappropriate attire**—shorts, sleeveless shirts, cropped tops, and skirts above the knee. Note also that you cannot enter the basilica with luggage, and that photos and filming inside are forbidden. Although the basilica is open Sunday morning for anyone wishing to attend Mass, non-worshippers cannot enter merely to tour the site.

below and replicas of the celebrated *Triumphal Quadriga,* four gilded bronze horses dating from the 2nd or 3rd century A.D.; the Roman originals were moved inside in the 1980s for preservation. (The word *quadriga* actually refers to a car or chariot pulled by four horses, though in this case there are only the horses.) The horses were transported to Venice from Constantinople in 1204, along with lots of other loot from the Fourth Crusade.

The basilica's greatest treasure is the magnificent altarpiece known as the **Pala d'Oro (Golden Altarpiece),** a Gothic masterpiece encrusted with over 2,000 precious gems and 83 enameled panels. It was created in 10th-century Constantinople and embellished by Venetian and Byzantine artisans between the 12th and 14th centuries. Second to the Pala d'Oro in importance is the 10th-century **"Madonna di Nicopeia,"** a bejeweled icon also purloined from Constantinople and exhibited in its own chapel. Also worth a visit is the **Tesoro (Treasury),** a collection of crusaders' plunder from Constantinople and other icons and relics amassed over the years. Much of the loot has been incorporated into the interior and exterior of the basilica in the form of marble, columns, capitals, and statuary.

Between April and October, it's worth taking one of the informative 45-minute tours Monday to Saturday (4–5 daily, from 10am; guides speak English). Book tours (from 21€) online at www.venetoinside.com. The church also organizes free tours, but these run for limited periods (mostly late July)—see the website for details.

Piazza San Marco. www.basilicasanmarco.it. © **041/2708311.** Basilica free; Museo di San Marco (includes Loggia dei Cavalli) 5€, Pala d'Oro 2€, Tesoro (Treasury) 3€. Basilica Mon–Sat 9:30am–5pm, Sun 2–4:30pm (Jun–Nov opens 9:45am Mon–Sat; closes Sun 5pm). Tesoro and Pala d'Oro Mon–Sat 9:45am–4:45pm, Sun 2–4:30pm (Jun–Nov closes 5pm daily). Museo di San Marco daily 9:45am–4:45pm. *Vaporetto:* San Marco.

Campanile di San Marco (Bell Tower) ★★★ ICON   An elevator whisks you to the top of this 97m (318-ft.) brown brick bell tower where you get an awe-inspiring view of St. Mark's cupolas. With a gilded angel atop its spire, it is the highest structure in the city, offering a pigeon's-eye panorama that includes the lagoon, neighboring islands, and the red rooftops and church domes and bell towers of Venice. Originally built in the 9th century, the bell tower was reconstructed in the 12th, 14th, and 16th centuries, when the pretty marble loggia at its base was added by Jacopo Sansovino. It collapsed in 1902, miraculously hurting no one except a cat. It was rebuilt exactly as before, using most of the same materials, even one of the five historical bells that it still uses today.

Piazza San Marco. www.basilicasanmarco.it. (C) **041/2708311.** 8€. Daily May–Aug 8:30am–9pm; early–mid Sept 8:30am–8:15pm, late Sept 8:30am–7:45pm; Oct–Mar 9:30am–5:30pm, Apr 9am–5:30pm. *Vaporetto:* San Marco.

Canal Grande (Grand Canal) ★★★ NATURAL ATTRACTION A leisurely cruise along the "Canalazzo" from Piazza San Marco to the Ferrovia (train station), or the reverse, is one of Venice's (and life's) must-do experiences (see box, p. 230). Hop on the **no. 1** *vaporetto* in the late afternoon (try to get a coveted outdoor seat in the prow), when the weather-worn colors of the former homes of Venice's merchant elite are warmed by the soft light and reflected in the canal's rippling waters, and the busy traffic of delivery boats, *vaporetti,* and gondolas that fills the city's main thoroughfare has eased somewhat.

Best stations to start/end a tour of the Grand Canal are Ferrovia (train station) or Piazzale Roma on the NW side of the canal and Piazza San Marco in the southeast. Tickets 7.50€.

Palazzo Ducale and Ponte dei Sospiri (Doge's Palace and Bridge of Sighs) ★★★ PALACE The pink-and-white marble Gothic-Renaissance **Palazzo Ducale,** residence of the doges who ruled Venice for more than 1,000 years, stands between the Basilica di San Marco and the sea. A symbol of prosperity and power, the original was destroyed by a succession of fires, with the current building started in 1340, extended in the 1420s, and redesigned again after a fire in 1483. If you want to understand something of this magnificent place, the fascinating history of the 1,000-year-old maritime republic, and the intrigue of the government that ruled it, take the **Secret Itineraries tour** ★★★ (see "Secrets of the Palazzo Ducale," p. 267). Failing that, at least download the free iPhone/Android app (see the website) or shell

---

Tip: St. Mark's & the Doge's Palace in 1 day?

Yes, it is possible (and not too exhausting) to see the Basilica di San Marco and the Palazzo Ducale in 1 day. Start at the church, arriving 30 minutes before opening (ideally get an online reservation in advance; see p. 264). Take a break before heading across to the Doge's Palace, where you can spend the rest of the day. You can buy palace tickets in advance online (www.vivaticket.it); there's no express entry option, unless you book a third-party tour, but there's not usually a wait to get inside here. Your palace ticket also includes entry to the Museo Correr and Museo Archeologico Nazionale, but it's safe to save these for another day—tickets are valid for up to 3 months

out for the audioguide tour (available at entrance, 5€) to help make sense of it all. Unless you can tag along with an English-speaking tour group, you may otherwise miss out on the importance of much of what you're seeing.

The 15th-century **Porta della Carta (Paper Gate)** opens onto a splendid inner courtyard with a double row of Renaissance arches (today visitors enter through a doorway on the lagoon side of the palace). The self-guided route through the palace begins on the main courtyard, where the **Museo dell'Opera** contains assorted bits of masonry preserved from the Palazzo's exterior. Beyond here, the first major room you'll come to is the spacious **Sala delle Quattro Porte (Hall of the Four Doors),** with a worn ceiling by Tintoretto. The **Sala dell'Anticollegio,** where foreign ambassadors waited to be

The Bridge of Sighs.

received by the doge and his council, is covered in four works by Tintoretto, including "Mercury & the Three Graces" and **"Bacchus and Ariadne"** ★★, the latter deemed one of his best by some critics. The Tintorettos are outshone, however, by Veronese's **"Rape of Europa"** ★★, considered one of the palazzo's finest. The highlight of the adjacent **Sala del Collegio** (the Council Chamber itself) is the spectacular cycle of **ceiling paintings** ★★ by Veronese, completed between 1575 and 1578 and one of his masterpieces. Next door lies the most impressive of the interior rooms, the richly adorned **Sala del Senato (Senate Chamber),** with Tintoretto's ceiling painting "The Triumph of Venice." After passing again through the Sala delle Quattro Porte, you'll come to the Veronese-decorated **Stanza del Consiglio dei Dieci (Room of the Council of Ten),** where justice was dispensed and decapitations ordered by the Republic's dreaded security police. Formed in the 14th century to deal with emergency situations, the Ten were considered more powerful than the Senate and feared by all. In the **Sala della Bussola (the Compass Chamber),** notice the **Bocca dei Leoni (Lion's Mouth),** a slit in the wall into which secret denunciations and accusations of enemies of the state were placed for quick action by the much-feared Council.

The main sight on the next level down—indeed, the main sight in the entire palace—is the **Sala del Maggior Consiglio (Great Council Hall).** This enormous space is animated by Tintoretto's huge **"Paradiso"** ★ at the far end of the hall above the doge's seat. Measuring 7×23m (23×75 ft.), it is said to be the world's largest oil painting; together with Veronese's gorgeous **"Il Trionfo di Venezia" ("The Triumph of Venice")** ★★ in the oval panel on the ceiling, it affirms the power emanating from the council sessions held here. Tintoretto also did the portraits of the 76 doges encircling the top of this chamber; note that the picture of the Doge Marin Falier, who was convicted of treason and beheaded in 1355, has been blacked out—Venice has never forgiven him. Tours culminate at the enclosed **Ponte dei Sospiri (Bridge of Sighs),** built in 1600, which connects the Doge's Palace with the grim **Palazzo delle Prigioni (Prison).** The bridge took its current name in the 19th century, when visiting northern European poets romantically imagined the prisoners' final breath of resignation upon viewing the outside world one last time. Some attribute the name to Casanova, who, following his arrest in 1755 (he was accused of being a Freemason and spreading antireligious propaganda), crossed this very bridge. One of the rare few to escape, he did so 15 months after his imprisonment began; it was 20 years before he dared return to Venice. Some of the cells still have the original graffiti of past prisoners, many of them locked up interminably for petty crimes.

San Marco, Piazza San Marco. www.palazzoducale.visitmuve.it. ☏ **041/2715911.** Admission only with San Marco Museum Pass (20€; see "Venice Discounts," p. 273). For an Itinerari Segreti (Secret Itineraries) guided tour in English, see "Secrets of the Palazzo Ducale," below. Daily 8:30am–7pm (Nov–Mar until 5:30pm). *Vaporetto:* San Marco.

Piazza San Marco ★★★ SQUARE   Dubbed "The finest drawing-room in Europe" by Napoleon, the San Marco Square is undeniably one of Italy's most beautiful spaces, despite being terribly congested in high season (and often flooded during *acqua alta*). Today, the square is a focal point for Carnevale, as well as the spectacular Basilica and the most historic cafes in Venice: venerable **Caffè Florian,** Wagner's **Caffè Lavena,** and **Gran Caffè Quadri** (all on pp. 287–288).

Vaporetto: San Marco.

Rialto Bridge ★★ ICON   This graceful arch over the Grand Canal, linking the San Marco and San Polo districts, is lined with overpriced boutiques

---

secrets **OF THE PALAZZO DUCALE**

The **Itinerari Segreti (Secret Itineraries)** ★★★ guided tours of the Palazzo Ducale are a must-see for any visit to Venice of more than 1 day. The tours offer an unparalleled look into the world of Venetian politics over the centuries and are the only way to access the otherwise restricted quarters and hidden passageways of this enormous palace, such as the doges' private chambers and the torture chambers where prisoners were interrogated. The tour must be reserved in advance online (www.vivaticket.it), by phone (☏ **041/4273-0892**), or in person at the ticket desk. Tours often sell out at least a few days ahead, especially from spring through fall. Tours in English are daily at 9:55am, 10:45am and 11:35am and cost 20€ for adults, 14.50€ for children ages 6 to 14 and students ages 15 to 25. There are also tours in Italian at 9:30am and 11:10am, and French at 10:20am and noon. The tour lasts about 75 minutes.

and teeming with tourists and overflow from the daily market on the San Polo side. Until the 19th century, it was the only bridge across the Grand Canal, originally built as a pontoon bridge at the canal's narrowest point. Wooden versions of the bridge followed; the 1444 incarnation was the first to include shops, interrupted by a drawbridge in the center. In 1592, this graceful stone span was finished to the designs of Antonio da Ponte (whose last name fittingly enough means bridge), who beat out Sansovino, Palladio, and Michelangelo with plans that called for a single, vast, 28m-wide (92-ft.) arch in the center to allow trading ships to pass.

Ponte del Rialto. *Vaporetto:* Rialto.

Scala Contarini del Bovolo ★★ VIEW

Artfully restored and opened in 2016, this is one of the city's newest attractions. Part of a palazzo built in the late 15th century, this multi-arch spiral staircase (a mini Tower of Pisa) leads to a belvedere with fabulous views of Venice. Halfway up, the **Sala del Tintoretto (Tintoretto Room)** contains the rare portrait of Lazzaro Zen, an African who converted to Christianity in Venice in 1770, as well as a preparatory painting by Tintoretto of his monumental "Paradise" (the final version is in the Palazzo Ducale). You can buy **timed entry tickets** in advance at www.ticketlandia.com (advisable in peak season).

Corte Contarini del Bovolo 4299, San Marco. www.scalacontarinidelbovolo.com. ⓒ **041/3096605.** Admission 7€; audioguide 1€. Daily 10am–6pm. Vaporetto: Rialto.

Teatro La Fenice ★★★ THEATER

One of Italy's most famous opera houses (it ranks third after La Scala in Milan and San Carlo in Naples), La Fenice was originally completed in 1792 but has been completely rebuilt twice after devastating fires; in 1837 and most recently in 2004. Self-guided tours (audioguides included) take in the opulent main theater, ornate side rooms, the gilded "royal box," and a small exhibit dedicated to feted soprano Maria Callas. For seeing a show at La Fenice, see p. 287.

Campo San Fantin 1965, San Marco. www.teatrolafenice.it. ⓒ **041/2424.** Admission 10€. Daily 9:30am–6pm. Vaporetto: Giglio.

T Fondaco dei Tedeschi ★★ STORE/VIEW

The Harrods of Italy? In 2016, architect Rem Koolhaas and friends converted one of the city's great 16th-century *palazzi* into a posh department store, centered on an elegant courtyard (featuring cafe/restaurant **AMO,** run by the Alajmo brothers). The **Rooftop Terrace** has rotating art exhibitions and quite possibly the city's greatest view of Venice. It's worth making reservations for the terrace in advance in peak season, either on the store website or via the iPads on the 3rd and the 4th floors. The building is actually owned by Benetton and leased by the LVMH–owned luxury travel company DFS.

Calle de Fontego dei Tedeschi, Ponte di Rialto, San Marco. www.dfs.com/en/venice. ⓒ **041/3142000.** Daily 10am–8pm (roof deck free; visits limited to 15 min). Vaporetto: Rialto.

Torre dell'Orologio (Clock Tower) ★★ MONUMENT As you enter the magnificent **Piazza San Marco,** it is one of the first things you see, standing on the north side, the centerpiece of the stately white **Procuratie Vecchie** (the ancient administration buildings for the Republic). The Renaissance **Torre dell'Orologio,** with its distinctive blue face ringed by astrological symbols, was built between 1496 and 1506, and the clock still keeps perfect time (although most of its original workings have been replaced). On top, two bronze figures, known as "Moors" because of the dark color of the bronze, pivot to strike the hour. Visits inside are by guided tour only (included in the price of admission), but unless you are interested in the clock's history, these are easily skipped, especially if you've already been up the Campanile di San Marco.

Piazza San Marco. www.torreorologio.visitmuve.it. ℭ **848/082000** or 041/42730892. 12€, 7€ for children 6–14 and students 15–25; ticket also includes Museo Correr, Museo Archeologico Nazionale, and Biblioteca Nazionale Marciana. Tours (1 hr.) in English Mon–Wed 10am and 11am, Thurs–Sun 2pm and 3pm (must be reserved in advance online); tours start at Museo Correr ticket office. *Vaporetto:* San Marco.

Castello

Though the highlight of this neighborhood is the huge **Santi Giovanni e Paolo,** within a few minutes' walk from here are two more magnificent Renaissance churches: **Santa Maria Formosa** (3€; Mon–Sat 10am–5pm), on Campo Santa Maria Formosa, and **San Zaccaria** (free; Mon–Sat 10am–noon and 4–6pm, Sun 4–6pm), at Campo San Zaccaria, which contains Giovanni Bellini's **San Zaccaria Altarpiece** ★, and early work from Tintoretto.

Basilica SS. Giovanni e Paolo ★ CHURCH This massive Gothic church was built by the Dominican order from the 13th to the 15th century and, together with the Frari Church in San Polo, is second in size only to the Basilica di San Marco. An unofficial Pantheon where 25 doges are buried (a number of tombs are part of the unfinished facade), the church, commonly known as Zanipolo in Venetian dialect, is also home to many artistic treasures.

The brilliantly colored **"Polyptych of St. Vincent Ferrer"** (ca. 1465), attributed to a young Giovanni Bellini, is in the right aisle. You'll also see the mummified foot of St. Catherine of Siena—considered a holy relic—encased

---

The Biennale

Venice hosts the latest in contemporary art and sculpture from dozens of countries during the prestigious **Biennale d'Arte** ★★★ (www.labiennale.org; ℭ **041/5218711**), one of the world's top international art shows. It fills the pavilions of the **Giardini** (public gardens) at the east end of **Castello** and at the **Arsenale,** as well as in other spaces around the city from May to November every odd-numbered year (usually open Tues–Sun 10am–6pm). Tickets cost around 25€, 20€ for those 65 and over, and 15€ for students and all those 26 and under.

in glass near here. Visit the **Cappella del Rosario** ★, through a glass door off the left transept, to see three restored ceiling canvases and one oil painting by Paolo Veronese, particularly "The Assumption of the Madonna."

Anchoring the large and impressive *campo* outside the church, a popular crossroads for this area of Castello, is the **statue of Bartolomeo Colleoni** ★★, the Renaissance *condottiere* (mercenary) who defended Venice's interests at the height of its power until his death in 1475. The 15th-century sculpture by the Florentine **Andrea Verrocchio** is considered one of the world's great equestrian monuments and Verrocchio's best.

Campo Santi Giovanni e Paolo 6363. www.basilicasantigiovanniepaolo.it. ℗ **041/ 5235913**. 3.50€. Daily 7:30am–7pm (open to tourists Mon–Sat 9am–6pm, Sun noon– 6pm). *Vaporetto:* Rialto.

Scuola di San Giorgio degli Schiavoni ★★ MUSEUM   One of the most mesmerizing spaces in Europe, the tiny main hall of this *scuola* once served as a meeting house for Venice's Dalmatian community (Dalmatia is a region of Croatia, and *schiavoni* means "Slavs"). Venetian *scuole,* or schools, were Middle Age guilds that brought together merchants and craftspeople from certain trades or similar religious devotions. Guilds functioned as social clubs, credit unions, even sources of spiritual guidance, and many commissioned elaborate headquarters, hiring the best artists of the day to decorate them. The *scuole* that remain in Venice today house some of the city's finest art treasures. Built beside its sister church, San Giovanni di Malta, in the early 16th century, San Giorgio degli Schiavoni offers a big reason to visit: to admire the awe-inspiring narrative painting cycle on its walls, created by Renaissance master **Vittore Carpaccio** between 1502 and 1509. The paintings depict the lives of the Dalmatian patron saints George (of dragon-slaying fame), Tryphon, and Jerome. In the upper hall (Sala dell'Albergo), you'll also find Carpaccio's masterful "Vision of St. Augustine."

Calle dei Furlani 3259A. ℗ **041/5228828**. 5€. Mon 1:30–5:30pm, Tues–Sat 9:30am– 5:30pm, Sun 9:30am–1:30pm. *Vaporetto:* Rialto.

Dorsoduro

Gallerie dell'Accademia (Academy Gallery) ★★★ MUSEUM Along with San Marco and the Palazzo Ducale, the **Accademia** is one of the highlights of Venice, a magnificent collection of European art and especially Venetian painting from the 14th to the 18th centuries. Visitors are currently limited to 300 at one time, so lines can be long in high season—advance reservations are essential (these are timed entry, so you can skip the line). In general, at opening in the morning, and around 2 hours before closing, tend to be the least crowded times.

There's a lot to take in here, so buy a catalog in the store, as these contain detailed descriptions of the core paintings and plenty of context—the audio guides are a little muddled and not worth 6€. Note also that Da Vinci's iconic **Vitruvian Man** ★★★ (*L'Uomo Vitruviano*), one of the museum's prize holdings, is an extremely fragile ink drawing and rarely displayed in public; check the website before you visit, as exhibitions featuring the painting are rare but well publicized.

Rooms are laid out in rough chronological order, though on-and-off-again renovations and closures mean some rooms may be off-limits when you visit (call ahead to check on specific paintings; the website is not updated regularly). The museum unveiled renovated galleries on the ground floor at the end of 2013, but the main rooms on the first floor remain in a parlous state. The following artworks should be on display somewhere in the museum, though locations may change.

Visits normally begin upstairs on the first floor, where room 1 (the grand meeting room of the Scuola Grande di Santa Maria) displays a beautifully presented collection of lavish medieval and early Renaissance art, primarily religious images and altarpieces on wood panels from 1300 to 1450.

The giant canvases in room 2 include Carpaccio's "Presentation of Jesus in the Temple," and works by Giovanni Bellini (one of Bellini's images of St. Peter lies in room 3).

Rooms 6 to 8 feature Venetian heavyweights Tintoretto, Titian, Veronese and Lorenzo Lotto, while Room 10 is dominated by Paolo Veronese's mammoth **"Feast in the House of Levi"** ★★. Vast Tintoretto canvases make up the rest of the room, including his four paintings of the legends of St. Mark. Opposite is Titian's last painting, a "Pietà" intended for his own tomb.

Room 11 contains work by Tiepolo, the master of 18th-century Venetian painting, but also several paintings by Tintoretto, including a "Crucifixion."

The next rooms contain a relatively mediocre batch of 17th- and 18th-century paintings, though Canaletto's **"Capriccio: A Colonnade"** ★ (Room 17), which he presented to the Academy when he was made a member in 1763, certainly merits a closer look for its elegant contrast between diagonal, vertical, and horizontal lines.

Room 19 has traditionally contained the monumental cycle of nine paintings by Carpaccio illustrating the **Story of St. Ursula** ★★; most of these continue to undergo restoration, with "Arrival in Cologne" the only one likely to be displayed for some time. Room 20 is filled by Gentile Bellini's cycle of **"The Miracles of the Relic of the Cross"** ★, painted around 1500.

While renovations are ongoing, room 23 will contain some of the museum's most famous paintings, including a gorgeous "St. George" by Mantegna, Della Francesca's "St. Jerome," a "St. John the Baptist" by Antonio Viviani, plus a series of Bellini Madonnas and his monumental "Martyrdom of St. Mark." Pride of place goes to Giorgione's enigmatic and utterly mystifying **"Tempest"** ★★. Finally, room 24 is adorned with Titian's "Presentation of the Virgin," created between 1534 and 1538 specifically to hang in this space.

Downstairs, the new ground-floor galleries cover the late 18th to 19th centuries, a far more mediocre collection of baroque and romantic works, though delicate paintings by Tiepolo share space with his large tondo "Feast of the Cross" in gallery 2, along with Veronese's "Venice Receives Homage from

Hercules and Ceres." Sculpture galleries (featuring the work of Canova) should also be open on this level.

Campo della Carità 1050, at foot of Ponte dell'Accademia. www.gallerieaccademia. org. ℓ **041/5200345.** 15€ adults (during temporary exhibitions admission price subject to change); free on first Sun of the month (check in advance). Reservations by phone or online incur a 1.50€ charge. Daily 8:15am–7:15pm (Mon until 2pm). *Vaporetto:* Accademia.

I Gesuati (Santa Maria del Rosario) ★ CHURCH   Built from 1724 to 1743 by Giorgio Massari to mirror the Redentore across the Canale della Giudecca, this cavernous church counters the latter's Palladian sobriety with rococo flair. The interior is graced by airy 1738–39 ceiling frescoes (some of the first in Venice) by **Giambattista Tiepolo.** Tiepolo also created the "Virgin with saints Rosa of Lima, Catherine of Siena, and Agnes of Montepulciano" on the first altar on the right. The third altar on the left is adorned with a Tintoretto "Crucifixion" (1565).

Fondamenta delle Zattere ai Gesuati. ℓ **041/2750462.** 3€ adults, free for children 5 and under. Mon–Sat 10am–5pm. *Vaporetto:* Zattere.

Peggy Guggenheim Collection ★★ MUSEUM   Though the **Peggy Guggenheim Collection** is one of the best museums in Italy exhibiting American and European art of the 20th century, you might find the experience a little jarring, given its location in a city so heavily associated with the High Renaissance and the baroque.

A sculpture from the Peggy Guggenheim Collection.

Nevertheless, art aficionados will find some fascinating work here, and the galleries occupy Peggy Guggenheim's wonderful former home, the 18th-century Palazzo Venier dei Leoni, right on the Grand Canal. Guggenheim bought the mansion in 1949 and lived here, on and off, until her death in 1979. Highlights include Picasso's extremely abstract "Poet" and his more gentle "On the Beach," several works by Kandinsky ("Landscape with Red Spots No. 2" and "White Cross"), Miró's expressionistic "Seated Woman II," Klee's mystical "Magic Garden," and some unsettling works by Max Ernst ("The Kiss," "Attirement of the

VENICE discounts

Venice offers a somewhat bewildering range of passes and discount cards. For short stays, we recommend buying an **ACTV travel card** (p. 229) and combining that with one of the first two passes listed below. The more complex Venezia Unica card scheme is convenient once you've worked out what you want online and is recommended if you intend to stay up to 7 days and do a lot of sightseeing. The Venezia Unica website (www. veneziaunica.it) is a one-stop shop for all the passes listed below.

The **Museum Pass** (www.vivaticket.it) grants admission to all the city-run museums over a 6-month period—it also lets you skip any ticketing lines, a useful perk in high season. The pass includes the museums of St. Mark's Square—**Palazzo Ducale, Museo Correr, Museo Archeologico Nazionale,** and the **Biblioteca Nazionale Marciana**—as well as the **Museo di Palazzo Mocenigo (Costume Museum), the Ca' Rezzonico, the Ca' Pesaro, the Museo del Vetro (Glass Museum)** on Murano, and the **Museo del Merletto (Lace Museum)** on Burano. The Museum Pass is available online (for an extra 0.50€), or at any of the participating museums and costs 24€ for adults, and 18€ for students under 30 and kids ages 6 to 14. It's a good deal, as the Doge's Palace will set you back 20€ alone; visit one more major museum (the Ca' Rezzonico and Ca' Pesaro are both 10€ each) and you've made a decent saving.

If churches are your interest, consider the **Chorus Pass** (www.chorusvenezia. org), which grants admission to almost every major church in Venice, 18 in all, for 12€ (8€ for students under 30), for up to 1 year. For 24€, the **Chorus Pass Family** gives you the same perks for two adults and their children up to 18 years old. Most churches charge 3€ admission, which means you'll need to visit more than four to make this pass worthwhile.

The **Venezia Unica** card (www.venezia unica.it) combines the above passes, transport, discounts, and even Internet access on one card via a "made-to-order" online system, where you choose the services you want. The most useful option is the **City Pass,** which combines the Museum Pass and Chorus Pass plus free entry to the Jewish Museum and discounts on temporary exhibits for 39.90€ for 7 days (29.90€ for ages 6–29). Assuming you visit the Doge's Palace, a couple of major city museums, the Jewish Museum, and more than four churches, this should save you 20€ or more. You can also buy various transportation packages and Wi-Fi access (from 5€ for 24 hr.). Once you've paid, you simply print out a voucher to use at museums and sights in Venice; to use public transport you must collect tickets by entering your booking code at one of the ACTV automatic ticket machines or by visiting one of the official Points of Sale in in the city, including one in the train station (open 7am–9pm) and at the Rialto *vaporetto* stop (open 7am–11pm).

Also, for visitors between the ages of 6 and 29, there is the **Rolling Venice** card (also available at www.veneziaunica. it). It's valid until the end of the year in which you buy it, costs just 6€, and entitles the bearer to significant (20%–30%) discounts at participating restaurants (but applies only to cardholder's meal) and a similar discount on ACTV travel cards (22€ for 3 days). Holders of the Rolling Venice card also get discounts at museums, stores, language courses, hotels, and bars across the city (it comes with a thick booklet listing everywhere that you're entitled to get discounts).

Bride"), who was briefly married to Guggenheim in the 1940s. Look for Magritte's "Empire of Light," Dalí's typically surreal "Birth of Liquid Desires," and a couple of gems from Pollock: his early "Moon Woman," which recalls Picasso, and "Alchemy," a more typical "poured" painting. The Italian Futurists are also well represented here, with a rare portrait from Modigliani ("Portrait of the Painter Frank Haviland"). *Tip:* It's not a good idea to visit the Guggenheim and St. Mark's on the same day—it's a fairly long walk between the two. We also don't advise seeing it on the same day as the Accademia, even though they are only 10 minutes apart; the artistic overload is likely to prove too much for even the most avid art aficionado.

Calle San Cristoforo 701. www.guggenheim-venice.it. ℂ **041/2405411.** 15€ adults, 13€ 65 and over (and for those who present an Alitalia ticket to or from Venice dated no more than 7 days previous), and 9€ students 26 and under and children ages 10–18. Wed–Mon 10am–6pm. *Vaporetto:* Accademia (walk around left side of Accademia, take 1st left, and walk straight ahead following the signs).

Punta della Dogana ★★★ MUSEUM   The eastern tip *(punta)* of Dorsoduro is crowned by the distinctive triangle of the 17th-century **Dogana di Mare** (Customs House), which once monitored all boats entering the Grand Canal. Transformed by architect Tadao Ando into a beautiful exhibition space, it's now a showcase for the contemporary art collection of billionaire François Pinault (officially dubbed the **Centro d'Arte Contemporanea Punta della Dogana**). It's pricey, but you can expect to see quality work from Cindy Sherman, Cy Twombly, Jeff Koons, and Marlene Dumas, among many others.

Fondamenta della Dogana alla Salute 2. www.palazzograssi.it. ℂ **041/2719031.** 18€ (includes admission to Palazzo Grassi). Wed–Mon 10am–7pm (sometimes closes between shows; check ahead). *Vaporetto:* Salute.

San Sebastiano ★★ CHURCH   Lose the crowds as you make a pilgrimage to this monument to **Paolo Veronese,** his parish church and home to some of his finest work. Veronese painted the coffered nave ceiling with the florid "Scenes from the Life of St. Esther." He also decorated the organ shutters and panels in the chancel in the 1560s with scenes from the life of St. Sebastian. Although Veronese is the main event here, don't miss Titian's sensitive "St. Nicholas" (just inside the church on the right). Veronese's sepulchral monument (with bust by Mattia Carneri) is to the left of the altar. The real highlight is the sacristy (go through the door under the organ), a tiny jewel box of a room adorned with more wonderful Veronese paintings of the "Coronation of the Virgin" and the "Four Evangelists."

Campo San Sebastiano. ℂ **041/2750462.** 3€. Mon–Sat 10:30am–4:30pm. *Vaporetto:* San Basilio.

Santa Maria della Salute (Church of the Virgin Mary of Good Health) ★ CHURCH   Generally referred to as "La Salute," this crown jewel of 17th-century baroque architecture proudly reigns at a commercially and aesthetically important point, almost directly across from the Piazza San Marco, where the Grand Canal empties into the lagoon.

The first stone was laid in 1631 after the Senate decided to honor the Virgin Mary for delivering Venice from a plague that had killed around 95,000 people. They accepted the revolutionary plans of a young, relatively unknown architect, Baldassare Longhena. He dedicated the next 50 years of his life to overseeing its progress (he would die one year after its inauguration but 5 years before its completion). Today the dome of the church is an iconic presence on the Venice skyline, recognized for its exuberant exterior of volutes, scrolls, and more than 125 statues. The most revered image inside is the **Madonna della Salute,** a rare black-faced sculpture of Mary brought back from Candia in Crete in 1670 as war booty. The otherwise sober interior is enlivened by the **sacristy,** with a number of important ceiling paintings and portraits by **Titian.** On the right wall of the sacristy, which you have to pay to enter, is Tintoretto's **"Marriage at Cana"** ★, often considered one of his best paintings.

Campo della Salute. ✆ **041/5225558.** Church free; sacristy 4€. Daily 9am–noon and 3–5:30pm. *Vaporetto:* Salute.

Scuola Grande dei Carmini ★★ CHURCH The former Venetian base of the Carmelite religious order, finished in the 18th century, is now a shrine of sorts to **Giambattista Tiepolo,** who painted the ceiling of the upstairs hall

THE ART OF THE gondola

Putting together one of these sleek black boats is a fascinatingly exact science that is still done in the revered traditional manner at boatyards such as the **Squero di San Trovaso** (see p. 276). Gondolas have been painted black since the 16th century, when local legislators passed a law designed to restrict the gaudy outlandishness so prevalent at the time.

Propelled by the strength of a single *gondoliere,* these boats, unique to Venice, have no modern equipment. They move with no great speed but with unrivaled grace. The right side of the gondola is lower because the *gondoliere* always stands in the back of the boat on the left.

The San Trovaso *squero,* or boatyard, is the city's oldest and one of only three remaining (the other two are immeasurably more difficult to find). Its predominant focus is on maintenance and repair, although they will occasionally build a new gondola (which takes some 40–45

working days), carefully crafting it from the seven types of wood—mahogany, cherry, fir, walnut, oak, elm, and lime— necessary to give the shallow and asymmetrical boat its various characteristics. After all the pieces are put together, the painting, the *ferro* (the iron symbol of the city affixed to the bow), and the woodcarving that secures the oar are commissioned out to various local artisans.

Although some 10,000 of these elegant boats floated on the canals of Venice in the 16th century, today there are only around 425, almost all catering to the tourist trade. The job of *gondoliere* remains a coveted profession, passed down from father to son over the centuries, but nowadays it's open to anyone who can pass 400 hours of rigorous training—Giorgia Boscolo passed the exam in 2010, becoming the first ever *gondoliera;* her father was also in the profession.

between 1739 and 1744. It's truly a magnificent sight. Tiepolo's elaborate rococo interpretation of "Simon Stock Receiving the Scapular" is now fully restored along with various panels throughout the building.

Campo San Margherita 2617. www.scuolagrandecarmini.it. ⓒ **041/5289420.** 5€. Daily 11am–5pm (Nov–Mar until 4pm). *Vaporetto:* San Basilio.

Squero di San Trovaso ★★ HISTORIC SITE   One of the most intriguing sights in Venice is this small *squero* (boatyard), which first opened in the 17th century. Just north of the Zattere (the wide, sunny walkway that runs alongside the Giudecca Canal in Dorsoduro), the boatyard lies next to the Church of San Trovaso on the narrow Rio San Trovaso (not far from the Accademia Bridge). It is surrounded by Tyrolean-looking wooden structures (a true rarity in this city of stone built on water) that are home to the multigenerational owners and original workshops for traditional Venetian boats (see "The Art of the Gondola," p. 275). Aware that they have become a tourist site themselves, the gondoliers don't mind if you watch them at work from across the narrow Rio di San Trovaso, but don't try to invite yourself in. *Tip:* It's the perfect midway photo op after a visit to the Accademia and a trip to **Gelateria Nico** (Zattere 922; see p. 260), whose chocolate *gianduiotto* is every bit as decadent as Venice just before the fall of the Republic.

Dorsoduro 1097 (on the Rio San Trovaso, southwest of the Accademia). *Vaporetto:* Zattere.

San Polo & Santa Croce

Santa Maria Gloriosa dei Frari (Church of the Frari) ★★ CHURCH
Known simply as "i Frari," this immense 14th-century Gothic basilica was built by the Franciscans and is the largest church in Venice after San Marco. It houses a number of important artworks, including two Titian masterpieces: the **"Assumption of the Virgin"** ★★ over the main altar, painted when the artist was only in his late 20s, and "Virgin of the Pesaro Family" in the left nave. For the latter work, Titian's wife posed for the figure of Mary (and died soon afterward in childbirth). Don't miss Giovanni Bellini's **"Madonna & Child"** ★★ over the altar in the sacristy, of which novelist Henry James wrote, "it is as solemn as it is gorgeous." The grand **mausoleum of Titian** is on the right as you enter the church, opposite the incongruous 18th-century monument to sculptor **Antonio Canova,** shaped like a pyramid—designed by Canova himself, this was originally supposed to be Titian's tomb.

Campo dei Frari 3072. www.basilicadeifrari.it. ⓒ **041/2728611.** 3€, audioguide 2€. Mon–Sat 9am–6pm; Sun 1–6pm. *Vaporetto:* San Tomà (walk straight ahead on Calle del Traghetto, turn right and immediately left across Campo San Tomà; walk straight on Ramo Mandoler, then Calle Larga Prima, and turn right when you reach Salizada San Rocco).

Scuola Grande di San Rocco (Confraternity of St. Roch) ★★★
MUSEUM   Like many medieval saints, French-born St. Rocco (St. Roch) died young, but thanks to his work healing the sick in the 14th century, his cult became associated with the power to cure the plague and other serious

illnesses. When his body was brought to Venice in 1485, this *scuola* began to reap the benefits, and by 1560 the current complex was completed. Work soon began on more than 50 paintings by **Tintoretto,** and today the *scuola* is primarily a shrine to the masterful Venetian artist. You enter at the **Ground Floor Hall (Sala Terrena),** where the paintings were created between 1583 and 1587, led by one of the most frenzied "Annunciations" ever made. The "Flight into Egypt" here is undeniably one of Tintoretto's greatest works. Upstairs is the **Great Upper Hall (Sala Superiore),** where Old Testament scenes such as "Moses Striking Water From the Rock" cover the ceiling. The paintings around the walls, based on the New Testament, are generally regarded as a master class of perspective, shadow, and color. In the **Sala dell'Albergo,** an entire wall is adorned by Tintoretto's mind-blowing "Crucifixion" (as well as his "Glorification of St. Roch," on the ceiling, the painting that actually won him the contract to paint the *scuola*). Way up in the loft, the **Tesoro** (Treasury) is a tiny space dedicated primarily to gold reliquaries containing venerated relics such as the fingers of St. Peter and St. Andrew, and one of the thorns that crowned Christ during the crucifixion.

Campo San Rocco 3052, adjacent to Campo dei Frari. www.scuolagrandesanrocco.it. ☏ **041/5234864.** 10€ adults (includes audioguide); 8€ ages 18–26; free 18 and under. Daily 9:30am–5:30pm. *Vaporetto:* San Tomà (walk straight ahead on Calle del Traghetto, turn right and immediately left across Campo San Tomà; walk straight on Ramo Mandoler, Calle Larga Prima, and Salizada San Rocco, which leads into the *campo* of the same name—look for the crimson sign behind Frari Church).

Cannaregio

Galleria Giorgio Franchetti alla Ca' d'Oro ★★ MUSEUM   This magnificent *palazzo* overlooking the Grand Canal, the "golden house," was built between 1428 and 1430 for the noble Contarini family. Baron Giorgio Franchetti bought the place in 1894, and it now serves as an atmospheric art gallery for his exceptional collection (mostly early Renaissance Italian and Flemish). The highlight is **"St. Sebastian"** ★★ by Paduan artist Andrea Mantegna, displayed in its own marble chapel built by the overawed baron. The so-called "St. Sebastian of Venice" was the third and final painting of the saint by Mantegna, created around 1490 and quite different to the other two (in Vienna and Paris, respectively); it's a bold, deeply pessimistic work, with none of Mantegna's usual background details to detract from the saint's suffering. Don't miss also the three panels from Carpaccio's "Stories of the Virgin" series on the first floor.

Strada Nuova 3932. www.cadoro.org. ☏ **041/520-0345.** 11€, plus 1.50€ reservation fee (price increases during special exhibitions). Mon 8:15am–2pm; Tues–Sat 8:15am–7:15pm; Sun 9am–7pm. *Vaporetto:* Ca' d'Oro.

Museo Ebraico di Venezia (Jewish Museum of Venice) ★ MUSEUM/SYNAGOGUE   In the heart of the Ghetto Nuovo, the Jewish Museum contains a small but precious collection of artifacts related to the long history of the Jews in Venice, beginning with an exhibition on Jewish

Il Ghetto & the Jews of Venice

Jews began settling in Venice in great numbers in the 15th century, and the Republic soon came to value their services as moneylenders, physicians, and traders. In 1516, however, fearing their growing influence, the Venetians forced the Jewish population to live on an island with an abandoned foundry (*ghetto* is old Venetian dialect for "foundry"), and drawbridges were raised to enforce a nighttime curfew. By the end of the 17th century, as many as 5,000 Jews lived in the Ghetto's cramped confines. Napoleon tore down the Ghetto gates in 1797, but it wasn't until the unification of Italy in 1866 that Jews achieved equal status. Il Ghetto remains the spiritual center for Venice's ever-diminishing community of Jewish families, with two synagogues and a Chabad House; although accounts vary widely, it's said that anywhere from 500 to 2,000 Jews live in all of Venice and Mestre, though very few now live in the Ghetto.

Aside from its historic interest, this is also one of the less touristy neighborhoods in Venice (although it has become something of a nightspot) and makes for a pleasant and scenic place to stroll. Venice's first kosher restaurant, **Gam Gam**, opened here in 1996, at 1122 Ghetto Vecchio right on the canal (www. gamgamkosher.com; ⓒ **366/2504505**), close to the Guglie *vaporetto* stop. Run by Orthodox Jews, it is open Sunday to Thursday noon to 10pm, Friday noon to 2 hours before Shabbat (sunset), and on Saturday from 1 hour after Shabbat, until 11pm (excluding summer).

festivities in the first room; chandeliers, goblets, and spice-holders used to celebrate Shabbat, Shofàrs (ram's horns) and a Séfer Torà (Scroll of Divine Law). The second room contains a rich collection of historic textiles, including Torah covers, and a rare marriage contract from 1792. A newer area explores the immigration patterns of Jews to Venice, and their experiences once here. For many, the real highlight is the chance to tour three of the area's five historic synagogues (ladies must have shoulders covered and men must have heads covered; no photos): **German** (Scuola Grande Tedesca), founded in 1528; **Italian** (Scuola Italiana), founded in 1575; **Sephardic** (Scuola Levantina), founded in 1541 but rebuilt in the second half of 17th century; **Spanish** (Scuola Spagnola), rebuilt in the first half of 17th century; and the baroque-style **Ashkenazi** (Scuola Canton), largely rebuilt in the 18th century. It's difficult to predict which three you'll visit on any given day, as it depends on which synagogues are being used; the Levantina and the Spanish are the most lavishly decorated, with one usually included on the tour.

Cannaregio 2902B (on Campo del Ghetto Nuovo). www.museoebraico.it. ⓒ **041/715359.** Museum 8€ adults, 6€ children and students ages 6–26; museum and synagogue tour 12€ adults, 10€ children and students ages 6–26. Museum Sun–Fri 10am–7pm (Oct–May until 5:30pm); synagogue guided tours in English hourly 10:30am–5:30pm (Oct–May last tour 4:30pm). Closed on Jewish holidays. *Vaporetto:* Guglie.

Santa Maria dei Miracoli ★ CHURCH   Hidden in a quiet corner of the residential section of Cannaregio northeast of the Rialto Bridge, the small and exceedingly attractive 15th-century Miracoli has one side of its precious polychrome-marbled facade running alongside a canal, creating colorful and shimmering reflections. It was built from 1481 to 1489 by Pietro Lombardo, a local artisan whose background in monuments and tombs is obvious. He would go on to become one of the founding fathers of the Venetian Renaissance.

The less romantic are inclined to compare it to a large tomb with a dome, but the untold couples who have made this jewel-like church their choice for weddings will dispel such insensitivity. The small square in front is the perfect place for gondolas to drop off and pick up the newly betrothed. The inside is decorated with early Renaissance marble reliefs, its pastel palette of pink, gray, and white marble making an elegant venue for all those weddings. The church was constructed for a venerated image of the Virgin Mary, credited with working miracles—including bringing back to life someone who spent half an hour at the bottom of the Giudecca Canal. The icon is now displayed over the main altar.

Campiello di Miracoli, Rio di Miracoli. No phone. 3€. Mon–Sat 10am–5pm. *Vaporetto:* Rialto (located midway btw. Rialto Bridge and Campo SS. Giovanni e Paolo).

Giudecca & San Giorgio

Il Redentore ★★ CHURCH   Many consider this the finest church ever designed by Andrea Palladio, the great Renaissance architect from nearby Padua most known for his country villas built for Venice's wealthy merchant families. It was commissioned by Venice to give thanks for being delivered from the great plague (1575–77), which claimed over a quarter of the population (some 46,000 people). The doge established a tradition of visiting this church by crossing a long pontoon bridge made up of boats from the Dorsoduro's Zattere on the third Sunday of each July, a tradition that survived the demise of the doges and remains one of Venice's most popular festivals ("Festa del Redentore").

The church interior is done in austere but elegant classical Palladian style. The artworks tend to be workshop pieces (from the studios or schools, but not the actual brushes, of Tintoretto and Veronese), but there is a fine "Baptism of Christ" by Veronese himself in the sacristy (accessed through a door in the last chapel on the right), which also contains Alvise Vivarini's "Madonna with Child & Angels" alongside works by Jacopo da Bassano and Palma il Giovane.

Campo del Redentore 195. ⓒ **041/523-1415**. 3€. Mon–Sat 10:30am–4:30pm (Mon closes at 4pm). *Vaporetto:* Redentore.

San Giorgio Maggiore ★★ CHURCH   This magnificent church sits on the little island of San Giorgio Maggiore across from Piazza San Marco. Andrea Palladio (see "Il Redentore," above) designed the church in 1565 and it was completed in 1610. To impose a classical front on the traditional church structure, Palladio designed two interlocking facades, with repeating triangles, rectangles, and columns that are harmoniously proportioned. Palladio also reinterpreted the interior with whitewashed stucco surfaces, an unadorned but harmonious space. The main altar is flanked by two epic paintings by Tintoretto, "The Fall of Manna," to the left, and the more noteworthy **"Last Supper"** ★★ to the right, famous for its chiaroscuro. Accessed by free guided tour only (usually Apr–Oct only, times vary), the adjacent Cappella dei Morti (Chapel of the Dead) contains Tintoretto's "Deposition," and the upper chapel contains Carpaccio's St. George Killing the Dragon." To the left of the choir is an elevator that you can take to the top of the 1791 campanile—for a charge of 6€—to experience an unforgettable view of the island, the lagoon, and the Palazzo Ducale and Piazza San Marco across the way.

On San Giorgio Maggiore island, across from Piazza San Marco. ℂ **041/5227827.** Free. Daily 9am–7pm Apr–Oct, 8:30am–6pm Nov–Mar. *Vaporetto:* Take Giudecca-bound *vaporetto* no. 2 from Riva degli Schiavoni (San Marco/San Zaccaria) and get off at 1st stop.

Exploring Venice's Islands

Venice shares its lagoon with four other principal islands: **Murano, Burano, Torcello,** and the **Lido.** Guided tours of the first three are available (20€ to 35€ for 3 to 4 hours), but while these can be informative, unless you are very short of time you'll enjoy exploring the islands in far more leisurely fashion on your own, easily done using the *vaporetti.*

Line nos. 4.1 and 4.2 make the journey to Murano from Fondamente Nove (on the north side of Castello). For Murano, Burano, and Torcello, Line no. 12 departs Fondamente Nove every 30 minutes; for Torcello change to the shuttle boat (Line 9) that runs from Burano, timed to match the arrivals from Venice. The islands are small and easy to navigate, but check the schedule for the next island-to-island departure (usually hourly) and your return so that you don't spend most of your day waiting for connections.

Vaporetto line nos. 1, 2, 5.1, 5.2, and LN cross the lagoon to the Lido from the San Zaccaria–Danieli stop near San Marco. Note that the Lido becomes chilly, windswept and utterly deserted from October to April.

MURANO ★★

The island of **Murano** has long been famous throughout the world for the products of its glass factories. The illuminating **Museo del Vetro (Museum of Glass)** ★★, Fondamenta Giustinian 8 (www.museovetro.visitmuve.it; ℂ **041/739586**), provides context, charting the history of the island's glass-making, and definitely worthwhile if you intend to purchase a lot of glass-ware, providing plenty of background so you know what you're buying in the stores outside. Daily hours are 10am to 6pm (Nov–Mar to 5pm), and admission is 10€ for adults and 7.50€ children 6 to 14 and students 25 and under.

Dozens of *fornaci* (kilns) offer free shows of mouth-blown glassmaking, almost invariably hitched to a hard-sell tour of their factory outlet. Once you're on the island, you can't miss these places (and they're pretty much of equivalent quality), but **Original Murano Glass** (9:30am–5pm daily; reserve free tours and demonstrations at www.originalmuranoglass.com), at the Ellegi Glass *fornaci*, Fondamenta San Giovanni dei Battuti 4, is a dependable choice (it's a few minutes' walk from the Murano Faro *vaporetti* stop). Almost all the shops will ship their goods, but that often doubles the price. On the other hand, these pieces are instant heirlooms.

Murano is also graced by two worthy churches (both free admission): the largely 15th-century **San Pietro Martire** ★ (Mon–Sat 9am–5:30pm, Sun noon–5:30pm), with its paintings by Veronese and Giovanni Bellini, and the ancient **Santa Maria e Donato** ★ (Mon–Sat 9am–6pm, Sun 12:30–6pm), with its intricate Byzantine exterior apse, 6th-century pulpit, stunning mosaic of Mary over the altar, and a fantastic 12th-century inland floor.

BURANO ★★★

Lace is the claim to fame of tiny, historic **Burano,** a craft kept alive for centuries by the

Traditional glassblowing in Murano.

wives of fishermen waiting for their husbands to return from the sea. Sadly, most of the lace sold on the island these days is made by machine elsewhere. It's still worth a trip if you have time to stroll the back streets of the island, whose canals are lined with the brightly colored, simple homes of the Buranesi fishermen—it's quite unlike anything in Venice or Murano. The local government continues its attempt to keep its centuries-old lace legacy alive with subsidized classes.

Visit the **Museo del Merletto (Museum of Lace Making)** ★, Piazza Galuppi 187 (www.museomerletto.visitmuve.it; ✆ **041/730034**), to understand why something so exquisite should not be left to fade into extinction. It's open Tuesday to Sunday 10am to 6pm (Nov–Mar to 5pm), and admission is 5€ adults, 3.50€ children 6 to 14 and students 25 and under.

Butter biscuits known simply as *buranelli* are also a famous product of the island—expect to be offered them in almost every store.

TORCELLO ★★

Torcello is perhaps the most charming of the islands, though today it consists of little more than one long canal leading from the *vaporetto* landing to a clump of buildings at its center.

Torcello boasts the oldest Venetian monument, the **Basilica di Santa Maria dell'Assunta ★★★**, whose foundation dates from the 7th century (☎ 041/2702464). It's justly famous for its spectacular 11th- to 12th-century Byzantine mosaics—a "Madonna and Child" in the apse and a monumental "Last Judgment" on the west wall—rivaling those of Ravenna's and St. Mark's basilicas. The cathedral is open daily 10:30am to 6pm (Nov–Feb to 5pm), and admission is 5€ (audioguide an extra 2€). Also of interest is the adjacent 11th-century church of **Santa Fosca** (free admission), a simple Byzantine brick church with a plain interior, and the **Museo di Torcello** (☎ 041/730761), with two small galleries showcasing archaeological artifacts from the Iron Age to medieval period, many found on the island. The church closes 30 minutes before the basilica, and the museum is open Tuesday to Sunday 10:30am to 5:30pm (Nov–Feb to 5pm). Museum admission is 3€. You must buy tickets for all attractions at the Basilica entrance.

Peaceful Torcello is uninhabited except for a handful of families (plus a population of feral cats) and is a favorite picnic spot. You'll have to bring food in from Venice—there are no stores on the island and only a handful of bars/trattorias plus one fabulous destination restaurant, **Locanda Cipriani ★★★** (Wed–Mon noon–3pm and 7–9pm; closed Jan to mid-Feb; www.locandacipriani.com), of Hemingway fame, which opened in 1935 and is definitely worth a splurge. Once the tour groups have left, the island offers a very special moment of solitude and escape.

THE LIDO ★

Although a convenient 15-minute *vaporetto* ride away from San Marco (see transport details above), Venice's **Lido beaches** are not much to write home about and certainly no longer a chic destination. For bathing and sun-worshipping there are much better beaches nearby—in Jesolo, to the north, for example. But the parade of wealthy Italian and foreign tourists (plus a good number of Venetian families) who still frequent this coastal area is an interesting sight indeed.

A beach on the Lido.

The Lido has two main beach areas. **Bucintoro** is at the opposite end of Gran Viale Santa Maria Elisabetta (referred to as the Gran Viale) from the *vaporetto* station Santa Elisabetta. It's a 10-minute stroll; walk straight ahead along Gran Viale to reach the beach. **San Nicolò,** about 1.5km (1 mile) away, can be reached by bus B. Renting loungers and parasols can cost from 10€ to 20€ per person (per day) depending on the time of year (it's

THE film FESTIVAL

The **Venice International Film Festival ★**, in late August and early September, is the most respected celebration of celluloid in Europe after Cannes. Films from all over the world are shown in the **Palazzo del Cinema** on the Lido as well as at various venues—and occasionally in some of the *campi*. Ticket prices vary, but those for the less-sought-after films are usually modest. See www.labiennale.org/en/cinema for more details.

just 1€ to use the showers and bathrooms). Keep in mind that if you stay at any of the hotels on the Lido, most have some kind of agreement with the different *bagni* (beach establishments).

Organized Tours

Because of the sheer number of sights to see in Venice, some first-time visitors like to start out with an organized tour. Although few things can really be covered in any depth on these overview tours, they're sometimes useful for getting your bearings. **Avventure Bellissime** (www.tours-italy.com; ✆ **041/970499**) coordinates a plethora of tours (in English), by boat and gondola, though the walking tours are the best value, covering all the main sights around Piazza San Marco in 2 hours for 25€ (discounts available online). For something with a little more bite (literally), **Urban Adventures** (www.urbanadventures.com; ✆ **348/9808566**) runs enticing tours that feature snacking on *cicchettí*, Venice's version of tapas (80€ for 2.5 hr. tour).

For those with more energy, learn to "row like a Venetian" (yes, literally standing up) at **Row Venice** (www.rowvenice.com; ✆ **347/7250637**), where 1½-hour lessons take place in traditional, hand-built "shrimp-tail" or *batele coda di gambero* boats for 85€ for up to 2 people.

Especially for Kids

It goes without saying that a **gondola ride** (p. 230) will be the thrill of a lifetime for any child (or adult). If that's too expensive, consider the far cheaper alternative: a **ride on the no. 1** *vaporetto* (p. 225).

Judging from the squeals of delight, **feeding the pigeons in Piazza San Marco** (purchase a bag of corn and you'll be draped in pigeons in a nanosecond) could be the high point of your child's visit to Venice, and it's the ultimate photo op. Be sure your child won't be startled by all the fluttering and flapping.

A jaunt to the neighboring **island of Murano** (p. 280) can be as educational as it is recreational—follow the signs to any *fornace* (kiln), where a glassblowing performance of the island's thousand-year-old art is free entertainment. But be ready for the guaranteed sales pitch that follows.

Take the elevator to the **top of the Campanile di San Marco** (p. 264) for a scintillating view of Venice's rooftops and cupolas, or get up close and

carnevale **A VENEZIA**

Carnevale traditionally was the celebration preceding Lent, the period of penitence and abstinence prior to Easter; its name is derived from the Latin *carnem levare,* meaning "to take meat away." Today Carnevale in Venice builds for 10 days until the big blowout, Shrove Tuesday (Fat Tuesday), when fireworks illuminate the Grand Canal, and Piazza San Marco is turned into a giant open-air ballroom for the masses. The festival is a harlequin patchwork of musical and cultural events, many of them free of charge, which appeals to all ages, tastes, nationalities, and budgets. Musical events are staged in some of the city's dozens of *piazze*—from reggae and zydeco to jazz and baroque. Special art exhibits are mounted at museums and galleries. Book your hotel months ahead, especially for the 2 weekends prior to Shrove Tuesday. Check **www.carnevalevenezia.com** for details on upcoming events.

personal with the four bronze horses on the facade of the Basilica San Marco. The view from its **outdoor loggia** is something you and your children won't forget. Scaling the **Torre dell'Orologio** (p. 269) or the bell tower at **San Giorgio Maggiore** (p. 279) is also lots of fun.

The **winged lion,** said to have been a kind of mascot to St. Mark, patron saint of Venice, was the very symbol of the Serene Republic and to this day appears on everything from cafe napkins to T-shirts. Keep a running tab of who can spot the most flying lions—you'll find them on facades, atop columns, over doorways, as pavement mosaics, on government stamps, and on the local flag.

SHOPPING

In a city that for centuries has thrived almost exclusively on tourism, remember this: **Where you buy cheap, you get cheap.** Venetians, centuries-old merchants, aren't known for bargaining. You'll stand a better chance of getting a good deal if you pay in cash or buy more than one item. In our limited space below, we've listed some of the more reputable places to stock up on classic Venetian items.

Shopping Streets & Markets

A mix of low-end trinket stores and middle-market-to-upscale boutiques line the narrow zigzagging **Mercerie** running north between Piazza San Marco and the Rialto Bridge. More expensive boutiques make for great window-shopping on **Calle Larga XXII Marzo,** the wide street that begins west of Piazza San Marco and wends its way to the expansive Campo Santo Stefano near the Accademia. The narrow **Frezzaria,** just west of Piazza San Marco and running north-south, offers bars, souvenir shops, and tony clothing stores like Louis Vuitton and Versace. The non-produce part of the **Rialto Market** is as good as it gets for basic souvenirs, where you'll find cheap T-shirts, glow-in-the-dark plastic gondolas, and tawdry glass trinkets.

The **Mercatino dei Miracoli** (© **041/2710022**), held only six times a year in Campo Santa Maria Nova (Cannaregio), is a fabulous flea market with all sorts of bric-a-brac and antiques sold by ordinary Venetians—haggling, for once, is acceptable. It usually takes place on the second Saturday or Sunday of March, April, May, September, October, and December, from 8:30am to 8pm. The **Mercatino dell'Antiquariato** (www.mercatinocamposanmaurizio. it) is a professional antiques market in Campo San Maurizio, San Marco; it takes place 4 to 5 times a year (usually Mar–Apr, May, Sept, Oct, and Dec; check the website for dates).

Arts & Crafts

Venice is uniquely famous for local crafts that have been produced here for centuries and are hard to get elsewhere: the **glassware** from Murano, the **delicate lace** from Burano, and the *cartapesta* (**papier-mâché**) **Carnevale masks** you'll find in endless *botteghe* (shops), where you can watch artisans paint amid their wares.

Now here's the bad news: There's such an overwhelming sea of cheap glass that buying **Venetian glass** can become something of a turnoff (shipping and insurance costs make most things unaffordable; the alternative is to hand-carry anything fragile). Plus, there are so few women left on Burano willing to spend countless tedious hours keeping alive the art of **lace-making** that the few pieces you'll see not produced by machine in China are sold at stratospheric prices; ditto the truly high-quality glass (although trinkets can be cheap and fun). The best place to buy glass is Murano itself—the **"Vetro Artistico Murano"** trademark guarantees its origin, but expect to pay as much as 60€ for just a wine glass.

Atelier Segalin di Daniela Ghezzo ★★   Founded in 1932 by master cobbler Antonio Segalin and his son Rolando, this old leather shoe store is now run by Daniela Ghezzo (the star apprentice of Rolando), maker of exuberant handmade shoes and boots, from basic flats to crazy footwear designed for Carnevale (shoes from 650€–1,800€). Calle dei Fuseri 4365, San Marco. www. danielaghezzo.it. © **041/5222115.** Mon–Fri 10am–1pm and 3–7pm. Sat 10am–1pm. Vaporetto: San Marco.

Ca' del Sol Maschere ★★   Run by a group of artists since 1986, this shop is a treasure trove of Venetian masks (prices 35€–360€), along with elaborate 18th-century costumes; you can even take mask-making courses here. Fondamenta de l'Osmarin 4964, Castello. www.cadelsolmascherevenezia.com. © **041/5285549.** Daily 10am–8pm. Vaporetto: San Zaccaria.

Il Canovaccio ★   Remember the creepy orgy scenes in Stanley Kubrick's film *Eyes Wide Shut?* The ornate masks used in the movie were made by the owners of this vaunted store. All manner of traditional, feathered, and animal masks are knocked out in their on-site workshop. Calle delle Bande 5369 (near

8

VENICE

Shopping

Campo Santa Maria Formosa), Castello. ☏ **041/5210393.** Daily 10am–7pm. Vaporetto: San Zaccaria.

Il Grifone ★★★ Toni Peressin's handmade leather briefcases, satchels, bound notebooks, belts, and soft-leather purses have garnered quite a following, and justly so—his craftsmanship is truly magnificent (he makes everything in the workshop out back). Small items start at around 25€. Fondamenta del Gaffaro 3516, Dorsoduro. www.ilgrifonevenezia.it. ☏ **041/5229452.** Tues and Fri 10am–6pm, Wed, Thurs, Sat 10am–1pm and 4–7pm. Vaporetto: Piazzale Roma.

La Bottega dei Mascareri ★★ High-quality, creative masks—some based on Tiepolo paintings—crafted by the brothers Sergio and Massimo Boldrin since 1984. Basic masks start at around 15€ to 20€, but you'll pay over 75€ for a more innovative piece. The smaller, original branch lies at the foot of the Rialto Bridge (San Polo 80; ☏ **041/5223857**). Calle dei Saoneri 2720, San Polo. www.mascarer.com. ☏ **041/5242887.** Both locations daily 9am–6pm. Vaporetto: Rialto.

Marco Polo International ★ This vast showroom, just west of the Piazza San Marco, displays quality glass direct from Murano (although it's more expensive than going to the island yourself), including plenty of easy-to-carry items such as paperweights and small dishes. Frezzaria 1644, San Marco. www.marcopolointernational.it. ☏ **041/5229295.** Daily 10am–7pm. Vaporetto: San Marco.

Venini ★ Convenient, classy, but incredibly expensive, Venini has been selling quality glass art since 1921, supplying the likes of Versace and many other designer brands. Venini's **workshop** on Murano is at Fondamenta Vetrai 50 (☏ **041/2737211**). Piazzetta Leoncini 314, San Marco. www.venini.it. ☏ **041/5224045.** Both locations Mon–Sat 9:30am–5:30pm. Vaporetto: San Marco.

ENTERTAINMENT & NIGHTLIFE

If you're looking for serious nocturnal action, you're in the wrong town—Verona and Padua are far livelier. Your best bet is to sit in the moonlit Piazza San Marco and listen to the cafes' outdoor orchestras, with the illuminated basilica before you—the perfect opera set—though this pleasure comes with a hefty price tag. Other popular spots to hang out include **Campo San Bartolomeo,** at the foot of the Rialto Bridge (although it is a zoo here in high season), and nearby **Campo San Luca.** In late-night hours, for low prices and low pretension, the absolute best place to go is **Campo Santa Margherita,** a huge open *campo* about halfway between the train station and the Accademia Bridge.

Visit one of the tourist information centers for current English-language schedules of the month's special events. The monthly *Ospite di Venezia* is distributed free or online at **www.unospitedivenezia.it** and is extremely helpful, but it's usually available only in the more expensive hotels.

Performing Arts & Live Music

Venice has a long and rich tradition of classical music; this was, after all, the home of Vivaldi. People dressed in period costumes stand around in heavily trafficked spots near San Marco and Rialto passing out brochures advertising classical music concerts, so you'll have no trouble finding up-to-date information.

Santa Maria della Pietà ★★ The so-called "Vivaldi Church," built between 1745 and 1760, holds concerts throughout the year, mostly performed by lauded ensemble **I Virtuosi Italiani;** check the website for specific dates. Full-price tickets are usually 28€ to 30€. Riva degli Schiavoni 3701, Castello. www.chiesavivaldi.it. ✆ **041/5221120.** Vaporetto: San Zaccaria.

Teatro La Fenice ★★★ The opera season runs from late November through June, but there are also ballet performances and classical concerts. Tickets are expensive for the major productions (80–110€ for the gallery and 130€ to 220€ for a decent seat). Those on a budget can opt for obstructed-view seats (from 35€) or listening-only seats (from 15€). Campo San Fantin 1965, San Marco. www.teatrolafenice.it. ✆ **041/2424.** Vaporetto: Giglio.

Cafes

For tourists and locals alike, Venetian nightlife mainly centers on the many cafes in one of the world's most remarkable *piazze:* Piazza San Marco. It is also a most expensive and touristed place to linger over a spritz, but it's a splurge that should not be dismissed too readily.

Caffè dei Frari ★★★ Established in 1870, this inviting bar and cafe overlooking the Frari church has walls adorned with original murals, an antique wooden bar, and a wrought-iron balcony upstairs. The seafood is especially good here, and at least three excellent German beers are usually on tap. Fondamenta dei Frari 2564, San Polo. ✆ **041/5241877.** Tues–Sat 9am–10pm, Sun and Mon 9am–4pm. Vaporetto: San Tomà.

Caffè Florian ★★ Occupying prime *piazza* real estate since 1720, this is one of the world's oldest coffee shops, with a florid interior of 18th-century mirrors, frescoes, and statuary. Sitting at a table, expect to pay 10€ for a cappuccino, 19.50€ for a Bellini (Prosecco and fresh peach nectar in season), and 13€ for a spritz—add another 6€ if the orchestra plays (Mar–Nov). Standing or sitting at the bar is much cheaper (5€ for a cappuccino, 9.50€ for a Bellini, etc.). Piazza San Marco 57. www.caffeflorian.com. ✆ **041/5205641.** Mon–Thurs 10am–9pm, Fri & Sat 9am–11pm, Sun 9am–9pm. Vaporetto: San Marco.

Caffè Lavena ★★ Said to be Wagner's favorite cafe and the hangout of fellow composer Franz Liszt in the 19th century, Lavena lies on the opposite side of the *piazza* to Florian and was founded just a few decades later in 1750. Expect the same high prices and surcharges here (cappuccino 12€, cocktails 20€), though as with Florian, if you stand and drink at the bar you'll pay much less than sitting at a table (espresso is just 1.50€). Piazza San Marco 133–134. www.lavena.it. ☎ **041/5224070.** Daily 9:30am–midnight (closed Tues in winter). Vaporetto: San Marco.

Gran Caffè Quadri ★   The final member of the San Marco "big three," (next door to Lavena), Quadri opened in 1638 as "Il Rimedio" ("The Remedy"), but it was more of a retail coffee operation at first, with the cafe upstairs added in 1830. It's been revitalized by chef Max Alajmo of Le Calandre restaurant in Padua, with a fancy restaurant upstairs **(Ristorante Quadri).** Most coffees are 8€ to 12€, with set breakfasts from 30€ to 45€. Beer is 13 to 16€ and Bellinis are 19€. April to October, guests are serenaded by the 121 St. Mark's Band (an extra 6€). Piazza San Marco 121. www.alajmo.it. ☎ **041/5222105.** Daily 9am–midnight (closed Mon in winter). Vaporetto: San Marco.

Il Caffè (aka Caffè Rosso) ★★★   Established in the late 19th century, Il Caffè has a history almost as colorful as its clientele, a mixture of students, aging regulars, and lost tourists. This is an old-fashioned, no-nonsense Venetian cafe/bar, with reasonably priced drinks and sandwiches, and plenty of seating on the *campo.* Campo Santa Margherita 2963, Dorsoduro. www.cafferosso.it. ☎ **041/5287998.** Mon–Sat 7am–1am. Vaporetto: Ca'Rezzonico.

Marchini Time ★★   The outlet for the famed Marchini *pasticcerie* (it opened in 1938), this plush modern cafe offers a range of addictive pastries, *biscotti,* chocolates, coffees, cakes, and savory *pizzette.* Campo San Luca 4589, San Marco. ☎ **041/2413087.** Mon–Sat 7am–8.30pm. Vaporetto: Rialto.

Pasticceria Nobile ★★   Founded in the 1930s, this is the most happening cafe in this section of town, celebrated for its tempting range of sweets, snacks, pastries, and chocolate. Locals congregate here for breakfast and for *aperitivo* after work. Calle del Pistor 1818, Cannaregio. www.pasticcerianobile.it. ☎ **041/720731.** Tues–Sun 7am–8:30pm (closed Jul). Vaporetto: San Marcuola.

Birreria, Wine & Cocktail Bars

Although Venice boasts an old and prominent university, dance clubs barely enjoy their 15 minutes of popularity before changing hands or closing down (some are open only in the summer months). Young Venetians tend to go to the Lido in summer or mainland Mestre. Evenings are better spent lingering over a late dinner, having a pint in a *birrerie,* or nursing a glass of prosecco in one of the pricey outdoor bars and cafes in Piazza San Marco or Campo Santa Margherita. (*Note:* Most bars are open Mon–Sat 8pm–midnight.)

Al Prosecco ★★   Get acquainted with all things bubbly at this smart enoteca, a specialist, as you'd expect, in Veneto prosecco. It features plenty of tasty *cicchetti* to wash down the various brands, and a gorgeous terrace from which to observe the *campo* below. Most drinks run 3€ to 5€. Campo San Giacomo da l'Orio 1503, Santa Croce. www.alprosecco.com. ☎ **041/5240222.** Mon–Sat 10am–10:30pm (closes 8pm in winter; closed Aug and Jan). Vaporetto: San Stae.

Caffè Centrale ★★ Not really a cafe but a super-hip bar and restaurant (with iPad menus), this spot is located within the 16th-century Palazzo Cocco Molin, just a short walk from Piazza San Marco. It's got an intriguing selection of local and foreign beers (5.50€–7.50€), and a huge cocktail list (12€–18€)—cover is an extra 4€ per person. Get a table by the canal or lounge on one of the comfy leather sofas. Piscina di Frezzaria 1659, San Marco. www.caffe centralevenezia.com. ✆ **041/8876642.** Daily 7pm–1am. Vaporetto: Vallaresso.

Harry's Bar ★ Possibly the most famous bar in Venice (and now a global chain), Harry's was established in 1931 by Giuseppe Cipriani and frequented by the likes of Ernest Hemingway, Charlie Chaplin, and Truman Capote. The Bellini was invented here in 1948 (along with *carpaccio* 2 years later), and you can sip the signature concoction of fresh peach juice and prosecco for a mere 21€. Go for the history but don't expect a five-star experience—most first-timers are surprised just how ordinary it looks inside. It's more a restaurant than a bar these days, serving very expensive food (the soup is 32€), but just stick to the drinks. Calle Vallaresso 1323, San Marco. www.harrysbarvenezia.com. ✆ **041/5285777.** Daily 10:30am–11pm. Vaporetto: Vallaresso.

Margaret DuChamp ★★ This popular student and *fashionista* hangout has plenty of chairs on the *campo* for people-watching, cocktails, and a spritz or two (spritz is just 3€). It also serves decent panini (from 5€) and *tramezzini* (2€ at the table/1.50€ at the bar) and has free Wi-Fi. Campo Santa Margherita 3019, Dorsoduro. ✆ **041/5286255.** Wed–Mon 9am–2am. Vaporetto: Ca' Rezzonico.

Paradiso Perduto ★★ "Paradise Lost" is the most happening bar in Cannaregio, crammed with students most nights and featuring the occasional live jazz or blues set (full concerts every Mon and every first Sun of the month), great *cicchetti* (piled in mountains at the bar) and cheap(ish) wine. Some people come to dine on the tasty seafood, but it's usually too busy and noisy to enjoy a proper meal here—stick to the drinks and the snacks. Fondamenta della Misericordia 2540, Cannaregio. www.ilparadisoperduto.wordpress.com. ✆ **041/720581.** Thurs–Mon noon–midnight (closed Tues–Wed). Vaporetto: Madonna dell'Orto.

DAY TRIPS FROM VENICE

By Stephen Keeling

If you only have 3 days or so, you will probably want to spend them in the center of Venice. However, if you are here for a week—or on your second visit to the city—head over to the mainland to see some fascinating old towns in the historic Veneto region.

9 PADUA ★★★

40km (25 miles) W of Venice

Tucked away within the ancient heart of **Padua** lies one of the greatest artistic treasures in all Italy, the precious Giotto frescoes of the **Cappella degli Scrovegni.** Although the city itself is not especially attractive (it was largely rebuilt after bombing during World War II), don't be put off by the urban sprawl that now surrounds it; central Padua is refreshingly bereft of tourist crowds, a workaday Veneto town with a large student population and a small but intriguing ensemble of historic sights.

Like much of the region, Padua prospered in the Middle Ages, and Italy's second oldest university was founded here in 1222. Its fortunes grew further when St. Antony of Padua died in the city in 1231, making it a place of pilgrimage ever since. In the 14th century, the da Carrara family presided over the city's golden age, but in 1405 Padua was conquered and absorbed by Venice, losing its independence. With the fall of the Venetian Republic in 1797, the city was ruled by Napoleon and then became part of the Austrian Empire in 1814. Finally annexed to Italy in 1866, the city boomed again after World War II, becoming the industrial dynamo of northeast Italy.

Essentials

ARRIVING The most efficient way to reach Padua is to take the train from the Santa Lucia station. Trains depart every 10 to 20 minutes and take 26 to 50 minutes depending on the class (tickets 4.25€–14.90€ one-way). The main Padua station ("Padova" in Italian) is a short walk north up Corso del Popolo from the Cappella degli Scrovegni and the old city.

VISITOR INFORMATION   The **tourist office** at the train station is usually open Monday to Saturday 9am to 7pm and Sunday 10am to 4pm (www.turis-mopadova.it; *©* **049/2010080**). The office in the old city at Vicolo Pedrocchi (same telephone) is open Monday to Saturday 9am to 7pm.

Exploring Padua

The one unmissable sight in Padua is the **Cappella degli Scrovegni ★★★** (www.cappelladegliscrovegni.it; *©* **049/2010020;** daily 9am–7pm; check website for evening openings 7–10pm) at Piazza Eremitani, an outwardly unassuming chapel commissioned in 1303 by Enrico Scrovegni, a wealthy banker. Inside, however, the chapel is gloriously decorated with an astonishing cycle of frescoes by Florentine genius **Giotto.** The frescoes depict the life of the Virgin Mary and the life of Jesus, culminating with the Ascension and Last Judgment. Seeing Giotto's powerful work in the flesh is spine-tingling; this is where he made the decisive break with Byzantine art, taking the first important steps toward the realism and humanism that would characterize the Renaissance in Italy.

Entrance to the chapel is limited, involving groups of 25 visitors spending 15 minutes in a climate-controlled airlock, used to stabilize the temperature, before going inside for another 15 minutes. To visit the chapel, you must **make a reservation at least 24 hours in advance.** You must then arrive 45 minutes before the time on your ticket. Tickets cost 13€ (6€ for kids ages 6–17 and students under 27).

Basilica of Saint Anthony of Padua.

If you have time, try to take in Padua's other historic highlights. The vast **Palazzo della Ragione** on Piazza del Erbe (6€; Tues–Sun 9am–7pm, closes 6pm Nov–Jan) is an architectural marvel, a cavernous town hall completed in 1219, decorated by 15th-century frescoes by Nicola Miretto. Pay a visit also to the **Basilica di Sant'Antonio** (Piazza del Santo; www.sant antonio.org; ☏ **049/8225652;** admission free; daily 6:20am–7:45pm, closes 6:45pm Nov–Mar), the stately resting place of **St. Anthony of Padua,** the Portuguese Franciscan best known as the patron saint of finding things or lost people. The exterior of the church is a bizarre 14th-century mix of Byzantine, Romanesque, and Gothic styles, while the interior is richly adorned with statuary and murals. In the piazza outside, don't miss **Donatello**'s stupendous 1453 equestrian statue of the Venetian *condottiere* **Gattamelata** (Erasmo da Narni), the first large bronze sculpture of the Renaissance.

Where to Eat in Padua

Padua offers plenty of places to eat, and you'll especially appreciate the overall drop in prices compared with Venice. It's hard to match the location of **Bar Nazionale ★★**, Piazza del Erbe 40 (Mon and Sat 7am–10:30pm; Tues, Thurs, and Fri 7am–11:30am; Wed 7am–midnight; Sun 9am–9:30pm), on the steps leading up to Palazzo della Ragione, though it's best for drinks and snacks (excellent *tramezzini* from 2€) rather than a full meal. For that, make for **Osteria dei Fabbri ★**, Via dei Fabbri 13, just off Piazza del Erbe (www. osteriadeifabbri.it; ☏ **049/650336;** Mon–Sat noon–3pm and 7–11pm), which cooks up cheap, tasty pasta dishes for under 15€.

VERONA ★★

115km (71 miles) W of Venice

The affluent city of **Verona,** with its gorgeous red- and peach-colored medieval buildings and Roman ruins, is one of Italy's major tourist draws, though its appeal owes more to **William Shakespeare** than real history. He immortalized the city in his (totally fictional) *Romeo and Juliet, The Two Gentlemen of Verona,* and *The Taming of the Shrew.* Despite its popularity with tourists, Verona is not Venice; it's a booming commercial center with vibrant science and technology sectors.

Verona emerged as a city-state in the 12th century, ruled primarily by the bloodthirsty (and, in Renaissance tradition, art-loving) Scaligeri family until 1387. After a brief period of Milanese rule, Verona fell under the control of Venice in 1405. Like the rest of the region, the city fell to Napoleon in 1797, then Austria, and became part of Italy in 1866.

Essentials

ARRIVING The best way to reach Verona from Venice is by **train.** Direct services depart every 30 minutes and take anywhere from 1 hour and 10 minutes to 2 hours and 20 minutes, depending on the type of train you catch (tickets 9.05€–31.80€ one-way). From Verona station (Verona Porta Nuova), it's a 15-minute walk to the historic center.

VISITOR INFORMATION The tourist office is off Piazza Bra at Via Degli Alpini 9 (www.tourism.verona.it; ℂ **045/8068680;** Mon–Sat 10am–1pm & 3–5pm, Sun 10am–2pm) and can supply maps, hotel reservations, discount cards, and guided tour information.

Exploring Verona

"Two households, both alike in dignity, in fair Verona…" So go the immortal opening lines of *Romeo and Juliet,* ensuring that the city has been a target for love-sick romantics ever since. Though Verona is crammed with genuine historic goodies, one of the most popular sites is the ersatz **Casa di Giulietta,** Via Cappello 23 (6€; Mon 1:30–7:30pm, Tues–Sun 8:30am–7:30pm), a 14th-century house (with balcony, naturally), claiming to be the Capulets' home. In the courtyard, the chest of a bronze statue of Juliet has been polished to a gleaming sheen thanks to a legend claiming that stroking her right breast brings good fortune. **Juliet's Wall,** at the entrance, is quite a spectacle, covered with the scribbles of star-crossed lovers; love letters placed here are taken down and, along with 5,000 letters annually, are answered by the Club di Giulietta (a group of locally based volunteers). There's not much to see inside the house, though plenty of visitors line up for a chance of a selfie on the balcony.

Once you've made the obligatory Juliet pilgrimage, focus on actual historic sights. The 1st-century **Arena di Verona ★** (10€; Mon 1:30–7:30pm and Tues–Sun 9am–7:30pm), in the spacious Piazza Bra, is the third largest

"Juliet" statue at Casa di Giulietta.

classical arena in Italy after Rome's Colosseum and the arena at Capua—it could seat some 25,000 spectators and still hosts performances today (see www.arena.it).

To the northwest on Piazza San Zeno, the **Basilica di San Zeno Maggiore** ★★ (3€; Mar–Oct Mon–Sat 8:30am–6pm, Sun 12:30–6pm; Nov–Feb Mon–Sat 10am–1pm and 1:30–5pm, Sun 12:30–5pm) is the greatest Romanesque church in northern Italy. The present structure was completed around 1135, over the 4th-century shrine to Verona's patron saint, St. Zeno (who died 380). Its massive rose window represents the Wheel of Fortune, while the impressive lintels above the portal represent the months of the year. The highlight of the interior is "Madonna and Saints" by Mantegna.

Where to Eat in Verona

Even in chic Verona, you'll spend less on a meal than in Venice. The most authentic budget Verona restaurant is **Osteria Sottoriva,** Via Sottoriva 9 (✆ **045/8014323;** Thurs–Tues 11am–11pm), one of the most popular places in town for lunch or dinner; try the *trippa alla Parmigiana* (braised tripe) or the hopelessly rich gorgonzola melted over polenta (main courses 8€–15€). The **Caffè Monte Baldo,** Via Rosa 12 (✆ **045/8030579;** noon–11pm daily), is an old-fashioned cafe transformed into a trendy *osteria,* serving classic pastas, and scrumptious *crostini* with wine in the evenings (try a bottle from a nearby vineyard).

TREVISO ★★

30km (19 miles) N of Venice

Long overshadowed by Venice, **Treviso** is a small, prosperous city of narrow medieval streets, Gothic churches, and an enchanting network of canals, replete with weeping willows and waterwheels (it's known as "piccola Venezia" or "little Venice"). Giotto's follower **Tomaso da Modena** (1326–79) frescoed many of its churches, and its maze of back streets makes for pleasant, often tourist-free exploring.

Essentials

ARRIVING Trains run two to four times an hour from Venice's Santa Lucia station; it's a 30- to 40-minute trip, definitely your fastest option. Tickets start at 3.45€ one-way. Arriving at Treviso Centrale station, you'll have an easy 10- to 15-minute walk to Piazza dei Signori, north across the River Sile (follow signs to "Centro"). Note also that most Ryanair **budget flights to Venice** actually arrive at Treviso airport (p. 223).

VISITOR INFORMATION The **tourist office** at Via Fiumicelli 30 (www.visittreviso.it; ✆ **0422/547-632**) is open Monday from 10am to 1pm, Tuesday to Saturday 10am to 5pm, and Sunday 10am to 4pm.

Exploring Treviso

The historic heart of Treviso, **Piazza dei Signori** ★ is anchored by the **Palazzo del Podestà,** rebuilt in the 1870s with a tall clock tower, and the **Palazzo dei Trecento,** the 13th-century town council hall (chic **Bar Beltrame** nestles beneath the arches). Just beyond the square, on adjacent Piazza San Vito, sit two handsome medieval churches: **Santa Lucia** ★ (www.santaluciatreviso.it; ✆ **0422/5457200**), with a superb Tomaso da Modena fresco of the "Madonna del Pavegio" in the first shrine on the right; and **San Vito** ★, with its fine 13th-century Byzantine-style frescoes. Both are open daily 8am–noon; admission is free.

Historic **Via Calmaggiore,** lined with posh boutiques, runs northwest from Piazza dei Signori towards Treviso's **Duomo** ★ (admission free; Mon–Sat 7:30am–noon and 3:30–7pm; Sun 8am–1pm and 3:30–8pm). Its relatively dull neoclassical facade dates only from 1836, but its flanking Romanesque lions and seven Venetian-Byzantine style green copper domes testify to the cathedral's 12th-century origins. The crypt is the most compelling part of the interior, with tombs of the city's bishops amid a forest of columns and fragments of 14th-century frescoes and mosaics. The cathedral also has a fine 1520 Titian altarpiece, the "Malchiostro Annunciation." Stroll southwest from the Duomo to the massive Italian Gothic **San Nicolò** church ★ (admission free; daily 8am–noon & 3:30–6pm), with its intriguing Gothic frescoes. Tomaso da Modena and his school decorated the huge round columns with a series of saints, notably St. Jerome and St. Agnes. Antonio da Treviso painted the gargantuan St. Christopher—his .9m-long (3-ft.) feet strolling over biting fish—in 1410.

East of Piazza dei Signori, in Piazzetta Mario Botter, the **Museo di Santa Caterina** (www.museicivicitreviso.it; ✆ **0422/658442;** 6€; Tues–Sun 9am–12:30pm and 2:30–6pm), housed in a deconsecrated church, displays another Tomaso da Modena fresco cycle, the "Story of the Life of Saint Ursula." There's also a cache of local archaeological finds, plus minor works by Titian, Lorenzo Lotto, and Francesco Guardi. South of there, the 15th-century church of **Santa Maria Maggiore** (admission free; daily 8am–noon and 3:30–6pm) houses a venerated frescoed image of Mary (the "Madonna Granda"), an ancient Byzantine-style image later touched up by Tomaso and members of his school.

Where to Eat in Treviso

For atmosphere it's hard to beat the **Hosteria Dai Naneti** ★★, Vicolo Broli 2 (www.dainaneti.it; ✆ **3403/783158;** Mon–Fri 9am–2:30pm and 5:30–9pm, Sat 9:30am–2pm and 5:30–9pm, Sun 11am–2pm and 5–8pm; May–Sept closed Sun), a cozy tavern, deli, and cheese shop where you can grab a delicious baguette and glass of wine, or just snack at the bar for around 5€ (standing room only).

For a full meal in the center, reserve a table at **Trattoria All'Antico Portico** ★★, overlooking the church at Piazza Santa Maria Maggiore 18 (www.anticoportico.it; ✆ **0422/545259;** Mon 9am–4pm, Wed–Sun 9am–11pm), which serves local specialties such as radicchio risotto and *baccalà alla veneziana* (salt cod); main courses are 15€ to 18€.

PLANNING YOUR TRIP

By Donald Strachan

This chapter provides a variety of planning tools, including information on how to get there, how to get around, and the inside track on local resources. If you do your homework on special events, pick the right place for the right season, and pack for the climate, preparing for a trip to Italy should be pleasant and uncomplicated. For "When to Go," see p. 37.

GETTING THERE

By Plane

10

If you're flying across an ocean, you'll most likely land at Rome's **Leonardo da Vinci–Fiumicino Airport** (FCO; www.adr.it/fiumicino), 40km (25 miles) from the center. This is almost always the cheapest intercontinental destination. Rome's much smaller **Ciampino Airport** (CIA; www.adr.it/ciampino) serves low-cost airlines connecting to European cities and other destinations in Italy. For information on getting to central Rome from its airports, see p. 42.

Carriers within Europe fly direct to several smaller Italian cities, including Venice's **Marco Polo Airport** (VCE; www.veniceairport.it), Bologna's **Marconi Airport** (BLQ; www.bologna-airport.it), and Pisa's **Galileo Galilei Airport** (PSA; www.pisa-airport.com). For information on getting into central Venice from the airport, see p. 223. For reaching Florence from the Pisa or Bologna airports, see p. 147.

By Train

Italy's major cities are well-connected to Europe's rail hubs. You can arrive in Milan on direct trains from France—including Nice, Paris, and Lyon—by **TGV** (http://en.oui.sncf/en/tgv), or Swiss intercity services from Zurich, and connect to Venice or Rome (see "Getting Around," p. 298). **Nightjet** rail routes (www.nightjet.com) go from Munich, Germany, and Vienna, Austria to Venice, Florence and Rome. Direct trains from elsewhere in central Europe also arrive at Verona and Venice.

Thello (www.thello.com) operates an overnight service connecting Paris with Venice. After crossing the Alps in the dead of night, the train calls at Milan, Brescia, Verona, Vicenza, and Padua before arriving in Venice around 9:30am. For Florence, Rome, and points south, alight at Milan (around 6am) and switch to Italy's national high-speed rail lines; see p. 301. Accommodation on the Thello train is in sleeping cars, as well as in six- and four-berth couchettes. Prices range from 35€ per person for the cheapest advance fare in a six-berth couchette to a maximum of 290€ for sole occupancy of a better-quality sleeping car. It's worth paying the extra for these rather than the couchette, if you can; they accommodate one, two, or three passengers.

You can book in advance online with **Loco2** (www.loco2.com) or with an agent such as **Rail Europe** (www.raileurope.com; ✆ **800/622-8600**) or **International Rail** (www.internationalrail.com; ✆ **+44-871/231-0790**).

GETTING AROUND

By Car

Much of Italy is accessible by public transportation, but to explore vineyards, countryside, and smaller towns, a car is essential. You'll get the **best rental rate** if you book your car far ahead of arrival. Try the website **AutoSlash.com** which applies any coupons on the market to your rental; and then monitors your booking. If the price drops, they'll make you a new reservation. We've found AutoSlash.com to be the best search engine for rentals by far, although it's a bit clunky to use: You must wait for an email back before you can see the options, but thankfully it usually comes within minutes of your request. Car-rental search companies usually report the lowest rates available between 6 and 8 weeks ahead of arrival. Rent the smallest car possible and request a diesel rather than petrol engine to minimize fuel costs. You must be 25 or older to rent from many agencies (although some accept ages 21 and up, at a premium price).

The legalities and contractual obligations of renting a car in Italy (where accident rates are high) are more complicated than those in almost any other country in Europe. You also must have nerves of steel, a sense of humor, a valid domestic driver's license, and, strictly speaking (for non-EU citizens) an **International Driving Permit** (see below). Insurance on all vehicles is compulsory. *Tip:* If you're planning to rent a car in Italy during high season, you should **book well in advance.** It's not unheard of to arrive at Rome airport in June or July to find that every agent is all out of cars, perhaps for the whole week.

It can sometimes be tricky to get to the *autostrada* (fast highway) from the city center or airport, so consider renting or bringing a GPS-enabled device or installing an offline satellite-navigation app on your smartphone. In bigger cities you will first have to get to the *tangenziale,* or "beltway," which will eventually lead to your highway of choice. The beltway in Rome is known as the *Grande Raccordo Anulare,* or "Big Ring Road."

The going can be slow on Friday afternoons leaving the cities and Sunday nights on the way back into town, and rush hour around the cities any day of the week can be epic. Although European fuel prices fell significantly in 2015–16, gas remains around 1.60€ *per liter* at time of writing. (Diesel is usually around .10€ cheaper.) Add in the price of car rental, and it's often cheaper to take the train, even for two people.

PERMITS & AUTO CLUBS Before leaving home, you can apply for an **International Driving Permit** from the **American Automobile Association** (**AAA;** www.aaa.com; © **800/622-7070** or 650/294-7400). In Canada, the permit's available from the **Canadian Automobile Association** (**CAA;** www. caa.ca; © **800/222-4357**). Technically, you need this permit and your driver's license to drive in Italy, although at the rental desk, your license itself generally suffices. Traffic police can fine you for driving without an IDP, however. Visitors from within the EU need only take their domestic driver's license.

Italy's equivalent of AAA is the **Automobile Club d'Italia** (**ACI;** www.aci. it). They're the people who respond when you place an emergency call to © **803-116** for road breakdowns, though they charge for this service if you're not a member.

ROAD TYPES **Autostrade** are toll highways denoted by green signs and a number prefaced with an *A,* like the A1 from Milan to Florence, Rome, and Naples. A few fast highways aren't numbered and are simply called a *raccordo,* a connecting road between two cities (such as Florence–Siena and Florence–Pisa). Autostrada tolls can get expensive, costing about 1€ for every 14km (8½ miles), which means it costs around 18€ for a trip from Rome to Florence. See **www.autostrade.it** for live traffic updates and a road-toll calculator.

Strade statali (singular is *strada statale*) are state roads, usually without a center divider and two lanes wide (although sometimes they can be a divided four-way highway), indicated by blue signs. Their route numbers are prefaced with an *SS,* as in the SS11 from Milan to Venice. On signs, however, these official route numbers are frequently omitted. Usually, you'll just see blue signs listing destinations by name with arrows pointing off in the appropriate directions. It's impossible to predict which of all the towns that lie along a road will be the ones chosen to list on a particular sign. Sometimes the sign gives only the first minuscule village that lies past the turnoff. At other times it lists the first major town down that road. Some signs mention only the major city the road eventually leads to, even if it's hundreds of kilometers away. It pays to study the map before coming to an intersection, or better yet, carry a GPS device or download an **offline GPS app** for your smartphone. Because they bisect many towns, the *strade statali* can be frustratingly slow: When feasible, pay and take the autostrada.

DRIVING RULES   Italian drivers aren't maniacs; they only appear to be. Spend any time on a highway and you will have the experience of somebody driving up insanely close from behind while flashing their headlights. Take a deep breath and don't panic: This is the aggressive signal for you to move to the right so he (invariably, it's a he) can pass, and until you do he will stay mind-bogglingly close. On a two-lane road, the idiot swerving into your lane to pass someone in opposing traffic expects you to veer obligingly toward the shoulder so three lanes of traffic can fit. He would do the same for you. Probably. Many Italians seem to think turn signals are optional, so be aware the car in front could be ready to turn at any moment.

A few important rules:

It is compulsory to **keep your headlights illuminated**—set to dip—even during the day.

The **speed limit** on roads in built-up areas around towns and cities is 50 kmph (31 mph). On two-lane roads it's 90 kmph (56 mph) and on the highway it's 130 kmph (81 mph). Italians have an astounding disregard for these limits. However, police can ticket you and collect a fine on the spot.

The **blood-alcohol limit** in Italy is 0.05%, often achieved with just two drinks; driving above the limit can result in a fine, driving ban, or imprisonment. The blood-alcohol limit is set at zero for anyone who has held a driver's license for less than 3 years.

Seat belts are obligatory in both front and back seats; ditto child seats or special restraints for minors under 1.5 meters (5 ft.) in height—although this latter regulation is often ignored.

Drivers may not use a **cellphone** while driving, but this is yet another law locals seem to treat as optional.

ROAD SIGNS   Here's a brief rundown of the road signs you'll most frequently encounter:

○ **Speed limit sign:** Black number inside a red circle on a white background

○ **End of a speed zone:** Black and white, with a black slash through the number

○ **Yield to oncoming traffic:** Red circle with a white background, a black arrow pointing down, and a red arrow pointing up

○ **Yield ahead:** Point-down, red-and-white triangle

○ **Pedestrian zone:** Simple white circle with a red border, or the words *zona pedonale* or *zona traffico limitato* (if your hotel is in a pedestrian zone, ask if you can prearrange to drop your baggage off by car)

- **One-way streets:** White arrow on a blue background
- **Do not enter:** Mostly red circle with a horizontal white slash
- **No parking:** Circular sign in blue with a red circle-slash
- Any image in black on a white background surrounded by a red circle means that image is **not allowed** (for instance, if the image is two cars next to each other, it means no passing; and so on).

PARKING On streets, **white lines** indicate free public spaces, **blue lines** are pay spaces, and **yellow lines** indicate spots where only residents are allowed to park. Meters don't line the sidewalk; rather, there's usually a machine on the block where you punch in how long you want to park. The machine spits out a ticket for placing on your dashboard. If you park in an area marked *parcheggio disco orario,* root around in your rental car's glove compartment for a cardboard parking disc. With this device, you dial up the hour of your arrival and display it on your dashboard. You're allowed *un'ora* (1 hr.) or *due ore* (2 hr.), or whatever the sign advises. If you do not have a disk, write your arrival time clearly on a sheet of paper and leave it on the dash.

   Parking lots have ticket dispensers, but exit booths are not usually manned. When you return to the lot to depart, first visit the office or automated payment machine to exchange your ticket for a paid receipt. You then use this to get through the exit gate.

FUEL Gasoline (gas or petrol), *benzina* in Italian, can be bought at pull-in gas stations along major roads and on the outskirts of towns, as well as in 24-hour stations along the autostrada. Almost all are closed for the *riposo* and on Sundays (except on the autostrada), but most have an automatic machine that accepts cash. Unleaded gas is *senza piombo*. Diesel is *gasolio* (or just *diesel*).

By Train

Italy, especially the northern half, has one of the best train systems in Europe, with most destinations connected. Consequently, the train is an excellent option if you're looking to visit the major sites without the hassle of driving. The vast majority of lines are run by state-owned **Ferrovie dello Stato,** or **Trenitalia** (www.trenitalia.com; ☏ **89/2021**). A private operator **Italo** (www.italotreno.it; ☏ **06/07-08,** or 89/2020) operates on the main Milan–Florence–Rome–Naples high-speed line, a branch from Bologna to Padua and Venice, and from Turin eastward to Venice via Milan and Verona.

Travel Times Between the Major Cities

CITIES	DISTANCE	(FASTEST) TRAIN TRAVEL TIME	DRIVING TIME
Florence to Venice	261km/162 miles	2 hr.	3 hr.
Rome to Florence	277km/172 miles	1½ hr.	3 hr.
Rome to Naples	219km/136 miles	1 hr., 10 min.	2½ hr.
Rome to Venice	528km/327 miles	3 hr., 20 min.	5¼ hr.

Travel durations and the price of tickets vary considerably depending on what type of train you choose. The country's principal north–south, high-speed line links Milan to Bologna, Florence, Rome, and Naples. Milan to Rome, for example, takes under 3 hours on the fast train, and costs 99€—though you can find tickets as low as 25€ if you buy ahead and travel in off-peak hours. Rome to Naples takes 70 minutes and costs 45€ (walk-up fare) on the fast train, or you can spend 12€ for a trip on a slower train that takes just over twice as long. *Tip:* To bag the cheapest fares on high-speed trains, try to **book around 100 to 120 days before your travel dates.** The **Italo news-letter** (and homepage) also regularly advertises limited-time promo code discounts offering up to 50% off its advanced fares—making them crazy cheap.

TYPES OF TRAIN   The speed, cleanliness, and overall quality of Italian trains vary. **High-speed trains** usually have four classes: Standard, Premium, Business, and Executive on Trenitalia; Smart, eXtra Large, First, and Club Executive on Italo. The cheapest of these, on both operators, is perfectly comfortable, even on long legs of a journey. These are Italy's premium rail services. *Tip:* Business class on the state railway is well worth paying a little extra for, if it's reduced for advanced ticket purchase.

Trenitalia's **Frecciarossa,** as well as Italo's rival high-speed train, is the fastest of the fast, Italy's bullet train. These trains operate on the Milan–Florence–Rome–Naples line, and normally run up to 300 kmph (186 mph). Frecciarossa services also connect Milan with Venice (with halts in Verona and Vicenza). The **Frecciargento** uses slightly lesser hardware and is a bit slower; it links Naples, Rome, Florence, Verona, and Venice at speeds of up to 250 kmph (155 mph). Speed and cleanliness come at a price, however, with tickets for these high-speed trains usually around three times the cheapest "regional" train. On high-speed services you **must make a seat reservation** when you buy a ticket. If you are traveling with a rail pass (see p. 303), you must pay a 10€ reservation fee to ride (which you can do from the automated Trenitalia ticket machines in stations, as well by queuing for a teller window). Rail passes are not accepted (for now) on Italo.

Intercity (IC) trains are one step down, in both speed and comfort; specific seat reservations are also compulsory on IC services. The slower *Regionale* **(R)** and *Regionale Veloce* **(RV)** make many stops and are occasionally on the grimy side, but are also cheap: A Venice–Verona second-class ticket will put you back only 9€ compared with 26€ on a high-speed service. There's no need to book R or RV trains ahead of time, and no price advantage in doing so. Just turn up, buy a ticket, and ride.

Old *Regionale* trains are slowly being replaced, and comfort is improving. However, **overcrowding** is often a problem on standard services (that is, not the prebookable trains) on Friday evenings, weekends, and holidays, especially in and out of big cities, or just after a strike. In summer, crowding escalates, and any train going toward a beach in August bulges like an over-stuffed sausage.

TRAIN TRAVEL TIPS   If you don't have a ticket with a reservation for a particular seat on a specific train, then you must **validate your ticket by stamping it in the little yellow box** on the platform before boarding the train. If you board a train without a ticket, or without having validated your ticket, you'll have to pay a hefty fine on top of the ticket or supplement, which the conductor will sell you. If you board a train without a ticket or realize once onboard that you have the wrong type of ticket, your best bet is to let the conductor know; she is likely to be more forgiving because you sought her out and made it clear you weren't trying to ride for free.

Schedules for all trains leaving a given station are printed on yellow posters tacked up on the station wall (a corresponding white poster lists arrivals). These are good for getting general information, but keep your eye on electronic boards and screens that are updated with delays and track *(binario)* changes. You can get official schedules (also in English) and buy tickets at www.trenitalia.com and www.italotreno.it, or at an online agent like **Loco2.com**.

In big cities and tourist destinations, ticketing lines can be dreadfully long. Don't be intimidated by the **automatic ticket machines.** They are easy to navigate, offer instructions in English, accept cash and credit cards, and save the stress of waiting in a slow line. *Note:* You can't buy international tickets at automatic machines.

Rail **apps** for state and Italo services offer paperless ticketing and convenient in-app payment for tickets via credit card or PayPal. You can just show a copy (paper or electronic) of your booking confirmation e-mail, which has a unique PNR code.

SPECIAL PASSES & DISCOUNTS   To buy the **Eurail Italy Pass,** available only outside Europe and priced in U.S. dollars, contact **Rail Europe** (www.raileurope.com). You have a month in which to use the train a set number of days; the base number of days is 3, and you can add up to 5 more. For adults, the first-class pass costs $246, second class is $199. Additional days each cost $40 to $45 more for first class, around $35 for second class. For youth tickets (27 and under), a 3-day second-class pass is $164 and additional days about $30 each. Buying your pass early in the year is often rewarded with an extra day's travel at no additional cost (such as, pay for 3 days, get 4). Saver passes are available for groups of two to five people traveling together *at all times,* and amount to a savings of about 15% on individual tickets. There are also Italy–Austria, Italy–Spain, Italy–France, and Italy–Switzerland rail pass combinations.

Note: Booking individual rail journeys online ahead of arrival will usually beat a pass on price, especially if you factor in the costs (and hassle) of making compulsory seat reservations on every high-speed train. However, the cheapest online fares are nonrefundable: You gain flexibility with a pass.

If you plan to do a lot of regular-ticket train travel around Italy over a longer period of time, and if you're aged **25 and under,** you can buy a 40€ **Carta Verde (Green Card)** at any Italian train station—it'll get you a 10% discount on walk-up fares for domestic trips and 25% on international connections for

1 year. Present it each time you buy a ticket. A similar deal is available for anyone **61 and over** with the **Carta d'Argento (Silver Card):** 15% off domestic walk-ups and 25% off international, for 30€ (the Carta d'Argento is free for those 76 and over).

Children 11 and under always ride half-price and kids 3 and under don't pay, although they also do not have the right to their own seat. On state railways, there are sometimes free tickets for children 14 and under traveling with a paying adult; ask about "Bimbi gratis" when buying your ticket (this option will also appear automatically when it's available on automatic ticket machines). The **Italo Famiglia** fare, available at the station and online, includes free travel for kids 13 and under accompanying an adult (in Smart [2nd] class only, Mon–Sat).

By Bus

Although trains are quicker and easier, you can get just about anywhere in Italy on a network of local, provincial, and regional bus lines. In bigger cities, the **bus station** for intercity trips is usually near the main train station. A small town's **bus stop** is usually either in the main square, on the edge of town, or on a bend in the road just outside the main town gate. You should always try to find the local ticket vendor—if there's no office, it's invariably the nearest newsstand or *tabacchi* (signaled by a sign with a white т), or occasionally a bar—but you can usually also buy tickets on the bus. You can sometimes flag down a bus as it passes on a country road, but try to find an official stop (a small sign, sometimes tacked onto a telephone pole).

Two particular convenient long-distance bus routes are the efficient **Florence–Siena** service and slightly more awkward **Florence–San Gimignano** run (see p. 147). If you are traveling on a tight budget, check intercity fares of **FlixBus** (www.flixbus.it; ✆ **02/947-59208**) and **Baltour** (www.baltour.it; ✆ **0861/199-1900**), which often significantly undercut train prices. A long-distance bus is *un pullman*.

For details on urban bus transportation, see individual chapters—for Rome, p. 50; for Florence, p. 152; and for Venice's water buses, p. 228.

[Fast FACTS] ITALY

Area Codes The **country code** for Italy is **39.** City **codes** (for example, Florence is 055, Venice is 041, Rome is 06) are incorporated into the numbers themselves. Therefore, you must dial the entire number, *including the initial zero,* when calling from *anywhere* outside or inside Italy and even within the same town.

To call Florence from the United States, dial **011-39-055,** then the rest of the phone number. Numbers in Italy can range anywhere from 6 to 12 digits in length.

ATMs The easiest and best way to get cash is from an ATM, referred to in Italy as a *bancomat.* ATMs are easy to find in Italian cities;

smaller towns usually have one, but it's good practice to fuel up on cash in urban centers before traveling to villages or rural areas.

Be sure to confirm with your bank that your card is valid for international withdrawals and that you have a four-digit PIN. (Some ATMs in Italy will not accept any other number of digits.)

Also, be sure you know your daily withdrawal limit before you depart.

If at the ATM you get an on-screen message saying your card isn't valid for international transactions, don't panic: It's most likely the bank just can't make an electronic connection to check it (occasionally this can be a citywide epidemic). Try another ATM or another town.

Business Hours Banks tend to be open Monday through Friday 8:30am to 1:30pm and 2:45 to 4:15pm. General opening hours for **stores, offices,** and **churches** are from 9:30am to noon or 1pm and again from 3 or 3:30pm (or later) to 7:30 or 8pm. The early afternoon shutdown is the *riposo*, the Italian siesta (in the downtown area of large cities, stores don't usually close for the *riposo*). Most stores close all day Sunday and some also on Monday (morning only or all day). Some public services and business offices are open to the public only in the morning.

Traditionally, **state museums** are closed Mondays. Most of the large museums stay open all day long otherwise, although some close for *riposo* or are only open in the morning (9am–2pm is popular).

Cell Phones See "Mobile Phones," p. 307.

Credit Cards The evolution of international computerized banking and consolidated ATM networks has led to the triumph of plastic throughout Italy. It remains a good idea to carry some cash—small businesses may accept only cash or may claim their credit card machine is broken to avoid paying card fees. **Visa** and **Mastercard** are almost universally accepted, and some businesses, typically at the luxe end, take **American Express. Diners Club** tends not to be accepted in Italy. Be sure to let your bank know you'll be traveling abroad to avoid having your card blocked after a few days of big purchases far from home. **Note:** Many banks assess a 1% to 3% "transaction fee" on **all** charges you incur abroad, whether you're using the local currency or your native currency.

Customs Foreign visitors can bring into the country most items for personal use duty-free, including merchandise valued up to 450€. Returning to the United States, U.S. citizens can bring with them up to $800 of goods, including 1 liter of alcohol, but no meats or fresh fruits and vegetables. Vinegars, oils, jams, chocolates, and certain cheeses are permissible (vacuum-packed cheeses yes; raw milk cheese no).

Disabled Travelers Most of the top museums and churches have installed ramps at their entrances, and many hotels have converted first-floor rooms into accessible units. Other than that, expect to find some of the most charming parts of Italy a little tricky to tackle.

Builders in the Middle Ages and the Renaissance didn't have wheelchairs or mobility impairments in mind when they built narrow doorways and spiral staircases, and heritage preservation laws keep Italians from being able to do much about this.

Public transportation is improving, however. There is generally better access for passengers in wheelchairs, particularly on modern local buses and new transit developments like Florence's tram. There are usually dedicated seats or areas for those with disabilities, and Italians are quick to give up their place for somebody who looks like they need it. **Trenitalia** has a special number that disabled travelers should call for assistance on the rail network: ✆ **199/303060.** The private rail network **Italo** has dedicated wheelchair spaces on every train: Call ✆ **060708** for any station assistance you need.

Accomable (www.accomable.com) is an agency connecting travelers with accessible properties for rent and is now part of the Airbnb empire.

Drinking Laws People of any age can legally consume alcohol in Italy, but a person must be 16 years old to be served alcohol in a restaurant or a bar. Bars generally close around 2am, though alcohol is often served in clubs after that. Supermarkets carry beer, wine, and liquor.

Electricity Italy operates on a 220-volt AC (50

cycles) system, as opposed to the U.S. 110-volt AC (60 cycles) system. You'll need a simple adapter plug to make the American flat pegs fit Italian round holes, and unless your appliance is dual-voltage (as some hair dryers, travel irons, and almost all gadgets are), you'll need an electrical converter.

Embassies & Consulates   The **Australian Embassy** is in Rome at Via Antonio Bosio 5 (www.italy.embassy.gov.au; © **06/852-721**).

The **Canadian Embassy** is in Rome at Via Zara 30 (www.italy.gc.ca; © **06/854-442-911**). The **New Zealand Embassy** is in Rome at Via Clitunno 44 (www.nzembassy.com/italy; © **06/853-7501**).

The **U.K. Embassy** is in Rome at Via XX Settembre 80a (www.gov.uk/government/world/italy.it; © **06/4220-0001**).

The **U.S. Embassy** is in Rome at Via Vittorio Veneto 121 (http://italy.usembassy.gov; © **06/46-741**). There is also a **U.S. Consulate General** in Florence at Lungarno Vespucci 38 (© **055/266-951**).

Emergencies   The best number to call with a **general emergency** is © **112,** which connects you to the **carabinieri,** who will transfer your call as needed. For the **police,** dial © **113;** for a **medical emergency** and to call an **ambulance,** the number is © **118;** for the **fire department,** call © **115.** If your car breaks

down, dial © **116** for **roadside aid** courtesy of the Automotive Club of Italy. All are free calls, but roadside assistance is a paid service for nonmembers.

Family Travel   Italy is a family-oriented society. A crying baby at a dinner table is greeted with a knowing smile rather than a stern look. Children almost always receive discounts, and maybe a special treat from the waiter, but the availability of such accoutrements as child seats for dinner tables is more the exception than the norm. There are plenty of parks, offbeat museums, markets, ice-cream parlors, and vibrant street life to amuse even the youngest children.

Health & Hospitals
Italy offers universal health care to its citizens and those of other European Union countries. (While they remain inside the EU, U.K. nationals should remember to carry an EHIC: See **www.nhs.uk/ehic**). Others should be prepared to pay medical bills upfront. Before leaving home, find out what medical services your **health insurance** covers. *Note:* Even if you don't have insurance, you will be treated in an emergency.

Insurance   Italy may be one of the safer places you can travel in the world, but accidents and setbacks can and do happen, from lost luggage to car crashes. We recommend looking at the following online marketplaces for insurance: **SquareMouth.com,**

InsureMyTrip.com, and **TripInsurance.com.** All three allow users to quickly and easily compare policies from different, vetted travel insurance companies. We find the user interface at SquareMouth to be the more intuitive, but all three are excellent resources.

Internet Access   If you're traveling with your own computer or smartphone, you'll find Wi-Fi in almost every hotel, but if it is essential for your stay, make sure you ask before booking. In a pinch, hostels, local libraries, and some cafes and bars have web access. Several spots around Venice, Florence, Rome, and other big cities are covered with free Wi-Fi access provided by the local administration, but at these and any other Wi-Fi spots around Italy, antiterrorism laws make it obligatory to register before you can log on. Take your passport or other photo ID when you go looking for an Internet point. **High-speed trains** often have free Wi-Fi (but throttle Skype, video streaming, file sharing, and similar data-hungry services).

LGBT Travelers   Italy as a whole, and northern Italy in particular, is gay-friendly. Homosexuality is legal, and the age of consent is 16. Same-sex civil unions became legal in 2016. Italians are generally more affectionate and physical than North Americans in all their friendships, and even straight men occasionally walk down the street with their arms around each other. However, kissing anywhere other than on the cheeks at greetings and goodbyes may draw attention.

Italy's national associations and support networks for gays and lesbians are **Arcigay and Arcilesbica.** The national websites are **www.arcigay.it** and **www. arcilesbica.it**, and most cities have a local office. See **www.arcigay.it/comitati** for a searchable directory of local affiliates.

Mail & Postage Sending a postcard or letter up to 20 grams, or a little less than an ounce, costs 1€ to European countries, 2.20€ to North America, and a whopping 2.90€ to Australia and New Zealand.

Mobile Phones **GSM** (Global System for Mobile Communications) is a cellphone technology used by most of the world's countries that makes it possible to turn on a phone with a contract based in Australia, Ireland, the U.K., Pakistan, or almost every other corner of the world and have it work in Italy without missing a beat. (In the U.S., service providers like Sprint and Verizon use a different technology—CDMA—and phones on those networks also need GSM and/or 4G/LTE compatibility to work in Italy. Most current, high-end models do; older phones may not work.) Also, if you are coming from the U.S. or Canada, you may need a multiband "world" phone.

All travelers should activate "international roaming" on their account, so check with your home service provider before leaving.

But—and it's a *big* but—using roaming can be very expensive, especially if you access the Internet on your phone. It is usually much cheaper, once you arrive, to buy an Italian SIM card (the fingernail-size removable plastic card found in all GSM phones that is encoded with your phone number). This is not difficult and is an especially good idea if you will be in Italy for more than a week. You can **buy a SIM card** at one of the many cellphone shops you will pass in every city. The main service providers are **TIM** (www.tim.it), **Vodafone** (www.vodafone.it), **Wind** (www.wind.it), and **3** (www.tre.it). If you have an Italian SIM card in your phone, local and national calls may be as low as .10€ per minute, and incoming calls are free. Deals on each network change regularly; check the individual websites or walk into a branded store or an electronics chain such as **Euronics** (www. euronics.it). **Note:** U.S. contract cellphones are often "locked" and will only work with a SIM card provided by the service provider back home, so check first that you have an unlocked phone.

Buying a phone is another option, and you shouldn't have any trouble finding one for about 20€. Use it, then recycle it or eBay it when you get home.

It will save you a fortune versus alternatives such as roaming or using hotel telephones.

Money & Costs Frommer's lists exact prices in local currency. The currency conversions quoted below were correct at press time. However, rates fluctuate, so before departing, consult a currency exchange website, such as **www.oanda.com/ currency/converter**, to check up-to-the-minute rates.

Like many European countries, Italy uses the **euro** as its currency. Euro coins are issued in denominations of .01€, .02€, .05€, .10€, .20€, and .50€, as well as 1€ and 2€; bills come in denominations of 5€, 10€, 20€, 50€, 100€, 200€, and 500€. You'll get the best rate if you **exchange money** at a bank or take cash out from one of its **ATMs** (see p. 303).

Traveler's checks have gone the way of the Stegosaurus.

Newspapers & Magazines "The New York Times International Edition" and "USA Today" are available at most newsstands in the big cities. At larger kiosks you can also find the "Wall Street Journal Europe," European editions of "Time," the "Economist," and most major European newspapers and magazines.

Pharmacies Pharmacies are ubiquitous (look for the green cross) and serve almost like miniclinics, where pharmacists diagnose and treat minor ailments, like flu symptoms and general aches and pains, with over-the-counter drugs. Carry the generic name of any prescription medicines, in case a local pharmacist is unfamiliar with your overseas brand. Pharmacies in cities take turns covering the night shift; normally a list is posted at the entrance of each pharmacy informing customers which are open each night of the week.

Police For emergencies, call 𝄡 **112** or 𝄡 **113.** Italy has several different police forces, but you'll likely need to deal with only two. The first is the *carabinieri* (𝄡 **112;** www.carabinieri.it), who normally only concern themselves with serious crimes, but point you in the right direction. The *polizia* (𝄡 **113;** www.poliziadistato.it), whose city headquarters is called the *questura,* is the place to go for help with lost and stolen property or petty crimes.

Safety Italy is a remarkably safe country. The worst threats you'll likely face are pickpockets who sometimes frequent touristy areas and public buses; keep your hands on your camera at all times and valuables in an under-the-clothes money belt or inside zip-pocket. Don't leave anything valuable in a rental car overnight, and leave nothing visible in it at any time. If you are robbed, you can fill out paperwork at the nearest police station (*questura),* but this is mostly for insurance purposes or to get a passport issued—don't

expect them to spend any resources hunting the perpetrator. In general, avoid public parks at night. Areas around rail stations are often unsavory, but rarely any worse than that. Other than that, there's a real sense of personal security for travelers in Italy.

Senior Travel Seniors and older people are treated with a deal of respect and deference, but few specific programs or concessions are made for them. The one exception is on admission prices for museums and sights, where those ages 60 or 65 and older will often get in at a reduced or even free. There are also special train passes and reductions on bus tickets in some towns (see "Getting Around," p. 297). As a senior in Italy, you're *un anziano* (if you're a woman: *un'anziana*)—it's a term of respect, and you should let people know if you think a discount may be due.

Smoking Smoking has been eradicated from inside restaurants, bars, and most hotels, so smokers tend to take outside tables at bars and restaurants. If you pick an outdoor table, you are essentially choosing a seat in the smoking section; requesting that your neighbor not smoke may not be politely received.

Student Travelers An **International Student Identity Card (ISIC)** qualifies students for savings on rail passes, plane tickets, entrance fees, and more.

The card is valid for 1 year. You can apply for the card online at **www.myisic.com** or in person at **STA Travel** (www.statravel.com; 𝄡 **800/ 781-4040** in North America). If you're no longer a student but are still 30 or under, you can get an **International Youth Travel Card (IYTC)** or an **International Teacher Identity Card (ITIC)** from the same agency, which entitles you to some discounts.

Taxes No sales tax is added to the price tag of purchases in Italy, but a 22% value-added tax (in Italy: IVA) is automatically included in just about everything, except food and a few specific goods and services, where rates of 4% and 10% apply. Entertainment, transport, hotels, and dining are among a group of goods taxed at a lower rate of 10%. For major purchases, non–E.U. residents can get IVA refunded. Several city governments have also introduced an **accommodation tax.** For example, in Florence, you will be charged 2€ per person per night for a 1-star hotel plus .80€–1€ per night per additional government-star rating of the hotel, up to a maximum of 10 nights. So, in a 3-star joint, the tax is 4€ per person per night. Children 11 and under are exempt. Venice, Rome, and many other popular localities also levy their own taxes. This tax is not usually included in a published room rate.

Tipping In **hotels,** service is usually included in your bill. In family-run operations, additional tips are unnecessary and sometimes considered rude. In fancier places with a hired staff, however, you may want to leave a .50€ daily tip for the maid and pay the bellhop or porter 1€ per bag. In **restaurants,** a 1€ to 3€ per person "cover charge" is automatically added to the bill, and in some tourist areas, especially Venice, another 10% to 15% is tacked on (except in the most unscrupulous of places, this will be noted on the menu somewhere; if unsure you should ask, è incluso il servizio?). It is not necessary to leave any extra money on the table, though it is not uncommon to leave up to 5€, especially for good service. Locals generally leave nothing. At **bars and cafes,** you can leave something very small on the counter for the barman (maybe 1€ if you have had several drinks), though it is not expected; there is no need to leave anything extra if you sit at a table, as they are likely already charging you double or triple the price you'd have paid standing at the bar. It is not necessary to tip **taxi** drivers, though it is common to round up the bill to the nearest euro or two.

Toilets Aside from train stations, where they cost about .50€ to use, and gas/petrol stations, where they are free (with perhaps a basket seeking gratuities for the cleaners), public toilets are few and far between. In an emergency, standard procedure is to enter a cafe, make sure the bathroom is not fuori servizio (out of order), and then order a cup of coffee before bolting to the facilities. It is advisable to always make use of toilets in a hotel, restaurant, museum, or bar before setting off around town. Public toilets—and often those in bars, too—can be dirty, with no seat or toilet paper. It's best to carry a pack of tissues with you, especially if you're traveling with children or teens who are easily grossed-out.

USEFUL ITALIAN PHRASES

English	Italian	Pronunciation
Thank you	Grazie	**graht-tzee-yey**
You're welcome	Prego	**prey-go**
Please	Per favore	**pehr fah-vohr-eh**
Yes	Si	**see**
No	No	**noh**
Good morning/Good day	Buongiorno	**bwohn-djor-noh**
Good evening	Buona sera	**bwohn-ah say-rah**
Good night	Buona notte	**bwohn-ah noht-tay**
My name is ____.	Mi chiamo ____.	**mee kyah-moh**
And yours?	E lei?	**eh lay**
Do you speak English?	Parla inglese?	**pahr-lah een-gleh-seh**
How are you?	Come sta?	**koh-may stah**
Very well	Molto bene	**mohl-toh behn-ney**
Goodbye	Arrivederci	**ahr-ree-vah-dehr-chee**
Excuse me (to get attention)	Scusi	**skoo-zee**
Excuse me (to get past someone)	Permesso	**pehr-mehs-soh**

GETTING AROUND

English	Italian	Pronunciation
Where is . . . ?	Dovè . . . ?	*doh*-vey
the station	la stazione	lah stat-tzee-*oh*-neh
a hotel	un albergo	oon ahl-*behr*-goh
a restaurant	un ristorante	oon reest-ohr-*ahnt*-eh
I am looking for . . .	Cerco . . .	*chehr*-koh
the check-in counter	il check-in	eel check-in
the ticket counter	la biglietteria	*lah beel-lyeht-teh-ree-ah*
gate number	l'uscita numero	loo-*shee*-tah *noo*-meh-roh
the restroom	la toilette	lah twa-*leht*
the information booth	l'ufficio informazioni	loof-*fee*-choh een-*fohr*-mah-*tsyoh*-nee
an ATM/cashpoint	un bancomat	oon *bahn*-koh-maht
baggage claim	il ritiro bagagli	eel ree-*tee*-roh bah-*gahl*-lyee
a restaurant	un ristorante	oon ree-stoh-*rahn*-teh
a bookstore	una libreria	*oo*-nah lee-breh-*ree*-ah
To the left	A sinistra	ah see-*nees*-tra
To the right	A destra	ah *dehy*-stra
Straight ahead	Avanti (or sempre diritto)	ahv-*vahn*-tee (*sehm*-pray dee-*reet*-toh)

DINING

English	Italian	Pronunciation
Breakfast	Prima colazione	*pree*-mah coh-laht-tzee-*ohn*-ay
Lunch	Pranzo	*prahn*-zoh
Dinner	Cena	*chay*-nah
How much is it?	Quanto costa?	*kwan*-toh *coh*-sta
The check, please	Il conto, per favore	eel kon-toh *pehr* fah-*vohr*-eh

A MATTER OF TIME

English	Italian	Pronunciation
When?	Quando?	*kwan*-doh
Yesterday	Ieri	ee-*yehr*-ree
Today	Oggi	*oh*-jee
Tomorrow	Domani	doh-*mah*-nee
What time is it?	Che ore sono?	kay *or*-ay *soh*-noh
It's one o'clock.	È l'una.	eh loo-nah
It's two o'clock.	Sono le due.	*soh*-noh leh *doo*-eh
It's two-thirty.	Sono le due e mezzo.	*soh*-noh leh *doo*-eh eh *mehd*-dzoh
in the morning	al mattino	ahl maht-*tee*-noh
in the afternoon	al pomeriggio	ahl poh-meh-*reed*-joh
at night	alla notte	dee *noht*-the

DAYS OF THE WEEK

English	Italian	Pronunciation
Monday	Lunedì	loo-nay-*dee*
Tuesday	Martedì	mart-ay-*dee*
Wednesday	Mercoledì	mehr-cohl-ay-*dee*
Thursday	Giovedì	joh-vay-*dee*
Friday	Venerdì	ven-nehr-*dee*
Saturday	Sabato	*sah*-bah-toh
Sunday	Domenica	doh-*mehn*-nee-kah

NUMBERS

English	Italian	Pronunciation
1	uno	*oo*-noh
2	due	*doo*-ay
3	tre	tray
4	quattro	*kwah*-troh
5	cinque	*cheen*-kway
6	sei	say
7	sette	*set*-tay
8	otto	*oh*-toh
9	nove	*noh*-vay
10	dieci	dee-ay-chee
11	undici	*oon*-dee-chee
20	venti	*vehn*-tee
21	ventuno	vehn-*toon*-oh
22	venti due	*vehn*-tee *doo*-ay
30	trenta	*trayn*-tah
40	quaranta	kwah-*rahn*-tah
50	cinquanta	cheen-*kwan*-tah
60	sessanta	sehs-*sahn*-tah
70	settanta	seht-*tahn*-tah
80	ottanta	oht-*tahn*-tah
90	novanta	noh-*vahnt*-tah
100	cento	*chen*-toh
1,000	mille	*mee*-lay
5,000	cinque milla	*cheen*-kway *mee*-lah
10,000	dieci milla	dee-ay-chee *mee*-lah

Index

See also Accommodations and Restaurant indexes, below.

General Index

A

Accessibility, 305
Accommodations. *See also* Accommodations index
  best of, 4–5
  in Florence, 153–163
  in Rome, 53–67
  in Venice, 233–245
Addresses, 150, 226
Ai Tre Scalini, 134
Air travel
  to Florence, 147–148
  to Italy, 297
  to Rome, 42–43
  to Venice, 223–224
Al Prosecco, 288
Alexanderplatz Jazz Club, 133
All Saints' Anglican Church, 133
Amorino, 174
Ancient Rome, 46
  accommodations, 57–59
  attractions, 95–107
  dining, 70–72
Anfiteatro, 144
Apartment rentals. *See* self-catering apartments
Aperitivo, 8, 135
Appartamento Borgia (Borgia Apartments), 90–91
Arch of Constantine (Arco di Costantino), 95
Area codes, 304
Arena di Verona, 2, 293–294
Atelier Segalin di Daniela Ghezzo, 285
ATMs, 304–305
Auditorium–Parco della Musica, 133
Augustus, 26
Authentic experiences, best of, 2–3
Aventine Hill, 100

B

Bacari, 246
Banks in Rome, 53
Bar del Fico, 134
Barnum Café, 134
Baroque, 31–34
Bars
  aperitivo, 8
  best of, 3
  in Florence, 208–209
  in Rome, 134–136
  in Venice, 288–289
Basilica di San Clemente, 104
Basilica di San Giovanni in Laterano, 104

Basilica di San Marco (St. Mark's Cathedral), 261, 264
Basilica di San Zeno Maggiore, 294
Basilica di Sant'Antonio, 292
Basilica SS. Giovanni e Paolo, 269–270
Baths of Caracalla (Terme di Caracalla), 95–96
Battistero (Baptistery), 175, 178
Beer, 28. *See also* bars
Beer House Club, 208
Biblioteca delle Oblate, 202
Biennale d'Arte, 269
Biking, 152
Bir and Fud, 135
Bitter Bar, 3, 208
Books, 33, 37
Breakfast tours of Vatican museums, 94
Brunelleschi, Filippo, 9, 180
Burano, 281
Buses
  in Florence, 152
  in Italy, 304
  to Rome, 43–44
  in Rome, 50–51, 52
  to Venice, 225
Business hours, 53, 153, 305

C

Ca' del Sol Maschere, 285
Cafes
  in Florence, 207–208
  in Rome, 134
  in Venice, 287–288
Caffè Centrale, 289
Caffè dei Frari, 287
Caffè Florian, 287
Caffè Lavena, 287
Caffetteria delle Oblate, 207
Calcio Storico (Historic Football), 39
Calendar of events, 39–40
Caligula, 26
Campanile di Giotto (Giotto's Bell Tower), 178
Campanile di San Marco (Bell Tower), 264–265
Campo de' Fiori, 111–112, 131
Campo dei Miracoli, 216–217
Campo Santa Margherita, 259
Canal cruises in Venice, 230
Canal Grande (Grand Canal), 265
Cannaregio, 8, 228
  accommodations, 244–245
  attractions, 277–279
  dining, 257–258
Cantinetta dei Verrazzano, 208
Capitoline Museums (Musei Capitolini), 96–98
Capitolium, 138
Cappella degli Scrovegni, 291
Cappelle Medicee (Medici Chapels), 190
Carnevale, 39, 284
Carta d'Argento (Silver Card), 304
Carta Verde (Green Card), 303

Casa dei Vettii, 143
Casa del Fauno, 143
Casa del Poeta Tragico, 143
Casa della Venere in Conchiglia, 144
Casa di Giulietta, 293
Casa Diana, 139
Case Romane del Celio, 105
Castel Sant'Angelo, 94–95
Castello, 227
  accommodations, 238–240
  attractions, 269–270
  dining, 251–253
Castle Caetani, 126
Catacombe di Domitilla, 127–128
Catacombe di San Callisto (Catacombs of St. Callixtus), 127
Catacombe di San Sebastiano (Catacombs of St. Sebastian), 128
Cavour 313, 135
Celio, 46
  accommodations, 57–59
  attractions, 95–107
  dining, 70–72
Cenacolo di Sant'Apollonia, 193
Centrale Montemartini, 5–6, 125
Centro Storico, 46
  accommodations, 59–62
  attractions, 107–112
  dining, 72–75
Children. *See* family activities
Chiostro dello Scalzo, 193
Chorus Pass, 273
Christmas Blessing of the Pope, 40
Cicchetti, 246
Circus Maximus (Circo Massimo), 98
City Pass, 273
Claudius, 26
Cocktails. *See* bars
Collegiata, 218–219
Collezione d'Arte Contemporanea (Collection of Modern Religious Art), 91
Colosseum (Colosseo), 98–99
Come il Latte, 83
Concorso Ippico Internazionale (International Horse Show), 39
Consulates, 306
Context Travel, 129
Convents, staying in, 55, 156
Coopculture, 84
Corridoio Vasariano (Vasari Corridor), 188
Costs, 307
Credit cards, 305
Cruises in Venice, 230
Crypta Balbi, 110
Cuisines. *See* food
Currency exchange, 307
Customs, 305

D

"David," where to see, 193–194
Day trips

Map List

Photo Credits

Frommer's EasyGuide to Rome, Florence & Venice 2019, 6th Edition

Published by
FROMMER MEDIA LLC

ISBN 978-1-62887-430-3 (paper), 978-1-62887-431-0 (e-book)

Editorial Director: Pauline Frommer
Editor: Holly Hughes
Production Editor: Heather Wilcox
Cartographer: Elizabeth Puhl
Photo Editor: Meghan Lamb
Cover Design: Dave Riedy

For information on our other products or services, see www.frommers.com.

Frommer Media LLC also publishes its books in a variety of electronic formats. Some content that appears in print may not be available in electronic formats.

Manufactured in the United States of America

5 4 3 2 1

ABOUT THE AUTHORS

Donald Strachan is a travel writer and journalist who has written about Italy and Europe for publications worldwide, including *National Geographic Traveller*, the *Guardian*, *Telegraph*, and CNN.com. He lives in London, England.

Stephen Keeling has been traveling to Italy since 1985 (when a serving of gelato was 1000 lire) and covering his favorite nation for Frommer's since 2007. He has written for the *Independent*, *Daily Telegraph*, various travel magazines, and numerous travel guides as well as authoring the award-winning *Frommer's Family Travel Guide to Tuscany and Umbria*. Stephen resides in New York City.

A long-time contributor to Frommer's guides, **Elizabeth Heath** has served as editor-in-chief to several regional magazines and writes articles on travel, business, celebrities, politics, and lifestyle for online, local, regional, and national outlets. Liz fell in love with Italy on her first visit 18 years ago. She now lives in the green hills of Umbria with her family, five dogs, several hundred olive trees, and acres of grapevines. She writes about the peculiarities of life in the Italian countryside in her award-winning blog, *My Village in Umbria*.